Transdermal Drug Delivery

Concepts and Application

Transdermal Drug Delivery

Concepts and Application

Kevin Ita
College of Pharmacy, Touro University California,
Mare Island-Vallejo, CA, United States

ELSEVIER

ACADEMIC PRESS
An imprint of Elsevier

Academic Press is an imprint of Elsevier
125 London Wall, London EC2Y 5AS, United Kingdom
525 B Street, Suite 1650, San Diego, CA 92101, United States
50 Hampshire Street, 5th Floor, Cambridge, MA 02139, United States
The Boulevard, Langford Lane, Kidlington, Oxford OX5 1GB, United Kingdom

British Library Cataloguing-in-Publication Data
A catalogue record for this book is available from the British Library

Library of Congress Cataloging-in-Publication Data
A catalog record for this book is available from the Library of Congress

ISBN: 978-0-12-822550-9

For Information on all Academic Press publications
visit our website at https://www.elsevier.com/books-and-journals

Publisher: Andre Gerhard Wolff
Acquisitions Editor: Erin Hill-Parks
Editorial Project Manager: Barbara Makinster
Production Project Manager: Maria Bernard
Cover Designer: Victoria Pearson

Typeset by MPS Limited, Chennai, India

Dedication

I dedicate this book to my wife Stella and
my children Precious-Mary and Treasure-Daniel.
I am grateful for their love and support.

Contents

List of figures

List of tables

Preface

I was inspired to write this book because of the tremendous achievements recorded in the area of transdermal drug delivery over the past few decades. Advances in biotechnology, nanotechnology, chemical, and biological assays have combined to make this research area even more exciting. Even though the number of approved products remains low compared to the quantum of research carried out, there are several developments that will lead ultimately to more approvals by regulatory authorities in different countries. This book (Transdermal Drug Delivery: Concepts and Applications) is divided into 12 chapters that deal with different aspects of percutaneous drug transport. Chapter 1 gives a general introduction of the subject area of "Transcutaneous Drug Administration" where the rationale for this mode of drug delivery is discussed.

The benefits and limitations of transdermal drug delivery are described. With the transdermal route of drug permeation, presystemic metabolism (first-pass effect) can be avoided, leading to enhanced bioavailability. Other advantages include painlessness, improved patient compliance, convenience, the possibility of self-administration, and noninvasiveness [or minimal invasiveness in the case of microneedles (MNs)]. Despite the aforementioned benefits, there are also disadvantages. The amount of drug that can cross the stratum corneum (SC) and enter into systemic administration is limited. This has resulted in the approval by regulatory authorities of less than 25 drug molecules as active pharmaceutical ingredients in transdermal patches. There are also safety concerns linked with the use of chemical penetration enhancers, iontophoresis or electroporation. Furthermore, there is a need to strike a fine balance between the need for systemic administration of medications through the skin and the physiologic function of this organ which includes protection from the external microorganisms and dangerous chemicals. These concerns will definitely be addressed as more research advances are recorded.

Chapter 2 examines the anatomy of human skin. The different layers of the human skin are described. This is important from a drug delivery standpoint because the outermost layer of the skin (the SC) forms the major permeability barrier. There are some studies that also document the role of the viable epidermis. The viable epidermis is subdivided into the stratum lucidum, stratum granulosum, stratum spinosum, and stratum basale. The dermis, in turn, is made up of two parts: (1) the upper or papillary dermis with a loose connective tissue and high cell density and (2) the reticular dermis in the deeper layers, which is densely packed with collagens and other connective tissue proteins but possesses a low cell density. Ultimately, the permeant has to cross the epidermis, dermis, and subcutaneous layers. The subcutis is the adipose-rich skin layer that is composed of lipocytes and provides insulation. This skin layer also provides an energy and fluid reserve that protects deeper tissues and organs and supports the dermis and epidermis.

Chapter 3 discusses the basic principles of transdermal drug delivery. When a medication is applied to the skin for systemic therapy, it must penetrate the structural layers of the human skin, encountering several lipophilic and hydrophilic regions until it gets to the dermis where absorption into blood circulation is fast because of the presence of a large capillary bed. Only few medications can cross the skin into the bloodstream at therapeutically significant rates because of the permeability barrier provided by the SC. It is critical to have a good knowledge of the pharmacokinetic and physicochemical parameters of an active pharmaceutical ingredient to determine that it is feasible for it to be delivered via the transdermal route. Compounds for transdermal drug delivery should, among other properties, possess low molecular weight (ideally less than 500 Da), lipophilicity between 1 and 3, aqueous solubility of more than 1 mg/mL, and a daily dose of less than 1 mg. Other physicochemical as well as biological determinants of transdermal drug delivery are also highlighted in Chapter 3.

Elastic liposomes and other vesicles are evaluated in Chapter 4. Elastic liposomes are phospholipid vesicles with deformable (flexible) bilayers. The elasticity is achieved through the introduction of edge activators (surfactants). There is still some controversy regarding the ability of these vesicles to cross the SC. Some investigators are of the opinion that hydration gradient provides adequate force to "push" these vesicles across skin pores. Ethosomes (with a higher percentage of ethanol) and transethosomes (ethosomes formulated with penetration enhancers) are also described in this chapter.

Chapter 5 focuses on chemical penetration enhancers. These are substances that facilitate transdermal drug transport through a variety of mechanisms including the ability of these compounds to disrupt or fluidize SC structure leading to enhanced drug diffusivity. Other mechanisms include enhancing drug partitioning and drug solubility. Chemical permeation enhancers are compounds that are diverse from the standpoint of chemical structure. Clearly, it is challenging to predict their mechanisms of action a priori based on molecular descriptors. Nevertheless, this is an exciting and expanding research domain. Chapter 6 describes microemulsions that are monophasic, optically isotropic, thermodynamically stable and clear dispersions formulated from oil, water, surfactant, and a cosurfactant. Microemulsions are easy to prepare, possess a high solubilization capacity, and can enhance drug transport into the skin. The microemulsion system has been shown to increase transdermal drug delivery and several examples are discussed in this chapter.

Chapter 7 focuses on prodrugs, which are drug precursors that can be biotransformed into active pharmaceutical ingredients inside the body, either through a spontaneous mechanism such as hydrolysis or a biocatalytic process. Typically, a molecule (termed "promoiety") is grafted onto an active pharmacological agent and this enhances drug transport to a biological target, after which the promoiety is eliminated and the drug "liberated." Prodrugs can be synthesized via a bioprecursor or through carrier-linked methods techniques. When the carrier-linked approach is used, the active pharmaceutical ingredient (API) is bound to a carrier moiety using a transient covalent bond. Cleavage of a carrier prodrug subsequently creates a molecule with enhanced biological activity and at least one side product, the carrier, which may possess targeting properties or is pharmacologically inert. On the other hand, bioprecursors are activated by the enzymatic biotransformation of a functional group. Bioprecursor-based prodrugs are usually transformed chemically into the active therapeutic agent via oxidation, hydration, or reduction. From an experimental standpoint, two methods for making prodrugs—the synthesis of either a simple acyl-type derivative or a soft alkyl derivative—have also been described in Chapter 7.

In Chapter 8, MNs are discussed. MNs are ultrasmall needles (usually less than 1000 μm) that are used to create pores in the skin and facilitate the transcutaneous delivery of medications into the bloodstream. These microscaled projections are able to painlessly disrupt the SC and reach the epidermal and dermal layer facilitating drug release. Five different types of MNs are described in the book: solid, dissolving, coated, hollow, and hydrogel-forming. The practical utility of these devices is demonstrated by discussing the effect of MNs on the transdermal delivery of different therapeutic agents. Chapter 9 focuses on three distinct types of physical enhancement techniques: iontophoresis, magnetophoresis, and electroporation. The differences between the three approaches are highlighted. Iontophoresis is the utilization of a weak electric current for the transport of charged drug molecules across the skin. The overall aim of using this approach is to enhance transdermal drug delivery. Magnetophoresis, on the other hand, involves the use of utilization of a magnetic field (5−300 mT) to increase drug permeation across the skin. Diamagnetic compounds can be repelled from an external magnetic field across the human skin. Electroporation refers to the use of high-voltage electric pulses to facilitate drug transport across the skin. Iontophoresis, magnetophoresis, and electroporation have been used to increase the transdermal delivery of several drugs and specific examples are discussed in this chapter.

Sonophoresis is described in Chapter 10. This is a transdermal drug delivery method that uses ultrasound as the external driving force for transdermal flux increase. In most percutaneous drug transport studies, low-frequency ultrasound is used. Ultrasound causes vibrations within the epidermal layers, thereby increasing the kinetic energy of drug molecules. The specific mechanisms through which ultrasound increases transcutaneous drug penetration are still poorly understood even though the following phenomena are known to take place: cellular-level effect, acoustic streaming, cavitation, and rectified diffusion. Ultrasound-mediated increase in transcutaneous flux is a function of several parameters including duty cycle (the ON time for ultrasound), application time, frequency, radiating diameter of the transducer, and intensity.

Chapter 11 focuses on lasers and other ablation techniques. Laser ablation is a thermal technique that eliminates the SC layer via temporal application of laser beam to the skin. High-energy light source is typically used to form well-defined ablated regions. Laser-assisted ablation of the SC can be used to facilitate (trans)dermal drug delivery. Another interesting method of increasing skin permeability involves heating the skin via short exposures to high temperatures or long exposures to moderate temperatures. Thermal ablation involves the noninvasive removal of small sections of the SC leading to enhanced transdermal drug delivery. Radiofrequency (RF) can also be used for heating. This occurs in materials via energy transferred from the electric field to the charges in the material. RF can be categorized as high frequency ($>$500 kHz), medium frequency (25–500 kHz), and low frequency (1–25,000 Hz). RF ablation uses high-frequency electrical current for localized heating of the outer skin layer. Abrasion utilizes sandpaper or pressurized particles to remove the SC. Microdermabrasion, on the other hand, uses negative pressure and Al_2O_3 crystals to superficially peel off the outer surface of the skin.

Mathematical models of transdermal drug delivery are discussed in Chapter 12. Several methods, including analytical and numerical statistical techniques such as finite element modeling, finite-difference modeling, finite volume modeling, as well as quantitative structure–permeation relationship modeling are routinely used to characterize transdermal permeation. By using these mathematical modeling techniques, the number of transdermal drug delivery experiments can be substantially reduced.

Acknowledgment

I thank my PhD Advisor Professor Jeanetta du Plessis (Deputy Dean, Research and Innovation in the Faculty of Health Sciences, North-West University, South Africa) and my PhD Co-Advisor Professor Jonathan Hadgraft (Emeritus Professor of Biophysical Chemistry at the School of Pharmacy, University of London) for introducing me to the field of transdermal drug delivery. I am equally grateful to Touro University California, United States (Dean Rae Matsumoto, former Dean Katherine Knapp, former Associate Dean for Academic Affairs and Research Paul Goldsmith, current Interim Associate Dean of Academic Affairs and Research Nathalie Bergeron, former Department Chair Professor Michael Ellerby, and current Department Chair Professor David Evans) for giving me the opportunity to teach pharmaceutics and conduct research in the area of transdermal drug delivery. I thank my former students in the Master of Science in Medical Health Sciences program for the time spent on transdermal drug delivery research. These students include Monika Kaur, Kathy Nguyen, Mylien Hoang, Emmy Luu, Julia Nguyen, Iqra Ahmad, Ifeoma Anne Abiandu, and Karna Ghimirey.

Chapter 1

Transcutaneous drug administration

Over the last few decades, it has been asserted that the transdermal route of drug administration represents an attractive approach in comparison to oral or parenteral drug delivery [1–3]. Delivering medications through the skin is important because it circumvents presystemic metabolism (first-pass effect), which is typically observed with the oral route. First-pass effect can lead to low bioavailability, adverse secondary effects, and uncomfortable drug dosing schedules [4]. Bacterial enzymes, gut wall enzymes, gastrointestinal lumen enzymes, and hepatic enzymes have all been implicated in the first-pass effect [5]. Recent experimental evidence has demonstrated the utility of transcutaneous drug transport in bypassing the first-pass effect, avoiding intestinal degradation, and providing transcutaneous permeation at controlled rates [6,7]. Percutaneous drug transport is also useful from a pharmacotherapeutic standpoint because there is no pain during drug administration, patients can self-administer, there is no chance of disease transmission by needle sharing, and a slow drug release can be achieved [8]. Transdermal drug delivery can provide effective blood levels for drugs [9]. A drug initially diffuses across the stratum corneum (SC), enters into the viable epidermis/dermis, and then becomes available for systemic absorption through dermal blood capillaries [10]. Transcutaneous drug administration is beneficial in comparison with the traditional administration routes such as oral or parenteral injections due to a number of factors: the oral route is characterized by partial drug absorption, gastrointestinal irritation, and slow onset of action, while hypodermic injections are invasive and painful, generates medical waste, pose risks of infection, and requires administration by medically trained professionals [11]. In contrast, transcutaneous drug administration is painless, noninvasive [12], or minimally invasive (in the case of transdermal microneedles). In addition, percutaneous drug administration usually requires a lower dosage of medications than oral administration due to a shorter diffusional length required to reach the vasculature [13]. Another advantage is the avoidance of side effects caused by erratic absorption and metabolism of the drug in the gastrointestinal tract [13]. Furthermore, transdermal therapeutic systems can be easily applied to the skin, are well accepted, and are relevant

Transdermal Drug Delivery. DOI: https://doi.org/10.1016/B978-0-12-822550-9.00001-6

options when oral drug delivery is challenging (instances of coma or difficulty in swallowing) [9]. From an economic standpoint, it has been calculated that the global transdermal drug delivery market will grow to approximately $95.57 billion by the year 2025 [14]. The global transdermal drug delivery market is worth $32 billion [15].

The human skin, an organ that receives one-third of the total blood supplied throughout the body, was not used as a drug delivery route for systemic administration until the late 20th century [14]. Scopolamine-loaded transdermal patch was the first commercial patch, and it was approved for clinical use in 1979 [16]. After nearly 40 years of extensive transdermal drug delivery research, only 22 active pharmaceutical ingredients have been approved by regulatory authorities in the United States in the form of transdermal patches [12]. Only low molecular weight, low-dose, lipophilic medications can be developed into transdermal drug delivery systems (TDDSs) with a good chance of therapeutic efficacy and regulatory approval [4,17]. In addition, the daily dose of most approved transdermal medications is typically in the milligram range [4]. Another point worthy of emphasis is that skin sensitivity varies among patients and therefore it is difficult to predict the effect of a transdermal patch. Also, skin occlusion with a patch may induce erythema at the administration site [4]. Furthermore, some medications are intrinsically irritating and early investigation of such compounds should be undertaken early enough in the transdermal drug development [4].

The skin functions as an effective barrier that hinders the ingress of harmful substances from the environment and the efflux of body fluid [18]. This barrier function is ascribed to the intercellular lipids present in the outermost layer of the skin called the SC. One of the obvious limitations of the transdermal route is that externally introduced chemicals (including medications) have to overcome the SC before entering into the bloodstream [19]. The successful transcutaneous permeation of a drug is a function of the partition coefficient (1–3), molecular weight (<500 Da), and the potency of the drug [19]. Equally important is the water solubility of the drug which should preferably be more than 1 mg/mL with the dose being less than 1 mg per day [7]. It is not surprising that all drugs commercially available in the form of TDDSs are very potent and typically, their molecular weights are lower than 500 Da [9]. Even after the drug successfully crosses the SC, it may be degraded prematurely by epidermal enzymes, leading to a reduced bioavailability [13].

From the standpoint of pharmacotherapy, this is an obvious disadvantage as proteins, peptides, and genes are hydrophilic, electrically charged, or large molecules and therefore cannot cross the skin in therapeutic quantities [20]. Various techniques have been utilized over the years to surmount the barrier presented by the SC. Vesicles (elastic liposomes, ethosomes, etc.), chemical penetration enhancers, iontophoresis, sonophoresis, microneedles, electroporation, and other techniques have been used to overcome the SC barrier and increase transdermal drug delivery. The terms TDDSs, transdermal therapeutic systems, and transdermal patches can be used interchangeably. There are two major classes of TDDS: those that are based on passive delivery and those that are based on microneedles, electroporation, sonophoresis, or other physical methods.

Passive transdermal therapeutic systems

There has been a surge in the utilization of transdermal drug therapeutic systems over the past 40 years. The first generation of transdermal delivery systems focused on medications that traversed the skin through passive diffusion [16,21]. Scopolamine-loaded adhesive transdermal therapeutic system was given the FDA approval in 1979 for the management of kinetosis [22]. Subsequently, nitroglycerin patch was approved in 1981 and the nicotine TDDS in 1991 [22]. Developments in science and technology have enabled the utilization of mild electric current (iontophoresis), ultrasound (sonophoresis), and chemical penetration enhancers for enhanced transport of drug molecules that cannot be transported across the skin in therapeutic amounts via passive diffusion alone [16,21]. Third generation transdermal therapeutic systems utilize microscopic needles (microneedles) for transport of medications including high molecular weight agents [16,21]. These TDDSs breach the SC facilitating the transport of the drug molecules [16,21].

Passive transdermal systems belong to three major categories: the reservoir (membrane-controlled) [23], matrix without a rate-controlling membrane [22,24], and matrix systems with a rate-controlling membrane [7,24,25]. A schematic representation of a reservoir transdermal system is shown in Fig. 1.1.

Reservoir systems depend on the transport of the drug out of or through a nonporous or microporous polymer layer [26]. Diffusion through the membrane or the static aqueous diffusion layer may determine the rate of transport [26]. It is important to note that molecular mass and pore size also have significant effect on the diffusion coefficient [26]. In reservoir transdermal

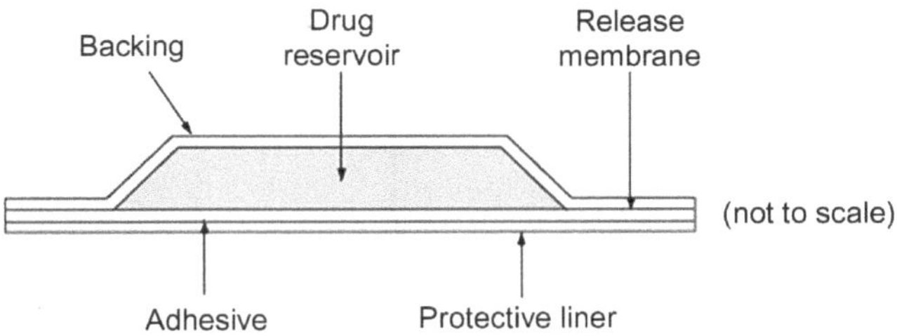

FIGURE 1.1 A schematic representation of a transdermal patch. *Reproduced with permission from D'Orazio JL, Fischel JA, Recurrent respiratory depression associated with fentanyl transdermal patch gel reservoir ingestion. J Emerg Med 2012;42(5):543–48 (Chapter 1).*

systems, the permeation rate is a function of the rate-determining polymer membrane [22]. An adhesive, a rate-controlling membrane, and a drug reservoir are normally used for the design and fabrication of reservoir systems [24]. The active pharmaceutical ingredient(s) as well as excipients are incorporated into the drug reservoir [24]. The adhesive component of the transdermal therapeutic system facilitates the adhesion of the patch to the skin [24]. There are two modes of adhesion: continuous and peripheral. If it is continuous, the adhesive completely covers the drug release area but in the case of a peripheral adhesive, a perimeter is created around a nonadhering drug release surface [24]. Examples of membrane-controlled transdermal therapeutic systems are Transderm Scop and Nicoderm CQ [27].

In a matrix transdermal system, the drug is introduced into an adhesive polymer, from which the medication diffuses transdermally into systemic circulation [22]. This transdermal delivery system is based on the following mechanisms: porosity (tortuous path) and polymer erosion [26]. Researchers typically fabricate matrix systems via drug dispersion in a lipophilic or hydrophilic polymer and subsequent molding of the drug-loaded polymer into a drug-loaded disk with a defined thickness and surface area [28]. The polymeric disk is then placed on a base plate with subsequent spread of an adhesive polymer to create a strip of rim along the drug-loaded disk [28]. The amount of transported medication is a function of the area of the TDDS administered to the skin and the quantity of the medication in the matrix [22].

Matrix systems are mostly thinner than reservoir systems and can provide greater comfort and cosmetic applicability [25]. One of the drawbacks of matrix transdermal systems is that the formulation of such devices is challenging, especially for medications in adhesive systems, since the adhesive incorporates the medication and regulates its delivery while being adhered to the skin [25]. Drug delivery rates are better controlled with reservoir TDDS but sometimes there may be an initial burst of drug release [22]. In addition, if the membrane is damaged, there is also a concomitant risk of overdose induced by the sudden release of the active pharmaceutical ingredient [22]. In matrix-based transdermal systems, an inactive polymer modulates drug delivery from the therapeutic system [27]. Commercially available transdermal matrix-based therapeutic systems include Nicotrol and Vivelle [27]. It is important to note that a drug is distributed evenly in a matrix patch [22]. A hybrid patch refers to a matrix patch with a silicon reservoir and a membrane [7,25]. Hair and coworkers published a paper describing a hybrid transdermal patch from which fentanyl was released over a 72-h delivery period [29]. The hybrid patch had a silicon matrix with a rate-modifying membrane [29]. Most TDDSs deliver medications into the skin at a constant rate over a specific time interval based on Fickian diffusion [27]. There is usually a zero-order drug release as long as the concentration gradient across the skin is constant [27]. As previously stated, the SC is the major impediment to percutaneous drug absorption.

Liu and coworkers formulated a transdermal patch loaded with benzoylaconitine [30]. The drug-in-adhesive patch was formulated using the solvent evaporation method [30]. The drug and skin sorption promoters were dissolved in ethyl acetate and then stirred thoroughly with pressure-sensitive adhesive (PSA) to obtain a homogeneous drug-PSA mixture [30]. The obtained mixture was coated onto the release liner using a laboratory coating unit. The fabric backing film was laminated onto the dry PSA layer with a rolling device to ensure the flatness of the backing film on the PSA layer [30]. Malaiya et al. loaded a transdermal delivery system with rivastigmine [31]. The backing membrane was prepared using an aqueous solution of a 6% w/v of polyvinyl alcohol. The solution was poured into a glass bangle placed on the surface of aluminum foil in a petri dish. Ethyl cellulose and polyvinylpyrrolidone were dissolved in chloroform and a homogeneous solution was prepared with the aid of a magnetic stirrer. The authors then added the drug and a plasticizer dibutyl phthalate to the mixture and stirred for 20 min until a homogeneous suspension was formed [31]. The authors next cast 5 mL of the homogeneous suspension on the backing membrane and dried the suspension at room temperature for 24 h, until a flat and uniform matrix patch was formed [31].

A matrix-type transdermal system loaded with lamivudine has also been formulated [32]. The authors prepared transdermal patches from Scotchpak 9733 (the backing membrane) and CoTran 9764 (polyethylene foam tape) and attached the system to each other using CoTran 9766 [32]. Then, the lamivudine-loaded polymeric monolithic films were attached to the hypoallergenic, pressure-sensitive acrylate adhesive coat of CoTran 9764 [32]. The drug layer was protected by Scotchpak 1022 (release liner).

References

[1] Levintova Y, Plakogiannis FM, Bellantone RA. An improved in vitro method for measuring skin permeability that controls excess hydration of skin using modified Franz diffusion cells. Int J Pharm 2011;419(1–2):96–106.

[2] Abiandu I, Ita K. Transdermal delivery of potassium chloride with solid microneedles. J Drug Deliv Sci Technol 2019;53:101216.

[3] Dillon C, et al. Dissolving microneedle based transdermal delivery of therapeutic peptide analogues. Int J Pharm. 2019;565:9–19.

[4] Wiedersberg S, Guy RH. Transdermal drug delivery: 30 + years of war and still fighting!. J Control Release 2014;190:150–6.

[5] Pereira de Sousa I, Bernkop-Schnurch A. Pre-systemic metabolism of orally administered drugs and strategies to overcome it. J Control Release 2014;192:301–9.

[6] Nguyen HX, et al. Poly (vinyl alcohol) microneedles: fabrication, characterization, and application for transdermal drug delivery of doxorubicin. Eur J Pharm Biopharm 2018;129:88–103.

[7] Ita KB. Transdermal drug delivery: progress and challenges. J Drug Deliv Sci Technol 2014;24(3):245–50.

[8] Robertson J, Squire M, Becker S. A thermoelectric device for coupling fluid temperature regulation during continuous skin sonoporation or sonophoresis. AAPS PharmSciTech 2019;20(4):147.
[9] Delgado-Charro MB, Guy RH. Effective use of transdermal drug delivery in children. Adv Drug Deliv Rev 2014;73:63–82.
[10] Alkilani AZ, McCrudden MT, Donnelly RF. Transdermal drug delivery: innovative pharmaceutical developments based on disruption of the barrier properties of the stratum corneum. Pharmaceutics 2015;7(4):438–70.
[11] Economidou SN, Lamprou DA, Douroumis D. 3D printing applications for transdermal drug delivery. Int J Pharm 2018;544(2):415–24.
[12] Szunerits S, Boukherroub R. Heat: a highly efficient skin enhancer for transdermal drug delivery. Front Bioeng Biotechnol 2018;6:15.
[13] Lee H, et al. Device-assisted transdermal drug delivery. Adv Drug Deliv Rev 2018;127:35–45.
[14] Ng LC, Gupta M. Transdermal drug delivery systems in diabetes management: a review. Asian J Pharm Sci 2019;.
[15] Singh P, et al. Polymeric microneedles for controlled transdermal drug delivery. J Control Release 2019;315:97–113.
[16] Paudel KS, et al. Challenges and opportunities in dermal/transdermal delivery. Ther Deliv 2010;1(1):109–31.
[17] Munch S, Wohlrab J, Neubert RHH. Dermal and transdermal delivery of pharmaceutically relevant macromolecules. Eur J Pharm Biopharm 2017;119:235–42.
[18] Uche LE, et al. Barrier capability of skin lipid models: effect of ceramides and free fatty acid composition. Langmuir 2019;35:15376–88.
[19] Singh I, Morris AP. Performance of transdermal therapeutic systems: effects of biological factors. Int J Pharm Investig 2011;1(1):4–9.
[20] Zorec B, et al. Combinations of nanovesicles and physical methods for enhanced transdermal delivery of a model hydrophilic drug. Eur J Pharm Biopharm 2018;127:387–97.
[21] Prausnitz MR, Langer R. Transdermal drug delivery. Nat Biotechnol 2008;26(11):1261–8.
[22] Margetts L, Sawyer R. Transdermal drug delivery: principles and opioid therapy. Contin Educ Anaesth Crit Care Pain 2007;7(5):171–6.
[23] D'Orazio JL, Fischel JA. Recurrent respiratory depression associated with fentanyl transdermal patch gel reservoir ingestion. J Emerg Med 2012;42(5):543–8.
[24] Wokovich AM, et al. Transdermal drug delivery system (TDDS) adhesion as a critical safety, efficacy and quality attribute. Eur J Pharm Biopharm 2006;64(1):1–8.
[25] Lane ME. The transdermal delivery of fentanyl. Eur J Pharm Biopharm 2013;84(3):449–55.
[26] Stevenson CL, Santini Jr. JT, Langer R. Reservoir-based drug delivery systems utilizing microtechnology. Adv Drug Deliv Rev 2012;64(14):1590–602.
[27] Prodduturi S, et al. Transdermal delivery of fentanyl from matrix and reservoir systems: effect of heat and compromised skin. J Pharm Sci 2010;99(5):2357–66.
[28] Alexander A, et al. Approaches for breaking the barriers of drug permeation through transdermal drug delivery. J Control Release 2012;164(1):26–40.
[29] Hair PI, Keating GM, McKeage K. Transdermal matrix fentanyl membrane patch (matrifen): in severe cancer-related chronic pain. Drugs 2008;68(14):2001–9.

[30] Liu C, et al. Investigation of the permeation enhancer strategy on benzoylaconitine transdermal patch: the relationship between transdermal enhancement strength and physicochemical properties of permeation enhancer. Eur J Pharm Sci 2019;138:105009.

[31] Malaiya MK, et al. Controlled delivery of rivastigmine using transdermal patch for effective management of Alzheimer's disease. J Drug Deliv Sci Technol 2018;45:408–14.

[32] Ramadan E, et al. Design and in vivo pharmacokinetic study of a newly developed lamivudine transdermal patch. Future J Pharm Sci 2018;4:166–74.

Chapter 2

Anatomy of the human skin

The largest organ in the human body is the skin [1], which makes up 16% of the total body weight with a corresponding surface area of 1.5–2.0 m^2 [2]. The anatomy of the human skin is shown in Fig. 2.1. It is the body's natural obstacle against harmful chemical (e.g., mercury), biological (e.g., staphylococcal enterotoxin), or physical (e.g., asbestos) agents [4,5]. In addition to providing a permeability barrier, lipids in the epidermis also block the invasion and colonization of the skin by pathogenic microorganisms [6]. If there is no competent permeability barrier, survival can be compromised as observed by the clinical disorders seen in burn patients and premature infants where the skin permeability barriers are dysfunctional [6]. The skin comprises the epidermis, dermis, and subcutaneous layers [7]. The epidermis has an ectodermal origin, while the dermis and the hypodermis are derived from the mesoderm [8]. The epidermis is a terminally differentiated and layered squamous epithelium, the main cell type of which is the keratinocyte [9]. Keratinocytes from the stratum basale (SB) typically differentiate to form the stratum spinosum (SS), stratum granulosum (SG), and stratum corneum (SC) [10]. Apart from the SC, the human skin is also made up of viable epidermis, which is further subdivided into SG, stratum lucidum (SL), stratum germinativum, and SS [8]. A scleroprotein (keratin) is produced by keratinocytes. Keratin is made up of coiled polypeptide chains that subsequently associate into supercoils bound by disulfide bonds [9]. Cytokines are usually produced by keratinocytes in response to injury [8,9].

The epidermis also contains Langerhans cells (LCs), which is a subclass of dendritic cells [11]. LCs are the first immune barrier against invading pathogens and are also known to induce tolerance [11]. LCs are antigen-presenting cells with the ability to capture protein antigens and bacterial toxins via dendrites, and this induces protective humoral responses [12]. The SC is postulated to be the main barrier against drug transport [13]. The peculiar anatomy of the SC, comprising intercellular lipids and corneocytes, provides the "brick and mortar" structure that is linked to the barrier function of the human skin [14]. The "bricks" refer to the corneocytes, while several lipid bilayers of cholesterol esters, cholesterol, ceramides and fatty acids constitute the "mortar" [15]. When epidermal keratinocytes undergo terminal

Transdermal Drug Delivery. DOI: https://doi.org/10.1016/B978-0-12-822550-9.00002-8

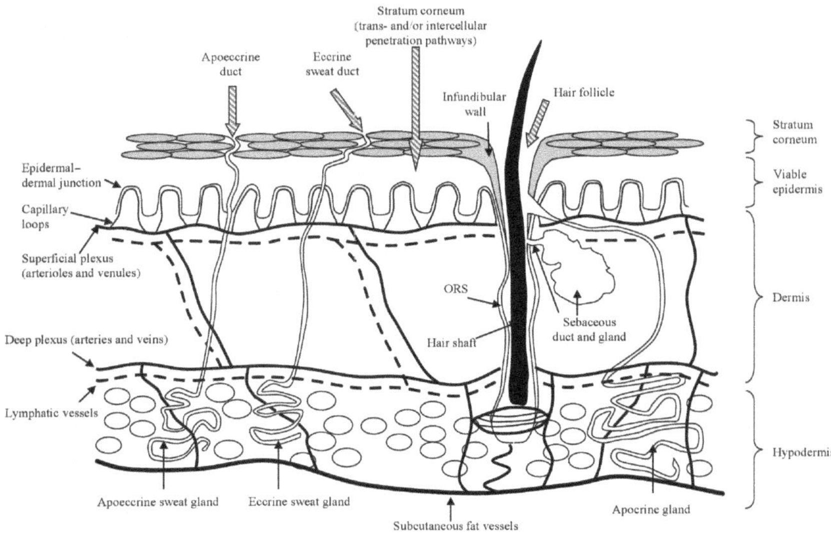

FIGURE 2.1 Anatomy of the human skin. *Reproduced with permission from Jepps OG, et al., Modeling the human skin barrier—towards a better understanding of dermal absorption. Adv Drug Deliv Rev 2013;65(2):152–168 (Chapter 2).*

differentiation, highly ordered, gel-phase lipids are secreted into the intercellular portion, and this structure results in an effective diffusion barrier [16]. By limiting the trans-epidermal water loss, the SC also prevents dehydration [5]. Appropriate lipid composition and lipid organization in this matrix are essential for an efficient skin barrier [17].

The SC comprises fully keratinized corneocytes embedded in a lipid matrix, which is the only continuous route through the SC [18]. The SC is made up of 10–15 layers of corneocytes 0.5 μm thick and 40 μm in diameter [19]. Multiple layers of corneocytes separated by lipid bilayers are present in the SC [20]. Approximately 10 lipid bilayers are compressed between two adjoining corneocytes layers [20]. The water concentration in the SC is about 18–58 wt.% [5]. Corneocytes are essentially flat hexagonal-shaped cells [9,21] with neither cytoplasmic organelles nor nuclei, and these are flattened structures with keratin filaments ordered into disulfide cross-linked microfibers [9]. Corneodesmosomes are an adhesion structure of the SC, comparable to desmosomes in viable epidermal keratinocytes [22]. Desmosomes and corneodesmosomes are linked directly with transmembrane desmosomal desmogleins (Dsgs), desmocollins (Dscs), and cadherins [22]. The main proteins are Dsg1/Dsc1 and Dsg3/Dsc3 in desmosomes, and Dsg1/Dsc1 with corneodesmosin in corneodesmosomes [22]. Corneodesmosomes covalently link corneocytes [19,21,23]. The main lipid groups in the SC are cholesterol (CHOL), ceramides (CERs), and free fatty acids (FFAs) [24]. In the human

SC, these lipids exist in an approximately equimolar ratio [24]. Filaggrin is also cross-linked into a rugged cornified cell envelope (CE) that supports the extracellular lipid matrix [19,23]. It is important to note that the cross-linkage of involucrin and loricrin is catalyzed by transglutaminase and that this process leads to the creation of CE just inside the corneocyte plasma membrane [19].

The CE is a densely cross-linked protein structure, which impedes the transport of many compounds [25] including medications. The CE forms an external membrane monolayer, which is called the corneocyte-bound lipid envelope (CLE) [26]. The CLE is made up of long-chain, omega-acylated-hydroxy-ceramides (ω-OH-Cer or ω-OH-acyl-sphingosine), with small quantities of omega-hydroxy-fatty acids (ω-OH-FA), covalently bound to involucrin via glutamyl residues [26]. Ceramides are composed of two parts: an acyl chain and a sphingoid base [27]. The molecular structure of ceramide and its hydrophilic head group defines the subclass of the ceramide [27]. The corneocytes in the SC are sealed with lipid lamellae [28] and an intricate multilamellar lipid structure occupies the extracellular space between the corneocytes [5]. Stacked bilayers of ceramides form a lamellar lipid structure [29]. In the lamellae, cholesterol is positioned in the sphingoid region, while FFAs are in the ceramide portion of the molecule [29]. The lipid matrix has many compounds such as CHOL, diacylglycerol (DAG), ceramides (CERs), FFAs, triacylglycerol (TAG), and cholesterol esters [28]. There are only traces of phospholipids—the major building block of most other biomembranes [5].

About three FFA and 17 ceramide subclasses are present in the human SC [21]. Each of these subclasses varies in chain length distribution [30]. The diverse class of ceramides is known to partake in the anatomical organization of the SC with subsequent influence on skin barrier [31]. There are several ceramide classes in the SC including acylceramides [32]. Ceramides are usually transformed into glucosylceramides (acyl-glucosylceramides in the case of acylceramides) or sphingomyelins and kept in lamellar bodies [32]. Glucosylceramides and sphingomyelins are subsequently converted back to ceramides/acylceramides by β-glucocerebrosidase or sphingomyelinase and a sufficient amount of cholesterol obtained from cholesteryl sulfate via the effect of sterol sulfatase [32]. Together with fatty acids (most likely obtained from phospholipids via phospholipases), these compounds form the skin lipid lamellae [32]. The interrelationship between the lipid lamellae and the CER subclasses has evoked considerable interest [31]. The number of specific lipids in the SC is more than 1000 [21]. They can be identified by the structure of the head group [6-hydroxysphingosine (H), sphingosine (S), phytosphingosine (P) base] coupled to α-hydroxy fatty acid (A) or a nonhydroxylated fatty acid (N) with different hydrocarbon chain lengths [33]. SC intercellular lipids are organized as crystalline lamellar phases [5,21] with short (6 nm) and long (13 nm) periodicities [21]. SC barrier lipids (fatty acids, ceramides, and cholesterol) usually adopt a dense orthorhombic lateral packing, while a smaller lipid fraction takes on a less dense hexagonal packing [17]. Within the lipid lamellae, the lipids can also assemble into liquid/fluid phases with clear-cut packing densities [24]. The formation of a hexagonal lateral packing is associated with increased presence of CERs with a shorter chain length as well as increased presence of monounsaturated CERs [18].

The viable epidermis(VE) (50–100 μm thick) does not possess blood vessels, and it is located directly below the SC [3,33]. The VE is composed of keratinocytes with about 15%–20% lipids, 40% water, and 40% protein [3]. The VE is subdivided into SG, SS, SB, and SL [33]. The keratinocytes in the SG contain keratohyalin [9]. SG derives its name from the granules present in the cells [34]. Even though this layer only has a few cells in terms of thickness, it is an important part of the epidermis because it is here that the major changes leading to the formation of the SC barrier take place [34]. There are two categories of granules in the SG: protein-filled keratohyalin granules and lipid-filled Odland (lamellar) bodies [34]. Odland bodies are secretory organelles, which are 200–300 nm in size and ovoid in shape [35]. They are absent in the SB but are present in the keratinocytes of the granular and the upper spinous layers [35]. These lamellar bodies contain glucosylceramides, phospholipids, sphingomyelin, and cholesterol. Several enzymes such as β-glucocerebrosidase, acidic sphingomyelinase, as well as secretory kallikreins and cathepsins are present in Odland bodies [35]. Keratohyalin granules are the main reservoirs for profilaggrin [32]. Several filaggrin units joined by linker peptides make up profilaggrin (a large, highly phosphorylated, insoluble protein). Profilaggrin is dephosphorylated and cleaved by serine proteases to form monomeric filaggrin during the terminal differentiation of epidermal keratinocytes in the SC [32]. Subsequently, filaggrin binds to keratin fibers, leading to the flattening of the corneocytes [32].

When present in human skin, the SL (usually seen in thick skin only) is usually observed as a clear layer consisting of eleidin (derived from keratohyalin) [36] (palms, soles). The SL is a thin clear layer consisting of eleidin [36]. Overlying the SB is a layer of the epidermis that is 5–10 cells thick and referred to as the squamous cell layer or SS [37]. The SS also called the prickle cell layer comprises irregular, polyhedral cells with outwardly extending "spines" [36]. The stratum germinativum, which is also called stratum basale (SB), is the deepest layer of the viable epidermis. A basement membrane (BM; basal lamina) separates SB from the dermis [36]. Specialized junctional complexes that mediate adhesion SB cells to the basal lamina are called hemidesmosomes [38]. The basal layer is made up of Merkel cells (with sensory functions), keratinocytes with stem cell-like properties, and melanocytes [30]. There is also a BM, which is located between the dermal and epidermal layers, and this is a thin layer of specialized extracellular matrix (ECM) to which the epidermis is attached [39]. It is an intricate collection of nidogen, type IV collagen, heparin sulfate proteoglycans, and laminin [39]. Anchoring fibril collagen type VII collagen links the epidermis to the dermis [39]. Anchoring fibrils bind the dermal-epidermal BM to the dermis below [40]. Type VII collagen molecules use tail-to-tail interactions via their carboxy terminals to agglomerate into centrosymmetric dimers [40]. Basal keratinocytes and dermal fibroblasts first synthesize type VII collagen as a 290-kDa polypeptide, and a triplex molecule is formed via three of these chains [40]. Hydroxylysyl residues are created from lysyl groups via hydroxylation, and in the next step, there is stepwise glycosylation resulting in the formation of either galactosyl-hydroxylysine (GHL) or glucosyl-galactosyl-hydroxylysine (GGHL) or [40].

The middle layer of the skin, the dermis, is composed up of the fibrillar structural protein known as collagen [37]. The dermis lies on the subcutaneous tissue (panniculus) [37]. The subcutis contains small lobes of fat cells known as lipocytes. The dermis is the load-handling portion of the human skin and it is formed from collagen (about 70% of the dry weight of skin) and elastin (about 2%–4% of the dry weight of skin) fibers [41]. Tropocollagen molecules, with a diameter of about 1.5 nm and a length of approximately 300 nm, have a staggered structure and they are components of collagen fibrils (CFs) [42]. CFs possess a d-period of 67 nm and a diameter of approximately 50–500 nm [41]. Collagen fibers, with diameters between 2 and 7 μm are formed from bundled fibrils [41]. The thickness of the dermis varies from 0.5 to 5 mm, and this is a function of the anatomical site: a thick dermis is located on the skin of the human back, while the eyelids have a thin dermis [43].

The dermis is mostly composed of fibroblasts/fibrocytes, which in turn form dense fibrous/elastic components [30]. There are also glycoproteins, proteoglycans, water, hyaluronic acid, and other compounds that combine to form the ECM [30]. The dermis is an integrated system with fibroblasts, macrophages, mast cells, vascular, lymphatic, and nervous networks [44]. Morphologically, the dermis is made up of two parts: (1) the upper or papillary dermis with a loose connective tissue and high cell density and (2) the reticular dermis in the deeper layers, which is densely packed with collagens and other connective tissue proteins but possesses a low cell density [45]. The 100–200 μm thick papillary layer of the dermis is composed of fibrocytes, elastin fibers, collagen bundles, and ground substance (GS). GS consists of plasma proteins, water, polysaccharides–polypeptide complexes, and electrolytes [3]. Below the papillary portion is the reticular layer, which consists mainly of elastic fibers and thick collagen bundles [3]. The dermis of the bare (hairless) human skin contains Merkel cell–neurite complexes, free nerve endings, and sensory corpuscles (Ruffini's corpuscles, Krause's corpuscles Meissner's corpuscles, and Pacinian corpuscles [46]). A central axon, differentiated nonmyelinating Schwann-related cells and endoneurial–perineurial-related cells combine to form a sensory corpuscle [46]. Periaxonal cells create distinct morphotypes of sensory corpuscles based on the configuration of corpuscular components with each component possessing the immunohistochemical properties of the corresponding nerve fiber [46]. The microstructure of the Pacinian corpuscles is made up of concentric lamellae, while within the Meissner's corpuscle, Schwann lamellae form sacs and a flattened axon ending [47]. There are adjoining sacs of dermal collagen [48]. There are also free nerve terminals that invaginate the epidermis and hair follicles (HFs) [30].

The subcutis (subcutaneous layer) is the adipose-rich skin layer that provides insulation for the conservation of internal body heat. It is also an energy and fluid reserve that protects deeper tissue and organs and supports the dermis and epidermis [49]. The subcutis is the innermost layer of the skin, and it comprises lipocytes (adipocytes) [43]. The lipocytes form a network of fat lobules, which are separated from one another by fibrous septa [43]. Fibers emanating from the dermis and extending into the subcutis (hypodermis) enforce the interactions between these two skin layers [43]. The hypodermis facilitates the passage of cutaneous nerves, lymph vessels, and blood vessels. It connects the dermis and fascia of the muscles [50]. Thus the ductile and energy-rich lipocytes, the vascular and neuronal network that support and innervate the skin, and the vast connective tissue that facilitates skin structural integrity are all components of the subcutaneous layer [49].

The skin also possesses numerous appendages—sweat glands, sebaceous glands and HFs [30]. SGs are acinar holocrine-secreting appendages of the epidermis linked to the junctional zone of the HF [51]. It is positioned to the upper permanent part of the HF and lies beneath the infundibulum and above the isthmus and the bulge region of the HF [51]. The basal layer of the SG comprises rapidly dividing cells that adjoin the outermost layer of the HF. Sebocytes are found in the inner portion of the gland [51]. Lysis of these cells leads to the secretion of sebum onto the skin's surface via a specialized canal [51]. During development, keratinocytes are drawn into the dermis, resulting in the creation of epidermal appendages [52]. HF comprises dermal (mesenchymal) and epidermal (epithelial) portions and the interaction of these two parts of this mini-organ influences its growth and morphogenesis [53]. HFs are complex and dynamic three-dimensional structures [54] that vary significantly in shape and size, but they all possess the inner root sheath (IRS), hair shaft (HS), dermal papilla (DP), and outer root sheath (ORS) [55].

The IRS is subdivided into three layers: the cuticle of the IRS, Huxley's layer, and Henle's layer [42]. These layers are structurally different and express layer-specific keratins, the main proteins of the HF [42]. The medulla, the cuticula, and the cortex (with melanosomes) constitute the HS [56]. The DP, derived from local fibroblasts during embryogenesis, is a specialized mesenchymal component of the HF that plays key roles in HF morphogenesis and regeneration [53,57]. The IRS covers the HS. The DP carries out several functions during cyclic adult hair regeneration including replication, the stimulation of epithelial growth, differentiation, as well as the specification of epithelial cell fates [58]. The ORS covers the entire HS and is subject to trichilemmal keratinization around the level of the isthmus [47]. Matrix cells in the lower portion of the hair bulb undergo a high rate of mitosis, while the mitotic rate in the upper part of the hair bulb is lower and can be transformed into six different groups of cells (e.g., cuticle of the IRS, Henle's layer of IRS, cuticle of hair, cortex, Huxley's layer of IRS, and medulla), each of which differentiates at a different rate [59]. HFs, which contain the differentiated cells of the HS, are first formed from hair germs during embryonic development [60]. The pilosebaceous unit (PU) is an integrated structure that incorporates the sebaceous gland, the HF, the HS, and the adjoining arrector pili muscle [61]. Several cell populations contribute to the organization of the PU [61]. The HF is composed of the permanent part—infundibulum, the isthmus, and the bulge region [61]. The transient segment of the HF includes the bulb and suprabulbar region [61]. A single HF undergoes successive growth cycles with the following phases: quiescence (telogen), growth (anagen) apoptosis and regression (catagen), and old hair fiber shedding (exogen) [60].

There are three main classes of sweat glands in the human skin: eccrine, apocrine, and apoeccrine [62]. Eccrine sweat glands are coiled, tubular glands widely distributed throughout the body, especially on the soles of the feet [63]. This class of sweat gland is made up of acrosyringium, secretory coil, and dermal duct [55,64]. The secretory coil contains three primary cells: the dark (mucoid), the secretary (clear), and the supportive (myoepithelial) cells [55]. Clear cells are thought to be the main source of sweat secretion due to the large number of mitochondria within the cells [55]. The participation of dark cells in membrane-cellular transport has been postulated, while myoepithelial cells are known to function as a supportive network [55]. Typically, eccrine gland duct opens onto the skin surface facilitating secretions, whereas the apocrine sweat gland is an appendage of the HF and secretes fluid through the infundibular portion of the HF [54,65]. Apocrine sweat glands secrete an oily material by shearing off cell parts in a process involving necrobiotic process [54]. Eccrine sweat glands populate the body surface with as many as $700/cm^2$ in the adult skin [54]. In contrast to the branched duct of the mammary gland, the eccrine gland duct is a straight channel, whereas the secretory part of the eccrine gland has a peculiar, coiled tube-shaped structure and a contracted lumen [54]. The secretory coils are formed from myoepithelial and secretory cells [66]. Secretory coils release isotonic fluid into the lumen from which the ducts reabsorb sodium, thereby converting sweat from an isotonic solution to a hypotonic one [66]. It has been shown that sweat glands from both hairy and depilated skin regions respond to changes in temperature [67]. The sweat made by the eccrine glands contains neither proteins nor fatty acids [62]. In the human skin, apoeccrine glands are positioned in close proximity to apocrine glands but they produce sweat with a composition comparable to that made by the eccrine glands [62].

References

[1] Wang Y, et al. NF-κB signaling in skin aging. Mech Ageing Dev 2019;184:111160.
[2] Chen Z, et al. Overcoming or circumventing the stratum corneum barrier for efficient transcutaneous immunization. Drug Discov Today 2018;23(1):181–6.
[3] Jepps OG, et al. Modeling the human skin barrier—towards a better understanding of dermal absorption. Adv Drug Deliv Rev 2013;65(2):152–68.
[4] Chen X. Current and future technological advances in transdermal gene delivery. Adv Drug Deliv Rev 2018;127:85–105.
[5] Schmitt T, et al. Impact of the ceramide subspecies on the nanostructure of stratum corneum lipids using neutron scattering and molecular dynamics simulations. Part I: impact of CER[NS]. Chem Phys Lipids 2018;.
[6] Feingold KR, Elias PM. Role of lipids in the formation and maintenance of the cutaneous permeability barrier. Biochim Biophys Acta Mol Cell Biol Lipids 2014;1841(3):280–94.
[7] Chen X. Current and future technological advances in transdermal gene delivery. Adv Drug Deliv Rev 2017;.
[8] Tsakovska I, et al. Quantitative structure-skin permeability relationships. Toxicology 2017;387:27–42.
[9] Venus M, Waterman J, McNab I. Basic physiology of the skin. Surgery 2011;29 (10):471–4.
[10] Erdo F, et al. Critical evaluation and methodological positioning of the transdermal microdialysis technique. A review. J Control Release 2016;233:147–61.
[11] Hieronymus T, et al. The clash of Langerhans cell homeostasis in skin: should I stay or should I go? Semin Cell Dev Biol 2015;41:30–8.
[12] Kitashima DY, et al. Langerhans cells prevent autoimmunity via expansion of keratinocyte antigen-specific regulatory T cells. EBioMedicine 2018;27:293–303.
[13] Ronnander P, et al. Modelling the in-vitro dissolution and release of sumatriptan succinate from polyvinylpyrrolidone-based microneedles. Eur J Pharm Sci 2018;125:54–63.
[14] Ita K. Dissolving microneedles for transdermal drug delivery: advances and challenges. Biomed Pharmacother. 2017;93:1116–27.
[15] Alexander A, et al. Approaches for breaking the barriers of drug permeation through transdermal drug delivery. J Control Release 2012;164(1):26–40.
[16] Miller MA, et al. Uptake and desorption of hydrophilic compounds from human stratum corneum. J Controlled Rel 2017;261:307–17.
[17] Berkers T, et al. Compromising human skin in vivo and ex vivo to study skin barrier repair. Biochim Biophys Acta Mol Cell Biol Lipids 2019;1864(8):1103–8.
[18] Mieremet A, et al. Unravelling effects of relative humidity on lipid barrier formation in human skin equivalents. Arch Dermatol Res 2019;311(9):679–89.
[19] Ita K. Ceramic microneedles and hollow microneedles for transdermal drug delivery: two decades of research. J Drug Deliv Sci Technol 2018;44:314–22.
[20] Mitragotri S. Modeling skin permeability to hydrophilic and hydrophobic solutes based on four permeation pathways. J Control Release 2003;86(1):69–92.
[21] Gooris GS, et al. Interactions of dipalmitoylphosphatidylcholine with ceramide-based mixtures. Biochim Biophys Acta 2018;1860(6):1272–81.
[22] Kitajima Y. Implications of normal and disordered remodeling dynamics of corneodesmosomes in stratum corneum. Dermatol Sin 2015;33(2):58–63.
[23] Kezic S, Jakasa I. Filaggrin and skin barrier function. Curr Probl Dermatol 2016;49:1–7.

[24] Uche LE, et al. New insight into phase behavior and permeability of skin lipid models based on sphingosine and phytosphingosine ceramides. Biochim Biophys Acta Biomembr 2019;1861(7):1317–28.

[25] Bouwstra JA, Honeywell-Nguyen PL. Skin structure and mode of action of vesicles. Adv Drug Deliv Rev 2002;54(Suppl 1):S41–55.

[26] Elias PM, et al. Formation and functions of the corneocyte lipid envelope (CLE). Biochim Biophys Acta 2014;1841(3):314–18.

[27] Boiten W, et al. Selectivity in cornified envelop binding of ceramides in human skin and the role of LXR inactivation on ceramide binding. Biochim Biophys Acta Mol Cell Biol Lipids 2019;1864(9):1206–13.

[28] Sadowski T, et al. Large-scale human skin lipidomics by quantitative, high-throughput shotgun mass spectrometry. Sci Rep 2017;7:43761.

[29] Lundborg M, et al. Predicting drug permeability through skin using molecular dynamics simulation. J Control Release 2018;.

[30] Slominski AT, Manna PR, Tuckey RC. On the role of skin in the regulation of local and systemic steroidogenic activities. Steroids 2015;103:72–88.

[31] Eichner A, et al. Influence of the penetration enhancer isopropyl myristate on stratum corneum lipid model membranes revealed by neutron diffraction and 2H NMR experiments. Biochim Biophys Acta Biomembr 2017;1859(5):745–55.

[32] Hirabayashi T, Murakami M, Kihara A. The role of PNPLA1 in ω-O-acylceramide synthesis and skin barrier function. Biochim Biophys Acta Mol Cell Biol Lipids 2019;1864 (6):869–79.

[33] Bouwstra JA, Ponec M. The skin barrier in healthy and diseased state. Biochim Biophys Acta Biomembr 2006;1758(12):2080–95.

[34] Wickett RR, Visscher MO. Structure and function of the epidermal barrier. Am J Infect Control 2006;34(10, Supplement):S98–110.

[35] Joshi R. Learning from eponyms: George F. Odland and Odland bodies. Indian Dermatol Online J 2014;5(3):334–8.

[36] Yousef H, Sharma S. Anatomy, skin (integument), epidermis. StatPearls. Treasure Island, FL: StatPearls Publishing LLC; 2018.

[37] Kolarsick PAJ, Kolarsick MA, Goodwin C. Anatomy and physiology of the skin. J Dermatol Nurses Assoc 2011;3(4):203–13.

[38] Nievers MG, Schaapveld RQJ, Sonnenberg A. Biology and function of hemidesmosomes. Matrix Biol 1999;18(1):5–17.

[39] Mikesh LM, et al. Proteomic anatomy of human skin. J Proteomics 2013;84:190–200.

[40] Vahidnezhad H, et al. Mutations in PLOD3, encoding lysyl hydroxylase 3, cause a complex connective tissue disorder including recessive dystrophic epidermolysis bullosa-like blistering phenotype with abnormal anchoring fibrils and type VII collagen deficiency. Matrix Biol 2019;81:91–106.

[41] Pissarenko A, et al. Tensile behavior and structural characterization of pig dermis. Acta Biomater 2019;86:77–95.

[42] Miyai M, et al. c-Maf and MafB transcription factors are differentially expressed in Huxley's and Henle's layers of the inner root sheath of the hair follicle and regulate cuticle formation. J Dermatol Sci 2010;57(3):178–82.

[43] Lai-Cheong JE, McGrath JA. Structure and function of skin, hair and nails. Medicine 2017;45(6):347–51.

[44] Kamble P, et al. Nanofiber based drug delivery systems for skin: a promising therapeutic approach. J Drug Deliv Sci Technol 2017;41:124–33.

[45] Korosec A, et al. Lineage identity and location within the dermis determine the function of papillary and reticular fibroblasts in human skin. J Investig Dermatol 2019;139 (2):342–51.
[46] Feito J, et al. The development of human digital Meissner's and Pacinian corpuscles. Ann Anat 2018;219:8–24.
[47] Martel JL, Badri T. Anatomy, hair follicle. StatPearls. Treasure Island (FL): StatPearls Publishing LLC; 2019.
[48] Somer DD, et al. A multi-scale computational assessment of channel gating assumptions within the Meissner corpuscle. J Biomech 2015;48(1):73–80.
[49] Ahn AC, Kaptchuk TJ. Spatial anisotropy analyses of subcutaneous tissue layer: potential insights into its biomechanical characteristics. J Anat 2011;219(4):515–24.
[50] Ishida T, et al. Anatomical structure of the subcutaneous tissue on the anterior surface of human thigh. Okajimas Folia Anat Jpn 2015;92(1):1–6.
[51] Niemann C, Horsley V. Development and homeostasis of the sebaceous gland. Semin Cell Dev Biol 2012;23(8):928–36.
[52] Mancini M, et al. MicroRNAs in human skin ageing. Ageing Res Rev 2014;17:9–15.
[53] Yang CC, Cotsarelis G. Review of hair follicle dermal cells. J Dermatol Sci 2010;57 (1):2–11.
[54] Lu C, Fuchs E. Sweat gland progenitors in development, homeostasis, and wound repair. Cold Spring Harb Perspect Med 2014;4(2).
[55] Sonner Z, et al. The microfluidics of the eccrine sweat gland, including biomarker partitioning, transport, and biosensing implications. Biomicrofluidics 2015;9(3):031301.
[56] Wosicka H, Cal K. Targeting to the hair follicles: current status and potential. J Dermatol Sci 2010;57(2):83–9.
[57] Huang WY, et al. Stress-induced premature senescence of dermal papilla cells compromises hair follicle epithelial-mesenchymal interaction. J Dermatol Sci 2017;86 (2):114–22.
[58] Lei M, Yang L, Chuong CM. Getting to the core of the dermal papilla. J Investig Dermatol 2017;137(11):2250–3.
[59] Lee WS. Integral hair lipid in human hair follicle. J Dermatol Sci 2011;64(3):153–8.
[60] Mesler AL, et al. Hair follicle terminal differentiation is orchestrated by distinct early and late matrix progenitors. Cell Rep 2017;19(4):809–21.
[61] Patzelt A, et al. Hair follicles, their disorders and their opportunities. Drug Discov Today Dis Mech 2008;5(2):e173–81.
[62] Piotr F, Piotr L, Wojcicki JM. Monitoring of sweat secretion from eccrine sweat glands using electric conductivity method. Biocybern Biomed Eng 2012;32(4):47–57.
[63] Hodge BD, Brodell RT. Anatomy, skin, sweat glands. StatPearls. Treasure Island, FL: StatPearls Publishing LLC; 2019.
[64] Treister AD, Lio AP. Anatomy, skin, sudoriferous gland. StatPearls [Internet]. Treasure Island, FL: StatPearls Publishing; 2019. Available from: https://www.ncbi.nlm.nih.gov/books/NBK513244/.
[65] Borowczyk-Michalowska J, et al. Stage-specific embryonic antigen-4 (SSEA-4) as a distinguishing marker between eccrine and apocrine origin of ducts of sweat glands. J Investig Dermatol 2017;137(11):2437–40.
[66] Li H, et al. Combination of keratins and alpha-smooth muscle actin distinguishes secretory coils from ducts of eccrine sweat glands. Acta Histochem 2015;117(3):275–8.
[67] Machado-Moreira CA, Taylor NA. Thermogenic and psychogenic recruitment of human eccrine sweat glands: variations between glabrous and non-glabrous skin surfaces. J Therm Biol 2017;65:145–52.

Chapter 3

Basic principles of transdermal drug delivery

The stacked lamellae in the intercellular space between corneocytes constitute the probable location for the skin's permeability barrier [1]. Skin lamellar lipids are rich in ceramides [1]. The skin barrier is also attributed to lamellar granules that contain numerous enzymes, cholesterol, fatty acids, and sphingolipids [2]. Cathelicidin and human β-defensin 2 (HBD-2) in the lamellar bodies are also linked to the skin's permeability barrier [3]. The staggered architecture of corneocyte in a lipid continuum results in a highly circuitous lipid route making the skin 1000 times less permeable to water compared to most membranes in the body [4]. For a drug to be effectively delivered through the transdermal route, it must overcome the skin barrier. An applied medication must penetrate the structural layers of the human skin, encountering several lipophilic and hydrophilic regions on the way to the dermis where absorption into the systemic circulation is fast because of the presence of a large capillary bed [5]. The first step in the drug transport process involves crossing the stratum corneum (SC) followed by the permeation across the viable epidermis before being absorbed through the dermal vasculature [6]. The transport of compounds through the skin occurs through the appendageal, transcellular, or intercellular routes [7]. Compounds transported via the intercellular route depend mainly on passive diffusion through the circuitous intercellular lipids in the SC and this route is used principally by lipophilic drugs [7]. Most drugs enter the viable epidermis via intercellular absorption that entails passive diffusion through the intercellular lipid pathway of the SC [8]. The amphibious nature of the intercellular lipids facilitates the movement of substances with a wide range of polarity [8]. The transcellular route entails compounds passing through the cells and requires movement through the hydrophilic water environment within the cells as well as the hydrophobic sections of the skin (cell membranes and intercellular lipids) [7]. The third pathway is the appendageal route that involves drug permeation via glandular ducts and hair follicles [7].

The SC hinders the diffusion of polar solutes such as salts, water, and sugars [9]; this function is ascribed to bilayer lipids secreted into the

Transdermal Drug Delivery. DOI: https://doi.org/10.1016/B978-0-12-822550-9.00003-X

intercellular spaces following terminal differentiation of keratinocytes [9]. The SC is permeable to small quantities of polar solutes as demonstrated by SC conductivity under low constant electric fields but the degree to which large hydrophilic compounds can cross the SC without breaching the skin barrier is still controversial [9]. It has been postulated that hydrophilic molecules cross the skin mainly through the transcellular route while the follicular route is also important even though hair follicles constitute only 0.1% of the total area of the skin [6,10]. When penetrating the skin via the transcellular route, a drug molecule partitions and diffuses through keratinocytes [11]. There are 4–20 lipid lamellae present between adjoining keratinocytes. Transdermal transport of penetrants can change as a function of skin hydration levels as well as chemical properties, permeant sizes, hydrophilicities, and diffusivities [12]. There has been considerable debate in scientific circles regarding the relative significance of the three alternative routes of drug administration—through SC, the follicular route with their associated sebaceous glands or via the sweat ducts [13]. Furthermore, it has been demonstrated that nanotopography (surface features created at the nanoscale level) can significantly increase the paracellular transport of high molecular weight (MW) compounds in vitro [14]. Walsh and coworkers published data that showed, for the first time, that nanotopography applied to microneedles substantially increased transdermal delivery of etanercept, a 150-kD molecule, in both rats and rabbits [14]. It is still not clear from experimental data if lipid layers, corneocytes, or tight junctions are the main contributors to the skin permeability barrier [15].

Increasingly, it is being recognized that corneocytes are permeable while the lipid layers are anisotropic—their permeability being direction-dependent [15]. Indeed, Mitragotri has commented on the anisotropy and size dependence of solute transport in SC lipid bilayers [16]. According to the author, lipid bilayers display structural heterogeneity giving rise to spatial changes in the values of partition and diffusion coefficients of compounds [16]. Normally, transcutaneous permeation of medications entails diffusion through the intercellular lipids around the corneocytes, with hydrophilic molecules penetrating the lipid head groups and lipophilic compounds diffusing via the hydrophobic lipid chains [17]. Lipids between the corneocytes are configured in the form of multilamellar arrays, and that can lead to several modes of drug diffusion [18]. It is increasingly being accepted that intercellular diffusion constitutes the most preponderant route of drug diffusion through the skin [18]. In homogeneous media, drug molecules undergo flux (J; units = amount/(area/time), e.g., $g/cm^2/h^1$) as a function of concentration gradient [19]. Typically, diffusional flux is from region of high chemical potential to the region of low chemical potential, resulting in a diffusion flux at a position x at time being proportional (in a general case scenario) to the chemical gradient potential [19]. Chemical potential, μ, is a parameter that is used to quantify the rate of change of free energy of a system when particles are added or removed under constant pressure and temperature provided the number of the other particles is also constant [20–22]. It takes into consideration the change in entropy upon adding a particle to the system [20]. With the parenteral (injectable) route of administration, medications are usually absorbed into blood circulation through convection but with transdermal drug delivery, the main mechanism of transport is diffusion [19]. Only few medications can be transported percutaneously into the bloodstream at therapeutically significant rates due to the unique nature of the skin barrier [23,24]. A drug candidate for transdermal delivery must possess great potency, low MW, and moderate lipophilicity [23]. Interestingly, most medications do not fulfill these criteria [23] and enhancement techniques have to be used. In the laboratory setting, transdermal drug delivery experiments are typically conducted with in vitro with diffusion cells and in vivo using various rodents.

Transdermal drug delivery experiments

Most skin permeation experiments are conducted in vitro and/or in vivo. In the beginning of most research projects, in vitro diffusion experiments are first conducted before in vivo transcutaneous penetration studies [25]. Percutaneous drug delivery projects typically entail the experimental determination of transcutaneous flux values [24]. This can be done in vitro using human skin or different types of animal skin samples including guinea pig, rat, or pig skin [24]. Excised human skin is desirable for most in vitro permeation studies but because of ethics, most researchers use nonhuman skin models for preliminary experiments [26]. Although several reptile and rodent skin models have been used as substitutes for the human skin, animal skin is more permeable in comparison with human skin [27]. It is also important to emphasize that although monkey skin is a better model than rodent skin, the use of primates for experiments is controlled and may be difficult to obtain [28]. In contrast, porcine skin can be easily acquired as waste from an abattoir [27]. Several transdermal drug delivery research projects have been conducted with synthetic membranes, guinea pig, mouse, pig, rabbit, rat, shed snake skin, and cultured human skin models [26]. Several types of diffusion systems for in vitro transcutaneous experiments are available [25]. These include static (vertical and horizontal) and flow-through diffusion cells [29]. The most commonly used diffusion cells are the vertical Franz cells [29]. There are two compartments in these cells with one containing the investigated compound in solution (donor) and the other serving as the receptor compartment with the appropriate fluid [typically phosphate buffered saline (PBS)] and investigators use a membrane to separate the two compartments with the receptor compartment jacketed to control the temperature [25].

Porcine skin is commonly utilized for in vitro diffusion studies because the histologic, biochemical, and permeability properties are comparable to those of the human skin [26,27,29]. The SC lipids in the pig skin are comparable to human lipids, the hair density is comparable, and there is a similarity in the skin permeability [30]. However, freezing and then thawing the pig tissue can result in drug transport enhancement [30]. Another important consideration in conducting transdermal experiments with biological membranes using a receiver fluid is that there may be bacterial growth, decomposition, unrealistic swelling, and leaching out of skin components, especially if the transdermal studies are carried out for more than 24 h [25]. The skin is usually placed between the diffusion cells (vertical or horizontal) and a solution of the drug is put in the donor chamber [24]. At different times, the drug solution is taken from the receiver chamber and assayed with either enzyme-linked immunosorbent assay, liquid chromatography–mass spectrometry (LC-MS), ultraviolet spectrometry, high-performance liquid chromatography, inductively coupled plasma optical emission spectrometry (ICP-OES), or any other suitable analytical technique [24,31,32]. Once drug concentration is determined, the cumulative amount versus time curve is plotted and the slope of the linear portion of this curve is used to compute the flux value (*J*) [33]. The cumulative amount of a permeant, Q_n (μg/cm^2) can be computed as follows [34]:

$$Q_n = \left(\frac{C_n \cdot V + V_o \sum_{i=1}^{n-1} C_i}{A} \right) \tag{3.1}$$

where C_n is the concentration of sample *n*, *V* is the volume of medium in the receptor compartment, C_i is the concentration of sample *i*, *A* (cm^2) is the permeation area, and V_o is the withdrawn volume [34].

According to Fick's first law, transdermal flux depends on diffusion coefficient, partition coefficient, and drug concentration [35]:

$$J = \frac{DKCv}{h} \tag{3.2}$$

where *J* is the flux, *D* is the diffusion coefficient, *K* is the partition coefficient, *Cv* is the drug concentration, and *h* is thickness of the diffusion barrier. There are three possible transdermal drug delivery enhancement strategies based on Fick's first law: increase the diffusion coefficient, increase the partition coefficient, and increase the degree of drug saturation in the vehicle [36]. For any compound, the transdermal flux for a drug is the product of its solubility and diffusivity in the SC. The skin permeability of a drug can be calculated from the pseudo-steady-state portion of the cumulative amount versus time curve by using the following equation [37]:

$$J_T = PA\Delta C \tag{3.3}$$

where J_T is the total flux, P is the permeability coefficient (cm/h), A is the diffusional area (cm^2), and ΔC is the concentration gradient across the skin. Since $J_T = V(dc/dt)$, the permeability coefficient can be calculated from:

$$P = \frac{V\left(\frac{dc}{dt}\right)}{A\Delta C} \quad (3.4)$$

where V represents the receptor compartment volume and dc/dt is the steady-state slope of the cumulative amount versus time curve [37]. The permeability coefficient is frequently described as a parameter describing the concentration-independent and intrinsic ability of a molecule to penetrate the SC [38]. When estimating a drug's permeability coefficient, it is important to consider drug's partition into the SC and the molecular size of the compound [38]. A direct measurement of a drug concentration in the SC lipid is not easy to determine experimentally and can be replaced by the drug's partition coefficient ($K_{o/w}$) [38]. Apparent diffusion coefficient is usually obtained experimentally by measuring steady-state flux and equilibrium partitioning [39]. Another method of experiment-based estimation of apparent diffusion coefficient is by calculating lag time (t_{lag}) from the cumulative amount versus time curve via the following equation [39]:

$$D = \frac{h^2}{6t_{lag}} \quad (3.5)$$

It has, however, been pointed out that the determination of D from drug permeation profiles should be carried out with caution since it is error-prone [39,40].

For in vivo skin permeation experiments, drug delivery scientists typically use rodents such as hairless guinea pigs, hairless rat, or hairless mice due to their relatively low cost, availability, small size, and simple handling [26]. Miniature pigs have also been used for in vivo transdermal pharmacokinetic experiments [41]. An approval must be obtained from the Institutional Ethics Committee [42]. Typically, glycopyrrolate and buprenorphine are used to induce analgesia while ketamine and xylazine (or pentobarbital sodium) are administered to the rodents to induce anesthesia before surgery [43–45]. Next, catheters are surgically implanted into the jugular vein and transdermal patches are then administered to the back of the rodents [44]. Plasma samples are drawn following transdermal and intravenous drug administration [44]. In another experimental design involving iontophoresis, a GelSponge patch applied on the rat's abdomen [46]. At predetermined time intervals, blood samples are collected from the tail vein into microtainer tubes [46] and subsequently analyzed by HPLC, LC-MS, or any other suitable technique. The retro-orbital bleeding technique can also be used to draw blood that is subsequently transferred into micro-centrifuge tubes [42]. Following chemical analysis of blood samples, pharmacokinetic (PK) parameters the elimination rate constant (K), and the volume of distribution (Vd) are determined [45]. Some research laboratories use WinNonlin or a similar software to calculate PK parameters [45]. Parameter estimation is carried out via model fitting analysis using the appropriate algorithm [47]. Cazares-Delgadillo and others used Gauss–Newton algorithm with a Levenberg–Hartley modification to estimate elimination (k10) rate constants and input rate (k_{input}) for granisetron [48]. Noncompartmental parameters such as half-life, C_{max} and AUC_{0-inf}, were then calculated [48]. Valiveti et al. investigated the pharmacokinetics of naltrexone following intravenous bolus injection by fitting the data to a three-compartment model using the following equation [43]:

$$C = Ae^{-\alpha t} + Be^{-\beta t} + Ce^{-\gamma t} \tag{3.6}$$

where A, B, and C are preexponential constants; α and β are fast and slow distribution rate constants, respectively; C is the plasma concentration of drug; γ is the elimination rate constant; and t is time [43]. WinNonlin was used to calculate elimination half-life, $t_{1/2}(\gamma)$; steady-state Vd, V_{ss}; distribution half-lives, $t_{1/2(\alpha)}$ and $t_{1/2(\beta)}$; area under the curve from 0 to infinity, $AUC_{0-\infty}$ and total body clearance (Cl) [43]. The authors used the peak plasma concentration (C_{max}) after an intravenous dose of naltrexone (NTX) to estimate the initial Vd [43]:

$$V = \frac{\text{Dose}}{C_{max}} \tag{3.7}$$

The same authors also utilized noncompartmental analysis to determine peak concentration (C_{max}), lag time to steady-state concentration (t_{lag}) and area under the curve from 0 to 48 h, AUC_{0-48} [43]. Following the administration of transdermal patches, the authors calculated the steady-state plasma concentration [43]:

$$C_{ss} = \frac{AUC_{0-t}}{\text{time}} \tag{3.8}$$

Selection of transdermal drug delivery candidates

In spite of the large number of publications on transcutaneous drug delivery carried out over the past 40 years, less than 25 active pharmaceutical ingredients are formulated as transdermal patches [24]. Not all drugs can be therapeutically effective when administered through the skin as transdermal drug delivery systems. In comparison with other dosage forms, the few transdermal products commercially available can be ascribed to the limited number of compounds that can achieve therapeutic concentration via the transdermal route [49]. It is critical to have a good knowledge of the pharmacokinetic and physicochemical parameters of an active pharmaceutical ingredient to determine it is feasible for it to be delivered transdermally [50]. Compounds for transdermal drug delivery should have low MW ideally less than 500 Da, possess lipophilicity between 1 and 3, aqueous solubility of more than 1 mg/mL and the dose should be less than one milligram per day [24]. Furthermore, the melting point of the drug should ideally be less than 200°C [51,52] since a relationship exists between the solubility and melting point of a drug [53]. There is an equation that links the solubility constraint (δsc) in the SC by using the melting point of the drug [54]:

$$\text{Log}\delta sc = 1.911\frac{10^3}{\text{mp}} - 2.956 \tag{3.9}$$

where mp is the melting point (in K) and δsc is the solubility constraint in the SC. It has been emphasized that lowering the melting point of a drug (e.g., through the formation of eutectic mixtures) can result in an enhanced solubility in the SC and ultimately increased its transcutaneous penetration [53]. Indeed, permeant melting point is inversely proportional to lipophilicity [55,56].

The feasibility of transdermal delivery is a step-wise process involving the determination of a drug's target transdermal flux [57]. This target flux across the skin shows if the drug transcutaneous permeation rate can result in the required therapeutic plasma concentration [44]. The following equation can be used to calculate target flux:

$$J\text{ss} = \frac{C_{\text{SS}}XCLt}{A} \tag{3.10}$$

where C_{SS} is the drug's therapeutic concentration, CLt is total body clearance, and A is the area of the transdermal drug delivery system [45]. It is preferable that the area of the transdermal patch does not exceed 50 cm^2 [57].

Physico-chemical determinants of percutaneous penetration

Molecular weight

The effect of physicochemical factors on the skin delivery of drugs is complex [24,57,58]. It would be convenient to have a clear-cut relationship between these factors (MW, partition coefficient, hydrogen bonding, etc.) and transcutaneous flux. At present, that is not possible. Nevertheless, it is well known that the skin permeation of a compound depends on the MW, hydrophobicity, and hydrogen bonding [59]. Indeed, many authors have identified the MW of less than 500 as optimal for transdermal drug delivery [24,57,58,60]. The scientific literature is inundated with mathematical models that attempt to associate molecular size with skin permeability coefficient [61,62]. It has been documented that there is a relationship between MW and transdermal flux [63]. Indeed, Potts and Guy used the Flynn database [64] to develop an equation that links skin permeability coefficient with MW and partition coefficient [61]. The starting point for the Potts–Guy approach is the characterization of the skin as a simple lipophilic barrier [59,61]. The skin permeability is given by the equation [61]:

$$K_p = D\frac{K}{\delta} \tag{3.11}$$

where K is SC water partition coefficient; D is the compound's diffusion coefficient in the SC; and δ is the diffusion path length across the SC [61]. The authors also used the free-volume theory to relate permeability coefficient(k_p) to diffusion coefficient (D), MW, and partition coefficient (K) [61]. According to this mathematical model, the empirical equation linking K_p with K_{ow} and MW is [61]:

$$\text{Log } k_p = -2.74 + 0.71 \text{ Log } K_{ow} - 0.0061\, MW \tag{3.12}$$

In Eq. 3.10, the units of k_p are cm/s[1] and the experimental values used to derive the Potts–Guy equation were obtained from compounds with log P values spanning from −3 to +6 and MWs ranging from 18 to over 750 [40]. Cleek and Bunge modified this equation to take into consideration the contribution of the underlying viable skin for more lipophilic compounds [57,65]:

$$k_{p,w}^{\text{corr}} = \frac{k_{p.w}}{1 + \left(\frac{k_{p.w} \times \sqrt{MW}}{2.6}\right)} \tag{3.13}$$

where $k_{p,w}^{\text{corr}}$ is the corrected permeability coefficient and $k_{p.w}$ is the permeability coefficient of the drug from a vehicle [57,65].

Partition coefficient

When a drug's permeability coefficient, k_p, is derived from a set of transdermal experiments or estimated theoretically, it is assumed that the drug first partitions into the skin before diffusing through the SC, viable epidermis into the dermis where it is taken up by the vasculature into the bloodstream. Such assumptions, though simplistic, have helped in developing robust in silico models. Transcutaneous permeation entails partitioning between multiple phases—the corneocytes and the vehicle, the SC lipids and the vehicle, the SC, and deeper skin layers such as the viable epidermis and between lipids and the corneocytes [40]. It has been observed by Mitragotri et al. that skin lipid bilayers are more hydrophobic than the adjoining water environment and that the highly organized lipid chains limit the partition coefficient due to low free volumes [40]. It is challenging to measure water/skin partition coefficient, so an alternative that is often used is the oil-water partition coefficient (log P) obtained by measuring the ratio of the drug's concentration in l-octanol and water. Indeed, log P is a surrogate for log K_{ow} in Eq. 3.10 and it is documented that drugs with log P values between 1 and 3 [24] are more likely to traverse the skin faster. It has been postulated that drug candidates for transdermal delivery should possess both water and lipid solubility [66]. Furthermore, for highly lipophilic drug, the intracellular route is favorable, while hydrophilic medications permeate the skin predominantly through the intercellular route [66].

Solubility

Solubility also affects the transcutaneous flux of medications [67]. In accordance with Fick's law, the transdermal penetration of a drug is a function of the concentration of the drug in the vehicle: high solubility facilitates a high drug concentration in the donor compartment and that ultimately leads to increased skin permeation [67]. Ideally, transdermal drug delivery candidates should have solubility values higher than 1 mg/mL [68]. Skin permeation of a drug is directly proportional to the solubility of the drug in the lipid phase of the skin and a drug can only cross the skin if it is in a solution [24]. The maximum solute concentration depends on its solubility in a given solvent that is determined by solute–solvent molecular interactions [69]. Lipids make up a significant portion of the SC and the solubility of a drug in lipid (S_{lipid}) is an essential parameter. For solubility determination, an excess quantity of the drug is usually mixed with the solvent (frequently water) and the drug concentration is subsequently quantified [70]. The rationale is to use a saturated solution with the maximum thermodynamic activity [35]. Indeed, Kathe and coworkers have shown the relationship between drug flux and thermodynamic activity [35]:

$$J = \frac{\alpha D}{\gamma h} \tag{3.14}$$

where $\alpha =$ thermodynamic activity of drug within formulation, $\gamma =$ thermodynamic activity of drug within membrane, D is the diffusion coefficient, h is the thickness of the diffusional barrier.

Diffusion coefficient

Transdermal transport of drugs is also a function of diffusion coefficient [71]. When a drug is administered through the transdermal route, it enters the bloodstream through a simple diffusion process [72]. Percutaneous penetration of compounds across the SC occurs possibly via two mechanisms: extracellular diffusion within the intercellular lipids or transcellular diffusion through lipid layers and corneocytes in series [73]. Researchers have used

Fick's second law to describe drug diffusion within a transdermal drug delivery system (TDDS) or the SC [71]:

$$\frac{\partial C_A}{\partial t} = D\frac{\partial^2 C_A}{\partial x^2}, t \geq 0,\ x \geq 0 \quad (3.15)$$

where D is the diffusion coefficient in the transdermal patch or the skin, C_A is the drug concentration in the transdermal therapeutic system or the skin, t is the time, and x is the depth. The authors used confocal Raman depth scans to compute diffusion coefficients of a model drug Paeonol (2′-Hydroxy-4′-methoxyacetophenone) [71]. The concentration was determined with a Gaussian function [71]:

$$m(t,x) = \frac{\sqrt{D}}{\sqrt{\pi t}}(C_{A0} - C_{A\propto})\exp\frac{-x^2}{4Dt} \quad (3.16)$$

$$C_{A0}(t=0,x) = C_{A.\alpha} = \text{const} \quad (3.17)$$

$$C_A(x=0) = C_{A0} \quad (3.18)$$

Using an approach based on depth profiles, a diffusion coefficient of $2.85 \times 10^{-16} \pm 6.5 \times 10^{-17}$ m²/s was obtained [71]. The difficulty in using classical diffusion coefficient is linked to the anisotropy of the skin [40,74]. Mitragotri and coworkers observed that the basic modeling assumptions of averaging key skin parameters (partition coefficient, diffusion length, and diffusion coefficient) across the entire SC as well as rapid microtransport processes within the SC in comparison to diffusion across the membrane do not always hold due to the anatomic heterogeneity of the SC and the existence of slow reversible binding phenomena [40]. Lipid layers in the SC are anisotropic—their permeability depends on direction- and that has a significant influence on skin diffusivity [75]. It has been postulated that the vertical heterogeneity of the SC can be linked to increases in SC water content with depth (20%–60% for incompletely hydrated SC and 50%–70% for fully hydrated SC) [75] leading to enhanced corneocyte diffusivity in the deeper strata of the SC [75].

Ionization

pH has a significant effect on transdermal delivery because researchers can use a broad range of pH values to formulate transdermal patches as long as skin irritation or sensitization issues do not occur [76]. Indeed, Hadgraft and Valenta have linked the total transcutaneous flux (J_{tot}) of a permeant to the permeation of ionized and unionized portions [77]. The pKa and the ambient pH of the penetrant have a significant effect on the relative quantities of unionized and ionized moieties [77]. The same authors have observed that given a defined drug concentration or pH, the quantity of medication transported across the skin is likely to be dominated by the permeation of ionized species [77]. Recently, Song et al. studied the effect of the degree of ionization on the transport of cimetidine across microneedle-treated skin [78]. Cimetidine pKa is 6.8, therefore a formulation pH spectrum of 5–7.5 leads to 98.4% and 16.6% ionization of the drug, respectively [78]. Importantly, the authors noted that those pH values may not cause skin irritation [78]. The investigators utilized Tris base to alter the pH of the formulations to 5, 6.8, and 7.5. Diffusion studies were conducted across porcine skin. The authors reported that at pH 5, the use of gels led to enhanced permeation through the generated micro-channels [78]. The total quantity of cimetidine transported in 24 h was 28.20 ± 4.63 μg from 0.8% w/w gel at pH 5, and this was more than that obtained at pH 6.8 (16.89 ± 3.56 μg) and pH 7.5 (12.03 ± 1.66 μg) [78].

Biological factors and transdermal drug delivery

Age

Pediatric and geriatric patients require different considerations in the design, formulation, and administration of transdermal therapeutic systems. From the clinical standpoint, it is important to administer pediatric medications with extreme accuracy [79]. In addition, the application method should be easy and precise with simple-to-follow rules and procedures [79]. Furthermore, younger children need smaller doses than adults and this makes it easier for pediatric patients to attain therapeutic drug concentration [80]. Another issue is that there are insufficient studies in the transdermal drug delivery literature of the rapidly evolving and immature skin barrier properties in babies born prematurely [80]. It has been pointed out that the vernix caseosa, a film of lipoproteic material with embedded fetal corneocytes is absent in infants born at less than 28 wk (gestational age) [80]. Interestingly, the SC of a preterm new-born has a defective barrier while the SC of a term neonate has more developed barrier properties as shown by transepidermal water loss (TEWL) values that are analogous to that of adult skin [80]. This can affect transcutaneous flux. Percutaneous drug administration can be more impactful in the management of chronic diseases for children [79]. As an illustration, many pediatric patients need human growth hormone, hGH, (somatropin), which is usually administered via injection to treat growth disorders [79]. A transdermal drug delivery alternative will be useful for pediatric patients [79]. Juvenile diabetes is also another area that will benefit from specially designed pediatric transdermal patches [79].

In 1994, approximately one in eight people in the United States were elderly and it has been estimated that by the year 2030, that number will increase to one in five according to projections by the US Census Bureau [81]. The use of transdermal drug delivery systems by geriatric patients has increased tremendously but the quantitative evaluation of skin barrier function has not been adequately investigated in the elderly [81]. The permeability of fluorescein was seven times higher in skin samples from older subjects compared to younger ones [81]. On the other hand, the transdermal delivery rate of acetylsalicylic acid, benzoic acid, caffeine, and hydrocortisone, was markedly less in aged subjects, whereas the absorption of estradiol and testosterone was comparable in the two groups [82]. In another study, Roskos and Guy investigated age-associated alterations in skin barrier function in "old" (69–85 years) and "young" (19–42 years) subjects via the monitoring of TEWL rates [83]. TEWL can sometimes serve as a surrogate for skin permeability. The authors measured TEWL at the ventral forearm skin sites, under occlusive conditions (polypropylene chambers) [83]. The authors documented a slower return of TEWL to baseline values of perturbed TEWL in "old" skin [83]. This discrepancy in the effect of aging on percutaneous drug penetration highlights the need to delineate factors that play critical role in the transdermal delivery of drugs within the geriatric subpopulation.

Hydration

Even though the permeability of the SC is low, it is not completely impermeable as shown by TEWL values of intact healthy skin [84]. The normal water concentration in the SC is approximately 30% ± 5% [84] and if the water content of the skin is below 10%, the barrier properties of the skin may be compromised [85]. On the other hand, significant quantities of water can be bound to corneocytes under hydrating conditions, but the configuration of keratin fibrils does not allow substantial lateral swelling [86]. The degree of SC hydration is important as a fully hydrated SC (under occlusion) has lower diffusional resistance to externally administered compounds compared to a dehydrated SC [23]. It is well established that the transport properties of the skin can be modified by the SC water quantity, which in turn is related to the relative humidity of the environment [84]. Water activity gradient results in a large chemical potential gradient across the skin [86]. The implication is that transcutaneous drug permeation rises suddenly and this can be explained by increased rates of hydration [86]. It has been recently reported that the exposure of skin samples to liquids during conventional in vitro transport studies can change skin membrane features and the corresponding permeability values [25]. To test this hypothesis, Levintova and coworkers used an unstirred donor and receiver system to investigate the transport of doxepin hydrochloride across human skin [25]. The drug solution in an unstirred donor gel was transported via a membrane into an adjustable unstirred gel receiver that mimicked physiological conditions [1]. The authors reported that doxepin permeability (P) was 0.0026 ± 0.0001 cm/h while the permeability value obtained from a system with stirred receiver sampling was 0.0155 cm/h [25]. The authors ascribed the difference in values to skin hydration [25].

It is obvious that the main obstacle to transdermal drug permeation is the SC [87,88]. Consequently, researchers are constantly developing techniques to overcome this barrier. The methods available for facilitating transcutaneous flux of medications include the use of vesicles [28,34,89–92], prodrugs [43,93], chemical penetration enhancers [94–97], microemulsions [98,99], microneedles [17,100,101], iontophoresis [102–105], sonophoresis [106–109], laser [110,111], microwave [11,112], and others.

References

[1] Lundborg M, et al. Predicting drug permeability through skin using molecular dynamics simulation. J Control Release 2018;283:269–79.

[2] Menon GK, Cleary GW, Lane ME. The structure and function of the stratum corneum. Int J Pharma 2012;435(1):3–9.

[3] Lee SH, Jeong SK, Ahn SK. An update of the defensive barrier function of skin. Yonsei Med J 2006;47(3):293–306.

[4] Naik A, Kalia YN, Guy RH. Transdermal drug delivery: overcoming the skin's barrier function. Pharm Sci Technol Today 2000;3(9):318–26.

[5] Margetts L, Sawyer R. Transdermal drug delivery: principles and opioid therapy. Contin Educ Anaesth Crit Care Pain 2007;7(5):171–6.

[6] Liuzzi R, et al. Transport efficiency in transdermal drug delivery: what is the role of fluid microstructure? Colloids Surf B Biointerfaces 2016;139:294–305.

[7] Chen X. Current and future technological advances in transdermal gene delivery. Adv Drug Deliv Rev 2017;127:85–105.

[8] Erdo F, et al. Critical evaluation and methodological positioning of the transdermal microdialysis technique. A review. J Control Release 2016;233:147–61.

[9] Miller MA, et al. Uptake and desorption of hydrophilic compounds from human stratum corneum. J Control Release 2017;261:307–17.

[10] Liu X, et al. Hair follicles contribute significantly to penetration through human skin only at times soon after application as a solvent deposited solid in man. Br J Clin Pharmacol 2011;72(5):768–74.

[11] Wong TW. Electrical, magnetic, photomechanical and cavitational waves to overcome skin barrier for transdermal drug delivery. J Control Release 2014;193:257–69.

[12] Wen J, Koo SM, Lape N. How Sensitive Are Transdermal Transport Predictions by Microscopic Stratum Corneum Models to Geometric and Transport Parameter Input? J Pharm Sci 2018;107(2):612–23.

[13] Barry BW. Drug delivery routes in skin: a novel approach. Adv Drug Deliv Rev 2002;54: S31–40.

[14] Walsh L, et al. Nanotopography facilitates in vivo transdermal delivery of high molecular weight therapeutics through an integrin-dependent mechanism. Nano Lett 2015;15 (4):2434–41.

[15] Barbero AM, Frasch HF. Effect of stratum corneum heterogeneity, anisotropy, asymmetry and follicular pathway on transdermal penetration. J Control Release 2017;260:234–46.

[16] Mitragotri S. Modeling skin permeability to hydrophilic and hydrophobic solutes based on four permeation pathways. J Control Release 2003;86(1):69–92.

[17] Prausnitz MR, Langer R. Transdermal drug delivery. Nat Biotechnol 2008;26 (11):1261–8.

[18] Bunge AL, Guy RH, Hadgraft J. The determination of a diffusional pathlength through the stratum corneum. Int J Pharm 1999;188(1):121–4.

[19] Jepps OG, et al. Modeling the human skin barrier—towards a better understanding of dermal absorption. Adv Drug Deliv Rev 2013;65(2):152–68.

[20] Attard P. Chapter 7—Interacting particles. In: Attard P, editor. Thermodynamics and Statistical Mechanics. London: Academic Press; 2002. p. 153–79.

[21] Job G, Herrmann F. Chemical potential—a quantity in search of recognition. Eur J Phys 2006;27(2):353.

[22] <https://www.tf.uni-kiel.de/matwis/amat/def_en/kap_2/advanced/t2_4_1.html>.

[23] Paudel KS, et al. Challenges and opportunities in dermal/transdermal delivery. Ther Deliv 2010;1(1):109–31.

[24] Ita KB. Transdermal drug delivery: progress and challenges. J Drug Deliv Sci Technol 2014;24(3):245–50.

[25] Levintova Y, Plakogiannis FM, Bellantone RA. An improved in vitro method for measuring skin permeability that controls excess hydration of skin using modified Franz diffusion cells. Int J Pharm 2011;419(1–2):96–106.

[26] Todo H. Transdermal permeation of drugs in various animal species. Pharmaceutics 2017;9(3):E33.

[27] Barbero AM, Frasch HF. Pig and guinea pig skin as surrogates for human in vitro penetration studies: a quantitative review. Toxicol Vitro 2009;23(1):1–13.

[28] Ita KB, et al. Dermal delivery of selected hydrophilic drugs from elastic liposomes: effect of phospholipid formulation and surfactants. J Pharm Pharmacol 2007;59(9):1215–22.

[29] Simon A, et al. Comparative evaluation of rivastigmine permeation from a transdermal system in the Franz cell using synthetic membranes and pig ear skin with in vivo-in vitro correlation. Int J Pharm 2016;512(1):234–41.

[30] Sintov AC. Cumulative evidence of the low reliability of frozen/thawed pig skin as a model for in vitro percutaneous permeation testing. Eur J Pharm Sci 2017;102:261–3.

[31] Paul S, Jayan A, Sasikumar CS. Physical, chemical and biological studies of gelatin/chitosan based transdermal films with embedded silver nanoparticles. Asian Pac J Trop Dis 2015;5(12):975–86.

[32] Courtenay AJ, et al. Microneedle-mediated transdermal delivery of bevacizumab. Mol Pharm 2018;15(8):3545–56.

[33] Kaur M, et al. Microneedle-assisted delivery of verapamil hydrochloride and amlodipine besylate. Eur J Pharm Biopharm 2014;86(2):284–91.

[34] Pathan IB, et al. Curcumin loaded ethosomes for transdermal application: formulation, optimization, in-vitro and in-vivo study. J Drug Deliv Sci Technol 2018;44:49–57.

[35] Kathe K, Kathpalia H. Film forming systems for topical and transdermal drug delivery. Asian J Pharm Sci 2017;12(6):487–97.

[36] Moser K, et al. Passive skin penetration enhancement and its quantification in vitro. Eur J Pharm Biopharm 2001;52(2):103–12.

[37] Ruland A, Kreuter J. Transdermal permeability and skin accumulation of amino acids. Int J Pharm 1991;72(2):149–55.

[38] Milewski M, Stinchcomb AL. Estimation of maximum transdermal flux of nonionized xenobiotics from basic physicochemical determinants. Mol Pharm 2012;9(7):2111–20.

[39] Hansen S, Lehr CM, Schaefer UF. Improved input parameters for diffusion models of skin absorption. Adv Drug Deliv Rev 2013;65(2):251–64.

[40] Mitragotri S, et al. Mathematical models of skin permeability: an overview. Int J Pharm 2011;418(1):115–29.

[41] Sun L, et al. Formulation and in vitro/in vivo correlation of a drug-in-adhesive transdermal patch containing azasetron. J Pharm Sci 2012;101(12):4540–8.

[42] Maurya A, et al. Rapidly dissolving microneedle patches for transdermal iron replenishment therapy. J Pharm Sci 2018;107(6):1642–7.

[43] Valiveti S, et al. In vivo evaluation of 3-O-alkyl ester transdermal prodrugs of naltrexone in hairless guinea pigs. J Control Release 2005;102(2):509–20.

[44] Kiptoo PK, et al. In vivo evaluation of a transdermal codrug of 6-β-naltrexol linked to hydroxybupropion in hairless guinea pigs. Eur J Pharm Sci 2008;33(4–5):371–9.

[45] Kalaria DR, et al. Controlled iontophoretic delivery of pramipexole: electrotransport kinetics in vitro and in vivo. Eur J Pharm Biopharm 2014;88(1):56–63.

[46] Vemulapalli V, et al. In vitro and in vivo iontophoretic transdermal delivery of an antiparkinsonian agent. Int J Pharm 2011;420(1):20–5.

[47] Patel N, Jain S, Lin S. Transdermal iontophoretic delivery of tacrine hydrochloride: correlation between in vitro permeation and in vivo performance in rats. Int J Pharm 2016;513 (1–2):393–403.

[48] Cazares-Delgadillo J, et al. Using transdermal iontophoresis to increase granisetron delivery across skin in vitro and in vivo: effect of experimental conditions and a comparison with other enhancement strategies. Eur J Pharm Sci 2010;39(5):387–93.

[49] Strasinger C, et al. Navigating sticky areas in transdermal product development. J Control Release 2016;233:1–9.

[50] Green PG, Hadgraft J, Wolff M. Physicochemical aspects of the transdermal delivery of bupranolol. Int J Pharm 1989;55(2):265–9.

[51] Chandrashekar NS, Shobha Rani RH. Physicochemical and pharmacokinetic parameters in drug selection and loading for transdermal drug delivery. Indian J Pharm Sci 2008;70 (1):94–6.

[52] Szunerits S, Boukherroub R. Heat: a highly efficient skin enhancer for transdermal drug delivery. Front Bioeng Biotechnol 2018;6:15.

[53] N'Da DD. Prodrug strategies for enhancing the percutaneous absorption of drugs. Molecules 2014;20780–807.

[54] Hadgraft J, Cordes G, Wolff M. Prediction of the transdermal delivery of β-blockers. In: Rietbrock N, editor. Die Haut als Transportorgan Für Arzneistoffe. Darmstadt, Germany: Steinkopff Verslag; 1990. p. 133–43.

[55] Calpena AC, et al. A comparative in vitro study of transdermal absorption of antiemetics. J Pharm Sci 1994;83(1):29–33.

[56] Stott PW, Williams AC, Barry BW. Transdermal delivery from eutectic systems: enhanced permeation of a model drug, ibuprofen. J Control Release 1998;50 (1–3):297–308.

[57] Wiedersberg S, Guy RH. Transdermal drug delivery: 30 + years of war and still fighting!. J Control Release 2014;190:150–6.

[58] Alkilani AZ, McCrudden MT, Donnelly RF. Transdermal drug delivery: innovative pharmaceutical developments based on disruption of the barrier properties of the stratum corneum. Pharmaceutics 2015;7(4):438–70.

[59] Kupczewska-Dobecka M, Jakubowski M, Czerczak S. Calculating the dermal flux of chemicals with OELs based on their molecular structure: an attempt to assign the skin notation. Environ Toxicol Pharmacol 2010;30(2):95–102.

[60] Brown MB, et al. Dermal and transdermal drug delivery systems: current and future prospects. Drug Deliv 2006;13(3):175–87.

[61] Potts RO, Guy RH. Predicting skin permeability. Pharm Res 1992;9(5):663–9.

[62] Lian G, Chen L, Han L. An evaluation of mathematical models for predicting skin permeability. J Pharm Sci 2008;97(1):584–98.
[63] Magnusson BM, et al. Molecular size as the main determinant of solute maximum flux across the skin. J Investig Dermatol 2004;122(4):993–9.
[64] Flynn G. Physicochemical determinants of skin absorption. In: Gerrity TRG, Henry CJ, editors. Principles of route-to-route extrapolation for risk assessment. New York: Elsevier; 1990.
[65] Cleek RL, Bunge AL. A new method for estimating dermal absorption from chemical exposure. 1. General approach. Pharm Res 1993;10(4):497–506.
[66] Marwah H, et al. Permeation enhancer strategies in transdermal drug delivery. Drug Deliv 2016;23(2):564–78.
[67] Ceschel G, et al. Solubility and transdermal permeation properties of a dehydroepiandrosterone cyclodextrin complex from hydrophilic and lipophilic vehicles. Drug Deliv 2005;12(5):275–80.
[68] Gerber M, Breytenbach JC, du Plessis J. Transdermal penetration of zalcitabine, lamivudine and synthesised N-acyl lamivudine esters. Int J Pharm 2008;351(1–2):186–93.
[69] Anissimov YG, et al. Mathematical and pharmacokinetic modelling of epidermal and dermal transport processes. Adv Drug Deliv Rev 2013;65(2):169–90.
[70] Nicoli S, et al. Association of nicotinamide with parabens: effect on solubility, partition and transdermal permeation. Eur J Pharm Biopharm 2008;69(2):613–21.
[71] Meyer S, et al. Confocal Raman investigation of diffusion processes in monolithic type transdermal drug delivery systems. Drug Deliv 2015;22(8):1103–10.
[72] Caputo M, Cametti C. Fractional derivatives in the diffusion process in heterogeneous systems: the case of transdermal patches. Math Biosci 2017;291:38–45.
[73] Kodiweera C, et al. Characterization of water and a model lipophilic compound in human stratum corneum by NMR spectroscopy and equilibrium sorption. J Pharm Sci 2016;105(11):3376–86.
[74] Liu X, Cleary J, German GK. The global mechanical properties and multi-scale failure mechanics of heterogeneous human stratum corneum. Acta Biomater 2016;43:78–87.
[75] Barbero AM, Frasch HF. Modeling of diffusion with partitioning in stratum corneum using a finite element model. Ann Biomed Eng 2005;33(9):1281–92.
[76] Ghosh P, Brogden NK, Stinchcomb AL. Effect of formulation pH on transport of naltrexone species and pore closure in microneedle-enhanced transdermal drug delivery. Mol Pharm 2013;10(6):2331–9.
[77] Hadgraft J, Valenta C. pH, pK(a) and dermal delivery. Int J Pharm 2000;200(2):243–7.
[78] Song Y, et al. Transdermal delivery of cimetidine across microneedle-treated skin: effect of extent of drug ionization on the permeation. J Pharm Sci 2017;106(5):1285–92.
[79] Subramony JA. Needle free parenteral drug delivery: leveraging active transdermal technologies for pediatric use. Int J Pharm 2013;455(1–2):14–18.
[80] Delgado-Charro MB, Guy RH. Effective use of transdermal drug delivery in children. Adv Drug Deliv Rev 2014;73:63–82.
[81] Konda S, et al. Age-related percutaneous penetration part 2: effect of age on dermatopharmacokinetics and overview of transdermal products. Skin Ther Lett 2012;17(6):5–7.
[82] Roskos KV, Maibach HI, Guy RH. The effect of aging on percutaneous absorption in man. J Pharmacokinet Biopharm 1989;17(6):617–30.
[83] Roskos KV, Guy RH. Assessment of skin barrier function using transepidermal water loss: effect of age. Pharm Res 1989;6(11):949–53.

[84] Silva CL, et al. Stratum corneum hydration: phase transformations and mobility in stratum corneum, extracted lipids and isolated corneocytes. Biochim Biophys Acta 2007;1768(11):2647–59.

[85] Hamed SH, et al. Construction, in vitro and in vivo evaluation of an in-house conductance meter for measurement of skin hydration. Med Eng Phys 2012;34(10):1471–6.

[86] Alber C, et al. Effects of water gradients and use of urea on skin ultrastructure evaluated by confocal Raman microspectroscopy. Biochim Biophys Acta 2013;1828(11):2470–8.

[87] Economidou SN, Lamprou DA, Douroumis D. 3D printing applications for transdermal drug delivery. Int J Pharm 2018;544(2):415–24.

[88] Ita K. Transdermal delivery of drugs with microneedles: strategies and outcomes. J Drug Deliv Sci Technol 2015;29(Supplement C):16–23.

[89] Garg T, et al. Elastic liposomal formulation for sustained delivery of antimigraine drug: in vitro characterization and biological evaluation. Drug Dev Ind Pharm 2008;34(10):1100–10.

[90] Ita K. Current status of ethosomes and elastic liposomes in dermal and transdermal drug delivery. Curr Pharm Des 2016;22(33):5120–6.

[91] Chen Y-Y, et al. A novel elastic liposome for skin delivery of papain and its application on hypertrophic scar. Biomed Pharmacother 2017;87:82–91.

[92] Marto J, et al. Ethosomes for enhanced skin delivery of griseofulvin. Colloids Surf B: Biointerfaces 2016;146:616–23.

[93] Ita KB. Prodrugs for transdermal drug delivery—trends and challenges. J Drug Target 2016;24(8):671–8.

[94] Azagury A, et al. The synergistic effect of ultrasound and chemical penetration enhancers on chorioamnion mass transport. J Control Release 2015;200:35–41.

[95] Ita KB. Chemical penetration enhancers for transdermal drug delivery—success and challenges. Curr Drug Deliv 2015;12(6):645–51.

[96] Pham QD, et al. Chemical penetration enhancers in stratum corneum—relation between molecular effects and barrier function. J Control Release 2016;232:175–87.

[97] Polat BE, et al. A physical mechanism to explain the delivery of chemical penetration enhancers into skin during transdermal sonophoresis—insight into the observed synergism. J Control Release 2012;158(2):250–60.

[98] Alyoussef Alkrad J, Talhouni AA. In vivo and in vitro study of transdermal application of diclofenac sodium using nonionic microemulsions as colloidal drug delivery systems. J Drug Deliv Sci Technol 2018;43:27–33.

[99] Sintov AC. Transdermal delivery of curcumin via microemulsion. Int J Pharm 2015;481(1–2):97–103.

[100] Nguyen HX, et al. Poly (vinyl alcohol) microneedles: fabrication, characterization, and application for transdermal drug delivery of doxorubicin. Eur J Pharm Biopharm 2018;129:88–103.

[101] Ita K. Ceramic microneedles and hollow microneedles for transdermal drug delivery: two decades of research. J Drug Deliv Sci Technol 2018;44:314–22.

[102] Lemos CN, et al. Iontophoresis-stimulated silk fibroin films as a peptide delivery system for wound healing. Eur J Pharm Biopharm 2018;128:147–55.

[103] Ita KB, Banga AK. In vitro transdermal iontophoretic delivery of penbutolol sulfate. Drug Deliv 2009;16(1):11–14.

[104] Ita K. Transdermal iontophoretic drug delivery: advances and challenges. J Drug Target 2016;24(5):386–91.

[105] Djabri A, Guy RH, Delgado-Charro MB. Transdermal iontophoresis of ranitidine: an opportunity in paediatric drug therapy. Int J Pharm 2012;435(1):27–32.

[106] Herwadkar A, et al. Low frequency sonophoresis mediated transdermal and intradermal delivery of ketoprofen. Int J Pharm 2012;423(2):289–96.

[107] Yin L, et al. Enhancing percutaneous permeability of sinomenine hydrochloride using dual-frequency sonophoresis. J Drug Deliv Sci Technol 2016;36:62–7.

[108] Ita KB, Popova IE. Influence of sonophoresis and chemical penetration enhancers on percutaneous transport of penbutolol sulfate. Pharm Dev Technol 2016;21(8):990–5.

[109] Tezel A, Mitragotri S. Interactions of inertial cavitation bubbles with stratum corneum lipid bilayers during low-frequency sonophoresis. Biophys J 2003;85(6):3502–12.

[110] Ganti SS, Banga AK. Non-ablative fractional laser to facilitate transdermal delivery. J Pharm Sci 2016;105(11):3324–32.

[111] Zorec B, et al. The effect of pulse duration, power and energy of fractional Er:YAG laser for transdermal delivery of differently sized FITC dextrans. Int J Pharm 2017;516(1):204–13.

[112] Nawaz A, Wong TW. Microwave as skin permeation enhancer for transdermal drug delivery of chitosan-5-fluorouracil nanoparticles. Carbohydr Polym 2017;157:906–19.

Chapter 4

Elastic liposomes and other vesicles

Liposomes or lipid vesicles are lipid bilayers rolled up into spherical shells with enclosed liquid within shells, separated from the outer (surrounding) liquid solution [1]. On the other hand, elastic liposomes (ELs) are phospholipid vesicles similar to traditional liposomes but they are different from the latter because of the presence of edge activators (surfactants) that impart deformability and elasticity [2]. Usually, a deformable vesicle is made from at least one bilayer softener and at least one bilayer-forming amphipat with the favored bilayer-forming amphipats being phospholipids, especially phosphatidylcholine (PC) [3]. Egg PC ($\sim$10% w/w) and unsaturated soya PC are the most commonly utilized phospholipids [4]. ELs usually have in their compositions surfactants, such as Polysorbate 80 or Polysorbate 20 [5]. The surfactants function as an "edge activator" that destabilizes the lipid bilayers and increases vesicle deformability [6]. Edge activators (EAs) control the transdermal penetration properties of ELs by decreasing lipid bilayer transition temperature resulting in enhanced fluidity of the ELs [7]. Sometimes, ethanol (approximately 10%) is included in the composition of ELs that are frequently formulated from lipids (about 10% of the final formulation) [6]. In ELs, phospholipid bilayers surround an inner aqueous compartment and lipophilic or hydrophilic compounds can be encapsulated in either the lipid or aqueous compartment [7]. ELs are typically prepared via the thin-film technique by using rotary evaporation [8]. Initially, surfactants, hydrophilic drugs (in a hydration medium) or lipophilic drugs, and phospholipids are dissolved in an organic solvent (ethanol or chloroform) at 25°C [4]. A rotary evaporator is then used to evaporate the organic solvent with subsequent removal of solvent traces via vacuum drying overnight [8]. Phosphate-buffered saline (PBS) loaded with the drug is then used to hydrate the film [8]. Homogenously sized liposomes are obtained by passing the vesicles through an extruder [8].

Cevc and coworkers reported that deformable liposomes (Transfersomes) are elastic enough to permeate skin pores with relatively smaller sizes [9]. Because of the vesicle deformability induced by surfactants, it has been claimed that Transfersomes can cross through channels that have one-tenth

Transdermal Drug Delivery. DOI: https://doi.org/10.1016/B978-0-12-822550-9.00004-1

the diameter of the Transfersomes [6]. The authors postulated that these vesicles can penetrate narrow, skin pores as efficiently as water [9]. This, according to Cevc and colleagues, is different from what obtains with niosomes and liposomes, for which it is challenging to cross the skin barrier due to the inability of such vesicles to pass through the narrow (≤30 nm) intercellular channels in the skin [10].

The Cevc research group has published several papers suggesting that Transfersomes are transported transdermally by concentration-independent, naturally occurring, and most likely hydration-based, transepidermal gradient (s) that can drive several therapeutic agents across the skin [10–12]. The authors have postulated that one of the driving forces for vesicle transport into the skin is probably the osmotic gradient induced by the water gradient between the relatively dehydrated skin surface (approximately 20% water) and the aqueous viable epidermis [6]. The transepidermal osmotic gradient, which is the driving force for elastic vesicle penetration into the skin, is normally created by nonocclusive application of the vesicles [13]. To circumvent the challenge of low colloid concentration and transport following the transdermal application of a suspension, an external driving force must act upon all vesicle components simultaneously [14]. Hydration potential difference or hydration gradient across nonoccluded stratum corneum (SC) is one possible route for such force [14]. According to Cevc and coworkers, particulate material can also be transported across occluded skin by electrical driving gradient with the added condition that the colloids are stable, deformable, and charged, as flexibility alone is not adequate for successful penetration [14]. Cevc and Gebauer also published data postulating that a combination of hydrophilicity and high membrane elasticity with water activity gradient can lead to a spontaneous permeation of certain lipid vesicles across a semipermeable membrane [11]. The authors also carried out experimental and theoretical studies to measure and mathematically model the influence of hydration gradient across nano-porous barriers. It was postulated that the spontaneous trans-barrier transport of suitable lipid vesicles was induced by partial vesicle dehydration at the administration site and high vesicle surface hydrophilicity and extreme vesicle shape malleability [11].

Transfersomes continue to receive attention in numerous scientific reports and patents over the past 25 years. Various terms are used to describe these drug delivery systems: elastic, ultra-flexible, deformable, or highly deformable liposomes [6]. It has been reported that these vesicles can enter the bloodstream through the skin [6]. The claim that ELs can permeate intact skin is still controversial since skin pores can be opened without major impairment to only 20–40 nm [2]. It is hard to imagine how liposomes that are typically about 100 nm or more in size can cross the skin intact [2]. Indeed, Brewer and colleagues utilized Raster image correlation spectroscopy (RICS) to study the transport of dual-color fluorescently labeled liposomes and disclosed that intact liposomes do not penetrate the skin [15]. The liposomes were labeled with a hydrophilic fluorophore in the liposome lumen and an amphiphilic fluorophore in the lipid bilayer. The authors investigated the integrity of liposomes following transcutaneous delivery and with RICS, were able to discriminate between joint (correlated) and separate (uncorrelated) permeation of the two fluorescent probes [15]. In a recent review by Dragicevic and Maibach, it was pointed out that several authors did not find intact liposomal vesicles in the deeper skin layers [5]. In addition, the ability of deformable vesicles to penetrate intact skin is doubtful and their penetration is still a subject of investigation [5]. Chen et al. have emphasized that regardless of the debate over the precise permeation mechanism of ELs, these vesicles do increase drug permeation into or through skin in most cases [16]. Indeed, over the last two decades, numerous scientific reports have been published chronicling the influence of elastic vesicles on the skin transport of different therapeutic agents [8,9,12,13,17,18]. In the next section, representative examples of the use of ELs for transcutaneous administration will be highlighted. Table 4.1 shows the transdermal delivery of therapeutic agents from ELs, while Table 4.2 focuses on the percutaneous transport of drugs from elastic vesicles, niosomes, ethosomes (ESMs), and transethosomes (TELs).

TABLE 4.1 Transdermal delivery of therapeutic agents from elastic liposomes.

Therapeutic agent(s) or model compound	Skin model	Elastic liposome composition	References
Tocopherol acetate	Pig skin	Soybean phosphatidylcholine (SPC) (Lipoid S75); Tween 20, 40, 60, and 80	[13]
Insulin	Murine skin	SPC solution; sodium cholate, ethanol	[9]
Sodium stibogluconate	Rat skin	Phospholipon 90G and Tween 80	[25]
Caffeine and minoxidil	Rat skin	Lecithin, Polysorbate 80, and Polysorbate 20	[30]
Asenapine	Rat skin	SPC, sodium deoxycholate (SDC)	[35]
Gap junction protein	Murine skin	SPC, Lipid A, sodium cholate, sodium docecyl sulfate, ethanol	[18]
Tetanus toxoid	Rat skin	SPC, cholesterol (CH), SDC, Span-85	[37]
Ondansetron	Rat skin	Phosphatidylcholine and sodium taurocholate	[39]

TABLE 4.2 Percutaneous transport of drugs from elastic vesicles, niosomes, ethosomes, (ESMs) and transethosomes (TELs).

Therapeutic agent(s) or model compound(s)	Membrane	Formulation (composition)	References
$3H_2O$	Hairless mouse skin	Elastic vesicles [octaoxyethylene laurate ester (PEG-8-L) and laurate ester (L-595)]	[44]
Pergolide	Human skin	Elastic vesicles [octaoxyethylene laurate ester (PEG-8-L) and sucrose laurate ester (L-595)]	[45]
Rotigotine	Human skin	Elastic vesicles [octaoxyethylene laurate ester (PEG-8-L) and sucrose laurate ester (L-595)]	[46]
Salidroside	Rat skin	Niosomes (Span 40, cholesterol)	[50]
Ellagic acid	Human skin	Niosomes (Span 60, Tween 60, Solulan C24)	[51]
Gallidermin	Rat skin	Niosomes (Tween 61, cholesterol, dimethyldioctadecylammonium bromide dicetylphosphate)	[52]
Resveratrol	Rat skin	Niosomes (Span 80, cholesterol)	[53]
Rhodamine B	Rat skin	ESMs (lecithin, cholesterol, and ethanol)	[62]
Curcumin	Human skin	ESMs (lecithin, cholesterol and ethanol)	[59]
Ovalbumin	Synthetic membranes (cellulose, polyethersulfone, polyvinylidene fluoride)	ESMs [soybean phosphatidylcholine (SPC), ethanol and saponin]	[78]
Griseofulvin	Pig skin	ESMs (ethanol, SPC)	[63]
Terbinafine hydrochloride	Rat skin	ESMs (soya phosphatidylcholine, propylene glycol and ethanol)	[66]

(*Continued*)

TABLE 4.2 (Continued)

Therapeutic agent(s) or model compound(s)	Membrane	Formulation (composition)	References
Terbinafine hydrochloride	Rat skin	ESMs (Epikuron 200)]	[83]
Voriconazole	Mouse skin	TELs [SPC (Lipoid S100), ethanol and oleic acid]	[84]
Paeonol	Pig skin	TELs (ethanol injection method using PC and Tween 80)	[85]
Ferrous chlorophyllin	Mouse skin	SPC, ethanol, Cremophor-A25, Span 20, Tween 80 and Tween 20	[86]
Vitamin E and caffeine	Pig ear skin	SPC, sodium cholate, sorbitan laurate	[87]

Alpha-tocopherol

Alpha-tocopherol (AT) is a form of vitamin E, widely used as an antioxidant [19]. The pharmacological properties of AT are associated with its capacity to scavenge free radicals formed from lipids and the ability to interrupt free radical chain reaction [19]. The efficacy of tocopherol is, nevertheless, compromised by its chemical instability and poor aqueous solubility and this can be circumvented by formulating it into an appropriate delivery system [13]. Recently, Caddeo et al. investigated the skin delivery of tocopherol acetate-loaded ELs [13]. Various polysorbates (i.e., Tween 20, 40, 60, and 80) were used to formulate ELs with high entrapment efficiency (EE), which increased in correlation with Tween fatty acid chain length (from 72% to 90%) [13]. The Transfersomes were stable on storage, less than 100 nm in size, with high loading efficiency (up to 90%). The percutaneous penetration of transfersomes was examined under nonocclusive application scenarios, which allow the transepidermal osmotic gradient necessary to drive the delivery of these vesicles and the loaded active pharmaceutical ingredients into the skin [13]. The highest amounts of compounds were detected in the SC: about 8.5% for all the ELs, except those prepared with Tween 80, that had a higher level of skin deposition (>11%) (Fig. 4.1) [13]. The deposition values in the epidermis and dermis were 3.5% and 5.5%, respectively, and the differences between investigated formulations were not statistically significant [13]. The authors also reported that the quantity of transported tocopherol was about 6.5%, despite the type of formulation administered on the skin [13].

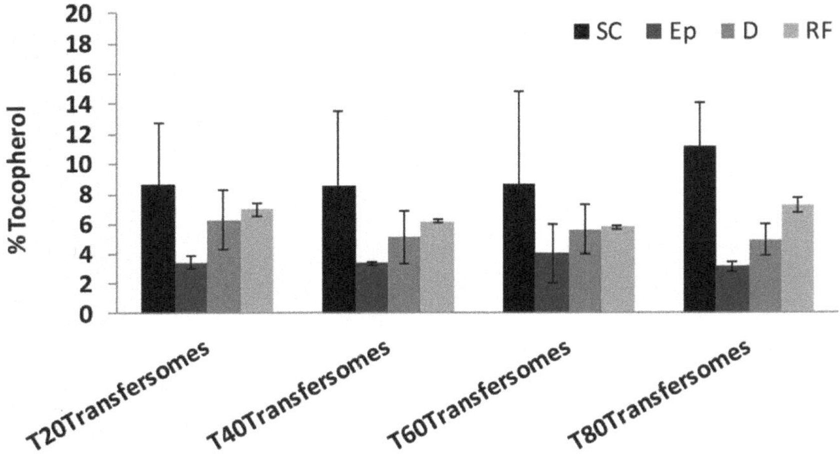

FIGURE 4.1 In vitro skin permeation studies: amount of tocopherol accumulated in the skin layers (SC, stratum corneum; Ep, epidermis; D, dermis) and receptor fluid (RF) after 8 h of non-occlusive application of the transfersomes. *Reproduced with permission from Caddeo C, et al. Tocopherol-loaded transfersomes: in vitro antioxidant activity and efficacy in skin regeneration. Int J Pharm 2018;551(1–2):34–41 (Chapter 4).*

Significantly, the authors also studied the antioxidant activity of the formulations by examining the capacity of these vesicles to protect fibroblasts and keratinocytes from being damaged by an oxidative agent (hydrogen peroxide) [13].

Insulin

Cevc et al. reported that Transfersomes prepared by mixing insulin solution with soybean phosphatidylcholine (SPC) solution, sodium cholate, and ethanol had an approximate radius of 90–110 nm and contained 84 ± 2 or 40 U/mL of the peptide [9]. The authors asserted that these ultra-deformable vesicles loaded with insulin were pushed by transepidermal water activity gradient into and across mouse skin and that these vesicles can spontaneously transport transdermally administered insulin, into the body [9]. The authors reported that epicutaneously administered, transfersome-associated insulin reduced the concentration of glucose in the blood by 20%–30% within 2–4 h [20]. In comparison, a simple liposome/insulin blend, an empty transfersome, or phospholipid/bile-salt micelles mixed with insulin did not alter serum glucose concentration significantly over the same time period [20]. The authors also pointed out that the net hypoglycemia caused by transfersulin was more than 30% and was close to 50% of the initial blood glucose level after 8 h [20]. The authors argued that high molecular–weight compounds can cross the skin if they are elastic enough to squeeze through skin pores [20]. Furthermore, the authors pointed to the lack of significant liposome fragmentation, which was supported by the fact that the mean liposome size before and after the pore transport was more or less constant [20].

Sodium stibogluconate

Leishmaniasis (LMS) is a global health challenge caused by the flagellate protozoan parasite of the genus Leishmania [21,22]. The genus Leishmania typically infects humans through the long and tiny phlebotomine called the sand fly [23]. There are three forms of LMS: visceral, mucocutaneous, and cutaneous (CL) depending on the immune response of the host and the species of the parasite [23]. Sodium stibogluconate (Pentostam) is a first-line therapeutic agent used for CL chemotherapy [24,25]. The drug possesses a high water solubility (100 mg/mL), a log P value of −3.41 and a high molecular−weight (910.9 g/mol) [25]. Dar and colleagues formulated nano-deformable liposomes (NDLs) for the skin transport of sodium stibogluconate (SSG) [25]. The elastic vesicles were formulated via a modified thin-film hydration technique and the Box−Behnken statistical design (BBSD) was used to optimize the composition of the formulation [25]. BBSD is a group of nearly rotatable or rotatable second-order designs based on three-level incomplete factorial designs [26]. This design is made up of three parts of four runs and within each part, two factors are organized in a full two-level design, while the level of the third factor is set at zero [26]. The three-factor Box−Behnken design (BBD) requires replicates at the center point and only 12 runs [26]. To provide easy administration, Dar and colleagues entrapped SSG-NDLs within carbopol gel and carried out ex vivo skin transport studies which showed that SSG-NDLs gel induced a 10-fold skin retention in deeper skin layers compared to the controls [25]. The authors attributed the driving force needed for the vesicle shape change to transepidermal hydration gradient [25]. It was also explained that the administration of NDLs also led to high skin retention because of lipid layer deformability that facilitates vesicle squeezing across the skin layers [25]. Significantly, SSG-NDLs (1.3 mg/mL) had a higher cytotoxic potential compared to the control SSG formulation(1.65 mg/mL) [25].

Minoxidil and caffeine

Minoxidil (MNX) is an antihypertensive medication that is also used for the reduction and slowing of androgenetic alopecia [27,28]. The drug is known to open ATP-sensitive potassium channel and has been employed for the management of severe hypertension as well as periodic paralysis [29]. The mechanism of hair growth induced by this drug is not completely elucidated, but it has been suggested that MNX facilitates the supply of blood to hair follicles, thus boosting nutrient and oxygen transport to the cells [30]. Topical caffeine is also used to stimulate hair growth and for the management of alopecia [30]. The enzyme 5-α-reductase converts testosterone to dihydrotestosterone (DHT), and caffeine is known to block this enzyme. It has been reported that DHT induces hair loss [30]. Ramezani and coworkers formulated an EL for the codelivery of caffeine and MNX [30]. The authors prepared transfersomes by using the thin-film hydration technique and mixing lecithin with different quantities of edge activators (Polysorbate 80 and Polysorbate 20) [30]. BBD was used to optimize the formulations and the authors found that utilizing 9.3% of polysorbate 20 and 22.2% of polysorbate 80 in the formulation facilitated drug transport to rat skin [30]. Even more important was the fact that the codelivery of caffeine and MNX in ELs increased hair weight and length in rats [30].

Asenapine

Second-generation antipsychotics are increasingly being used for the management of bipolar affective disorder [31]. Asenapine (ASPM) is an antipsychotic medication used for the pharmacotherapy of bipolar 1 disorder and schizophrenia. ASPM is used clinically either in the form of monotherapy or in combination with sodium valproate or lithium [31,32]. The drug is known to interact with several dopaminergic (D2, D3), histaminergic (H1, H2), serotonergic [5HT(7), 5HT(6), 5HT(5A), 5-HT(2A-C)], and alpha-adrenergic (α(1), α(2)) receptor subtypes [33]. ASPM has a higher binding affinity for the 5HT2A receptor in comparison with the D_2 receptors [34]. The drug is a member of the dibenzooxepinopyrrole class of atypical antipsychotics and it is used in the form of sublingual tablets [35]. One major challenge with ASPM is the low bioavailability caused by extensive presystemic metabolism and this can be addressed by formulating the drug into a transdermal formulation such as an EL [35]. Recently, Shreya et al. studied the effect of transfersomes on the percutaneous transport of ASPM [35]. The elastic vesicles were formulated via the thin-film method using SPC combined with the edge activator sodium cholate. The authors studied the influence of the vesicles on the penetration of ASPM across rat skin [35]. The authors revealed that the magnitude and rate of ASPM transport from a transfersomal gel loaded with 5 mg of ASPM (TG-2) were higher (Q24: 309.28 mg; flux: 12.1 ± 0.81 mg/cm^2/h) than that containing 2.5 mg of the drug (TG-1) (Q24: 220.16 mg; flux: 9.13 ± 0.72 mg/cm^2/h) [35]. Significantly, the Q24 and flux values achieved with TG-2 gel was significantly higher than (1) gel loaded with the drug without ethanol (CG-2NE-Q24: 51.28 ± 3.16 mg; flux: 2.0 8 ± 0.13 mg/cm^2/h), (2) gel loaded with the drug with 20% ethanol (CG-2-Q24: 145.29 ± 7.06 mg; flux: 6.00 ± 0.35 mg/cm^2/h), and (3) gel containing nano-transfersomes with no ethanol (TG-2NE-Q24: 132.89 ± 6.05 mg; flux: 5.57 ± 0.26 mg/cm^2/h).

Gap junction protein

The accessibility of the human skin in conjunction with its immunocompetence makes the organ attractive for vaccination [36]. Transcutaneous vaccination is beneficial because there is an abundance of immunocompetent Langerhans cells (LCs) along the transcutaneous permeation route [37]. LCs typically move from the epidermis into lymphatic vessels and then the regional lymph nodes transporting processed antigen [37]. Antigens are initially broken down into short segments that conjugate with major histocompatibility complex (MHC) molecules and are finally shown at the cell surface where they are recognized by T cells [36]. LCs are subdivided into dendritic cells that present antigens to naïve CD4 + T cells [18,37]. There are two other classes of antigen-presenting cells in the skin (B lymphocytes and macrophages) but these cells need to be activated for antigen presentation as well as T cell stimulation [18]. It is obvious that novel approaches for the noninvasive, transcutaneous administration of immunogens are desirable. Paul et al. used transfersomes for the transdermal delivery gap junction protein (GJP) [18]. The authors reported the transport of GJP across intact murine skin following epicutaneous administration [18]. It is noteworthy that specific antibody titers comparable to or higher than those obtained by repeated subcutaneous immunization were determined following the skin application of GJP-loaded transfersomes [18]. In addition, the delivery of immunogen across the skin creates a large amount of immunoglobulin A (IgAs), which is different from what obtains following subcutaneous injection [18]. The authors attributed this phenomenon to presence of stimulating components in the ELs, as well as the transdermal route of antigen presentation [18].

Tetanus toxoid

The anaerobic bacterium *Clostridium tetani* produces a neurotoxin that causes tetanus. This is an acute disease associated with symptoms such as convulsive spasms and muscle rigidity [38]. The incidence of tetanus can be decreased via vaccination with Tdap (adult tetanus, diphtheria, pertussis vaccines) and by adherence to hygienic delivery practices [38]. The intramuscular mode of tetanus vaccine administration is fraught with challenges as the weak antigenicity of tetanus toxoid (TT) and the logistic hurdle of providing a cold chain for the maintenance of vaccine stability [38]. Gupta et al. studied the noninvasive transport of TT using ELs and compared the elicited immune responses to that of liposomes and niosomes [37]. The authors measured the serum anti-TT immunoglobulin G (IgG) titer following topical administration of the toxoid as a way of studying the immune-stimulating activity of liposomes, transfersomes, and niosomes [37]. The deformability of transfersomal, niososmal and liposomal bilayers were determined via extrusion through a 50 nm polycarbonate filter [37]. The deformability(elasticity) values of transfersomes, niosomes, and liposomes were 124.4 ± 4.2, 29.3 ± 2.4, and 21.7 ± 1.9, respectively, while the corresponding optimal formulations of the abovementioned dosage forms entrapped $72.7\% \pm 3.4\%$, $42.5\% \pm 2.4\%$, and $41.3\% \pm 2.2\%$ of the antigen [37]. The transport of TT through full-thickness rat skin was investigated by the authors and after 48 h, the cumulative transport of TT from liposomes, niosomes, and transfersomes was $10.7\% \pm 0.9\%$, $12.5\% \pm 1.1\%$, and $16.4\% \pm 1.6\%$, respectively [37]. The effect of intramuscular and topical TT administration on humoral immune response in the rodents was also examined. Animal studies showed that dermally administered TT-loaded transfersomes induced immune response (anti-TT-IgG) that was comparable to the one obtained via intramuscular alum-adsorbed TT vaccination [37]. Liposomes and niosomes induced less potent immune response compared to ELs [37].

Ondansetron

Serotonin antagonists are efficacious in the management of emesis because they block both 5-HT3 receptors positioned centrally (the area postrema and chemoreceptor trigger zone of the nucleus tractus solitarius) and peripherally (enteric nervous system's enterochromaffin cells) [39]. Ondansetron (ON) is a 5HT-3 receptor blocker that has received approval by regulatory authorities for the prevention and management of emesis and nausea linked to cancer chemotherapy and surgery [40]. ON possesses low aqueous solubility and the oral dose is only 4–8 mg [39]. The elimination half-life of ON is short (3–3.5 h) and the drug is subject to considerable liver metabolism by the cytochrome P450 enzyme system [41]. Furthermore, ON has a low oral bioavailability of approximately 60% [42]. It has a log P value of 2.0, a pKa of about 7.4, and a molecular weight of 293 Da [39]. Taken together, these properties make ON a strong candidate for transdermal drug delivery. Habib et al. recently formulated elastic nanovesicles (NVs) loaded with ON [39]. The ON NVs were prepared from PC and sodium taurocholate via the conventional thin-film hydration technique with subsequent sonication of the prepared nanovesicular suspension [39]. The deformability of the vesicles was determined through extrusion via a 200 nm nylon filter at 2.5 bar. The deformability index (DI) was calculated using the following equation [37,39]:

$$\mathrm{DI} = J\left(\frac{r_v}{r_p}\right)^2 \tag{4.1}$$

where DI is the deformability index, J is the elastic liposomal dispersion weight of extruded in 10 min, r_v is the vesicle size following extrusion (nm), and r_p is the barrier pore size (nm) [39]. Box–Cox transformation was used for variable optimization. Box–Cox is a parametric method to nonlinearly transform a set of points with the goal of making their distribution approximately Gaussian [43]. A 2^3 full factorial design was utilized in the research project to compare transfersomes, ESMs, and TELs [39]. Ethanol concentration in ESMs is approximately 10%–40%, while one or more surface active agent or sorption promoter is typically combined with ethosomal ingredients in TELs [39]. The investigated independent variables were sodium taurocholate amount, sonication time, and ethanol volume in the hydration medium, while the dependent variables (responses) were: zeta potential (ZP), EE, and particle size (PS) [39]. The authors showed that ON transfersomes were more optimal than either TELs or ESMs. The transfersomes had a transdermal flux (through rat skin) of 4.19 $\mu g/cm^2/h$ and a good flexibility (deformability) of 18.35 g [39]. The lag time for transfersomes was 4.5 h $\pm$ 0.17, while the permeability coefficient (*kp*) was 1.309×10^{-3} cm/h [39].

Surfactant-based elastic vesicles

For many years, most elastic vesicles were made from phospholipids, especially fluid-chain PCs [3]. Elastic vesicles have also been made from the micelle-forming surfactant octaoxyethylene laurate ester (PEG-8-L) and the bilayer-forming surfactant sucrose laurate ester (L-595) [44,45]. By combining micelle-forming single-chain surfactants with bilayer-forming surface active agents, vesicles can be formulated with different deformability (elasticity) values based on the molar ratio of the constituents [44]. van den Bergh and coworkers prepared deformable (elastic) vesicles from the single-chain surfactant PEG-8-L and L-595 and studied the impact of these vesicles on the mouse skin ultrastructure [44]. The authors studied the interplay of the elastic vesicles (containing L-595 and PEG-8-L surfactants) with the mouse skin and made comparisons with those documented following skin treatment with sucrose stearate-ester (Wasag-7) rigid vesicles [44]. In addition, the authors also studied in vitro $3H_2O$ flux across hairless mouse skin following nonocclusive administration of the elastic vesicles, rigid vesicles, or PEG-8-L micelles [44]. Clearly delineated regions with lamellar stacks associated with deformable vesicles were observed in the SC intercellular spaces following the application of the vesicles [44]. Subsequently, skin bilayer organization was modified, resulting in enhanced skin permeability [44]. In contrast, there were no alterations in viable epidermis ultrastructure [44]. Significantly, application of the rigid Wasag-7 system did not influence skin permeability or cutaneous ultrastructure of the hairless mouse skin (rodent) [44]. Furthermore, pretreating the rodent skin with 70 mol% PEG-8-L deformable vesicles enhanced the transport of $3H_2O$ [44].

Honeywell-Nguyen et al. prepared elastic vesicles from surfactants and studied the influence of these vesicles on pergolide delivery across human skin [45]. The vesicles were made from PEG-8-L, L-595, and the charge inducer sulfosuccinate (TR-70). The transcutaneous delivery of the drug from various compositions was studied in vitro with a saturated buffer solution serving as the control [45]. Four different pergolide-loaded vesicles with a wide composition range (from very deformable to very rigid vesicles) were studied [45]. All the vesicle and micelle compositions had a longer lag time (t_{lag}) in comparison to the pergolide buffer solution. The difference was statistically significant for the L-595/PEG-8-L (70/30) and the L-595/PEG-8-L (50/50) deformable vesicles [45]. The most rigid vesicles L-595/PEG-8-L (100/0) substantially decreased the J_{ss} by half in comparison to the buffer solution but when the PEG-8-L concentration was increased—with a corresponding increase in the vesicle elasticity—there was a significantly higher J_{ss} for the L-595/PEG-8-L (70/30) deformable vesicles [45]. A threefold increase in flux relative to the buffer solution and a sixfold increase in comparison with the most rigid vesicle was documented [45]. When PEG-8-L content was increased further, J_{ss} was slightly decreased the but PEG-8-L micelles and L-595/PEG-8-L (50/50) deformable vesicles increased drug delivery by more than a factor 2 compared to the buffer control [45]. The authors attributed the enhanced elastic vesicle transport to transepidermal osmotic gradient [45].

In a related study, the same research group studied the influence of deformable vesicles on the transdermal delivery of rotigotine across human skin [46]. Elastic and rigid rotigotine-loaded vesicles were formulated and transdermal delivery was assessed in vitro with micelle and buffer solutions serving as controls [46]. The authors reported that the administration of the most flexible system L-595/PEG-8-L (50/50) resulted in a steady-state flux value of 214.4 ± 27.8 ng/h/cm^2 [46]. This flux value was higher than that of rigid vesicles (129 ± 24 ng/h/cm^2), micelles (38 ± 8 ng/h/cm^2), and buffer (5 ± 1 ng/h/cm^2) [46]. In another study, Uchino and colleagues prepared ketorolac-loaded deformable vesicles from L-595, PEG-8-L, and TR-70 [47]. The authors found that raising the PEG-8-L/L-595 ratio enhanced vesicle elasticity, while a rise in ketorolac loading reduced the elasticity of the vesicles [47].

Niosomes

When nonionic surface active agents self-assemble, they form vesicles called niosomes [48]. Nonionic surfactants such as polysorbates (Tweens), polyethoxy fatty ethers (Brij), and sorbitan fatty acid esters (Spans) are used to prepare niosomes [49]. Compared to liposomes, niosomes have a larger membrane flexibility, a higher chemical stability, and a low cost of production [49]. But niosomes also have limitations: these vesicles are subject to hydrolysis and degradation when stored for a long time. In addition, niosomes can fuse, aggregate, or sediment [49]. Niosomes promote cutaneous drug absorption through two mechanisms—modification of SC properties through the reduction of transepidermal water loss, loosening of its cellular structure, and increase in SC hydration. The second mechanism entails surface active agents serving as carriers and the enhancement of drug transport across the SC by nanosized niosomes [50]. Several investigators have studied the influence of niosomes on the transdermal delivery of drugs. In one study, Span 40-based niosomes were used to increase the transcutaneous permeation of salidroside [50]. Niosomes possessing a 4:3 molar proportion of Span 40 to cholesterol had the largest percutaneous permeation rate and dermal deposition for the drug. The transport rate of the salidroside from the 4:3 (Span 40:cholesterol) niosomal formulation was substantially higher compared to the solution of the drug in water. In another study, niosomes loaded with ellagic acid (a potent antioxidant) were prepared and the influence of chemical permeation enhancers on the permeability of the drug from niosomes was evaluated [51]. The authors used Solulan C24 as a steric stabilizer and Span 60, Tween 60, as well as cholesterol as vesicle forming agents to prepare EA-loaded niosomes via the reverse-phase evaporation technique [51]. *N*-methyl-2-pyrrolidone (NMP) or dimethylsulfoxide (DMSO) was employed as a chemical permeation enhancer, while polyethylene glycol 400 (PEG) was employed as a solubilizer [51]. The skin penetration promoters increased the flux of EA from the niosomes. The use of DMSO niosomes resulted in the largest amount of EA in the epidermis, while the utilization of NMP niosomes led to the greatest amount of EA in the receptor compartment [51].

The percutaneous penetration of gallidermin (Gdm)-loaded niosomes was also recently studied [52]. The authors prepared neutral niosomes from Tween 61/cholesterol using a molar ratio of 1:1, while cationic and anionic niosomes were formulated from Tween 61/cholesterol/dimethyldioctadecylammonium bromide and/or dicetylphosphate using the molar ratio of 1:1:0.05 [52]. There were higher cumulative amounts of Gdm from niosomes in the viable epidermis and dermis (VED) of rat skin (about two times more than unincorporated Gdm) [52]. The preparation of Gdm-loaded niosomes and subsequent formulation of these vesicles into a gel led to the highest cumulative amount ($82.42 \pm 9.28\ \mu g/cm^2$) and flux value ($13.74 \pm 1.55\ \mu g/cm^2/h^1$) in the SC, as well as cumulative amount ($183.16 \pm 30.32\ \mu g/cm^2$) and flux value ($25.74 \pm 5.05\ \mu g/cm^2/h^1$) in VED compared to the noisome-free Gdm loaded into a gel [52].

The polyphenolic compound resveratrol (RVL) possesses cardioprotective, antiobesity, neuroprotective, anticarcinogenic, and antiinflammatory effects [53]. Recently, Span 80 was used to prepare niosomes by ether injection and thin-film hydration methods. The RVL-loaded niosomal gel was formulated from carbopol [53]. In vitro release data followed the Korsmeyer–Peppas model, while ex vivo experiments showed high skin penetration and deposition of the drug in comparison with unloaded RVL [53]. The skin penetration level of optimized niosomal gel (88.4%) was higher than the unincorporated RVL suspension (62.7%) [53]. The following mechanisms were thought to be responsible for enhanced transdermal delivery of RVL across excised dorsal rat skin: (1) adsorption and subsequent fusion of niosomes on the skin surface, leading to a high interfacial thermodynamic activity gradient and (2) the decrease in rat skin barrier properties because of the enhanced permeation induced by niosomes [53]. Skin retention studies showed that the niosomal gel formulation possessed 4.85 times more transport (4.76 ± 0.21 μg/cm^2) than that of plain drug suspension (0.98 ± 0.01 μg/cm^2) [53]. In another research project, lacidipine-loaded niosomes were formulated via the thin-film hydration technique and the dosage form was optimized via the BBD [54]. The optimized drug delivery system had a EE, flux value, and vesicle size of 82.77% ± 4.34%, 38.43 ± 2.43 μg/cm^2/h, and 676.98 ± 10.92 nm, respectively [54].

Ethosomes

ESMs refer to lipid vesicles with relatively high ethanol content [2,55]. These vesicular systems can increase the skin permeation of medications [2,55]. Most ESMs are prepared from phospholipid, water, and ethanol [56,57]. ESMs may also contain propylene glycol (PG) or isopropyl alcohol along with ethanol [58]. When the concentration of ethanol approaches 45% in the formulation, PC acquires the shape of spherical bilayers with a line shape [57]. The ethosomal systems investigated by Touitou et al. were formulated from 2%–5% Phospholipon 90 (phospholipid), 20%–50% of ethanol, and up to 100% w/w of water [55]. Prior to the discovery of ESMs, researchers hypothesized that vesicles with high ethanol content were incapable of existing side-by-side because of the interdigitation influence of ethyl alcohol [55]. Higher concentration of ethanol can induce steric stabilization of the vesicles possibly because of negative charge, resulting in the deeper permeation of the loaded medication through the skin [59]. Ethanol interacts with lipids and subsequently decreases lipid melting temperature and increases fluidity, resulting in improved skin permeability [60]. ESMs possess fluidized phospholipid bilayers resulting in the formation of soft vesicles [57]. Furthermore, there is perturbation and fluidization of SC lipids [57]. Touitou and Godin have reported that ESMs penetrate the fluidized SC bilayers generating channels across the SC lipids and fusing with deeper skin layer cell membranes where they release their payload [57]. Due to a high degree of lamellarity, ESMs can efficiently incorporate lipophilic, amphiphilic, and hydrophilic molecules because of the presence of ethanol that enhances the solubility of many therapeutic agents [61].

Fluorescent anisotropy and paramagnetic-ion nuclear magnetic resonance (NMR) experiments with AVPC (9-antrivinyl labeled analog of PC) as well as differential scanning calorimetry (DSC) thermograms have demonstrated that ethosomal phospholipid bilayers are loosely packed with a lower transition temperature and a high degree of fluidity in comparison to liposomes [57].

Dayan and Touitou have reported in several publications that unlike conventional liposomes, that transport medications to the external skin layers, ESMs facilitate the transdermal transport of drugs through the SC [56]. ESMs are liquid and deformable, and the ethanol contained in the formulation is capable of loosening the configuration of lipid molecules in the SC [62]. Furthermore, the high ethanol content also increases the fluidity and flexibility of the ESM membrane [62]. The effects of ESMs can therefore be ascribed to the influence of ethanol on the SC, the higher adaptability, and elasticity of these vesicles as well as the interplay of these drug delivery systems with skin lipids [63]. Ethosomal systems are generally characterized by a limited size distribution that can vary from 30 nanometers to microns [57]. It is important to note that ESMs can encapsulate and deliver active agents with a wide range of physicochemical properties, including lipophilic molecules and high molecular–weight entities [57].

ESMs are usually made by thin-film dispersion technique [59]. In a typical experimental setup, ethanolic solutions of the phospholipid (e.g., soybean phosphatidylcholine) and the drug are prepared [63]. Water is then added slowly with constant stirring. Subsequently, the vesicle size is determined by filtration through 100 nm polycarbonate membranes under nitrogen [63]. The EE of ESMs can be determined by using the dialysis technique [64]. Ethosomal suspension is placed in a dialysis bag, which is then soaked in saline bottle and vibrated for 5 h [64]. Subsequently, the drug in the dialysis solution is assayed [64]. The percent EE can be calculated from the following equation [59]:

$$\text{Percent entrapment efficiency} = \frac{\text{Total amount of drug loaded free drug in supernatant}}{\text{Total amount of drug used in formulation}} \times 100 \tag{4.2}$$

ESMs are normally characterized by transmission electron microscopy (TEM) [65]. Zhang et al. prepared ESMs and studied them with TEM at room temperature staining them with 1% phosphotungstic acid buffer (pH 6.0) [65]. Samples were then observed with an electron microscope [65]. ZP can also be used to characterize ESMs [66].

ZP (ζ) is usually determined indirectly [67] and it can be estimated by measuring the mobility of particles via techniques such as electrophoretic mobility combined with the use of theoretical models [67]. The relationship between electrophoretic mobility and ZP is described by Henry equation [68]:

$$\mu = 2\zeta\varepsilon 3\eta f(\mathrm{Ka}) \tag{4.3}$$

where η is the viscosity of the dispersing liquid, f(Ka) is Henry's function (1 or 1.5), and ε is the dielectric constant [68]. An approximation called the Smoluchowski equation is often used [68]:

$$\mu = \zeta\varepsilon\eta \tag{4.4}$$

The velocity of a moving particle, which is under the effect of an electric field (electrophoretic mobility), can be determined in the laboratory [68,69]. There are different techniques available for electrophoretic mobility determination, namely phase analysis light scattering, electrophoretic light scattering, and laser Doppler anemometry [68]. The instruments used for ZP measurements are, in most instances, similar to those used for PS determination [68]. The surface charge of a vesicle can be measured by laser Doppler microelectrophoresis [70]. ZP can also be viewed as the electrostatic potential present at the electrical double layer that encloses a particle in solution [71]. A ZP ranging from -10 to $+10$ mV is considered almost neutral, while particles with ZP higher than $+30$ mV or lower than -30 mV are strongly cationic and strongly anionic, respectively [71]. It has been suggested that colloidal systems with a ZP higher than $|30\ \text{mV}|$ are strongly charged, and consequently, stable because of particle–particle repulsion while particles between -10 and $+10$ mV are almost neutral [68,71]. In the laboratory, different parameters are used to determine optimal ethosomal composition. As an example, Limsuwan and Amnuaikit prepared ESMs loaded with mycophenolic acid (MPA) and chose an optimized MPA ethosomal formulation with a ZP that was more than 30 mV, an encapsulation efficiency of more than 50%, PS of less than 500 nm, and a narrow size distribution [61]. It has been pointed out in the literature that ESMs have two major limitations [72]: the first is physical instability that leads to hydrophobic force-induced fusion of these vesicles. This fusion can result in the breakage of vesicles. The second disadvantage is the low viscosity of the ethosomal solution, which limits skin application as it cannot withstand physiological stress caused by the movement of skin or body movement [72].

Hyaluronic acid is a polysaccharide made up of repetitious units of D-glucuronic acid and *N*-acetyl-D-glucosamine [73]. The hyaluronic acid (HA) hydrophobic patch domain, comprising eight CH groups, may react with lipid constituents in SC during permeation and perturb skin barrier, increasing the permeability of HA derivatives [73]. Furthermore, the hygroscopic HA molecules can hydrate the skin and open the transdermal route more permeable for conjugated payloads [73]. The complex formed between phospholipids and the HA patch domain was used to prepare ESMs [62]. Xie and coworkers prepared ESMs from lecithin, cholesterol, rhodamine B, and ethanol via the ethanol injection method [62]. HA-ES-RB was formulated by mixing HA with ESMs [62]. The suspension was subsequently downsized and homogenized with ultrasound [62]. The authors then studied the drug loading, EE, surface morphology, and stability of the HA-ES-RB. The HA-ES-RB was, stable, spherical with the PS smaller than 100 nm [62]. Transcutaneous delivery studies across rat dorsal skin were also carried out in vitro and the permeation enhancing impact of HA-ES-RB was higher than that of rhodamine-loaded ethosomes (ES-RB) [62]. The penetration enhancing influence of HA-ES-RB was ascribed to the smaller vesicle size and the hydration effect of hyaluronic acid [62]. Furthermore, the HA-ES delivery system was biocompatible with normal cells [62]. Several investigators have used ESMs for transdermal drug delivery and only representative examples will be discussed in this chapter. Some studies are focused on only one active pharmaceutical ingredient, while others compare the influence of ESMs and other lipid-based vesicles on transcutaneous drug penetration.

Cucurmin

Curcumin (CUR), a natural polyphenol and low molecular–weight compound obtained from turmeric (*Curcuma longa*) rhizome has been investigated by several authors because of its broad spectrum of pharmacological activity [74,75]. The compound has antiinflammatory, antioxidant, antidiabetic antimicrobial, antiviral, and antitumor effects [75]. Several authors have documented the pharmacological activity of CUR in psoriasis, vitiligo, Crohn's disease, peptic ulcer, rheumatoid arthritis, ulcerative colitis, and gastric ulcer [75]. The compound, however, possesses poor water solubility (11 ng/mL in phosphate buffer at pH 5), low bioavailability, rapid metabolism, and excretion ($t_{1/} = 28.2$ and 44.5 min after i.v. and oral curcumin in rats, respectively) [75]. Pathan and coworkers recently developed curcumin-loaded ESMs [59]. The investigators studied the delivery of CUR from ESMs across human cadaver skin [59]. The ethosomal formulation was prepared from lecithin and cholesterol by thin-film dispersion method and sonicated at 500 J and 10% amplitude for 45 min (three cycles of 15 min each at 15 s ON/OFF) [59]. The percentage of ethanol in the dosage form varied from 3% to 6%. The authors used the BBD method with three independent variables (concentration of ethanol, cholesterol, and lecithin) and three response variables (flux, percent EE, and vesicle size) to optimize the composition of the vesicles [59]. Experimentally determined values for the response parameters were fitted to the quadratic, first-order and second-order models and the best fit was the quadratic model for all responses [59]. The formulation prepared from 4.5% ethanol, 10 mg cholesterol, and 10 mg lecithin had an optimal flux value (10.5 ± 2.6 μg/cm^2/h) through human skin, a smaller vesicle size (228.8 nm), and a higher drug encapsulation efficiency ($81.2\% \pm 3.12\%$) [59].

Ovalbumin

The protein ovalbumin (OVA), the main constituent in egg white, is often used as a model antigen as it is relatively inexpensive and accessible [76,77]. Zhang et al. developed an ethosomal transdermal gel loaded with OVA and studied the influence of solvent type on the forming and in vitro stability of the formulation [78]. The authors prepared the ESMs from soy PC, ethanol and saponin [78]. The gel base was made by dispersing carbopol 934 in 30%

ethanol-PBS or distilled water. In situ coalescence of ESMs was imaged and in vitro transport of the vesicles was quantified by using various synthetic membranes (cellulose, polyethersulfone, polyvinylidene fluoride) [78]. It was revealed that the hydrophobic polyvinylidene fluoride (PVDF) membrane had the highest transport-enhancing effect on OVA followed by the hydrophilic cellulose. Polyethersulfone was the least penetrated membrane [78]. The authors also investigated different carbomer concentrations and reported that the formulation with no carbomer had the highest transport rate followed by 0.3% carbomer gel [78]. The 0.5% carbomer gel had the lowest permeation rate, with less than 20% crossing the PVDF membrane after 24 h [78]. Furthermore, in vitro release studies showed a greater permeation rate for the ethosomal PBS gel compared to the aqueous ethosomal gel [78]. The authors also determined serum antibody titers following the administration of ESMs in 2-, 4-, and 6-week intervals. The investigators observed increased amount of antibody following the use of ESMs in comparison with the negative control, which showed a small or no change in the level of serum antibody [78]. The authors agreed with Touitou and coworkers that ethanol decreased phospholipid transition temperature and increased ethosome flexibility [55,78].

Griseofulvin

Griseofulvin (GRF) is a potent antifungal drug orally administered for the management of dermatophytosis [79]. The drug possesses pharmacological active against *Epidermophyton floccosum*, Microsporum, and Trichophyton, the fungi responsible for *Tinea corporis* [63]. The drug is poorly soluble in water (8.64 mg/L at 25°C) and mostly administered to patients orally [63]. Recently, Marto et al. prepared ESMs loaded with GRF [63]. The ethosomal systems were made from ethanol, SPC, and water. ESMs were formulated by the investigators from 45% (v/v) ethanol and 5% (w/v) SPC and loaded with different quantities of GRF (0.01%–0.5%). Subsequently, the suspension was filtered through 100 nm track-etched polycarbonate membranes under nitrogen pressure [63]. The flux of ethosomal suspension across a 30 nm polycarbonate filter was conducted by using two external pressures (0.7 and 1.0 MPa), formed by a nitrogen stream, and quantified at different times [63]. The authors carried out in vitro skin permeation experiments with newborn pig skin and employed a tape stripping technique to investigate SC deposition [63]. The formulation containing 0.1% (w/w) GRF displayed the highest incorporation efficiency (approximately 70%).

In the study, a pressure mimicking the hydrostatic pressure of the skin was used to study the permeation of the membrane by ESMs. It was observed by the investigators that the rise in pressure (0.7–1 MPa) led to enhanced vesicle transport across the membrane [63]. The introduction of GFR into vesicles did not modify their elasticity or other biomechanical properties and the vesicles size that was exposed to pressure was approximately sixfold higher than the diameter of the pores [63]. The use of hydroethanolic solution led to more GRF transport across the synthetic membranes after 1 h compared to ESMs, in accordance with theoretical predictions due to the drug's greater availability from a solution [63]. Following the administration of ESMs loaded with GRF, approximately 40% of the administered dose of the drug was deposited in the SC in 24 h. In contrast, the difference in the epidermal and dermal retention of the drug between GRF solution and GRF-loaded ESMs was not statistically significant [63]. The authors also examined the cytotoxicity potential of 0.1% GRF-loaded ESMs and GRF solution in HaCaT cells and reported that the cell viability was almost the same for the two formulations. However, there was a reduction in cell viability at 100 μg/mL of GRF [63]. The in vitro antifungal activity of GRF in hydroethanolic solution and ESMs was investigated against *Trichophyton rubrum* ATCC 28188 and the evaluated drug delivery systems showed a significant fungicidal action [63]. In contrast, there was no growth inhibition of the microorganism when empty ESMs were used, indicating that the quantity of GFR released from ESMs exceeded the minimum inhibitory concentration against *T. rubrum* [63].

Terbinafine

Terbinafine hydrochloride (TH) is administered orally for the management of onychomycosis and other superficial skin and nail fungal infections [80,81]. The drug has a molecular weight of 291 Da, and it is a synthetic allylamine with a pKa of 7 [82]. The octanol/water partition coefficient (log P) of TH is 3.3, and it is keratinophilic and lipophilic in nature [81,82]. Recently, Lizhar et al. investigated the skin delivery of TH from ethosomal vesicles [66]. The ESMs were prepared from soya PC, PG, and ethanol, while the drug incorporation efficiency was quantified by ultracentrifuging the dispersion at 20,000 rpm for 3 h [66]. Sonicated and unsonicated ESMs were formulated and the size of the vesicles was determined via dynamic light scattering, while in vitro drug diffusion study across cellophane dialysis membrane was conducted to choose the optimal ethosome composition for ex vivo permeation studies [66].

An ethosomal gel loaded with 3 mg of TH was administered on rat abdominal skin [66]. The authors reported that the EE in unsonicated ESMs increased from 60.59% ± 1.92% to 62.61% ± 2.13% when ethanol concentration went up from 40% to 50% w/v. In contrast, by raising ethanol content from 50% w/v to 60% w/v, the authors achieved a reduction in the encapsulation efficiency from 64.61% ± 2.13% to 55.33% ± 1.32% [66]. The size of ESMs obtained via a sonication method and without sonication was from 539 to 812 nm and from 227 to 695 nm, respectively [66]. The authors also reported that TH release declined with more phospholipid concentration, while elevated ethanol content in the formulation F2 (unsonicated with 5 mL of ethanol) led to an increased release of the drug [66]. Furthermore, elevating alcohol concentration from 40% to 60% w/v led to a substantial difference in drug transport, and this was attributed to the elevated bilayer membrane fluidity [66]. A formulated ethosomal gel prepared by adding carbopol 934P to the composition of the best formulation, F6 (prepared via sonication) was named F6*. The authors found that the proportion of the drug released from the sonicated ethosomal formulation F6 was 84.28% ± 1.03%, whereas 74.01% ± 0.62% of the drug was released from the formulation F6* in 12 h [66]. In contrast, the quantity of drug that permeated the skin from a commercially available cream was 61.45% ± 0.86% [66]. The percutaneous flux values for the ethosomal gel and commercially available cream were 144.61 ± 1.28 and 121.6 ± 1.16 μg/cm^2/h, respectively [66].

AbdelSamie and colleagues also investigated ethosomal gel loaded with terbinafine hydrochloride [83]. The authors prepared ESMs from terbinafine hydrochloride (TBN HCL) and phospholipid (Epikuron 200) via the classical mechanical dispersion method [83]. EE% was obtained via the centrifugation technique, while the deformability of the vesicles was determined via extrusion through polycarbonate filters at a constant pressure of 0.17 MPa [83]. The DI was calculated by using the following formula [83]:

$$\mathrm{DI} = \frac{j}{t}\left(\frac{r_v}{r_p}\right)^2 \tag{4.5}$$

where DI is the deformability index (mL/s), r_p is the filter membrane pore size (nm), t is the extrusion time (s), j is the quantity of suspension extruded (mL), and r_v is the vesicles size after extrusion (nm). The higher the DI value, the greater the deformability of the vesicles [83]. Ex vivo studies across rat abdominal skin were also undertaken. Compared to liposomes (LIPO), the presence of ethanol in ETH caused a threefold increase in EE% (from 20% to 59.25%) and this was attributed to the enhanced TBN solubility [83]. The deformability index for ETH was 0.38 [83]. ETH produced a substantially greater amount of TBN in the SC (10%) compared to liposomes (6%) but the amount of TBN delivered to the SC from the marketed cream was higher than that from the two vesicles (14%) [83]. However, the amounts of drug deposited in the epidermis following the administration of ETH and liposomes (LIPO) were higher (21% and 18%, respectively) compared to solution (11% ± 3.3%) or cream (11% ± 1.8%) [83].

Transethosomes

TELsare vesicles formulated by adding penetration enhancers or an edge activator (surfactant) to conventional ESMs [84]. TELs combine the advantages of ESMs and deformable liposomes [84]. Song et al. prepared ESMs from soybean phosphatidylcholine (Lipoid S100), ethanol, and water [84].

To obtain TELs, the authors added oleic acid, Tween 80, or sodium taurocholate [84]. The vesicles were loaded with 0.3% voriconazole. In skin permeation experiments, TELs were applied on hairless mouse skin, and transdermal flux values were compared with those of conventional liposomes (CLs), deformable liposomes (DLs), ESMs, and control (polyethylene glycol, PG) solutions [84]. The researchers used TEM to investigate TELs and found that the vesicles had irregular spherical shape, and this was attributed to higher fluidity because of the perturbed lipid bilayers [84]. The deformability values of TELs and ELs were substantially higher than those of DLs and CLs. Significantly, the in vitro transdermal delivery rate of the drug from TELs was the greatest among the vesicles, and the cumulative amount of voriconazole that was transported across the skin for 12 h (95.92 ± 10.20 $\mu g/cm^2$) was the highest when it was delivered from TEL (prepared from oleic acid) in comparison to that of the other vesicles [84]. The highest rate of transcutaneous transport (11.5 ± 1 $\mu g/cm^2/h$) was documented with the TEL prepared from oleic acid [84].

Chen and colleagues also investigated the delivery of paeonol from TEL [85]. Paeonol, which is the major pharmacologically active constituent in the root bark of *Paeonia lactiflora*, possesses antiinflammatory, antibacterial, and analgesic activities [85]. TELs loaded with paeonol were formulated via an ethanol injection method using PC and Tween 80. In vitro diffusion experiments were conducted with porcine ear skin sample in a Valia-Chien chamber [85]. The cumulative quantities of paeonol that penetrated the skin (Qn) from transfersomes, TEL, and a 35% saturated solution in ethanol at 28 h were 1995.2 ± 144.5, 2346.3 ± 195.8, and 1286.4 ± 75.7 $\mu g/cm^2$, respectively [85]. The authors also observed an enhanced paeonol transdermal flux of 82.9 $\mu g/cm^2/h$ and a greater skin retention amount in pig ear skin from TELs in comparison with transfersomes (71.2 $\mu g/cm^2/h$) and a 35% saturated ethanol solution of paeonol (46.8 $\mu g/cm^2/h$) [85]. The authors also carried out in vivo studies and the reported area under curve (AUC) of paeonol TEL was about 3.52- and 1.57-fold higher than those of a saturated solution of paeonol in 35% ethanol and transfersomes, respectively [85].

Rady et al. also investigated the impact of TEL on the skin permeation of a photosensitizer, ferrous chlorophyllin (Fe-CHL) [86]. TELs were prepared from soybean PC, ethanol, and an edge activator (Cremophor-A25, Span 20, Tween 80, and Tween 20) [86]. Skin permeation experiments revealed that 63.7% ± 5.5% and 19.2% ± 2.2% of Fe-CHL permeated from formulations E4 (150 mg of PC and 30 mg of Tween 80) and E7 (150 mg of PC and 30 mg of Tween 20), respectively [86]. Interestingly, skin deposition results demonstrated that formulation E3 (110 mg of PC and 10 mg of Cremophor) had the highest percentage of Fe-CHL deposited in the skin layers after 24 h (35.4% ± 1.6%) [86]. It was also reported that 29.1% ± 1.4%, and 13.7% ± 2.1% of Fe-CHL was retained in mouse skin after 24 h following the administration of E7 and E4, respectively [86]. In another study, three types of ultradeformable vesicles (transethosomes [TEL], ethosomes [E], and transfersomes [T]) were investigated for the delivery of vitamin E and caffeine across dermatomed pig ear skin [87]. For in vitro release of vitamin E, the following order was obtained: transethosomes (TEL) > ethosomes (ESMs) > transfersomes (T) [87]. The authors postulated that in the case of vitamin E, transethosomes were the most deformable vesicles (compared to transfersomes and ESMs), because TEL can easily alter their conformation and allow a higher membrane transport [87]. In contradistinction to vitamin E, the release profiles of caffeine formulations were greater and demonstrated the following order: T > E > TE. Permeation studies showed that although vitamin E was quantified in the receptor compartment after 24 h for all three (TEL, E, and T) formulations, its concentration (0.085–0.117 μg/mL) was negligible since it was less than the limit of quantification (1 μg/mL) [87]. The order of vitamin E-loaded ultradeformable vesicles deposited in the SC was T > E > TE, and the following order was observed for epidermis/dermis (ED) deposition (TE >T > E) expressed as $\%/cm^2$ [87]. The authors concluded that the release profile depends on the properties of the active pharmaceutical ingredients and their incorporation efficiency in the investigated formulations [87].

References

[1] Pandur Z, et al. Liposome destruction by hydrodynamic cavitation in comparison to chemical, physical and mechanical treatments. Ultrason Sonochem 2019;61:104826.

[2] Ita K. Current status of ethosomes and elastic liposomes in dermal and transdermal drug delivery. Curr Pharm Des 2016;22(33):5120–6.

[3] Elsayed MMA, Ibrahim MM, Cevc G. The effect of membrane softeners on rigidity of lipid vesicle bilayers: derivation from vesicle size changes. Chem Phys Lipids 2018;210:98–108.

[4] Hussain A, et al. Elastic liposome-based gel for topical delivery of 5-fluorouracil: in vitro and in vivo investigation. Drug Deliv 2014;1–15.

[5] Dragicevic N, Maibach H. Combined use of nanocarriers and physical methods for percutaneous penetration enhancement. Adv Drug Deliv Rev 2018;127:58–84.

[6] Benson HA. Elastic liposomes for topical and transdermal drug delivery. Methods Mol Biol 2017;1522:107–17.

[7] Hussain A, et al. Elastic liposomes as novel carriers: recent advances in drug delivery. Int J Nanomed 2017;12:5087–108.

[8] Ita KB, et al. Dermal delivery of selected hydrophilic drugs from elastic liposomes: effect of phospholipid formulation and surfactants. J Pharm Pharmacol 2007;59(9):1215–22.

[9] Cevc G, et al. Ultraflexible vesicles, Transfersomes, have an extremely low pore penetration resistance and transport therapeutic amounts of insulin across the intact mammalian skin. Biochim Biophys Acta 1998;1368(2):201–15.

[10] Cevc G. Transfersomes, liposomes and other lipid suspensions on the skin: permeation enhancement, vesicle penetration, and transdermal drug delivery. Crit Rev Ther Drug Carr Syst 1996;13(3–4):257–388.

[11] Cevc G, Gebauer D. Hydration-driven transport of deformable lipid vesicles through fine pores and the skin barrier. Biophys J 2003;84(2 Pt 1):1010–24.

[12] Cevc G, Blume G. Biological activity and characteristics of triamcinolone-acetonide formulated with the self-regulating drug carriers, Transfersomes®. Biochim Biophys Acta Biomembr 2003;1614(2):156–64.

[13] Caddeo C, et al. Tocopherol-loaded transfersomes: in vitro antioxidant activity and efficacy in skin regeneration. Int J Pharm 2018;551(1–2):34–41.

[14] Cevc G. Lipid vesicles and other colloids as drug carriers on the skin. Adv Drug Deliv Rev 2004;56(5):675–711.

[15] Brewer J, et al. Spatially resolved two-color diffusion measurements in human skin applied to transdermal liposome penetration. J Investig Dermatol 2013;133(5): 1260–8.

[16] Chen J, et al. Skin permeation behavior of elastic liposomes: role of formulation ingredients. Expert Opin Drug Deliv 2013;10(6):845–56.

[17] Chen Y-Y, et al. A novel elastic liposome for skin delivery of papain and its application on hypertrophic scar. Biomed Pharmacother 2017;87:82–91.

[18] Paul A, Cevc G, Bachhawat BK. Transdermal immunisation with an integral membrane component, gap junction protein, by means of ultradeformable drug carriers, transfersomes. Vaccine 1998;16(2–3):188–95.

[19] Qu Y, et al. α-Tocopherol liposome loaded chitosan hydrogel to suppress oxidative stress injury in cardiomyocytes. Int J Biol Macromol 2018.

[20] Schatzlein A, Cevc G. Non-uniform cellular packing of the stratum corneum and permeability barrier function of intact skin: a high-resolution confocal laser scanning microscopy study using highly deformable vesicles (Transfersomes). Br J Dermatol 1998;138 (4):583–92.

[21] Matera G, et al. Depression of lymphocyte activity during cutaneous leishmaniasis: a case report. Diagn Microbiol Infect Dis 2018;92(3):230–4.

[22] Sundar S. Visceral leishmaniasis. Trop Parasitol 2015;5(2):83–5.

[23] Purohit P, et al. An insight into tetrahydro-beta-carboline-tetrazole hybrids: synthesis and bioevaluation as potent antileishmanial agents. MedChemComm 2017;8(9):1824–34.

[24] Utaile M, et al. Susceptibility of clinical isolates of Leishmania aethiopica to miltefosine, paromomycin, amphotericin B and sodium stibogluconate using amastigote-macrophage in vitro model. Exp Parasitol 2013;134(1):68–75.

[25] Dar MJ, Din FU, Khan GM. Sodium stibogluconate loaded nano-deformable liposomes for topical treatment of leishmaniasis: macrophage as a target cell. Drug Deliv 2018;25 (1):1595–606.

[26] Ferreira SLC, et al. Statistical designs and response surface techniques for the optimization of chromatographic systems. J Chromatogr A 2007;1158(1):2–14.

[27] Gollasch M, Welsh DG, Schubert R. Perivascular adipose tissue and the dynamic regulation of Kv 7 and Kir channels: implications for resistant hypertension. Microcirculation 2018;25(1).

[28] Beach RA. Case series of oral minoxidil for androgenetic and traction alopecia: tolerability & the five C's of oral therapy. Dermatol Ther 2018;e12707.

[29] Tricarico D, et al. Characterization of minoxidil/hydroxypropyl-beta-cyclodextrin inclusion complex in aqueous alginate gel useful for alopecia management: efficacy evaluation in male rat. Eur J Pharm Biopharm 2018;122:146–57.

[30] Ramezani V, et al. Formulation and optimization of transfersome containing minoxidil and caffeine. J Drug Deliv Sci Technol 2018;44:129–35.

[31] Barak Y, Finkelstein I, Pridan S. The geriatric mania asenapine study (GeMS). Arch Gerontol Geriatr 2016;64:111–14.

[32] Oosterhof CA, El Mansari M, Blier P. Asenapine alters the activity of monoaminergic systems following its subacute and long-term administration: an in vivo electrophysiological characterization. Eur Neuropsychopharmacol 2015;25(4):531–43.
[33] McIntyre RS. Asenapine: a review of acute and extension phase data in bipolar disorder. CNS Neurosci Ther 2011;17(6):645–8.
[34] Minassian A, Young JW. Evaluation of the clinical efficacy of asenapine in schizophrenia. Expert Opin Pharmacother 2010;11(12):2107–15.
[35] Shreya AB, et al. Nano-transfersomal formulations for transdermal delivery of asenapine maleate: in vitro and in vivo performance evaluations. J Liposome Res 2016;26(3):221–32.
[36] Ita K. Transdermal delivery of vaccines—recent progress and critical issues. Biomed Pharmacother 2016;83:1080–8.
[37] Gupta PN, et al. Non-invasive vaccine delivery in transfersomes, niosomes and liposomes: a comparative study. Int J Pharm 2005;293(1–2):73–82.
[38] Esser ES, et al. Tetanus vaccination with a dissolving microneedle patch confers protective immune responses in pregnancy. J Control Release 2016;236:47–56.
[39] Habib BA, Sayed S, Elsayed GM. Enhanced transdermal delivery of ondansetron using nanovesicular systems: fabrication, characterization, optimization and ex-vivo permeation study-Box-Cox transformation practical example. Eur J Pharm Sci 2018;115:352–61.
[40] Danielsson B, Webster WS, Ritchie HE. Ondansetron and teratogenicity in rats: evidence for a mechanism mediated via embryonic hERG blockade. Reprod Toxicol 2018;81:237–45.
[41] Obata Y, et al. A statistical approach to the development of a transdermal delivery system for ondansetron. Int J Pharm 2010;399(1–2):87–93.
[42] Al Abood RM, et al. Microemulsion as a tool for the transdermal delivery of ondansetron for the treatment of chemotherapy induced nausea and vomiting. Colloids Surf B Biointerfaces 2013;101:143–51.
[43] Bicego M, Baldo S. Properties of the Box–Cox transformation for pattern classification. Neurocomputing 2016;218:390–400.
[44] van den Bergh BA, et al. Elasticity of vesicles affects hairless mouse skin structure and permeability. J Control Release 1999;62(3):367–79.
[45] Honeywell-Nguyen PL, et al. Transdermal delivery of pergolide from surfactant-based elastic and rigid vesicles: characterization and in vitro transport studies. Pharm Res 2002;19(7):991–7.
[46] Honeywell-Nguyen PL, Arenja S, Bouwstra JA. Skin penetration and mechanisms of action in the delivery of the D2-agonist rotigotine from surfactant-based elastic vesicle formulations. Pharm Res 2003;20(10):1619–25.
[47] Uchino T, et al. Physicochemical characterization of drug-loaded rigid and elastic vesicles. Int J Pharm 2011;412(1–2):142–7.
[48] Abdelkader H, Alani AW, Alany RG. Recent advances in non-ionic surfactant vesicles (niosomes): self-assembly, fabrication, characterization, drug delivery applications and limitations. Drug Deliv 2014;21(2):87–100.
[49] Yeom S, Shin BS, Han S. An electron spin resonance study of non-ionic surfactant vesicles (niosomes). Chem Phys Lipids 2014;181:83–9.
[50] Zhang Y, et al. Evaluation of transdermal salidroside delivery using niosomes via in vitro cellular uptake. Int J Pharm 2015;478(1):138–46.
[51] Junyaprasert VB, Singhsa P, Jintapattanakit A. Influence of chemical penetration enhancers on skin permeability of ellagic acid-loaded niosomes. Asian J Pharm Sci 2013;8(2):110–17.

[52] Manosroi A, et al. Transdermal absorption enhancement through rat skin of gallidermin loaded in niosomes. Int J Pharm 2010;392(1–2):304–10.
[53] Negi P, et al. Niosome-based hydrogel of resveratrol for topical applications: an effective therapy for pain related disorder(s). Biomed Pharmacother 2017;88:480–7.
[54] Qumbar M, et al. Formulation and optimization of lacidipine loaded niosomal gel for transdermal delivery: in-vitro characterization and in-vivo activity. Biomed Pharmacother 2017;93:255–66.
[55] Touitou E, Ainbinde D. Ethosomes—novel vesicular carriers for enhanced delivery: characterization and skin penetration properties. J Control Release 2000;65(3):403–18.
[56] Dayan N, Touitou E. Carriers for skin delivery of trihexyphenidyl HCl: ethosomes vs. liposomes. Biomaterials 2000;21(18):1879–85.
[57] Touitou E, Godin B. Ethosomes for skin delivery. J Drug Deliv Sci Technol 2007;17 (5):303–8.
[58] Nainwal N, et al. Transdermal applications of ethosomes—a detailed review. J Liposome Res 2018;1–11.
[59] Pathan IB, et al. Curcumin loaded ethosomes for transdermal application: formulation, optimization, in-vitro and in-vivo study. J Drug Deliv Sci Technol 2018;44:49–57.
[60] Meng S, et al. Preparation of osthole-loaded nano-vesicles for skin delivery: characterization, in vitro skin permeation and preliminary in vivo pharmacokinetic studies. Eur J Pharm Sci 2016;92:49–54.
[61] Limsuwan T, Amnuaikit T. Development of ethosomes containing mycophenolic acid. Procedia Chem 2012;4:328–35.
[62] Xie J, et al. Hyaluronic acid-containing ethosomes as a potential carrier for transdermal drug delivery. Colloids Surf B Biointerfaces 2018;172:323–9.
[63] Marto J, et al. Ethosomes for enhanced skin delivery of griseofulvin. Colloids Surf B Biointerfaces 2016;146:616–23.
[64] Yu X, et al. Improved anti-melanoma effect of a transdermal mitoxantrone ethosome gel. Biomed Pharmacother 2015;73:6–11.
[65] Zhang Z, et al. In vitro study of ethosome penetration in human skin and hypertrophic scar tissue. Nanomedicine 2012;8(6):1026–33.
[66] Iizhar SA, et al. In vitro assessment of pharmaceutical potential of ethosomes entrapped with terbinafine hydrochloride. J Adv Res 2016;7(3):453–61.
[67] Kohli R. Chapter 2—UV-ozone cleaning for removal of surface contaminants. In: Kohli R, Mittal KL, editors. Developments in surface contamination and cleaning. Oxford: William Andrew Publishing; 2015. p. 71–104.
[68] Fonte P, et al. Chapter fifteen—chitosan-coated solid lipid nanoparticles for insulin delivery. In: Düzgüneş N, editor. Methods in enzymology. Academic Press; 2012. p. 295–314.
[69] Rho H, Chon K, Cho J. Surface charge characterization of nanofiltration membranes by potentiometric titrations and electrophoresis: functionality vs. zeta potential. Desalination 2018;427:19–26.
[70] Ja'afar F, et al. Surface charge measurement of SonoVue, Definity and Optison: a comparison of laser Doppler electrophoresis and micro-electrophoresis. Ultrasound Med Biol 2015;41(11):2990–3000.
[71] Clogston JD, Patri AK. Zeta potential measurement. Methods Mol Biol 2011;697:63–70.
[72] Zhang Y, et al. Lipid vesicular nanocarrier: quick encapsulation efficiency determination and transcutaneous application. Int J Pharm 2017;516(1–2):225–30.
[73] Jung HS, et al. Enhancing the transdermal penetration of nanoconstructs: could hyaluronic acid be the key? Nanomedicine 2014;9(6):743–5.

[74] Kumari P, et al. Curcumin delivery by poly(lactide)-based co-polymeric micelles: an in vitro anticancer study. Pharm Res 2016;33(4):826–41.

[75] Sintov AC. Transdermal delivery of curcumin via microemulsion. Int J Pharm 2015;481 (1–2):97–103.

[76] Jankovicova B, et al. Epitope mapping of allergen ovalbumin using biofunctionalized magnetic beads packed in microfluidic channels: the first step towards epitope-based vaccines. J Chromatogr A 2008;1206(1):64–71.

[77] von Halling Laier C, et al. Spray dried cubosomes with ovalbumin and Quil-A as a nanoparticulate dry powder vaccine formulation. Int J Pharm 2018;550(1–2):35–44.

[78] Zhang Y, et al. Formulation and in vitro stability evaluation of ethosomal carbomer hydrogel for transdermal vaccine delivery. Colloids Surf B Biointerfaces 2018;163: 184–91.

[79] Paguigan ND, et al. Chemoselective fluorination and chemoinformatic analysis of griseofulvin: natural vs fluorinated fungal metabolites. Bioorg Med Chem 2017;25(20):5238–46.

[80] Stolmeier DA, et al. Utility of laboratory test result monitoring in patients taking oral terbinafine or griseofulvin for dermatophyte infections. JAMA Dermatol 2018;154:1409–16.

[81] Sachdeva V, et al. Iontophoresis mediated in vivo intradermal delivery of terbinafine hydrochloride. Int J Pharm 2010;393(1–2):112–18.

[82] Sachdeva V, et al. Transdermal iontophoretic delivery of terbinafine hydrochloride: quantitation of drug levels in stratum corneum and underlying skin. Int J Pharm 2010;388 (1–2):24–31.

[83] AbdelSamie SM, et al. Terbinafine hydrochloride nanovesicular gel: in vitro characterization, ex vivo permeation and clinical investigation. Eur J Pharm Sci 2016;88:91–100.

[84] Song CK, et al. A novel vesicular carrier, transethosome, for enhanced skin delivery of voriconazole: characterization and in vitro/in vivo evaluation. Colloids Surf B Biointerfaces 2012;92:299–304.

[85] Chen ZX, et al. Evaluation of paeonol-loaded transethosomes as transdermal delivery carriers. Eur J Pharm Sci 2017;99:240–5.

[86] Rady M, et al. Dermal delivery of Fe-chlorophyllin via ultradeformable nanovesicles for photodynamic therapy in melanoma animal model. Int J Pharm 2018;548(1):480–90.

[87] Ascenso A, et al. Development, characterization, and skin delivery studies of related ultradeformable vesicles: transfersomes, ethosomes, and transethosomes. Int J Nanomed 2015;10:5837–51.

Chapter 5

Chemical permeation enhancers

Chemical permeation enhancers (skin penetration promoters) refer to compounds that increase transdermal drug transport [1] by perturbing the stratum corneum (SC) and/or other components of the skin. These compounds facilitate transdermal delivery for medications that do not sufficiently permeate the skin [2]. Over 350 chemical penetration enhancers (CPEs) have been identified [3]. CPEs have several benefits including low cost, easy processing, and formulation flexibility [4]. Furthermore, permeation enhancers are beneficial compared to physical methods because they do not cause pain at the application site [5]. But there are also limitations as the use of CPEs is associated with safety concerns [3]. Skin irritation and cytotoxicity are disadvantages linked to CPEs [6].

Despite extensive research carried out by several laboratories, it has been challenging to elucidate the effects of CPE [7]. What has emerged from experimental work and theoretical postulates is that skin penetration promoters can (1) disrupt or fluidize SC structure, leading to enhanced drug diffusivity (Fig. 5.1) [8,9].

Minor fractions of the SC protein and lipid constituents become fluid in hydrated conditions [10]. Sorption promoters tend to enhance this fluidity [10]. Skin penetration enhancers may boost SC diffusion coefficient of the drug or increase the vehicle drug effective concentration [9]. (2) CPEs can interact with keratin to increase transport through the corneocytes, and (3) these enhancers can also improve the partitioning of drug in SC [8]. Another mechanism of flux enhancement entails boosting penetrant solubility in the SC by temporarily altering skin solubility parameter [11]. Many solvents used as CPEs enter the SC and increase the partitioning of a copenetrant (drug) [12]. Significant is the fact that several CPEs can interact with sebum, leading to increased follicular drug delivery [13]. Because of the multiplicity of CPE-mediated enhancing mechanisms, it has been suggested that several approaches be used in research to obtain a full picture of penetration enhancement [14].

Several structure–activity relationship investigations have demonstrated that the enhancing activity of CPEs is a function of their chemical structures [4]. Because of the variety in the chemical structure of CPEs, it is plausible that these compounds act via more than one mechanism and that the specific

Transdermal Drug Delivery. DOI: https://doi.org/10.1016/B978-0-12-822550-9.00005-3

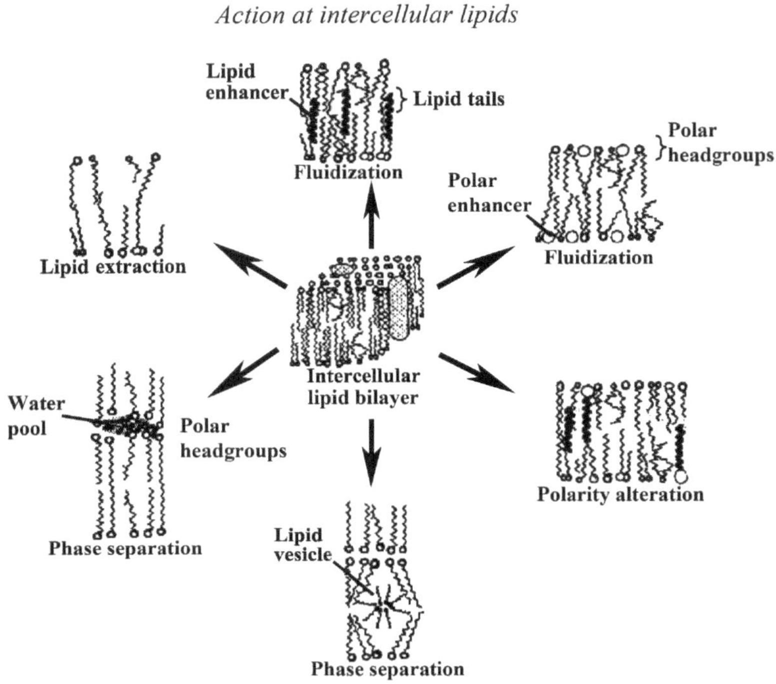

FIGURE 5.1 Effect of penetration enhancers on the intercellular lipid domain. *Reproduced with permission from Williams AC, Barry BW. Penetration enhancers. Adv Drug Deliv Rev 2012;64(Supplement):128–37.*

effect of the CPE is a function of the physicochemical properties of the sorption promoter as well as the permeant [2]. Barry has classified CPEs based on their chemical structures [12]. According to the author, enhancers used for percutaneous transport enhancement include pyrrolidones, alcohols, esters, water, esters sulfoxides (such as dimethyl sulfoxide) and their derivatives, hydrocarbons, terpenes and derivatives, Azone and its analogs, amides (including urea and its derivatives), fatty acids, surfactants (nonionic, cationic, and anionic), polyols, essential oils (EOs), oxazolidines, polymers, epidermal enzymes, and lipid synthesis inhibitors [12].

Another classification of CPEs has also been documented by Karande and colleagues [3]. The classes include zwitterionic surfactants, cationic surfactants, anionic surfactants, fatty acids, sodium salts of fatty acids, fatty amines, Azone-like compounds, fatty esters, nonionic surfactants, and others [3]. Nonionic surfactants enhance drug penetration by direct bonding with either proteins or skin lipids [15]. In addition, extraction of lipid components leads to membrane integrity loss and there is usually a correlation between an increase in membrane fluidity and acyl chain disorganization induced by the transport of surfactant molecules into the intercellular regions of the SC [15]. Furthermore, nonionic surfactants can interact with keratin filaments, leading to the disordering of corneocytes and facilitated skin or systemic drug delivery [15].

Lane has proposed a diffusion-partition-solubility postulate to characterize CPE mechanism of action [16]. According to this author, the effects of CPEs are caused by the intercalation of CPEs with skin lipid bilayers which leads to disruption or fluidization. In addition, these enhancers are present as discrete phases in the intercellular lipid regions of the skin [16]. The recommended properties for skin permeation enhancers have been enumerated by Williams and Barry [9] who emphasized that (1) these compounds should neither be toxic nor allergenic; (2) penetration enhancers should act promptly, and both the duration of action and activity should be reproducible and predictable; (3) accelerants (CPEs) should aid drug flux of into the body while preventing the efflux of endogenous compounds; (4) when sorption promoters (CPEs) are discarded, skin barrier properties should be restored promptly and completely; (5) CPEs are expected to be inert and also be compatible with excipients and medications; and (6) CPEs should be cosmetically acceptable [9]. Penetration enhancers should be evaluated for skin irritation, patient acceptability and dose control [17]. The action of CPEs can be grouped into direct or indirect [18,19]. Direct effects reduce the resistance offered by the intracellular keratin and the intercellular lipid region of the skin, while indirect effects optimize the drug thermodynamic activity as well as the partition coefficient of the drug, increase drug solubility, and can lead to the formation of drug reservoirs in the skin [18,19]. CPE molecules enter into the skin lipid bilayer vibrating, rotating, creating microcavities, translocating, and boosting the free volume available for drug penetration [12]. Ionic surface-active agents such as DMSO and decylmethylsulfoxide interact with keratin in corneocytes, loosening the dense protein structure, rendering it more porous and thus increasing the diffusion coefficient [12]. CPEs can also interact with sebum, leading to marked increase in follicular drug delivery [13]. Some CPEs have found widespread use in percutaneous drug transport research. In the next section, some of these sorption promoters will be discussed. The effect of chemical permeation enhancers on transdermal drug delivery is shown in Table 5.1.

Terpenes

Terpenes (TPNs), which are derived from EOs, consist of repeated isoprene (C_5H_8) units [20,21]. Two major types of terpenes have been identified: oxygen-containing molecules (OCMs) and nonpolar hydrocarbons [2]. OCMs can have ester, epoxy, keto, hydroxyl, or carboxyl functional groups as hydrogen-bond donors (HBDs) or hydrogen-bond acceptors (HBAs) [2]. Terpenes can also be grouped based on the amount of isoprene units

TABLE 5.1 Effect of chemical permeation enhancers on transdermal drug delivery.

Therapeutic agent (s) or model compound	Skin model	Chemical permeation enhancer	References
Dimethyl fumarate	Human skin	Cineole and Terpene	[1]
Lidocaine and diphenhydramine	Pig skin	Menthol	[8]
Diltiazem	Rat skin	1,8-Cineole, *N*-methyl pyrrolidone (NMP), dimethyl sulfoxide (DMSO), and capsaicin	[5]
Donepezil	Rat skin	Essential oil (EO), sabinene (SA), 4-terpineol (TE), *p*-cymene (CY), and cuminaldehyde (CU)	[27]
Zidovudine	Rat skin	Carvone, cineole, pulegone, menthol, menthone, alpha-terpineol, and ethanol	[28]
Fenoterol hydrobromide	Guinea pig skin	1-Dodecyl-2-pyrrolidinone, oleic acid	[44]
Levamisole hydrochloride	Rat skin	Azone, Tween 80	[39]
Methotrexate	Human skin	Azone	[43]
Memantine hydrochloride	Pig skin	Azone	[46]
Propranolol	Human skin	*N*-methylpyrrolidone	[50]
Flurbiprofen, indomethacin, triamcinolone acetonide, and 5-fluorouracil	Rat skin	1-Lauryl-2, 1-hexyl and 1-methyl-pyrrolidone	[51]
Buprenorphine	Rat skin	Lauryl alcohol	[56]
Hydrocortisone(HC)	Human stratum corneum	Isopropyl alcohol and isopropyl myristate	[59]
4-Benzylpiperidine	Human skin	Propylene glycol	[62]
Testosterone	Human cadaver skin	Isopropyl myristate	[17]

(*Continued*)

TABLE 5.1 (Continued)

Therapeutic agent (s) or model compound	Skin model	Chemical permeation enhancer	References
Ribavirin, gliclazide, nimesulide, and oxaprozin	Rat skin	Isopropyl palmitate	[71]
Methadone	Pig skin	Dimethylsulfoxide, ethanol, and Azone	[75]
5-Fluorouracil	Human skin	Oleic acid	[79]
Lumiracoxib	Pig skin	Oleic acid	[81]
Ibuprofen	Human skin	Transcutol (monoethyl ether of diethylene glycol)	[85]
Dexpanthenol	Pig skin	Tween 85, sodium dodecyl sulfate, and Span 80	[94]
Human epidermal growth factor	Rat skin	TD1	[96]
Ketoprofen	Mouse skin	Arginine terminated peptide dendrimers	[100]
Diclofenac sodium	Rat skin	Janus-type poly (propyl ether imine) dendrimers	[108]

(sesterterpenes, triterpenes, sesquiterpenes, monoterpenes, tetraterpenes, diterpenes, etc.) [21]. TPNs are regarded as less harmful compared with other commonly used CPEs such as surfactants, fatty acids/esters, dimethyl sulfoxide, urea, and ethanol [22]. Indeed, terpenes belong to the generally recognized as safe (GRAS) class of sorption promoters and can be utilized between 1% and 5% to boost either lipophilic or hydrophilic transcutaneous drug transport without adverse effects [5]. Although TPNs are composed of only oxygen, hydrogen and carbon atoms, these molecules are not aromatic [9]. It has been asserted that terpenes disrupt skin lipid bilayer by competitive hydrogen bonding with skin ceramides inducing the perturbation of SC lipid packing [23]. The consequence is an increased level of drug diffusivity [23].

Ameen and coworkers studied the effect of CPEs on the transdermal delivery of dimethyl fumarate [23]. The authors compared the skin permeation–boosting action of cineole (cin) and terpene (terp) on DMF and observed that the higher transdermal flux induced by cin was partially ascribed to the fact that cin is more hydrophilic than terp with the calculated log P values of 2.84 and 3.28, respectively [23]. Another perspective by the same authors was that the mechanisms of DMF flux enhancement by both CPEs may be different [23]. Terpenes may influence transdermal drug transport via distinct modalities due to the disparate physicochemical features controlling their interactions with the skin as well with drug molecules [23]. As a matter of fact, the permeability coefficient (P) resulting from the use of terp was almost twice compared to that obtained with cin, demonstrating that they have distinct skin permeating effect on DMF [23].

Menthol is a naturally occurring cyclic monoterpene with a lingering minty smell [24]. Menthol's analgesic effect is linked to the compound's conjugation with the transient receptor potential melastatin 8 (TRPM8) channel and it has been speculated that TRPM8 may also play a role in menthol's penetration enhancing effect [8]. Calcium partakes in the maintenance of cell–cell adhesion that impacts skin barrier properties. Because menthol binds to calcium through TRPM8 channel, is has been suggested that the skin permeation properties of menthol may be mediated by calcium [8]. Joshi et al. studied the potential role of calcium and linked that to the skin permeation enhancing property of menthol [8]. The authors wanted to know if the administration of the calcium channel blockers (CCBs) diltiazem and verapamil can negate the skin enhancing properties of menthol in relation to two model drugs (lidocaine and diphenhydramine) [8]. The authors prepared several gels: (1) drug with menthol; (2) drug, menthol, and CCB (verapamil or diltiazem); (3) drug and CCB; and (4) drug alone (diphenhydramine or lidocaine) [8]. Animal studies were carried out for each drug/menthol/CCB combination gel by administering four formulations on shaved rabbit's dorsum. The authors then used microdialysis to measure the concentration of the medications in the dermis. It was reported that the administration of menthol-loaded gel led to enhanced transdermal transport of the drugs compared to the formulations with no penetration enhancers [8]. In addition, the inclusion of a CCB in the composition blocked the permeation-boosting influence of menthol. These results point to the role of calcium in the skin transport-inducing effect of menthol [8].

The penetration-boosting influence of terpenes on drug transport is somewhat conflicting. Lane observed that terpenes have not found clinical relevance as sorption promoters most likely due to the relatively large quantities of these enhancers needed for transdermal drug delivery enhancement [16]. The authors emphasized that for menthol, there is no adequate evidence showing that it can facilitate topical or transcutaneous drug transport in humans [16]. In contrast, Barry and Williams pointed out that the utilization of eucalyptus oil resulted in a 34-fold enhancement in 5-fluorouracil permeability coefficient [25]. The main terpene in eucalyptus oil is 1,8-cineole [9]. In another study, it was shown that natural terpenes possess higher enhancement activity in comparison with synthetic CPEs

[26]. Interaction with SC intercellular lipids was suggested by the authors as the major mechanism of action for terpenes [26]. In another study, the ex vivo penetration of diltiazem (DTH) across hairless rat abdominal skin was investigated and the cumulative amount of the permeated drug ($\mu g/cm^2$) against time was plotted [5]. The greatest transport (2691 $\mu g/cm^2$) of DTH at 36 h was induced by the enhancer 1,8-cineole and this was significantly higher than that obtained with *N*-methyl pyrrolidone (NMP), dimethyl sulfoxide (DMSO), and capsaicin [5]. Furthermore, the highest flux (89.7 $\mu g/cm^2/h$) of DTH was achieved, when 1,8-cineole was used as the CPE in comparison with *N*-methyl pyrrolidone (NMP), dimethyl sulfoxide (DMSO), and capsaicin [5].

Nan et al. also investigated the chemical composition of *Ledum palustre* EO and reported that the oil contained p-cymene (CY), 4-terpineol (TE), sabinene (SA), and cuminaldehyde [27]. The authors subsequently studied the flux enhancement effects of these constituents via in vitro skin permeation experiments and reported that cuminaldehyde (the principal active constituent of the EO enhanced the skin permeation of donepezil (DNP) by reducing the interaction between DNP and the SC intercellular lipids, facilitating the mobility of the SC intercellular lipids, and enhancing the partition of DNP into the SC [27]. SA marginally enhanced the skin transport of DNP in comparison with the control group, but it was less than that obtained with EO [27]. The authors also used molecular docking and attenuated total reflection-Fourier transform infrared (ATR-FTIR) spectroscopy to evaluate the effects of CPEs on the intercellular lipids and reported that the EO induced a blue shift of $\upsilon_{as}CH_2$, which suggests that EO increased the mobility of the SC lipids. Intriguingly, DNP also engendered a blue shift of $\upsilon asCH_2$, which infers the interaction of DNP with SC lipids, and that the interaction may reduce the transport of the drug across the skin [27]. The skin penetration enhancement effect of oxygen-containing terpenes on drugs has been attributed to the perturbation of the SC hydrogen-bond network because of intermolecular interactions between HBD and HBA groups of terpenes on one side and the SC on the other side [2,28]. The influence of several oxygen-containing monoterpenes including carvone, cineole, pulegone, menthol, menthone, and alpha-terpineol on the transport of zidovudine (AZT) across rat skin was examined and it was reported that all the investigated terpenes substantially enhanced the percutaneous penetration of AZT compared to 66.6% aqueous solution of ethanol [28]. The interactions between terpenes and hydrocortisone (HC), diclofenac sodium (DFS), estradiol (ES), and 5-fluorouracil (5FU) have also been studied [2]. It was demonstrated that the creation and properties of the complexes between terpenes and these medications depended on the solvent environment [2]. The structures of over 60 complexes (1:1 drug–enhancer) were determined for three solvent environments (1-octanol, chloroform, and water) [2].

Water

The SC hinders water loss and chemical penetration [29]. The natural hydration level of SC in vivo is thought to be around 30%–50% of its dry weight [30]. A normal SC can restrict water egress to less than 25 mL/h in an adult skin surface subjected to dry air conditions [29]. Transepidermal water gradient hydrates the skin and determines its permeability at steady state [31]. With enhanced hydration, corneocytes swell mostly in the direction perpendicular to the skin surface [29]. The concentration of water in the SC is approximately 15%–20% although this can change as a function of the external environment especially humidity [9]. It has been observed that by immersing the skin in water, occluding or exposing it to high humidities, water content in the SC can be boosted [25], leading to enhanced skin permeability. When the skin is occluded, the water concentration in the SC may be close to 400% [32]. Water is an efficient natural sorption promoter and can enhance the transport of hydrophilic and lipophilic compounds [30]. The degree of SC hydration determines the skin permeation of a given medication as there is a relationship between increased hydration and enhanced transdermal flux of a variety of medications [33]. It is noteworthy that SC hydration is not uniform: when the skin is in the normal range of hydration, the bulk of water is in corneocytes, which contain "natural moisturizing factor" (NMF) [34]. This is a hygroscopic humectant mixture of salts, amino acids, and derivatives [35]. NMF helps in maintaining skin pliability. SC water may be "free" (can function as a solvent within the skin for polar penetrants) or "bound" [9]. Although water is known to enhance the delivery of some medications, the mechanisms of increased drug flux values are not sufficiently elucidated and warrant further studies [9]. As an illustration, it has been argued that increased hydrophilic drug fluxes occur under occlusive conditions but in contrast, it has also been emphasized that the repeat distance of lipid lamellae is essentially the same (even at 100% humidity), despite different hydration levels, suggesting the presence of low water level in the skin lipid lamella headgroup area [36].

Azone

In the Azone (AZ) molecule, a dodecyl carbon chain is linked to caprolactam (1-aza-2-cycloheptanone) ring [37]. Azone structure can be broken down into two parts: the polar cycle head (α carbon on the hydrophobic chain the heterocycle) and the hydrophobic chain [38]. It was the first compound skin permeation promoter developed by researchers [39]. Although FDA has not approved Azone (AZ) for use in clinical formulations, the skin permeation effects of this compound have been characterized for several lipophilic and hydrophilic medications including antibiotics and steroids [40]. AZ is soluble in several organic solvents, including propylene glycol and ethanol [39].

The compound is a lipophilic compound with a log P value of approximately 6.2 [39]. The skin penetration enhancement property of Azone is associated with the reduction of skin diffusional resistance [41]. Bouwstra et al. used several azones with different alkyl chain length (C6–C16) to study the thermal properties of human SC and documented a reduction in transition enthalpy with a corresponding enhancement in lipid bilayer fluidity [14]. Meng-Lund and coworkers have also pointed out that the skin permeation–boosting influence of AZ on the keratinized skin may be due to the disruptive influence of AZ on the intercellular lipids and subsequent enhanced diffusivity of drugs through the skin [42]. The "soup spoon" structure of AZ enables it to partition into skin lipid bilayers, where the enhancer disrupts the organized packing of lipids [38]. Following the application of AZ, there is increased disorganization of the ceramide bilayers with enhanced diffusion coefficient of the medication [43]. In another study, Elshafeey and colleagues studied the influence of Azone derivative (dodecyl pyrrolidinone) on the percutaneous transport of fenoterol [44]. According to the authors, the use of 1-dodecyl-2-pyrrolidinone (DPY) resulted in the highest drug permeation (404.69 $\mu g/cm^2$) compared to other enhancers [44]. The permeation enhancement provided by DPY was 40 times more than that offered by control patches without enhancer [44].

The impact of Azone dispersion states on the skin penetration of levamisole hydrochloride was recently investigated [39]. Levamisole possesses immunomodulatory actions and has also been used as an antiparasitic agent against leprosy and recalcitrant warts [45]. In addition, the drug is used for the pharmacotherapy of dermatologic diseases such as recalcitrant aphthous ulcers and lichen planus [45]. Chen and coworkers prepared hydroalcoholic gels containing levamisole hydrochloride (LH) and azone in different dispersion states by using various concentrations of Tween 80 and Azone in the formulations [39]. Azone was used in different forms as coarse or fine emulsion droplets in gels, dissolved molecules, or solubilized in micelles [39]. The authors investigated the in vitro transport of LH across excised rat skin and found out that there was a substantial increase in the percutaneous penetration of LH when azone concentration was between 0.25% and 0.75% indicating high transcutaneous enhancement by azone molecules or micelles [39]. It was also observed that azone in the form of oil droplets did not effectively increase the percutaneous transport of LH [39].

Čuříková et al. prepared artificial membranes (AMs) from cholesterol sulfate, cholesterol, stearic acid, and a ceramide (CER) constituent comprising *N*-stearoyl phytosphingosine (CER[NP]) and/or *N*-2-hydroxystearoyl phytosphingosine (CER[AP]) [40]. They studied the effect of (S)-*N*-acetylproline dodecyl ester (L-Pro2) and *N*-dodecyl azepan-2-one (Azone) on the delivery of theophylline (TH) and indomethacin (IND) across the AMs [40]. The steady-state flux values of (A) theophylline and (B) indomethacin through various model membranes and through porcine skin are shown in Fig. 5.2.

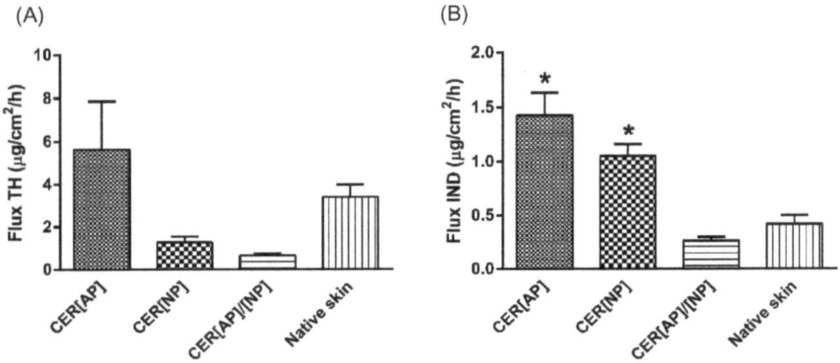

FIGURE 5.2 Steady-state flux values of theophylline (A) and indomethacin (B) through model membranes of various composition and through porcine skin. Data are presented as means ± SEM, $n > 6$. * indicates a significant difference ($P < .05$) compared to porcine skin. *Reproduced with permission from Curikova BA, et al. Simplified stratum corneum model membranes for studying the effects of permeation enhancers. Int J Pharm 2017;534(1–2):287–96.*

The authors compared the effect of L-Pro2 and Azone on the transport of TH and IND through CER[AP]/[NP] membrane compared to porcine skin. TH transport rate through the membrane was 0.64 ± 0.1 μg/cm^2/h, and this rose substantially to 216.12 ± 33.94 and 41.64 ± 2.11 μg/cm^2/h under the impact of L-Pro2 and Azone, respectively [40]. L-Pro2 and Azone also enhanced TH flux through pig skin from 3.4 ± 0.56 μg/cm^2/h to 45.28 ± 3.39 and 29.81 ± 2.75 μg/cm^2/h for L-Pro2 and Azone, respectively [40]. The permeation of IND through CER[AP]/[NP] membrane was 0.26 ± 0.03 μg/cm^2/h and this rose substantially to 21.06 ± 2.82 and 6.20 ± 1.31 μg/cm^2/h following the use of L-Pro2 and Azone, respectively. Both permeation promoters also enhanced IND flux through the pig skin from 0.42 ± 0.08 to 4.41 ± 0.53 and 0.83 ± 0.11 μg/cm^2/h for L-Pro2 and Azone, respectively [40].

The effect of 3% Azone (laurocapram) on the transport of methotrexate from a gel formulation has also been studied [43]. Ethanolic carbomer gels prepared from 1% methotrexate and 0 or 3% Azone were utilized in the experiments. When Azone was not used, the researchers did not find methotrexate in the receptor chamber of the diffusion cells after 48 h [43]. In contrast, when Azone was incorporated into the formulation, the transdermal flux across human abdominal skin was 189 ± 98 ng/cm^2. In another study, Rio-Sancho and coworkers investigated the effect of Azone on the transcutaneous delivery of memantine hydrochloride (MH) across pig ear skin and found out that pretreating the skin with laurocapram led to a statistically significant enhancement in the percutaneous permeation rate of MH in comparison with the control [46]. When laurocapram (Azone) was used, the transdermal flux of MH increased from 7.10 ± 1.50 to 38.4 ± 4.7 μg/cm^2/h [46].

Buspirone is a D3 receptor antagonist and a partial serotonin 1A agonist that is used as an anxiolytic agent [47]. The drug is utilized for the pharmacotherapy of attention-deficit/hyperactivity disorder, anxiety caused by smoking cessation or alcohol craving, as well as for the management of generalized anxiety disorder [48]. Meidan and colleagues investigated the influence of Azone on the transcutaneous permeation of buspirone hydrochloride (BH). The transcutaneous permeation rate of BH was significantly increased by the administration of 2.5% (v/v) Azone [48]. Pretreating the human skin with Azone yielded approximately 27-fold increase in BH flux [48].

Pyrrolidone and derivatives

Pyrrolidone is a constituent of natural moisturizing factor and its derivatives as well as structurally related compounds have been used to increase the percutaneous penetration of therapeutic agents [9,23,49]. These CPEs tend to exhibit a more significant impact on hydrophilic penetrants compared to lipophilic ones [9]. *N*-Methylpyrrolidone and 2-pyrrolidone are two compounds that have been used as solvents and can significantly partition into human SC and modify the solvent properties of the skin [16]. NMP is known to act as a solvent for SC lipids promoting the partitioning of the drug molecule [23]. Cilurzo and coworkers used experimental data in combination with molecular dynamic (MD) simulations to unravel the mechanism through which *N*-methylpyrrolidone (NMP) increases the percutaneous penetration of compounds [50]. The authors used ATR-FTIR to probe the interaction of NMP (dispersed in water or mineral oil) with human epidermis. There were no substantial changes in the structure of the SC [50]. Remarkably, there was a twofold enhancement in the permeation rate of propranolol (PR) through human epidermis following the addition of 10% NMP but there was no increase in the transcutaneous flux of HC [50]. It was also demonstrated by MD simulations that a complex was formed between propranolol's aromatic systems and NMP's amido group and this phenomenon may have been mediated by $\pi-\pi$ stacking interactions and H-bonds [50].

The use of pyrrolidones may also lead to depot formation within the skin. Such a reservoir is useful for the extended release of therapeutic agents [9]. Ameen et al. investigated the influence of NMP on the transdermal delivery of dimethyl fumarate (DMF) and found out that NMP significantly enhanced the permeation of DMF [23]. The lag time did not decline and the permeability coefficient of DMF increased with 20% NMP. In another study, transdermal permeation as a function of tadalafil solubility was investigated [49]. Tadalafil exhibited the greatest solubility in NMP in comparison to the other binary or pure vehicles. From skin transport experiments, it was documented that NMP, ethanol, or glycerin exhibited a greater effect on the skin transport of tadalafil over 12 h compared to PEG 400 or PG [49]. The transdermal flux value following the use of NMP was $0.34 \pm 0.02\ \mu g/cm^2/h$ [49] in comparison to the flux values achieved with PG (0.14 ± 0.01 μg/cm^2/h) or PEG 400 (0.10 ± 0.02 μg/cm^2/h). Of all the solvents and binary mixtures tested, the highest transdermal flux (0.41 ± 0.03 μg/cm^2/h) was recorded when tadalafil was dissolved in ethanol [49].

Sasaki and coworkers investigated the influence of 1-methyl (1), 1-hexyl (2), and 1 -lauryl-2-pyrrolidone (3) on the transcutaneous penetration of flurbiprofen, indomethacin, triamcinolone acetonide, and 5-fluorouracil across rat skin [49]. Pyrrolidone derivatives facilitated the transdermal delivery of the drugs, notably lipophilic compounds 2 and 3, which increased the penetration of 5-fluorouracil and indomethacin [51]. Furthermore, it was demonstrated by the authors that pyrrolidone derivatives increased permeant solubility in isopropyl myristate. It was also observed that compounds 2 and 3 increased the solubility and transcutaneous transport of hydrophilic permeants compared to the same parameters for lipophilic penetrants [51]. The authors postulated that pyrrolidone derivatives enhanced the transdermal transport of permeants by improving permeant solubility in the SC [51].

In another study, the Sasaki research group also showed that increased skin enhancer concentration improved the permeation rate and skin deposition of phenol [52]. There was also a reduction in the lag time for the model nonabsorbable permeant [52]. An interesting approach aimed at reducing the irritation potential of CPEs was suggested by Lambert and colleagues [53]. The authors suggested the use of a "soft" skin penetration promoter that can be biotransformed to inactive compounds in the viable epidermis after increasing penetration across the SC [53]. The authors prepared fatty acid esters of *N*-(2-hydroxyethyl)-2-pyrrolidone and these were used to increase the transdermal delivery of HC through mouse skin [53]. Increased permeability of the drug was reported by the authors. The cleavage of the esters by enzymes in the plasma and skin homogenates was documented and it was interesting that these CPEs had significantly less irritation potential compared to conventional skin sorption promoters [53].

Despite the wide range of investigations carried out with pyrrolidone and derivatives, the clinical use of this class of CPEs is impeded by adverse effects. As an illustration, a recent research showed that pyrrolidone derivatives induced erythema in some study participants, even though this adverse event was for a short period of time [9].

Alcohols

Compounds with one or more hydroxyl (−OH) groups conjugated to a single-bonded alkane are known as alcohols and these have been used to increase the percutaneous transport of medications [37]. Alcohols can increase the transdermal delivery of drugs via numerous mechanisms including the swelling of the SC, extraction of lipids and proteins, the enhancement of drug solubility in the formulation, or drug partitioning into the skin [3].

Certain compounds including polyglycols, glycerols, alkenols, alkanols, and glycols are classified as alcohols [33], but isopropyl alcohol and ethanol are among the most widely used short-chain alcohols for transdermal drug delivery [16]. Isopropyl myristate or propylene glycol may perturb the SC by intercalating into the skin lipids, which enhances skin fluidity and increases the diffusion coefficient of permeants [54]. Ethanol penetrates the human skin promptly with a steady-state flux of about 1 mg/cm^2/h and facilitates transdermal drug delivery through several mechanisms [9]. Ethanol is both a skin permeation promoter and a solvent. It is one of the components in Estraderm transdermal patch [16,37]. The capacity of ethanol or ethanol–water mixtures to alter skin barrier properties has been linked to several mechanisms such as lipid fluidization, lipid extraction, lipid ordering and the effects on keratin [16].

Williams and Barry have also pointed out that ethanol can improve drug solubility—even though the permeation rate of a drug from any nonenhancing and saturated vehicle should be comparable at steady state [9]. Ethanol diffusion into the SC can also modify the solubility properties of the skin leading to enhanced partitioning of a drug into the skin [9]. Another consideration is that the drug thermodynamic activity can be altered when ethanol is used as the penetration enhancer [9]. Solvent drag is another mechanism implicated in the drug penetration enhancement by ethanol [9]. Ethanol is a volatile solvent and when used at a high concentration for a long period of time, it is capable of extracting some of the lipids from within the SC [9]. Heard et al. studied the influence of ethanol on the percutaneous transport of mefenamic acid [55]. The authors prepared 5, 10 and 25% (v/v) solutions of ethanol or 1,8-cineole in PEG 400 and applied the solutions to pig ear skin under infinite conditions [55]. A concentration-dependent skin transport profile was documented for ethanol and a concomitant concentration-dependent facilitated transport of mefenamic acid was also reported [55]. The authors suggested that the tight correlation between the rates of enhancer permeation and solute was a result of the "pull" effect (also known as the "drag" effect) which entails CPE transport facilitating the transdermal delivery of the drug [55].

A recent study examined the influence of different skin penetration promoters on the transcutaneous flux of buprenorphine [56]. Box–Behnken experimental design was utilized to assess the influence of lauryl alcohol on the percutaneous penetration of buprenorphine [56]. The incorporation of lauryl alcohol into the mixture resulted in an enhanced flux (0.843 μg/cm^2/h) of the drug through rat abdominal skin [56]. Bounoure and coworkers investigated the influence of isopropyl myristate, propylene glycol, and ethanol on the transcutaneous penetration of metopimazine (MPZ) across porcine skin [54]. The effect of chemical permeation promoters was evaluated with the marketed solution of MPZ diluted with 48% ethanol-2% isopropyl myristate (ET-MYR), 25% ethanol-25% propylene glycol (ET-PG), 50% propylene glycol (PG), and 50% ethanol (ET) [54]. The authors revealed that the addition of a mixture of ET-PG (25%–25%), ET-MYR (48%–2%), PG (50%), and ET (50%) into the composition of the preparation facilitated MPZ absorption [54]. The authors used FTIR spectroscopy results to elucidate the low MPZ permeation following the use of the skin permeation promoters. There were no significant alterations in the conformational order of the SC lipids before and after application of the permeation promoters [54]. However, the combination of iontophoretic current (0.25 mA/cm^2), 48% ET 2% and MYR enhanced MPZ permeation rate from 3.22 to 4.772 μg/cm^2/h) [54]. In another set of experiments, we examined the influence of 50% ET on the skin transport of penbutolol sulfate [41]. When ET was used, there was a 2.2-fold (17.07 ± 3.24 μg cm/^{2}/ h) increase in the transdermal transport of penbutolol across pig skin in comparison with passive penetration (7.76 ± 2.9 μg cm/^{2}/ h) [41].

Raman spectroscopy is a vibrational method based on the inelastic scattering of incident photons by the functional groups of sample molecules [57]. It is useful for studying the effect of alcohol on transdermal drug delivery. Flufenamic acid (FluA) in propylene glycol/ethanol (75/25) or octanol was administered to the SC of human skin and confocal Raman microscopy was subsequently used to map drug and CPE penetration [58]. The authors used deuterated forms of the permeation promoters to spectroscopically differentiate externally introduced compounds from SC lipids that naturally exist in the human body [58]. The FluA route was monitored by the C=C stretching mode at approximately 1618 cm^{-1} [58]. High FluA concentrations coexisted with octanol regions that apparently provided a route for drug delivery to the viable epidermis. In comparison, FluA was observed in the upper SC when propylene glycol/ethanol was utilized and endogenous lipids in domains outside the CPE pockets were not perturbed [58].

Brinkmann and Müller-Goymann evaluated the influence of isopropyl alcohol (IPA) on the delivery of HC across the human SC [59]. IPA was included into the composition of water-containing hydrophilic ointment (WHS), and the influence of IPA on HC transport and on HC deposition in SC was studied. Furthermore, the effect of these compounds on the SC microstructure was also investigated [59]. It was observed by the authors that IPA perturbs and fluidizes the bilayer structure of the intercellular lipids and that these aftereffects, in combination with an increased quantity of dissolved HC within the WHS ointment, enhance the delivery of HC across the SC [59]. Another study examined the effect of isopropyl alcohol (IPA) concentration on the transcutaneous permeation of testosterone (T) from hydroalcoholic gels [60]. The authors used different quantities of IPA to prepare several hydroalcoholic gel formulations, loaded with carbopol as the gel-forming polymer and 1% T as the active pharmaceutical ingredient. A natural membrane (hairless guinea pig skin) and synthetic membranes (Celgard 2400 and cellulose ester) were used to investigate the release of T from each gel [60]. The authors reported that all the investigated gels were comparable to Androgel, implying that the incorporation of IPA did not influence the release of T from hydroalcoholic gels. The researchers also noted that even though there were no statistically significant differences, the permeation rates of T from the gels were higher when the concentration of IPA was increased [60].

Approximately 913,000 people aged 12 or older in the United States suffer from cocaine use disorder (CUD) [61]. CUD is a crippling neuropsychiatric disorder that is thought to be induced, at least partially, by dopamine system dysfunction [62]. The main mechanism for the reinforcing and euphorigenic effects of cocaine is its capability to elevate extracellular dopamine (DA) concentration via the inhibition of DA uptake [63]. 4-Benzylpiperidine (4-BP) is a dopamine/norepinephrine (DA/NE) releaser that can be utilized as a substitute agonist for the management of CUD [64]. Recently, Ganti et al. studied the percutaneous permeation of 4-benzylpiperidine across dermatomed human skin in vitro [64]. The authors probed the effect of different propylene glycol (PG) solutions (1, 10, 20, and 50 mg/mL) on the transdermal transport of 4-BP and reported that the use of 1, 10, 20, and 50 mg/mL of PG led to 16%–31% increase in the transport of 4-BP (49.45 ± 11.60, 258.47 ± 48.50, 600.26 ± 74.18, and 1945.20 ± 405.59 $\mu g/cm^2$, respectively) [64]. The enhancement effect of PG is associated with several mechanisms: the compound can alter the drug's thermodynamic activity; the solvent may partition into the skin and PG can perturb lipid packing within the SC [9]. Nair and coworkers also probed the influence of CPEs on the percutaneous transport of palonosetron [65]. The authors prepared transdermal patches using the following pressure-sensitive adhesives: Duro-Tak 87-2287, Duro-Tak 87-9301, Duro-Tak 87-900A, Duro-Tak 87-2074, and Duro-Tak 87-4098. The impact of oleic acid, diethylene glycol monoethyl ether propylene glycol and Tween 80 was assessed, and it was demonstrated that CPEs significantly increased the transdermal delivery of the drug [65]. The use of propylene glycol (5% w/w) led to the highest flux (53.12 ± 5.62 $\mu g/cm^2/h$), which was fourfold greater than that of the control solution.

Esters

The utilization of esters as chemical sorption promoters has generated a great deal of interest. Esters typically partition into the ordered lipid regions of the SC [33]. Isopropyl myristate (IPM) is one of the most widely investigated fatty acid esters [33]. Although lipophilic, IPM possesses a small polar moiety [66]. IPM can fluidize SC lipids and X-ray diffraction studies have shown IPM ester group in the polar membrane domain of SC models [66]. Indeed, Eichner and colleagues investigated the effect of IPM on a widely used SC lipid model membrane containing cholesterol, behenic acid, ultra long−chain CER[EOS]-br, and CER[AP]-C18 [66]. The authors reported that IPM reduced the state of order of the lamellae and also impacted the phase characteristics of the SC model membranes most likely due to the interaction with the lipid headgroups [66]. Remarkably, IPM perturbed the rigid lamellar lipid structure, hindered the formation of a long periodicity phase, and reduced the barrier characteristics of the model membranes [66]. CERs play a prominent role in the lipid matrix architecture and two of the most abundant of them are the [NP] and [AP] [67].

Differential scanning calorimetry (DSC) results showed a negative shift in the phase transition temperatures of SC lipids and reduced enthalpy induced by IPM [16,68]. These DCS effects point to the fact that there is an integration of IPM into the SC lipid bilayers [16,68]. To gain a more thorough understanding of the mechanism of transdermal drug delivery increase by CPEs, isolated sheets of human SC were probed by DSC, following the application of lipophilic liquids including IPM [68]. All samples were analyzed over a heating range of 10°C−130°C, and DSC curves were evaluated based on the peak maximum temperatures of the lipid phase transitions at approximately 75°C and 85°C as well as the peak areas of the phase transition enthalpies [68]. Recently, Zidan et al. studied the effect of isopropyl myristate (IPM) on the transport of testosterone from carbopol gels through human cadaver skin in vitro [17]. Six testosterone gel formulations were prepared using different concentrations of IPM (0%, 0.4%, 0.7%, 1%, 2%, and 3%) [17]. When the authors increased IPM concentration, there was a corresponding and enhanced increase in testosterone flux [17]. There was an 11-fold increase in transdermal flux from gels loaded with 2% IPM in comparison with the control formulation (no enhancer) [17]. When the researchers increased IPM concentration from 0.4% to 3% (w/w), the permeability coefficient of the drug increased considerably from 3.43×10^{-4} to 15.46×10^{-4} cm^2/h, while the transdermal flux went up from 0.65 to 2.88 $\mu g/h/cm^2$, respectively [17]. The authors ascribed the drug permeation enhancement by IPM to its synergistic binary actions with ethanol, which leads to an enhanced delivery of testosterone across the SC and epidermal layers [17].

IPM was also used to facilitate the release of blonanserin (BNN) from a drug-in-adhesive patch [69]. BNN, an antipsychotic drug approved for the treatment of schizophrenia in Japan and Korea, acts on dopamine D2 and serotonin 5-HT2A receptors [70]. IPM concentrations used in the experiments were 0, 4%, 8%, and 12% (w/w), while BNN concentration was 5% (w/w) based on dry adhesive weight [69]. The release rate of BNN increased with an increasing IPM concentration. BNN release profile from the dosage form was in consonance with the Higuchi model and the percentage of the drug released (%) was plotted against $t_{1/2}$. The shear adhesion and rolling ball tack tests showed declining values when IPM concentration was raised [69].

Another fatty acid ester that has been deployed to increase the transcutaneous transport of medications is isopropyl palmitate [71]. Guo studied the permeation enhancing activity of ethanolic solutions of isopropyl palmitate (IP) (5%, 10%, 15%, and 20%, w/w) on the transport of ribavirin, gliclazide, nimesulide, and oxaprozin across excised rat skin [71]. These model penetrants were used for experiments because they possess varying lipophilicities. Oxaprozin, nimesulide, and gliclazide are lipophilic, while ribavirin is hydrophilic [71]. Oxaprozin, nimesulide, and gliclazide permeability values went up as the concentration of Irritation potential (IP) was increased by the researchers. The maximum increase in permeability coefficient was 5.53-82.79-, and 54.74-fold for nimesulide, oxaprozin, and gliclazide, respectively [71]. The enhancer also increased the permeation of ribavirin. The permeability coefficient of ribavirin went up from 1.77×10^{-6} cm/s when IP was not used to 8.80×10^{-6} cm/s following the application of 20% (w/w) of the CPE [71]. The authors emphasized that ethanol and Isopropyl palmitate (IPP) can increase transdermal drug delivery synergistically [71].

Benzoate esters have also been investigated as CPEs. Octyl salicylate (OSAL) is conventionally utilized as a sunscreen and in concentrations up to 5%, and it is considered safe [72]. Recently, Paz-Alvarez et al. studied the influence of several solvents on the transcutaneous transport of climbazole (CBZ) [73]. Four solvents were tested on CBZ, namely polyethylene glycol 200 (PEG), Transcutol P (TC), octyl salicylate (OSAL, and propylene glycol (PG) [73]. CBZ is a fungicidal agent that is sometimes used in antidandruff shampoos [74]. CBZ as a 1% (w/v) solution was administered to human and porcine skin using infinite (250 μL/cm^2) and finite ($\sim$10 μL/cm^2) doses [73]. The administration of finite doses led to a higher extraction of CBZ from human skin in comparison with infinite doses [73]. The uptake of CBZ into the skin was a higher in pig skin ($>$sevenfold) in comparison with human skin. However, there were no statistically significant differences when comparing the quantities of the compound that was transported across pig and human skin into systemic circulation [73]. In a separate study, Santos and colleagues also investigated the transdermal penetration of fentanyl from supersaturated preparations containing OSAL [72]. Transdermal permeation of fentanyl from supersaturated and saturated solutions across human skin was investigated in vitro [72]. The magnitude of uptake of enhancers by the skin as well as mass balance studies were also carried out. By increasing the degree of saturation of fentanyl, the drug transport was enhanced for some OSAL systems [72].

Sucrose esters (SEs) refer to biocompatible, surface-active and nonionic molecules, prepared from easily biodegradable and naturally occurring compounds such as fatty acids and sucrose [15]. Marketed SEs are mixtures of mono-, di-, tri-, and other esters of sucrose with up to eight fatty acids per molecule [15]. Todosijević and coworkers used Brewster angle microscopy (BAM), infrared reflection-absorption spectroscopy (IRRAS) and surface pressure-area (π-A) isotherms to probe the interactions between SC intercellular lipids and SEs [15]. The bonding between SEs and SC lipids was probed using π-A isotherms of the mixed monolayers [15]. The acyl chains of SC lipids were perturbed by SEs as shown by IRRAS data and images obtained by BAM showed SC monolayer domain changes [15].

Dimethyl sulfoxide

Dimethyl sulfoxide (DMSO) has been widely investigated as a CPE. This compound is a potent aprotic solvent in which hydrogen does not bond with water but rather interacts with itself [9]. Several skin penetration enhancement mechanisms have been proposed for DMSO including bonding with SC lipid alkyl chains and/or changes in the structure of keratin [16]. Other proposed mechanisms are extraction of skin lipids and the displacement of bound water from keratin [16]. DMSO denatures proteins and when administered on human skin, this CPE alters intercellular keratin configuration (from an α-helix to a β-sheet) [9]. Munoz and coworkers recently investigated the effect of DMSO, ethanol, and Azone on the transdermal delivery of methadone [75]. Plastoid E35H adhesive (27%) and a plasticizer (12.4% PVA) were added to an aqueous solution of methadone, with 5% solutions of sorbitol and propylene glycol used as film-forming substances [75].

Diffusion studies were conducted with dermatomed porcine skin and the authors reported that when methadone (MTD) was formulated into transdermal patches without an enhancer, only 5% of the drug crossed pig skin in 24 h [75]. In contrast, ethanol and DMSO enhanced the transdermal delivery of MTD from a solution across porcine skin by 77% and 38% respectively [75]. The researchers subsequently prepared matrix-type transdermal patches with the two enhancers and reported that DMSO-based systems achieved an enhanced MTD transport of approximately 70% [75]. Interestingly, when ethanol was used, methadone transport through pig skin was 8%, and this was the same result obtained when no enhancer was utilized [75]. Although DMSO has been shown to be a good percutaneous penetration enhancer in some studies, it has limitations. The effects of DMSO depend on the concentration and used cosolvents with more than 60% DMSO required to increase transdermal drug delivery [9]. One major pitfall is that DMSO can denature certain proteins and induce erythema at relatively high concentrations [9]. In addition, dimethylsulfide, which is a metabolite of DMSO, produces a foul odor [9]. Due to the abovementioned limitations of DMSO, dimethylacetamide, and dimethylformamide (DMF) that are structurally related to DMSO have also been tested as CPEs [9]. It has been postulated that decylmethylsulfoxide (DCMS) enhances transcutaneous penetration due to interactions with lipids as well as protein–enhancer interaction [76]. The latter results in the formation of water channels [76].

Fatty acids

Fatty acids have also attracted the attention of researchers as CPEs. The influence of linoleic, oleic, dodecanoic, decenoic, and decanoic acids on the percutaneous transport of pizotifen malate was recently investigated [77]. The authors estimated partition, diffusion, and steady-state flux parameters by fitting the following equation (Eq. 5.1) [77,78] to experimental data:

$$Q = (KH)C_{\text{veh}}\left[\frac{D}{H^2}t - \frac{1}{6} - \frac{2}{\pi^2}\sum_{n=1}^{\infty}\frac{(-1)^n}{n^2}\exp\left(\frac{-Dn^2\pi^2 t}{H^2}\right)\right] \tag{5.1}$$

In Eq. 5.1, Q is the predicted accumulated quantity of drug that was transported per unit of area at time t, C_{veh} is the donor drug concentration, H is the diffusion path length, D is the diffusion coefficient, and K is the SC/vehicle partition coefficient [77,78]. It was reported that decenoic acid induced the highest permeation increase, which was attributed to the long alkyl chain and unsaturated ninth carbon [77]. In the same study, the authors prepared transcutaneous dosage forms loaded with pizotifen and containing CPEs (oleic acid and decenoic acid), propylene glycol, ethanol, the adhesive Plastoid E35H, and PVP. An occlusive layer (Scotchpack 9733) was used to prepare the transdermal system [77]. The authors then compared the results obtained with solutions with those obtained with the transdermal delivery system (TDS) and found out that increased permeation was obtained with CPEs possibly due to enhanced partitioning and diffusion of the drug [77].

Oleic acid (OA) has also been widely investigated as a CPE. Yamane and colleagues studied the effect of OA on the transport of 5-fluorouracil through human epidermal membrane and reported a 24-fold enhancement in transdermal drug permeation rate following the use of OA [79]. These authors also used differential thermal calorimetry to elucidate the mechanisms of flux enhancement by OA and other CPEs. Human SC thermogram typically has four principal endotherms: T1 at approximately 37°C, T2 at about 72°C, T3 at approximately 83°C, and T4 at about 100°C. It was documented that oleic acid exerted no significant influence on the enthalpy of T3, but it decreased the enthalpy of T2 after 6 h pretreatment by approximately 50%, which continued for a 12 h treatment period [79]. It was also postulated that oleic acid increases skin diffusivity of penetrants due to the disorganizing effect on skin lipids [16]. In vitro studies aimed at elucidating the mechanism of action of OA, have highlighted (1) lipid phase separation and (2) lipid fluidization as possible modes of action [80]. Porcine SC infrared spectroscopy indicated at physiologically suitable temperatures, the presence of OA in a liquid state, phase-separated from naturally occurring solid lipids [80]. The same research group also used attenuated total reflectance infrared spectroscopy to examine the mechanism of action of OA in animal studies [80]. The properties of endogenous lipids were assessed independently and compared to that of the exogenously administered OA by utilizing their spectrally distinct methylene group oscillations [80]. The authors found out that perdeuterated OA caused lipid disruptions only in the SC superficial layers. The authors also reported that [^{2}H] OA existed in a liquid phase at all levels of the SC that were spectroscopically investigated [80]. The authors concluded that skin penetration enhancement, following the application of OA, involved lipid phase separation and fluidization with the former being the predominant mechanism [80].

Moreira et al. also investigated the influence of oleic acid (OA) on the transport of lumiracoxib (LM) from poloxamer-based delivery systems to/through pig ear skin [81]. Polyoxyethylene–polyoxypropylene–polyoxyethylene (PEOn-PPOn-PEOn) tri-block copolymers are called poloxamers [81]. Nonionic poloxamers (including PF-127 gel) are used for the formulation of several drug delivery systems [82,83]. Transdermal penetration and skin deposition of LM across/into pig ear skin were quantified with or without OA in vitro [81]. The authors reported that LM flux through the skin from a 25% PF-127 gel containing OA 10% was about 6.5 times higher and the lag time remained the same in comparison with the control 25% PF-127 gel (without OA) [81]. In addition, the highest amount of LM retained in both SC ($14.31 \pm 0.52\ \mu g/cm^2$) and (epidermis without SC + dermis) ($199.1 \pm 4.26\ \mu g/cm^2$) was achieved following the application of 25.0% PF-127 containing 10.0% OA [81].

In an effort to elucidate the skin permeation enhancement mechanism of OA, two-photon fluorescence microscopy was used to visualize OA-induced percutaneous diffusion pathways [84]. The spatial distribution of fluorescent model drugs and skin autofluorescence were imaged concurrently over identical spatial coordinates [84]. Using dual channels, the authors detected distinct fluorescence emission wavelengths of intrinsic skin fluorophores, as well as the intensity emission of rhodamine-based model drug at different wavelengths. The hydrophobic rhodamine B hexyl ester and the hydrophilic sulforhodamine B exhibited oleic acid-induced changes in penetrant transport in relation to the skin anatomic characteristics over an 0.3 mm by 0.3 mm skin area imaged by the authors [84]. Oleic acid enhanced lipid to corneocyte partitioning of sulforhodamine B and also facilitated the localization of the rhodamine B hexyl ester to the lipid multilamellar domain [84]. It was explained that the skin penetration enhancing effect of oleic acid was a function of the model drug's physicochemical properties [84].

Glycol ethers

Transcutol (TL) is the monoethyl ether of diethylene glycol [16] and it has been studied as a sorption promoter in several transdermal therapeutic systems. The effect of TL on the percutaneous transport of ibuprofen (IBU) was recently investigated [85]. Formulations containing 2.64% of different sucrose esters (sucrose myristate C-1416, sucrose laurate D-1216) and/or Transcutol as well as 5% of IBU were evaluated to quantify the impact of these accelerants on the percutaneous transport of IBU across human skin as well as the parallel artificial membrane permeability assay (PAMPA) membrane [85]. The PAMPA membrane is created from free fatty acid, and a synthetic ceramide analog (certramide) and cholesterol to simulate the properties of ceramide in the human skin lipids [85]. From the experimental results, it was seen that sucrose ester gels significantly enhanced the transcutaneous transport of IBU compared to the control gel, but the TL gel did not increase IBU diffusion [85]. It has been postulated that TL increases transdermal drug delivery by enhancing drug solubility [85]. However, TL can also increase the skin deposition of topically applied medications without an associated percutaneous permeation enhancement. Furthermore, the use of TL can lead to intercellular SC lipid swelling with lipophilic drugs such as IBU encapsulated in the swollen SC lipids [85].

In another research project, TL was incorporated into diclofenac acid nanocrystals with Poloxamer 188 used as a stabilizer [86]. The authors studied the influence of TL on the transdermal diffusion of diclofenac (DCF) from nanosuspensions through porcine skin [86]. When no TL was incorporated into the nanosuspensions (NS-TL 0%), drug accumulation in the SC was about 2 and 16 times higher than that obtained following the application of a coarse suspension and a commercial gel, respectively [86]. Surprisingly, when TL concentration in the nanosuspension formulations was increased, there was reduced DCF skin delivery. Specifically, the nanosuspension formulation containing 0.5% TL (NS-TL 0.5%) led to SC drug accumulation comparable to that of coarse suspension (~12.5%), while the administration of NS-TL 1% and NS-TL 5% further decreased the DCF deposition (7.8% and 4.9%, respectively) [86]. Although TL is a potent solubilizing agent, increasing its concentration in the nanosuspensions negatively impacted DCF solubility. The authors ascribed this anomaly to the adverse interaction between the stabilizer, poloxamer 188, and TL [86]. This can stabilize the nanocrystal, via intercalation of the polyoxyethylene chains and nanocrystal encapsulation. Typically, the DCF nanocrystal is loosely coated by polymer/solvent coating, leading to an increased mean hydrodynamic diameter [86]. The formed "TL-P188 corona" can create a sterically hindered and viscous diffusion layer around the nanocrystals, which is an impediment to DCF dissolution [86]. The authors ruled out a synergistic influence of combining nanosizing and TL for enhanced transcutaneous permeation of diclofenac from a nanosuspension [86].

Surfactants

Surfactants or surface-active agents form an important group of penetration enhancers [20,87]. Although structurally diverse, they are amphiphiles, comprising hydrophobic (tail) and hydrophilic (head) groups [88]. The hydrophobic portion of the molecule is normally a straight or branched hydrocarbon chain comprising 8–18 carbon atoms [89]. Surface-active agents reduce the surface tension between two liquids and the interfacial tension between a liquid and a solid [90,91]. A surfactant is often utilized in combination with a solvent system and its activity is a function of the charge, lipid chain length, and the hydrophilic-to-lipophilic balance [33]. Traditionally, surfactants are added to dosage forms and drug delivery systems with the objective of solubilizing lipophilic active ingredients [9]. These same compounds can, therefore, solubilize SC lipids [9]. Furthermore, surfactants can form micelles, lower the drug's thermodynamic activity, and thus enhance its skin penetration [16]. Surface-active agents are made up of a hydrophilic headgroup and a lipophilic aryl or alkyl chain [9].

Surface-active agents can alter skin properties to enhance transdermal drug delivery [92]. These compounds can decrease the skin's resistance to diffusion by changing the physicochemical properties of the SC in a reversible manner and consequently enhancing transdermal drug delivery [92]. The type of polar headgroups is the basis for surfactant classification: zwitterionic (amphoteric), nonionic, anionic, or cationic [87]. When the hydrophilic portion of the molecule is negatively charged, the surfactant is termed anionic, while the hydrophilic portions of nonionic surfactants do not ionize in water [87]. A distinguishing feature of cationic surfactants is the presence of positively charged hydrophilic headgroups [89,93] whereas zwitterionic (amphoteric) is a term used to describe a surfactant with both cationic and anionic segments in the molecule [87]. Anionic surfactants can be phosphates (C_nH_{2n} + 1OPO (OH) O^-X), sulfonates (C_nH_{2n} + 1SO3$^-$X), sulfates (CnH2n + 1OSO3 − X), and carboxylates ($C_nH_{2n+1}COO^-X$), where n is the number of carbon atoms (i.e., $n = 8-18$) [89]. Cationic surfactants include quaternary ammonium compounds such as alkyl dimethyl benzyl ammonium chloride (benzalkonium chloride) and this compound is extensively utilized as a preservative agent in dosage forms [89]. Zwitterionic (amphoteric) surface-active agents possess both anionic and cationic functional groups and their properties are determined by the pH of the medium [89]. Zwitterions are positively charged in acidic medium and act like cations, while they are negatively charged in alkaline medium and act as anions [89].

Surfactant impact on the transdermal delivery of drugs is a function of their capacity to self-assemble into micelles as well as their interaction with the SC [88]. Skin barrier destruction and irritation are connected with the use of the anionic surfactant sodium lauryl sulfate (SLS) [16]. These effects are linked to SLS interaction with keratin and lipids in the skin as well as its influence on epidermal desquamation and differentiation [16]. Abruzzo and colleagues recently investigated two negatively charged surfactants (C18-OPK and C12-OPK), which were prepared via the condensation of fatty amines with itaconic acid [88]. The surfactants have C18 and C12 alkyl chains, respectively [88]. The authors examined the effect of various surfactant concentrations on the solubility and transdermal flux of on HC across pig skin [88]. It was revealed that there was an upsurge in HC solubility with increased concentrations of both surfactants, possibly as a result of the interaction between micelles and medication [88].

Skin permeation studies were conducted out with Franz diffusion cells. For each surfactant, the authors chose one concentration 10-fold greater than the critical micelle concentration (CMC) (3 mM for C18-OPK and 10 mM for C12-OPK), and in another set of experiments, the concentration was below the CMC (0.15 mM) [88]. The cumulative amount of the medication that diffused per unit area of porcine skin (mg/cm^2) was plotted against time (s). The use of 10 mM C12-OPK resulted in the greatest flux of HC through pig skin [88]. An important observation from this study was that when 10 and 3 mM of C12-OPK (above CMC) were used, HC permeability coefficients were less than those achieved with 0.15 mM (under CMC) [88]. The researchers had the same observation for C18-OPK: the Kp with 3 mM solution of the surfactant (above CMC) was less than the Kp obtained with the 0.15 mM solution (less than the CMC). Decrease in permeability coefficient following the use of a concentration higher than CMC was ascribed to the formation of micelles. It has been postulated that micelles have low skin penetration because of bulkiness [88].

The effect of Tween 85, sodium dodecyl sulfate (SDS) and Span 80 on the transport of dexpanthenol across porcine abdominal skin was investigated [94]. The amount of permeated drug was determined, and the following skin penetration enhancer activity ranking was established: SDS > Span > Tween [94]. The surfactants were studied in the concentrations of 0.5%, 1%, 2%, and 5% and the most promising results were obtained when a surfactant concentration of 1% (w/w) surfactant was used [94]. Flux enhancement at low enhancer concentrations was ascribed to their capacity to curtail the barrier function of the skin and increase transcutaneous drug transport [94]. In another study, Nokhodchi and colleagues investigated the skin permeation enhancing influence of different surface-active agents [Tween 80, benzalkonium chloride, cetyltrimethylammonium bromide (CTAB), and sodium lauryl sulfate (SLS)] on the delivery of lorazepam across rat skin [95]. Increased concentration of CTAB led to the transdermal flux enhancement of lorazepam compared to the control. Conversely, increased concentration of CTAB from 0.5% to 1% w/w or benzalkonium chloride from 1% to 2.5% w/w, respectively, decreased the enhancement ratio (ER) [95]. When the cationic surfactant benzalkonium chloride was used, there was a 7.66-fold increase in lorazepam flux in comparison with the control solution [95]. When the researchers used 5% w/w CTAB and sodium lauryl sulfate, there was increased percutaneous drug flux in comparison with the control (9.82- and 11.30-fold, respectively) [95]. Flux enhancement was linked to the deleterious influence of higher concentrations of cationic and anionic surface-active agents on the skin [95].

Peptides

Peptides with molecular weights between 1000 and 1500 Da were recently investigated as safer skin penetration enhancers [6]. Numerous research reports have documented the use of skin penetrating peptides (SPPs) and some studies have attempted to understand the underlying mechanisms of this class of CPEs: transient pore formation in appendages, as well as interactions with keratin or skin lipids [6]. Kumar and coworkers investigated the mechanism of action of five SPPs (a dermis-localizing peptide, skin penetrating and cell entering (SPACE) peptide, a skin penetrating linear peptide TD1, and polyarginine) on cyclosporine A (a model hydrophobic macromolecule) [6]. The authors studied the influence of these SPPs on keratinocytes, skin proteins, and lipids. Three SPPs TD1, SPACE, and polyarginine substantially increased cyclosporine A (CsA) transport across porcine skin [6]. The CPEs interacted with skin proteins and caused alterations in the secondary structures (turns, random coils, β-sheets, and α-helices) of the proteins as assessed by in silico docking as well as FTIR analysis [6]. It was revealed that SPPs enhanced the transdermal delivery of CsA transport via the transcellular route, increasing its partitioning into corneocytes through the simultaneous binding of SPP with CsA and keratin [6]. SPACE peptide was the least toxic to keratinocytes compared to other investigated peptides, and it was also among the most efficient at transporting CsA into the skin [6].

The peptide chaperon TD1 has enhanced the percutaneous penetration of several proteins. Ruan and colleagues studied the influence of TD1 on the flux of the human epidermal growth factor (hEGF) across rat skin [96]. A fusion protein (TD1-hEGF) was used in these studies and it was shown that TD1-hEGF had comparable bioactivity with the native hEGF and a significantly greater percutaneous flux than hEGF and that obtained via coadministration of TD1 and hEGF [96]. The influence of TD1 on the percutaneous flux of TD1-hEGF was depended on the dose, with a significant impact reported at 20 μg, and the maximum influence achieved at 100 μg [96]. In vivo experiments were also carried out and it was shown that the hEGF concentration in TD1-hEGF group attained a maximum value at 2 h after administration, which was approximately 14-fold in comparison with the hEGF group [96].

In another study involving a peptide, Lee and colleagues used a combination of sorbitan monolaurate with magainin-*N*-lauroylsarcosine to increase the percutaneous penetration of a model compound fluorescein [97]. Previous studies had shown a decrease in the irritation potential of *N*-lauroylsarcosine (NLS) when sorbitan monolaurate (S20) was used simultaneously [97]. Furthermore, it was shown in an earlier set of experiments that the combination of the pore-forming peptide magainin with *N*-lauroylsarcosine (NLS) enhanced skin permeability by 47-fold [97]. Lee et al. used a parameter called the enhancement ratio/irritation potential (ER/IP) to quantify the efficacy to toxicity ratio of the developed dosage form and showed that the mixture of magainin with NLS:S20 enhanced the permeability of fluorescein across pig skin and also reduced the toxicity of the transdermal system [97]. The dosage form containing 2% (w/v) NLS:S20 with a weight fraction of 0.6:0.4 had the highest ER/IP value [97]. The authors also used FTIR spectroscopy to elucidate penetration enhancer mechanisms and reported that both the transcellular route through SC protein and the intercellular lipid pathway were implicated in fluorescein transport [97].

Gennari and coworkers recently studied the effect of an SPP on the percutaneous permeation of unfractionated heparin (UFH) across human epidermis [98]. The authors used molecular dynamics simulation and ATR-FTIR spectroscopy to study the influence of a heptapeptide (DRTTLTN) on human SC microstructure. DRTTLTN induced both SC fluidization and keratin extension and this was attributed to the enhanced contribution of α-helices [98]. It was reported that the binding of DRTTLTN to UFH via sodium *N*-hydroxysulfosuccinimide and *N*-(3-(dimethylamino)propyl)-*N*′-ethylcarbodiimide hydrochloride resulted in a 24- to 36-fold percutaneous flux increase of UFH (depending on the synthetic technique used) in comparison with unconjugated UFH [98]. Intriguingly, the coadministration of DRTTLTN with UFH did not enhance skin transport due to the interaction between UFH and keratin [98].

Wedge-like branched or radial macromolecules comprising a peptidyl branching core and/or covalently attached surface functional units are called peptide dendrimers [99]. Recently, Manikkath et al. evaluated the effect of peptide dendrimers on the transcutaneous penetration of ketoprofen [100]. The authors prepared and characterized arginine-terminated peptide dendrimers possessing various charges (4 + , 8 + , and 16 + ; A4, A8, and A16, respectively) [100]. Ultrasound-mediated, peptide dendrimer-assisted and passive transport of ketoprofen across Swiss albino mouse skin was investigated, both in vitro and in animal studies. Peptide dendrimers significantly facilitated the in vitro transcutaneous penetration of the drug and ERs of up to 3.25 (with A16 dendrimer) were achieved, in comparison to passive transport. In addition, transdermal and oral absorption data showed that percutaneous permeation of ketoprofen-loaded A8 dendrimer resulted in absorption and plasma drug level profiles comparable to the oral route [100].

Amino acid derivatives

Amino acid derivatives represent an important category of skin penetration promoters [101]. These compounds possess hydrophobic chains attached to an amino acid headgroup via a biodegradable ester bond. Due to the amphiphilic nature of these derivatives, it is possible for them to enter into the SC lipid barrier and significantly disorganize skin membrane lipids [101]. The labile bond in a CPE is hydrolyzed when it enters into the enzymatically active epidermis. Subsequently, less toxic compounds with lower irritation potential are formed. By using this approach, several investigators have developed potent CPEs (Transkarbam 12, DDAIP) with optimal properties [101]. Recently, Janůšová et al. studied CPEs prepared from amino acids (glycine, β-alanine, alanine, sarcosine, and proline) that were conjugated to hydrophobic chain(s) through a biodegradable ester link [101]. D-proline (D-Pro), glycine (Gly), L-proline (L-Pro), sarcosine (Sar), L-alanine (L-Ala), β-alanine (β-Ala), and D-alanine (D-Ala) were used as headgroup constituents of the CPEs [101].

The conformationally hindered cyclic amino acid L-Pro as well as several double-chain skin permeation promoters based on the Gly homolog β-Ala, its isomers Sar, and L-Ala were synthesized and investigated. Single-chain CPEs derived from the same amino acids were also studied to provide evidence for the authors' previous postulate that removing one long hydrophobic chain will boost skin permeation enhancing activity. It was demonstrated that the lipid-like double-chain compounds did not increase skin permeability, while single-chain substances significantly enhanced the transdermal flux of theophylline (TH) [101]. When no CPE was used, the TH percutaneous permeation rate was 4.04 ± 0.41 μg/cm^2/h. Azone, which was employed as a standard CPE, increased TH flux 2.7-fold, while dodecyl 2-(dimethylamino) propanoate (DDAIP) displayed no skin penetration enhancing effect. The CPEs T12 and DDAK induced up to a sevenfold increase in TH flux [101]. A slight increase in flux (comparable to what was achieved with Azone) was reported following the application of all the double-chain CPEs. Significantly, single-chain CPEs, on the whole, possessed more skin enhancing properties than their double-chain equivalents (except for β-Ala2), with the most effective CPE being L-Pro2 (TH flux of 27.9 ± 3.1 μg/cm^2/h and a concomitant ER value of 6.9) [101]. The skin permeation activity of L-Pro2 was significantly greater than that of Azone and DDAIP and comparable to what was obtained with DDAK and T12. The CPE with the second-highest permeability enhancing activity was Sar2 with an ER value of 6.2. The third- and fourth-highest CPEs (ranked by skin permeation enhancement) were Gly2 (ER = 3.9) and L-Ala2 (ER = 3.6), respectively [101].

Ceramide-like penetration enhancers

Ceramides (CERs) are constituents of mammalian phospholipids and glycolipids [102]. Structurally, CERs are zwitterionic molecules with an acylamide polar head structure and two long hydrocarbon chains [38]. An amide group and two-to-four hydroxyls form the polar head structure [103]. Ceramide-like CPEs are usually prepared by isosterically replacing amide and 1-hydroxymethyl moieties of natural ceramides [102]. Metabolically more stable five-membered heterocyclic (1,2,4-oxadiazole, 1,2,4-triazole, tetrazole) and oxime analogs were synthesized by Takács and coworkers [102].

Novotný and coworkers also synthesized several short-chain ceramide derivatives with a polar headgroup similar to a naturally occurring nonhydroxy acyl sphingosine type (NS) ceramide [104]. The authors subsequently studied the effect of these compounds on the skin permeability of theophylline and indomethacin across pig skin. The effects of these compounds were compared to ceramide NS [104]. In the nomenclature of ceramides, [A] is an α-hydroxylated fatty acid, [N] refers to a nonhydroxylated fatty acid, while [O] represents ω-hydroxy fatty acid [105]. It was revealed that ceramides with 4- to 8-carbon acyl chain facilitated the transdermal penetration for both drugs up to 10.8 times with the highest impact obtained with the 6-carbon acyl chain [104]. The authors did not find an enhanced skin permeability of the drugs following the use of ceramide NS or 2- and 12-carbon acyl ceramides [104].

In another study, Školová and colleagues synthesized analogs of *N*-lignoceroylsphingosine with acyl chains (2, 4 and 6 carbons) and 12- and 15- carbon sphingosine [106]. The authors investigated the effect of these compounds on the skin [106]. 15C- sphingosine ceramides disrupted the skin barrier more than the 12C- and 18C-counterparts with the greatest impact belonging to the 4–6C acyls (up to 15 times higher skin penetrability in comparison with the control) [106]. Researchers have also studied the influence of acyl chain length in NS ceramides on the permeability of the skin [107]. It was observed that skin barrier function was neither altered by free sphingosine nor the long- to medium-chain ceramides (8–24C). However, short-chain ceramides reduced skin electrical impedance and enhanced the transdermal permeation of theophylline and indomethacin, with the highest effect observed with 4–6C acyl ceramides [107].

Oleodendrimers

Oleodendrimers have also been used to facilitate the transport of medications across the skin. With their tree-like shape, uncommon size, and several peripheral functionalities, this class of compounds can entrap medications, provide alternative sites for drug conjugation, and create and can be used to modify certain drug properties [108]. Dendrimers that are polar at one end and no-polar at the other (Janus-type) are zwitterionic molecules capable of attracting both hydrophilic a well as lipophilic compounds. Recently, Kalhapure and Akamanchi synthesized Janus-type poly (propyl ether imine) dendrimers and investigated these compounds as potential skin permeation enhancers [108]. The dendrimers were made by linking oleic acid and dendrons via amide and ester bonds. The compounds increased the transdermal delivery of diclofenac sodium (DSF) (model drug) compared to oleic acid and the control. Ester linked dendrimers displayed the highest flux ER of 3.33 ± 0.31 and 3.39 ± 0.21, respectively [108].

Ionic liquids and deep eutectic solvents

Traditional skin penetration enhancers may be effective for small drugs but hardly so for proteins [109]. Recently ionic liquids (ILs) and deep eutectic solvents (DESs) have been proposed as biocompatible transdermal sorption promoters and these compounds have demonstrated an excellent ability to enhance the permeation of macromolecules such as proteins, siRNAs, and polysaccharides [109]. Room-temperature ILs can be modified for various purposes including their utilization in transdermal drug delivery research as skin penetration enhancers [110]. Wu and colleagues studied the influence of ILs on the transdermal delivery of hydrophilic macromolecules. The ILs were formulated from malic acid and choline, which are commonly used as food additives and are GRAS [111]. Choline malate ionic liquid (CM-IL) was formed via ionic interactions and possessed a melting point of −65.2°C. CM-IL transported a model hydrophilic macromolecule dextran deeply into the skin. The quantity of dextran transported into the epidermis and dermis by CM-IL was about twofold compared to that achieved with dextran solution [111]. Increased in vivo skin delivery by CM-IL was also confirmed. The fluorescence of FITC-dextran permeated pervasively throughout the skin from 4 to 24 h, while in the control groups, it was mainly localized in the SC and hair follicles [111].

Qi and Mitragotri reported enhanced percutaneous delivery of dextrans of various molecular weights up to 150 kDa following the use of choline and geranic acid (CAGE)-based IL [109]. Furthermore, the authors showed the ability of CAGE to reduce the size-dependence of percutaneous skin delivery thus widening the application of this enhancer to a wide variety of solutes [109]. DESs are typically synthesized from quaternary ammonium salts and carboxylic acids [112]. In DESs, an organic halide is typically complexed with an organic agent, frequently a hydrogen-bond donor derived from nonionic moieties [110]. The physical properties such as viscosity, conductivity, and surface tension of these DES are comparable to those of ambient temperature ILs, while the physical properties are significantly affected by the structure of the carboxylic acid used for DES synthesis [112]. Several major properties of DESs including miscibility, viscosity, and drug delivery enhancement can be regulated via the selection of ions and their ratio in the DES [113]. Tanner et al. studied the influence of DES cation/anion ratio by utilizing a CAGE-based DES [113]. The authors prepared variants of CAGE by regulating the ratio of choline to geranic acid over a range of 1:4−2:1 [113]. Diffusivity and conductivity were determined. The influence of CAGE on skin transport was evaluated using insulin in ex vivo pig skin. Each variant displayed distinct properties, including viscosity, interionic interactions, and conductivity [113]. Furthermore, the influence of CAGE on SC lipids, as probed by FTIR, was a function of DES composition. Transdermal delivery increase also depended on the composition, as the variants with excess geranic acid (1:2 and 1:4, but not geranic acid alone) displayed higher insulin transport into the dermis in comparison to other compositions, showing the importance of ion ratios on drug transport [113].

References

[1] Ameen D, Michniak-Kohn B. Development and in vitro evaluation of pressure sensitive adhesive patch for the transdermal delivery of galantamine: effect of penetration enhancers and crystallization inhibition. Eur J Pharm Biopharm 2019;139:262–71.

[2] Drakulic BJ, et al. Role of complexes formation between drugs and penetration enhancers in transdermal delivery. Int J Pharm 2008;363(1–2):40–9.

[3] Karande P, et al. Design principles of chemical penetration enhancers for transdermal drug delivery. Proc Natl Acad Sci U S A 2005;102(13):4688–93.

[4] Liu X, et al. Time dependence of the enhancement effect of chemical enhancers: molecular mechanisms of enhancing kinetics. J Control Release 2017;248:33–44.

[5] Parhi R, Suresh P. Transdermal delivery of diltiazem HCl from matrix film: effect of penetration enhancers and study of antihypertensive activity in rabbit model. J Adv Res 2016;7(3):539–50.

[6] Kumar S, et al. Peptides as skin penetration enhancers: mechanisms of action. J Control Release 2015;199:168–78.

[7] Hadgraft J, et al. Mechanisms of action of skin penetration enhancers/retarders: Azone and analogues. Int J Pharm 1996;141(1):17–25.

[8] Joshi A, et al. Cutaneous penetration-enhancing effect of menthol: calcium involvement. J Pharm Sci 2017;106(7):1923–32.

[9] Williams AC, Barry BW. Penetration enhancers. Adv Drug Deliv Rev 2012;64:128–37.

[10] Pham QD, et al. Chemical penetration enhancers in stratum corneum — Relation between molecular effects and barrier function. J. Controlled Release 2016;232:175–87.

[11] Mohammed D, et al. Influence of skin penetration enhancers on skin barrier function and skin protease activity. Eur J Pharm Sci 2014;51:118–22.

[12] Barry BW. Novel mechanisms and devices to enable successful transdermal drug delivery. Eur J Pharm Sci 2001;14(2):101–14.

[13] Caserta F, Brown MB, McAuley WJ. The use of heat and chemical penetration enhancers to increase the follicular delivery of erythromycin to the skin. Eur J Pharm Sci 2019;132:55–62.

[14] Bouwstra JA, et al. Effect of N-alkyl-azocycloheptan-2-ones including Azone on the thermal behaviour of human stratum corneum. Int J Pharm 1989;52(1):47–54.

[15] Todosijevic MN, et al. Sucrose esters as biocompatible surfactants for penetration enhancement: an insight into the mechanism of penetration enhancement studied using stratumcorneum model lipids and Langmuir monolayers. Eur J Pharm Sci 2017;99:161–72.

[16] Lane ME. Skin penetration enhancers. Int J Pharm 2013;447(1–2):12–21.

[17] Zidan AS, et al. Effect of isopropyl myristate on transdermal permeation of testosterone from carbopol gel. J Pharm Sci 2017;106(7):1805–13.

[18] Maurya A, et al. Pre-treatment with chemical penetration enhancers in dermal/transdermal drug delivery. J Drug Deliv Sci Technol 2014;24(3):251–4.

[19] Escobar-Chávez JJ, Rodríguez-Cruz IS, Domínguez-Delgado CL. Chemical and physical enhancers for transdermal drug delivery. In: Gallelli L, editor. Pharmacology. IntechOpen; 2012 https://doi.org/10.5772/33194. Available from: <https://www.intechopen.com/books/pharmacology/chemical-and-physical-enhancers-for-transdermal-drug-delivery>.

[20] Ita K. Transdermal delivery of drugs with microneedles—potential and challenges. Pharmaceutics 2015;7(3):90–105.

[21] Aqil M, et al. Status of terpenes as skin penetration enhancers. Drug Discov Today 2007;12(23–24):1061–7.

[22] Kahraman E, et al. The combination of nanomicelles with terpenes for enhancement of skin drug delivery. Int J Pharm 2018;551(1):133–40.

[23] Ameen D, Michniak-Kohn B. Transdermal delivery of dimethyl fumarate for Alzheimer's disease: effect of penetration enhancers. Int J Pharm 2017;529(1–2):465–73.

[24] Kamatou GP, et al. Menthol: a simple monoterpene with remarkable biological properties. Phytochemistry 2013;96:15–25.

[25] Williams AC, Barry BW. Penetration enhancers. Adv Drug Deliv Rev 2004;56 (5):603–18.

[26] Chen J, et al. Natural terpenes as penetration enhancers for transdermal drug delivery. Molecules 2016;21(12).

[27] Nan L, et al. Investigation of the enhancement effect of the natural transdermal permeation enhancers from Ledum palustre L. var. angustum N. Busch: mechanistic insight based on interaction among drug, enhancers and skin. Eur J Pharm Sci 2018;124:105–13.

[28] Narishetty ST, Panchagnula R. Transdermal delivery of zidovudine: effect of terpenes and their mechanism of action. J Control Release 2004;95(3):367–79.

[29] Kodiweera C, Yang Y, Bunge AL. Characterization of water self-diffusion in human stratum corneum. J Pharm Sci 2018;107(4):1131–42.

[30] Bouwstra JA, et al. Water distribution and related morphology in human stratum corneum at different hydration levels. J Investig Dermatol 2003;120(5):750–8.

[31] Sparr E, et al. Controlling the hydration of the skin though the application of occluding barrier creams. J R Soc Interface 2013;10(80):20120788.

[32] Narasimha Murthy S, Shivakumar HN. Chapter 1—Topical and transdermal drug delivery. In: Kulkarni VS, editor. Handbook of non-invasive drug delivery systems. Boston: William Andrew Publishing; 2010. p. 1–36.

[33] Karande P, Mitragotri S. Enhancement of transdermal drug delivery via synergistic action of chemicals. Biochim Biophys Acta 2009;1788(11):2362–73.

[34] Das C, Olmsted PD. The physics of stratum corneum lipid membranes. Philos Trans A Math Phys Eng Sci 2016;374(2072).

[35] Björklund S, et al. Glycerol and urea can be used to increase skin permeability in reduced hydration conditions. Eur. J. Pharm. Sci. 2013;50(5):638–45.

[36] Groen D, et al. Disposition of ceramide in model lipid membranes determined by neutron diffraction. Biophys J 2011;100(6):1481–9.

[37] Ita KB. Chemical penetration enhancers for transdermal drug delivery—success and challenges. Curr Drug Deliv 2015;12(6):645–51.

[38] Chen Y, et al. Novel chemical permeation enhancers for transdermal drug delivery. Asian J Pharm Sci 2014;9(2):51–64.

[39] Chen HL, et al. Effect of the dispersion states of Azone in hydroalcoholic gels on its transdermal permeation enhancement efficacy. J Pharm Sci 2018;107(7):1879–85.

[40] Curikova BA, et al. Simplified stratum corneum model membranes for studying the effects of permeation enhancers. Int J Pharm 2017;534(1–2):287–96.

[41] Ita KB, Popova IE. Influence of sonophoresis and chemical penetration enhancers on percutaneous transport of penbutolol sulfate. Pharm Dev Technol 2015;1–6.
[42] Meng-Lund E, et al. Azone(R) decreases the buccal mucosal permeation of diazepam in a concentration-dependent manner via a reservoir effect. J Pharm Sci 2014;103(4):1133–41.
[43] Brain KR, et al. The influence of Azone® on the percutaneous absorption of methotrexate. Int J Pharm 1991;71(3):R9–11.
[44] Elshafeey AH, et al. In vitro transdermal permeation of fenoterol hydrobromide. J Adv Res 2012;3(2):125–32.
[45] Liu RF, et al. The effect of levamisole in the treatment of recalcitrant recurrent erythema multiforme major: an observational study. J Dermatol Sci 2018;92(1):38–44.
[46] del Rio-Sancho S, et al. Transdermal absorption of memantine—effect of chemical enhancers, iontophoresis, and role of enhancer lipophilicity. Eur J Pharm Biopharm 2012;82(1):164–70.
[47] Reynolds AR, et al. Buspirone maintenance does not alter the reinforcing, subjective, and cardiovascular effects of intranasal methamphetamine. Drug Alcohol Depend 2017;181:25–9.
[48] Meidan VM, Al-Khalili M, Michniak BB. Enhanced iontophoretic delivery of buspirone hydrochloride across human skin using chemical enhancers. Int J Pharm 2003;264(1–2):73–83.
[49] Hamishehkar H, et al. The relationship between solubility and transdermal absorption of tadalafil. Adv Pharm Bull 2015;5(3):411–17.
[50] Cilurzo F, et al. An insight into the skin penetration enhancement mechanism of N-methylpyrrolidone. Mol Pharm 2014;11(3):1014–21.
[51] Sasaki H, et al. Enhancing effect of pyrrolidone derivatives on transdermal penetration of 5-fluorouracil, triamcinolone acetonide, indomethacin, and flurbiprofen. J Pharm Sci 1991;80(6):533–8.
[52] Sasaki H, et al. Enhancing effect of pyrrolidone derivatives on transdermal drug delivery II. Effect of application concentration and pre-treatment of enhancer. Int J Pharm 1990;60(3):177–83.
[53] Lambert WJ, et al. A biodegradable transdermal penetration enhancer based on N-(2-hydroxyethyl)-2-pyrrolidone I. Synthesis and characterization. Int J Pharm 1993;95(1):181–92.
[54] Bounoure F, et al. Effect of iontophoresis and penetration enhancers on transdermal absorption of metopimazine. J Dermatol Sci 2008;52(3):170–7.
[55] Heard CM, Kung D, Thomas CP. Skin penetration enhancement of mefenamic acid by ethanol and 1,8-cineole can be explained by the 'pull' effect. Int J Pharm 2006;321(1–2):167–70.
[56] Taghizadeh SM, Moghimi-Ardakani A, Mohamadnia F. A statistical experimental design approach to evaluate the influence of various penetration enhancers on transdermal drug delivery of buprenorphine. J Adv Res 2015;6(2):155–62.
[57] Khan S, et al. Analysis of tuberculosis disease through Raman spectroscopy and machine learning. Photodiagnosis Photodyn Ther 2018;24:286–91.
[58] Pyatski Y, et al. Effects of permeation enhancers on flufenamic acid delivery in ex vivo human skin by confocal Raman microscopy. Int J Pharm 2016;505(1–2):319–28.
[59] Brinkmann I, Muller-Goymann CC. Role of isopropyl myristate, isopropyl alcohol and a combination of both in hydrocortisone permeation across the human stratum corneum. Skin Pharmacol Appl Skin Physiol 2003;16(6):393–404.

[60] Pabla D, Zia H. A comparative permeation/release study of different testosterone gel formulations. Drug Deliv 2007;14(6):389–96.

[61] Fries GR, et al. Anhedonia in cocaine use disorder is associated with inflammatory gene expression. PLoS One 2018;13(11):e0207231.

[62] Siciliano CA, Fordahl SC, Jones SR. Cocaine self-administration produces long-lasting alterations in dopamine transporter responses to cocaine. J Neurosci 2016;36(30):7807–16.

[63] Ferris MJ, et al. Cocaine self-administration produces pharmacodynamic tolerance: differential effects on the potency of dopamine transporter blockers, releasers, and methylphenidate. Neuropsychopharmacology 2012;37(7):1708–16.

[64] Ganti SS, et al. Transdermal formulation of 4-benzylpiperidine for cocaine-use disorder. J Drug Deliv Sci Technol 2018;47:299–308.

[65] Nair AB, et al. Influence of skin permeation enhancers on the transdermal delivery of palonosetron: an in vitro evaluation. J Appl Biomed 2018;16(3):192–7.

[66] Eichner A, et al. Influence of the penetration enhancer isopropyl myristate on stratum corneum lipid model membranes revealed by neutron diffraction and 2H NMR experiments. Biochim Biophys Acta Biomembr 2017;1859(5):745–55.

[67] Schmitt T, et al. Investigation of a CER[NP]- and [AP]-based stratum corneum modeling membrane system: using specifically deuterated CER together with a neutron diffraction approach. Langmuir 2018;34(4):1742–9.

[68] Leopold CS, Lippold BC. An attempt to clarify the mechanism of the penetration enhancing effects of lipophilic vehicles with differential scanning calorimetry (DSC). J Pharm Pharmacol 1995;47(4):276–81.

[69] Zhao C, et al. Effect of isopropyl myristate on the viscoelasticity and drug release of a drug-in-adhesive transdermal patch containing blonanserin. Acta Pharm Sin B 2016;6(6):623–8.

[70] Tachibana M, et al. Effectiveness of blonanserin for patients with drug treatment-resistant schizophrenia and dopamine supersensitivity: a retrospective analysis. Asian J Psychiatr 2016;24:28–32.

[71] Guo H, et al. Effects of isopropyl palmitate on the skin permeation of drugs. Biol Pharm Bull 2006;29(11):2324–6.

[72] Santos P, et al. Influence of penetration enhancer on drug permeation from volatile formulations. Int J Pharm 2012;439(1–2):260–8.

[73] Paz-Alvarez M, et al. Topical delivery of climbazole to mammalian skin. Int J Pharm 2018;549(1):317–24.

[74] Chen G, et al. Sensitive and simultaneous quantification of zinc pyrithione and climbazole deposition from anti-dandruff shampoos onto human scalp. J Chromatogr B 2015;1003:22–6.

[75] Muñoz MD, et al. Design, development and characterization of transdermal patch of methadone. J Drug Deliv Sci Technol 2017;42:255–60.

[76] Walker RB, Smith EW. The role of percutaneous penetration enhancers. Adv Drug Deliv Rev 1996;18(3):295–301.

[77] Serna-Jiménez CE, et al. Development of antimigraine transdermal delivery systems of pizotifen malate. Int J Pharm 2015;492(1–2):223–32.

[78] Scheuplein RJ. Mechanism of percutaneous adsorption. I. Routes of penetration and the influence of solubility. J Investig Dermatol 1965;45(5):334–46.

[79] Yamane MA, Williams AC, Barry BW. Effects of terpenes and oleic acid as skin penetration enhancers towards 5-fluorouracil as assessed with time; permeation, partitioning and differential scanning calorimetry. Int J Pharm 1995;116(2):237–51.
[80] Naik A, et al. Mechanism of oleic acid-induced skin penetration enhancement in vivo in humans. J Control Release 1995;37(3):299–306.
[81] Moreira TS, de Sousa VP, Pierre MB. A novel transdermal delivery system for the anti-inflammatory lumiracoxib: influence of oleic acid on in vitro percutaneous absorption and in vivo potential cutaneous irritation. AAPS PharmSciTech 2010;11(2):621–9.
[82] Choi SG, et al. Thermosensitive and mucoadhesive sol-gel composites of paclitaxel/dimethyl-beta-cyclodextrin for buccal delivery. PLoS One 2014;9(9):e109090.
[83] Maulvi FA, et al. Effect of surfactant chain length on drug release kinetics from microemulsion-laden contact lenses. Int J Pharm 2017;524(1–2):193–204.
[84] Yu B, et al. Visualization of oleic acid-induced transdermal diffusion pathways using two-photon fluorescence microscopy. J Investig Dermatol 2003;120(3):448–55.
[85] Balazs B, et al. Investigation of the efficacy of transdermal penetration enhancers through the use of human skin and a skin mimic artificial membrane. J Pharm Sci 2016;105(3):1134–40.
[86] Pireddu R, et al. The effect of diethylene glycol monoethyl ether on skin penetration ability of diclofenac acid nanosuspensions. Colloids Surf B Biointerfaces 2018;162:8–15.
[87] Som I, Bhatia K, Yasir M. Status of surfactants as penetration enhancers in transdermal drug delivery. J Pharm Bioallied Sci 2012;4(1):2–9.
[88] Abruzzo A, et al. Surfactants from itaconic acid: toxicity to HaCaT keratinocytes in vitro, micellar solubilization, and skin permeation enhancement of hydrocortisone. Int J Pharm 2017;524(1):9–15.
[89] Bnyan R, et al. Surfactant effects on lipid-based vesicles properties. J Pharm Sci 2018;107(5):1237–46.
[90] Liu H, et al. Foliar penetration enhanced by biosurfactant rhamnolipid. Colloids Surf B Biointerfaces 2016;145:548–54.
[91] Choulis NH. Chapter 14—Dermatological drugs, topical agents, and cosmetics. In: Aronson JK, editor. Side effects of drugs annual. Elsevier; 2014. p. 273–94.
[92] Carbone C, Pignatello R. 6—DSC in drug–biomembrane interaction studies. In: Pignatello R, editor. Drug-biomembrane interaction studies. Woodhead Publishing; 2013. p. 213–36.
[93] Gelardi G, et al. 9—Chemistry of chemical admixtures. In: Aïtcin P-C, Flatt RJ, editors. Science and technology of concrete admixtures. Woodhead Publishing; 2016. p. 149–218.
[94] Laffleur F, et al. Impact of surfactants on skin penetration of dexpanthenol. Curr Drug Deliv 2018;15(3):351–6.
[95] Nokhodchi A, et al. The effect of terpene concentrations on the skin penetration of diclofenac sodium. Int J Pharm 2007;335(1–2):97–105.
[96] Ruan RQ, et al. Transdermal delivery of human epidermal growth factor facilitated by a peptide chaperon. Eur J Med Chem 2013;62:405–9.
[97] Lee H, Park J, Kim YC. Enhanced transdermal delivery with less irritation by magainin pore-forming peptide with a N-lauroylsarcosine and sorbitan monolaurate mixture. Drug Deliv Transl Res 2018;8(1):54–63.
[98] Gennari CG, et al. Skin penetrating peptide as a tool to enhance the permeation of heparin through human epidermis. Biomacromolecules 2016;17(1):46–55.
[99] Sadler K, Tam JP. Peptide dendrimers: applications and synthesis. J Biotechnol 2002;90(3–4):195–229.

[100] Manikkath J, et al. Influence of peptide dendrimers and sonophoresis on the transdermal delivery of ketoprofen. Int J Pharm 2017.

[101] Janůšová B, et al. Amino acid derivatives as transdermal permeation enhancers. J Control Release 2013;165(2):91–100.

[102] Takács M, et al. Synthesis of novel ceramide-like penetration enhancers. Tetrahedron Lett 2011;52(16):1863–5.

[103] Vávrová K, et al. l-Serine and glycine based ceramide analogues as transdermal permeation enhancers: polar head size and hydrogen bonding. Bioorg Med Chem Lett 2003;13 (14):2351–3.

[104] Novotny J, et al. Short-chain ceramides decrease skin barrier properties. Skin Pharmacol Physiol 2009;22(1):22–30.

[105] Schmitt T, Neubert RHH. State of the art in stratum corneum research: the biophysical properties of ceramides. Chem Phys Lipids 2018;216:91–103.

[106] Skolova B, Janusova B, Vavrova K. Ceramides with a pentadecasphingosine chain and short acyls have strong permeabilization effects on skin and model lipid membranes. Biochim Biophys Acta 2016;1858(2):220–32.

[107] Janůšová B, et al. Effect of ceramide acyl chain length on skin permeability and thermotropic phase behavior of model stratum corneum lipid membranes. Biochim Biophys Acta Mol Cell Biol Lipids 2011;1811(3):129–37.

[108] Kalhapure RS, Akamanchi KG. Oleodendrimers: a novel class of multicephalous heterolipids as chemical penetration enhancers for transdermal drug delivery. Int J Pharm 2013;454(1):158–66.

[109] Qi QM, Mitragotri S. Mechanistic study of transdermal delivery of macromolecules assisted by ionic liquids. J Control Release 2019;311–312:162–9.

[110] Sidat Z, et al. Ionic liquids as potential and synergistic permeation enhancers for transdermal drug delivery. Pharmaceutics 2019;11(2).

[111] Wu X, et al. Improving dermal delivery of hydrophilic macromolecules by biocompatible ionic liquid based on choline and malic acid. Int J Pharm 2019;558:380–7.

[112] Abbott AP, et al. Deep eutectic solvents formed between choline chloride and carboxylic acids: versatile alternatives to ionic liquids. J Am Chem Soc 2004;126(29):9142–7.

[113] Tanner EEL, Ibsen KN, Mitragotri S. Transdermal insulin delivery using choline-based ionic liquids (CAGE). J Control Release 2018;286:137–44.

Chapter 6

Microemulsions

Microemulsions (MEs) refer to monophasic, optically isotropic, thermodynamically stable, and clear dispersions formulated from oil, water, surfactant, and a cosurfactant [1−3]. Certain microemulsions scatter light and the reflected light is whitish while the transmitted light is usually reddish [4]. Microemulsions are usually formulated from three different components: an oil phase, aqueous phase, and a mixture of surfactants [5]. When viewed with a microscope, water-rich and oil-rich regions separated by a zwitterionic layer can be identified in microemulsions [6]. The term microemulsion, which was first used in 1943 by Hoar and Schulman [7], is ambiguous because it is not clear from the term that several phases and structures can be formed [6]. Water or oily droplets and bicontinuous structures can form even within the microemulsion domains [6]. Different microemulsion microstructures, oil-in-water (o/w), bicontinuous, and water-in-oil (w/o) microemulsion, are shown in Fig. 6.1.

Various methods such as cryo-field emission scanning electron microscopy (Cryo-FESEM), freeze-fracture transmission electron microscopy (FF-TEM), small-angle nuclear magnetic resonance (NMR), X-ray scattering (SAXS), differential scanning calorimetry (DSC) as well as viscosity measurements and electrical conductivity can be used to characterize the complex microemulsion microstructure [8]. The characteristic property of all ME microstructures is that they are constantly undergoing spontaneous and continuous changes [9].

Microemulsions are effective drug delivery vehicles since they are simple to prepare (an external energy source is not required) and are thermodynamically stable (ME (microemulsion) phases do not easily separate over time and a majority of microemulsions are stable for many years) [5,10,11]. In addition, they possess a high solubilization capacity and can enhance drug transport into the skin [5,10,11]. A system is considered to be thermodynamically stable when the free energy of formation is mainly zero or negative [10]. In MEs, the constituents are at a greater energetic level compared to the final product [11]. As a result, energy is needed for the microemulsion to dissociate into the original constituents. Thus the formation of a microemulsion is a forward-driven process and, indeed, nearly all microemulsions are created spontaneously without an external energy source [11]. There is a

Transdermal Drug Delivery. DOI: https://doi.org/10.1016/B978-0-12-822550-9.00006-5

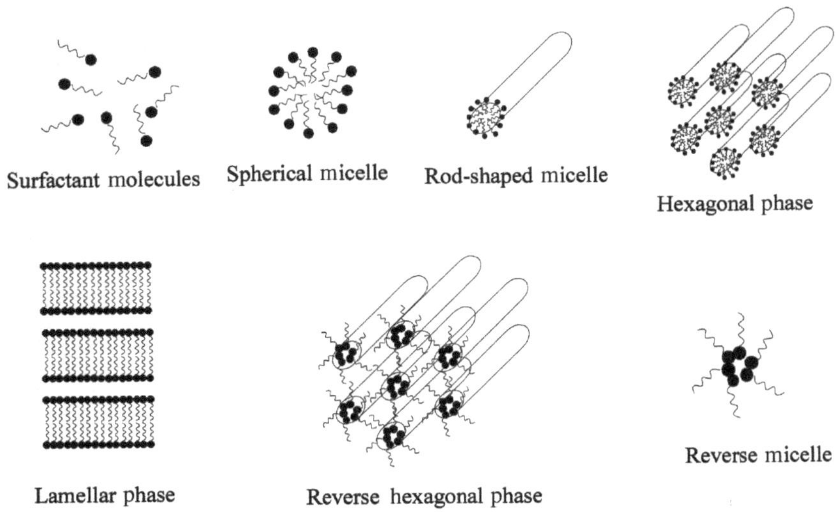

FIGURE 6.1 Schematic representation of the three most commonly encountered microemulsion microstructures: oil-in-water, bicontinuous, and water-in-oil microemulsion. *Reproduced with permission from Lawrence, MJ, Rees, GD. Microemulsion-based media as novel drug delivery systems. Adv Drug Deliv Rev 2012;64:175–93.*

postulate that the free energy of microemulsion formation is a function of the magnitude of the oil–water surface tension decrease by the surfactant and the system's entropy change such that,

$$\Delta G_f = \gamma \Delta A - T \Delta S \tag{6.1}$$

where γ is the surface tension of the oil–water interface, ΔG_f is the free energy of formation, ΔA is the change in interfacial area on microemulsification, T is the temperature, and ΔS is the change in entropy of the system that is the dispersion entropy [3]. When a microemulsion is created, ΔA is very large due to the considerable number of small droplets formed. Also, γ is positive at all times, very small (of the order of fractions of mN/m), and it is offset by the entropy [3]. Consequently, a negative free energy of formation is obtained when substantial decrease in surface tension occurs together with a favorable change in entropy. Under such circumstances, microemulsion formation takes place spontaneously and the formed system is stable from a thermodynamic perspective [3]. In microemulsion systems, hydrophilic medications are intercalated via solubilization in the water phase, while lipophilic medications dissolve in oleaginous or oil–surfactant mixtures [12]. Microemulsion stability depends on the low interfacial tension between the water and oil phases. The cosurfactants and surfactants utilized for the formulation of MEs lower interfacial tension [13]. Typically, the cosurfactant should reduce interfacial tension to less than 1 mN/m

(c. 10^{-2}–10^{-3} mN/m) [14]. One important factor with significant influence on the size of the ME droplet is the packing density of surfactant molecules in the interfacial film [11]. The compressibility and curvature of the interfacial film determine the interfacial tension and also contribute to the total free energy [11]. Specifically, smaller droplet size and higher packing density are achieved with the use of a more rigid film [11]. A short alkyl chain of the surface-active agent or cosurfactant will lead to enhanced droplet–droplet interaction and larger w/o droplets at constant oil alkyl chain length, which may influence the stability of the microemulsion [11]. Experiments using small-angle neutron scattering have shown that oil core formation in the microemulsion droplet depends upon both the quantity of oil introduced and the relative chain lengths of the oil and surfactant, with oils of comparable or longer chain length (compared to the surfactant) being more inclined to constitute a core [15]. Cosurfactants interpose with the surfactants at the oil–water interface, thus influencing droplet curvature [16]. Several molecules have been utilized as ME cosurfactants including alkyl amines, alkanediols, alkanoic acids, nonionic surface-active agents, and alcohols [3]. MEs are spontaneously constituted with no external energy source and the created droplet measurement is less than 200 nm [14]. These droplets are invisible because they are less than the wavelength of visible light (400–800 nm) and therefore cannot reflect visible light. As a consequence, microemulsions cannot be seen through an optical microscope [2].

Compared to regular emulsions, microemulsions form spontaneously following the mixing of the correct amounts of the constituents, with no need for a supplementary source of mechanical energy [17]. Another difference is that microemulsions are clear or translucent with droplet size in nanometers, while emulsions are coarse, milky dispersions with droplet size usually measured in micrometers and somewhat below [18]. Even though emulsions are kinetically stable, they are unstable from a thermodynamic perspective and are capable of phase-separating [3]. In contrast, microemulsions exhibit thermodynamic stability under the right conditions [18]. MEs are also different from self-microemulsifying drug delivery systems (SMEDDS), although these two systems are closely related [3]. An SMEDD is a mixture of oil, surfactant, and a drug that, when administered into the body, are transformed into droplets of comparable size with MEs [3].

MEs have limitations: larger amounts of surfactant are needed compared to emulsions, and this may increase the irritation potential of the formulation [18]. Since the concentration of the oil phase and surfactants in microemulsions is relatively high, irritancy of the excipients becomes an important consideration [17]. MEs can potentially be formulated from several oil–water–surfactant compositions depending on the characteristics of the excipients [17]. Nevertheless, microemulsions are usually formed from water, oil, and surfactant over a narrow concentration range and ME domain is graphically depicted in pseudo-ternary phase diagrams, as ratios between water, oil, and a mixture of cosurfactant–surfactant [17]. MEs are normally categorized as w/o, o/w, or bicontinuous. These drug delivery systems are clear mixtures in which either water is dispersed in oils (w/o) or oil is dispersed in water (o/w) [1]. Even though w/o droplets and o/w are mostly spherical in shape, these systems can also be ellipsoidal (asymmetric) [3]. Bicontinuous microemulsions are created when approximately equivalent volumes of oil and water are mixed leading to the formation of sponge-like regions hosting the other domains. The converse is also true (other domains hosting spongy domains) [19]. Given the right conditions, droplets can coalesce into a bicontinuous architecture comprising two intertwined 3D networks of oil and water [6].

In microemulsions, several phases often exist in equilibrium, with each phase possessing a distinct architecture [20]. These phases can be Winsor type I, Winsor II, or Winsor type III subject to salinity change at a specific temperature and pressure [20]. As Winsor-type systems, microemulsions can be in equilibrium with excess water, excess oil, or both [20]. Water–oil ratio (WOR), oil type, molecular structure, surfactant type, cosurfactant, temperature, and salinity have significant influence on the physicochemical properties and phase transition between different systems [20]. Winsor had earlier identified four classes of MEs [21]: (1) Type I—this dispersion possesses an upper excess oil phase and lower o/w emulsion; (2) Type II—upper w/o emulsion and lower excess aqueous phase; (3) Type III—upper surplus oil phase, middle bicontinuous microemulsion and lower excess water phase; and (4) Type IV—a single ME phase [21]. A very low interfacial tension between aqueous and oil phases is a distinct property of MEs and while these systems may have complex and assorted microstructures ranging from solutions, microdroplet to the bicontinuous form, ME particle size is characteristically less than 100 nm [22].

MEs possess many benefits including the ability to enhance drug permeability across the skin, low surface tension, high drug loading, and small droplet size [23]. Increased blood levels of medications (especially those with less than optimal physicochemical properties) following the use of MEs is attributed to the skin penetration enhancement of these thermodynamically stable systems [9]. Enhanced transdermal delivery of medications by MEs is linked to the existence of saturated or unsaturated fatty acids used as the oil phase [16]. MEs can solubilize poorly water-soluble drugs. The existence of a large proportion of hydrophilic and/or lipophilic phase can enhance drug solubility leading to increased drug partition into the skin because only the dissolved part of a drug can permeate the skin [24]. Furthermore, microemulsion-based formulations are liquid and this is preferable for patients who find it difficult to swallow solids [25]. Increased partitioning of medications from MEs into the stratum is also important [26]. It has been documented that the transdermal delivery and skin deposition of the drug are also facilitated by the interaction of MEs with the lipid layers of the stratum corneum (SC) [24]. Furthermore, the formulation of oleaginous chemical permeation enhancers (CPEs) as microemulsion has been shown to increase transcutaneous permeation thus allowing the use of a lesser concentration of potentially irritant oils [23].

In MEs, there are several regions with divergent polarity within the same phase, which makes it possible to solubilize either lipophilic or hydrophilic compounds [22]. Despite the aforementioned benefits, there are also certain limitations connected with the utilization of MEs for transdermal drug transport. A major shortcoming of MEs is low viscosity that makes skin administration challenging [27]. It must be emphasized that rheological properties affect MEs since viscosity not only facilitates formulation deposition on the skin but can also decelerate water evaporation [27]. The permeation enhancing mechanisms of MEs can be explained thus [1,28,29]: (1) the high concentration of surface-active agent leads to a higher quantity of dissolved drug and higher thermodynamic activity and (2) the skin permeation influence of individual components in MEs can increase drug loading and the ME components can also act as penetration enhancing agents [29]. In addition, ME constituents may disintegrate and permeate the skin as monomers thus enhancing drug solubility [28]. Furthermore, a large surface area for drug transport is provided by the ME microstructure and the phase transition of MEs can also enhance the formation of supersaturated systems. MEs can also dissolve the lipids in the SC, resulting in the destruction of the skin barrier function [30].

MEs are usually prepared via a variety of low-energy techniques including phase inversion composition (PIC) [31], phase inversion temperature (PIT) [32], or emulsion phase inversion point (EPI) [33] methods. PIT is based on the alterations in the relative solubility and/or molecular geometry of a nonionic surfactant as a function of temperature change [34]. PIT is the temperature at which a dispersion is transformed from an o/w emulsion to an w/o emulsion or vice versa because of alterations in surfactant solubility or curvature [34]. PIT is linked to the critical packing parameter (CPP) [34]. The CPP refers to the capability of a surface-active agent to self-agglomerate and form a surfactant monolayer based on their molecular geometry [34]. For a surfactant with hydrophobic chain partial molar volume, γ, surface area of the surface-active agent head group, a, and a hydrophobic surfactant tail length, l_c, the dimensionless number, CPP, can be calculated [34]:

$$\text{CPP} = \frac{\gamma}{a \cdot l_c} \tag{6.2}$$

PIC entails the optimization of surfactant curvature or solubility and this is achieved by changing the composition (altering the pH or adding salt) of the system [34]. EPI involves titrating a mixture containing surfactant and oil with water which initially results in the creation of a w/o emulsion that subsequently changes into an o/w emulsion [33]. Based on the composition of the ME and the physicochemical properties of the components, the system stability may be affected by the addition of polymers, preservatives, buffers, and electrolytes that may modify ME architecture and the area/extent of formation [17]. The phase properties of a simple microemulsion formulated from water, surfactant, and oil can be studied via ternary phase diagram with individual corners of the diagram representing 100% of that specific constituent [3]. When four or more constituents are involved, a corner of the pseudo-ternary phase diagram represents a binary mixture of two constituents such as oil/drug, water/drug, surfactant/cosurfactant, etc. [3].

Ionic liquids are salts, made up of ions, with a melting point lower than 100°C [35]. It has been postulated that ionic liquid-in-oil microemulsions can solubilize sparingly soluble drugs than its individual constituents. Poh and colleagues formulated 1-ethyl-3-methylimidazolium acetate-in-oil microemulsions and varied the weight ratios of Tween 80 and Span 20 [36]. The investigators meticulously mixed Span 20 with Tween 80 at the fixed weight ratios of 3:1, 3:2, 1:1, 1:2, and 1:3 to formulate several microemulsions. The hydrophilic-lipophilic balances of the surfactant mixtures were subsequently determined. The authors added Labrafac Lipophile WL 1349 (74 wt.%) to a 20 wt.% mixture of the surface-active agents. Then, 1 wt.% xanthan gum and 5 wt.% of the 1-ethyl-3-methylimidazolium acetate were added to the mixture. The microemulsion was then sonicated at 60 Hz for 5 min to homogenize the system [36]. The introduction of 1-ethyl-3-methylimidazolium acetate into the microemulsions led to a well-distributed particle size that ranged from 111.87 to 202.33 nm, conductivity that reflected the oil-continuous character of the microemulsions, and a pH of 5.66–5.89 [36]. The ME formulated from Tween 80 and Span 20 in a ratio of 3:2 showed significant thermodynamic stability and acceptable cytotoxicity [36].

With the dilution method, pseudo-ternary phase diagram is usually constructed for MEs formulated from oil, water, and surfactants [37]. A typical pseudo-ternary phase diagram is shown in Fig. 6.2.

These diagrams are produced after titrating homogenous liquid mixtures of oil, surfactant, and cosurfactant with water [1,39]. At certain predetermined weight ratios, the surfactant and oil mixture is mixed and slowly titrated as the aqueous phase is added dropwise [1,39]. The system is inspected for clarity either by means of ultraviolet transmittance or visually after adding each drop of the water phase. Subsequently, the ratio of each constituent is calculated for the ME regions (slightly viscous and transparent mixtures) [39]. The Kahlweit fish representation can also be used to draw phase diagrams [6]. In this instance, the phase regions are expressed with two variables: temperature and surfactant concentration [6]. Kahlweit fish diagrams are used to depict the effect of temperature on samples loaded with equivalent masses of oil and water as well as increasing quantities of the surface-active agent [6]. This provides pseudo-binary phase diagrams with monophasic, diphasic, and triphasic regions in a temperature surface–active agent concentration space [6]. Mixed surfactant concentration is usually depicted as its mass fraction in the sample. The entire shape of the diagram resembles a fish, where the body is the triphasic region and the tail is the monophasic region of MEs [6]. The phase

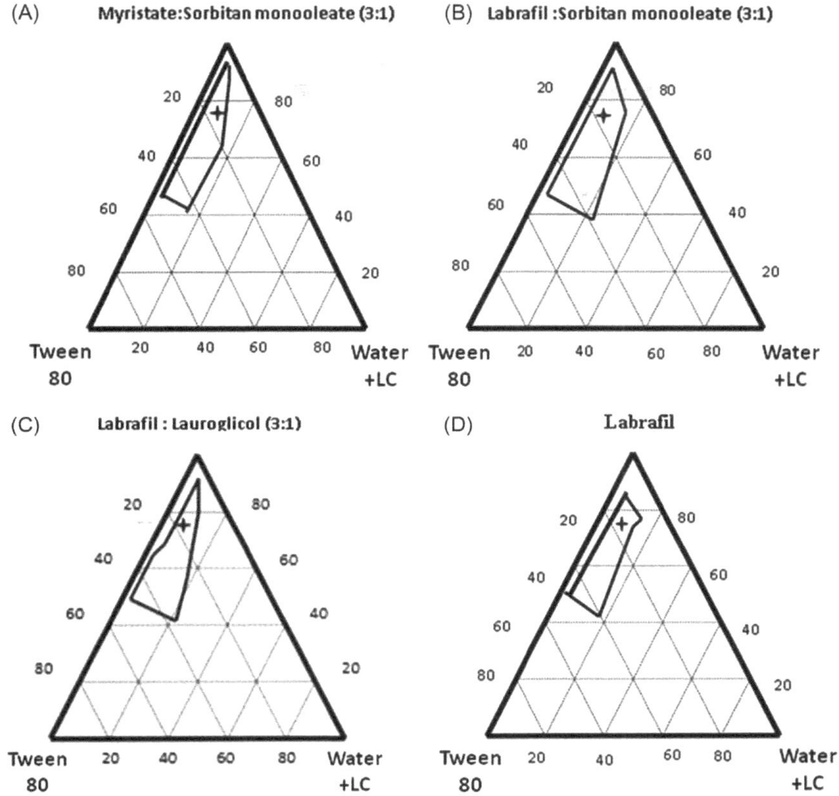

FIGURE 6.2 Representative pseudo-ternary phase diagrams of systems containing ME-1, ME-2, ME-3 and ME-4. *Reproduced with permission from Pineros, I., et al.,* Analgesic and anti-inflammatory controlled-released injectable microemulsion: Pseudo-ternary phase diagrams, in vitro, ex vivo and in vivo evaluation. *European Journal of Pharmaceutical Sciences, 2017. 101: p. 220–227.*

inversion point is an important feature of the Kahlweit fish diagram and this can be detected at the junction between the body and tail of the fish, the "PIT" [6]. The quantity of surface-active agent needed to achieve a homogeneous single phase is the lowest at this point, and the ME structure is bicontinuous [6]. Considerable attention is focused on the utilization of microemulsions for transdermal drug transport. These systems decrease the interfacial tension at the skin surface and can also enhance the solubility of the medication [40]. Furthermore, the chemical penetration enhancers used for formulating MEs (cosurfactant, surfactant, lipids) can disorder or dissolve the lipid bilayer structure of the epidermis, resulting in enhanced transdermal drug transport [40]. In the next section, concrete examples of drug-loaded MEs for percutaneous transport will be discussed. Table 6.1 shows the influence of microemulsions on transdermal drug delivery.

TABLE 6.1 The influence of microemulsions on transdermal drug delivery.

Therapeutic agent(s) or model compound	Skin model	Composition	References
Indomethacin	Rabbit skin	Eugenol oil, Tween 40, propylene glycol, ethanol, water	[23]
α-Santalol	Rat, pig and human skin	Isopropyl myristate, Phospholipid and Tween 80, water	[40]
Propranolol	Pig skin	Oleic acid, isopropyl palmitate, isopropyl myristate, isopropyl alcohol, ethanol and propylene glycol, water	[5]
Tetramethylpyrazine	Rat skin	Labrasol, Transcutol P, ethyl oleate, borneol, water	[42]
Testosterone	Pig skin	Tween 20, Transcutol, oleic acid, water	[43]
Methyl dihydrojasmonate	Mouse skin	Isopropyl myristate, Labrafil M, Labrafac CC, Labrafac PG, oleic acid or Capryol 90, Plurol Oleique, Tween 80, Labrasol, Transcutol P, water	[44]
Dencichine	Mouse skin	Isopropyl myristate, propylene glycol, 1-butyl-3-methylimidazolium dodecanesulfate, 1-hydroxyethyl-3-methylimidazolium chloride, water	[37]
Clotrimazole	Mouse skin	Isopropyl myristate, benzyl alcohol, oleic acid and lemon oil, Cremophor EL, Tween 80, *n*-butanol, water	[46]
Clotrimazole	Human skin	Cremophor EL, Labrasol, isopropyl myristate, water	[47]
Tetrapeptide PKEK	Human skin	Butylene glycol, TEGOSOFT P, TEGOSMO V, TEGO Care PL4, water	[9]

(*Continued*)

TABLE 6.1 (Continued)

Therapeutic agent(s) or model compound	Skin model	Composition	References
Bee-venom phospholipase A2	Pig skin	Caproylocaproylmacrogol-8 glycerides EP, polyglyceryl-6 dioleate, glycerol, butylene glycol, cetearyl ethylhexanoate, isopropyl palmitate, water	[48]
Repaglinide	Rat skin	Capryol 90, Cremophor EL, Transcutol P, water	[50]
Cyclosporine	Pig skin	Soluble derivative of vitamin E (TPGS), Tween 80, propanediol, propylene glycol, Transcutol, oleic acid, water	
Lapachol	Pig skin	Oleic acid, Cremophor EL, Tween 20, water	[52]
Zidovudine	Pig skin	Labrosol, Oleic Plurol, isopropyl myristate, water	[29]
Ropivacaine	Mouse skin	Capryol 90, Labrasol, ethanol, water	[53]
Celecoxib	Mouse skin	Transcutol P, triacetin, Tween 80, water	[54]
Imiquimod	Pig skin	Isostearic acid, D-α-Tocopheryl polyethylene glycol 1000 succinate, water	[55]

Transdermal delivery of indomethacin with microemulsion

Khayat and coworkers recently studied the effect of ME on indomethacin (IND) loading, release, and percutaneous penetration [23]. Eugenol was the oily phase and pseudo-ternary phase diagrams were drawn when propylene glycol or ethanol were employed as cosurfactants at 1:1 weight ratio with Tween 40 (surfactant) [23]. Mixtures of eugenol oil, cosurfactant (if present), and Tween 40 were titrated with water while monitoring the phase properties of the pseudo-ternary system [23]. Turbid dispersions were regarded as coarse emulsions while single-phase transparent fluid systems were considered as MEs. Percutaneous penetration studies were conducted with freshly excised rabbit ear [23]. The ME zone in the phase diagram occupied 38% of the total area of the phase diagram while the remaining portion was in the form of a coarse emulsion. The application of a saturated aqueous solution of IND resulted in a mean percutaneous flux of 1.66 μg/cm^2/h and a mean lag time of 2.06 h [23]. The use of a eugenol-based microemulsion formulation led to a significant enhancement in the transcutaneous flux of IND in comparison to that obtained with a saturated aqueous solution [23]. For the optimized ME formulation (TW PG ME 30), the percutaneous flux value was 21.98 ± 0.68 μg/cm^2/h [23].

Percutaneous transport of α-santalol through breast skin and mammary papilla

Most breast tumors begin as atypical hyperplasia in breast lobules and ducts [41]. Biologically active substances obtained from medicinal plants are potential breast cancer chemopreventive agents because they possess insignificant adverse events and low toxicity [41]. Terpenes derived from essential oils are known to have chemoprophilactic activities. Recently, Dave and coworkers investigated the transcutaneous transport of α-santalol (α-SL), a sesquiterpene [41]. α-SL blocks cell proliferation and cell viability in estrogen negative (MDA-MB231) and estrogen positive (MCF-7) breast cancer cells [41]. The optimal physicochemical features of α-santalol (liquid, log $P = 4.5$, MW = 220 Da) combine to make this compound interesting for transdermal administration [41]. The percutaneous transport of α-SL to the breast was recently studied [41].

In vitro transdermal experiments were conducted with excised rat, pig, and human breast tissues (breast skin and nipple). Phospholipid or Tween 80 was used to prepare o/w ME [41]. To formulate a microemulsion from Tween 80 (T80-ME), the authors added a mixture of isopropyl myristate and α-santalol to Tween 80: ethanol. The authors then added water to the mixture and vortexed the dispersion to obtain the microemulsion [41]. Similarly, the authors utilized phospholipid 90G to prepare microemulsion (PL-ME). α-santalol was added to an ethanolic solution of Phospholipon 90G under vortexing [41]. The researchers then incorporated water into the mixture under stirring to obtain two distinct PL-ME with 25% and 10% of the drug [41]. In vitro transdermal experiments were conducted with human breast and animal (rat and pig) tissue. The authors compared the delivery α-santalol from o/w ME, o/w vanishing cream, and a hydroalcoholic solution. α-SL permeated the nipple from the different dosage forms with the following permeability ranking: PL-ME10 > hydro alcoholic solution > cream > T80-ME [41]. The transdermal permeation rate and the cumulative amount of α-santalol delivered were 4- to 11-fold higher when PL-ME10 was used in comparison with other dosage forms. The use of T80-ME led to the least flux, but there was no statistically significant contrast between the vanishing cream and the hydroalcoholic solution [41]. Phospholipid, with a chemical structure similar to skin lipids, can also be used as a CPE. Tissue deposition was 3–8 times greater with PL-ME10 and hydroalcoholic solution in comparison with the other two dosage forms [41]. The phospholipid microemulsion (PL-ME10) led to increased drug transport compared to the Tween 80-based counterpart (T80-ME) [41]. The authors also showed that the percutaneous transport of α-SL through the entire breast led to a greater concentration in the mammary gland compared to permeation through the nipple or breast skin [41]. The results from the research project demonstrated the potential of utilizing transdermal ME loaded with α-SL for breast cancer prevention [41].

Skin delivery of propranolol-loaded microemulsions

Infantile hemangioma (IH) is a benign vascular neoplasm [42]. Propranolol (PL) is a beta-blocker used for the management of IH [5]. Optimization of propranolol formulation can significantly improve patient/caregiver compliance and also decrease adverse events in children. Kelchen and Brogden formulated and characterized several MEs for the skin delivery of PL [5]. The skin deposition and penetration of PL from MEs applied to intact and MN-treated pig skin were studied in vitro [5]. The authors chose the appropriate solubility-based oil and cosurfactant combinations by adding a surplus quantity of PL to three different oil phases (oleic acid, isopropyl palmitate, and isopropyl myristate) and three cosurfactants (isopropyl alcohol, ethanol, and propylene glycol) [5]. The authors reported that the solubility of the drug was considerably higher in oleic acid (269.0 ± 52.4 μg/mL) in comparison with isopropyl myristate (23.4 ± 0.5 μg/mL) or isopropyl palmitate (21.1 ± 0.7 μg/mL) [5]. The authors chose oleic acid as the ME oil phase. Propranolol was more soluble in ethanol (8.3 ± 0.3 mg/mL) in comparison with isopropyl alcohol (5.7 ± 0.4 mg/mL) or propylene glycol (1.3 ± 0.3 mg/mL) and therefore ethanol was chosen for ME preparation [5].

The authors drew a pseudo-ternary phase diagram showing ME domains [5]. Surfactant mixture (1:1 ratio of ethanol and Tween 80) and the oil phase (oleic acid) were incorporated into the formulations in different ratios from 1:9 to 9:1 [5]. The authors added water drop by drop under uninterrupted stirring until the translucent solution turned cloudy. The final volume of each constituent was recorded as a percentage and depicted in the pseudo-ternary phase diagram [5]. MEs were formed from solutions with low oil and high surfactant concentration. ME formulations were translucent and freely flowed following vial inclination at a 45° angle, while preparations outside the ME domain were cloudy and did not freely flow after tilting [5]. From what was depicted in the phase diagrams, the authors chose four formulations prepared from surfactant mixture, oil, and distilled water.

Skin transport and deposition parameters across MN-treated and intact skin were assessed following the administration of four microemulsions (ME3, ME4, ME6, ME9) loaded with 0.5% w/v propranolol [5]. The solubility of the drug was substantially greater in MEs in comparison with phosphate-buffered saline [5]. When administered to an imperforated skin, the phosphate buffered saline (PBS) solution produced considerably greater skin drug concentration (4.82 ± 1.45 μmol drug/g skin) compared to the MEs although the skin-to-receiver ratios were substantially greater for water-rich MEs in comparison to surfactant-rich microemulsions or PBS [5]. Of the investigated MEs, ME9 provided significantly higher skin concentration (0.040 ± 0.008 μmol drug/g skin) than ME3 (0.010 ± 0.009 μmol drug/g skin) and ME4 (0.012 ± 0.008 μmol drug/g skin) [5]. The cumulative drug transport into the Franz cell receptor after 24 h was significantly higher for the aqueous solution of PBS (188.6 ± 58.9 nmol) in comparison to the MEs. The authors did not observe any significant difference in cumulative drug penetration between the researched MEs [5]. Knowing that one of the objectives of local therapy for IH is to enhance skin concentration while reducing systemic transport, the authors compared skin-to-receiver ratios of the various investigated dosage forms. The average ± SD skin-to-receiver ratio for PBS was 6.04 ± 2.56 and this was comparable to skin-to-receiver ratios for the formulations rich in surfactants (ME6: 8.27 ± 6.48, ME4: 3.75 ± 1.73, and 4.20 ± 4.05) [5]. Water-rich MEs displayed a greater skin-to-receiver ratio (ME9: 25.50 ± 10.69), which was significantly higher than the PBS solution and all MEs [5]. When skin samples pretreated with MNs were studied, it was noted that the use of MEs led to significant alterations in skin concentration of the drug following MN utilization, with enhancement ratios (ERs) of 8.3, 7.9, 17.4, and 20.4 for ME9, ME6, ME4, and ME3, respectively [5]. Aqueous solution of PBS exhibited a moderate ER of 1.8 after the use of MNs [5].

The Influence of microemulsion on the percutaneous transport of tetramethylpyrazine

Recently, Hu et al. reported an increased brain distribution and transdermal delivery of tetramethylpyrazine (TMP) when the drug was delivered through the skin from a borneol-based ME [43]. TMP is a biologically effective compound obtained from the herb *Ligusticum wallichii* Franch [43]. The neuroprotective activity of TMP is associated with thrombolytic effects, enhancement of cell differentiation and neurogenesis, blocking of the inflammatory response, decrease of calcium overload, antioxidation, increase in dendritic plasticity, antiexcitotoxicity, and antiapoptosis [43]. Borneol (BN), which is a terpene isolated from *Dryobalanops aramatica* C.F. Gaertn, curtails brain insult following ischemic stroke by directly decreasing malondialdehyde (MDA) concentration as well as enhancing superoxide dismutase (SODase) and lactate dehydrogenase (LHD) activities [43].

It has also been postulated that BN can increase TMP bioavailability through enhanced brain distribution. Increased brain distribution is achieved by means of improved blood brain barrier absorption following intranasal administration [43]. When TMP is utilized for the management of ischemic stroke, a prolonged treatment schedule is usually implemented, and this may last from weeks in the acute phase of the disease to several years during the chronic stage [43]. TMP possesses low bioavailability as well as a very short biological half-life after oral ingestion and it is essential to dispense the compound three or four times daily [43]. A transdermal drug delivery system that was loaded with BN and TMP (TMP-BN-ME-TDDS) and was delivered through ME was formulated and tested on rats to assess the effect of BN on the pharmacokinetic profile of TMP [43]. Labrasol, Transcutol P, and ethyl oleate were employed as the surfactant (S), cosurfactant (Cos), and oil phase respectively for the preparation of TMP-BN-ME [43]. The weight ratio of S to Cos (Km) was fixed at 3:1, the weight ratio of oil to S and Cos was changed (9:1, 8:2, 7:3, 6:4, 5:5, 4:6, 3:7, 2:8, 1:9) while the ME zone was accordingly delineated [43]. The mixtures were gently vortexed at room temperature, while water was added drop by drop. The critical points that set apart the ME domain from other zones were noted when the system transitioned from translucent to cloudy. The collected data were used to draw a pseudo-ternary phase diagram. In vitro skin transport studies of TMP-BN-MEs across freshly excised male Sprague Dawley rat abdominal skin were conducted [43]. The pharmacokinetic profiles demonstrated that the TMP-BN-ME-TDDS treated rats had significantly greater C_{max} and area under curve (AUC) of TMP compared to the TMP-ME-TDDS treated rats, providing evidence that BN enhances the rate and magnitude of TMP transdermal permeation. Significantly, brain TMP AUC was significantly higher in the TMP-BN-ME-TDDS group, demonstrating that BN enhances the brain distribution of TMP [43].

The influence of microemulsion on the transcutaneous delivery of testosterone

The average lipophilicity (log $P_{o/w} = 3.3$) and the comparatively low molecular weight (MW = 288) as well as the water solubility (0.039 mg/mL at 37°C) of testosterone are positive determinants that the drug can be successfully delivered transdermally [44]. Another important consideration is that testosterone replacement should closely mimic the normal rate in humans (3−10 mg/day), which corresponds to a target transdermal permeation rate of about 1−10 μg/cm^2/h for a transdermal drug delivery system with an area of 30 cm^2 [44]. The formulation of an alternative drug delivery system for the percutaneous transport of testosterone is a global challenge. Hathout and colleagues investigated MEs, comprising known CPEs, for the transcutaneous transport of testosterone. MEs were formulated from Tween 20 (surfactant), Transcutol (cosurfactant), oleic acid (oil phase), and water [44]. NMR spectroscopy and DSC were utilized for the study of the dosage forms and conductivity determination showed the point at which the ME made the transition from the w/o to the bicontinuous type based on the weight fraction of water [44]. Physical parameters such as conductivity, pH, and viscosity as well as Fourier-Transform Infrared Spectroscopy (FTIR), 11H NMR, and 3C NMR were utilized for the assessment of changes in the ME microstructure, after loading the dosage form with testosterone. The authors conducted in vitro experiments to study testosterone transport from MEs across pig skin. Testosterone permeated porcine skin from the MEs, with the greatest transdermal flux (4.6 ± 0.6 g/cm^{-2}/h) obtained from the ME loaded with 3% (w/v) of the drug, 20% water, 32% Tween 20, 32% Transcutol, and 16% oleic acid [44].

In an interesting study, Hsieh and coworkers studied the influence of microemulsions on the solubilization of testosterone propionate [15]. Dilutable, o/w, cosurfactant-free MEs stabilized by the following amphoteric surfactants, 3-(*N*,*N*-dimethyldodecylammonio)propanesulfonate (DDAPS) as well as 3-(*N*,*N*-dimethyloctylammonio)propanesulfonate (DOAPS) and comprising four different ethyl ester oils were prepared [15]. The authors mixed the required amounts of oil [ethyl palmitate (EP), ethyl oleate (EO), ethyl caprylate (EC), and ethyl butyrate (EB)]; surfactant (DOAPS, DDAPS) with water and subsequently phase diagrams were constructed [15]. Both DDAPS and DOAPS displayed the highest degree of solubilization on the shortest chain oil (EB) while DDAPS had the least solubilization impact on the longest chain oil (EO). Because of the high surfactant concentration required to formulate DDAPS and DOAPS MEs. The authors used 35% w/w of surfactant for testoserone propionate (TP) solubilization [15]. The solubilization of TP was higher in all MEs studied in comparison with micelles independent of the quantity of oil added [15]. Furthermore, the ME prepared from EC and DDAPS solubilized TP at a higher degree than those formulated from EB with the same surfactant concentration [15].

Transdermal microemulsion loaded with methyl dihydrojasmonate

In another study, ME was utilized for the delivery of methyl dihydrojasmonate (a phytochemical agent), which is known to have anticancer activity [45]. The authors constructed pseudo-ternary phase diagrams via the water titration technique after using several combinations of cosurfactants, surfactants, and oils. Ratios between 1:9 and 9:1 were employed to mix the oil phase with a combination of the surface-active agent and the cosurfactant. The mixtures were evaluated visually as two-phase mixtures or multiple-phase MEs. Cloudiness was taken as an indication of the separation of phases. The authors used an experimental design (Simplex Lattice Mixture Design) to choose preparations for ex vivo transport experiments through mouse skin [45]. Methyl dihydrojasmonate (MDHJ) was incorporated into

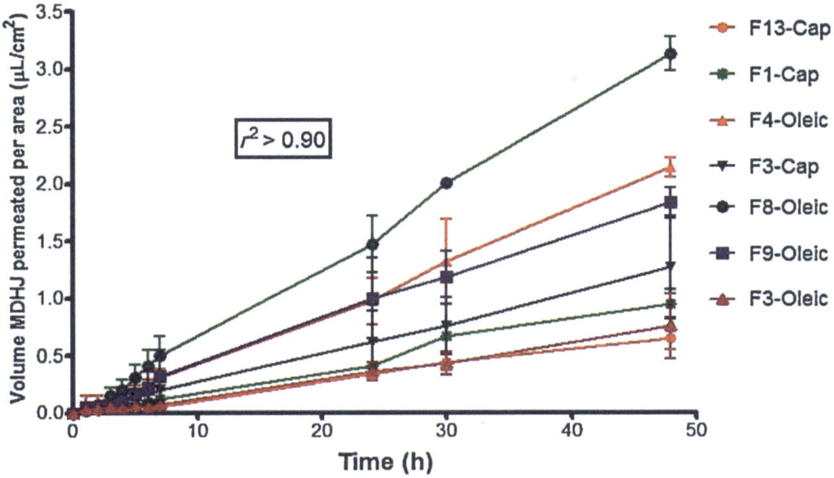

FIGURE 6.3 Cumulative amount permeated of methyl dihydrojasmonate per unit area from selected microemulsion systems. *Reproduced with permission from Yehia R, et al. Anti-tumor efficacy of an integrated methyl dihydrojasmonate transdermal microemulsion system targeting breast cancer cells: in vitro and in vivo studies. Colloids Surf B Biointerfaces 2017;155: 512–21.*

the oily phase made up of isopropyl myristate (IPM), Labrafil M, Labrafac CC, Labrafac PG, oleic acid, or Capryol 90 [45]. Plurol Oleique, Tween 80, Labrasol, or Transcutol P were utilized as cosurfactants or surfactants [45]. The mixing ratio for either the oily phase constituents with MDHJ or surfactant with cosurfactant was maintained at 1:1. The MEs loaded with oleic acid and Capryol in the oily phase as well as Labrasol/Transcutol as surfactant/cosurfactant produced the broadest ME domains in the pseudo-ternary phase diagrams [45]. The use of MDHJ/oleic acid/Labrasol/Transcutol/water system led to the greatest steady-state permeation flux (J_{ss}) and permeability coefficients (Kp) values that were 0.07 μL/cm^2/h and 3.39 μL/h, respectively, pointing to higher permeation parameters than the MDHJ/Capryol 90/Labrasol/Transcutol/water system (Fig. 6.3) [45].

The effect of microemulsion on the transcutaneous permeation of dencichine

Dencichine (β-*N*-oxalyl-L-α, β-diaminopropionic acid, Den) is an amino acid isolated from *P. notoginseng*, with significant hemostatic activity [38]. Recently, Wang et al. introduced two ionic liquids (1-butyl-3-methylimidazolium dodecanesulfate) ([BMIM])C12SO3 and 1-hydroxyethyl-3-methylimidazolium chloride ([HOEIM]Cl) into the surfactant and aqueous phases, respectively, and subsequently prepared Den-loaded ME [38]. The ME was made from 20% IPM as the oil phase, 10% propylene glycol as the cosurfactant, 50% water/[HOEIM]Cl mix (1:1) as the water phase and 20% Tween 80/[BMIM]C12SO3 mix (1:1) as the surfactant a [38]. The pH (6.71 ± 0.04), viscosity (31 ± 4 mPa), zeta potential (−14.83 ± 3.64 mV), and droplet size (47.7 ± 1.5 nm) of the o/w microemulsion were determined [38]. In vitro skin penetration experiments demonstrated the significant enhancement effect of ionic liquid-based MEs on the skin transport of Den, which was approximately 10-fold compared to the aqueous solution of the compound [38]. The authors reported that the ME can decrease skin barrier function by disorganizing corneocyte architecture and modulating SC surface properties as shown by ATR-FTIR, DSC, and transepidermal water loss (TEWL). Significantly, the in vivo pharmacodynamic profile showed considerable hemostatic effect of Den when administered topically with an ME [38].

Skin delivery of clotrimazole-loaded microemulsions

Clotrimazole (CTM) is used in clinical practice as an antimycotic agent with activity against pathogenic yeasts, dermatophytes, and certain species of *Malassezia, Epidermophyton, Microsporum, Tricophyton,* and *Candida* [46]. Several MEs loaded with CTM were formulated in gel as well as liquid forms and the physicochemical as well as skin transport properties of the drug were investigated [47]. Isopropyl myristate, benzyl alcohol, oleic acid, and lemon oil were investigated for use as an ME oil phase. Cremophor EL and Tween 80 were used as surfactants (S) while *n*-butanol was employed as a cosurfactant (Cos) in an S/Cos weight ratios of 1:1, 1:2, and 1:3 [47]. Next, the authors used the water titration method to formulate the dispersions and drew pseudo-ternary phase diagrams of each oil combined with the surfactants/cosurfactants. The mixtures were titrated with water drop by drop and mixed thoroughly by stirring until translucent ME phase domains were spotted. Chemix School 3.5 software was used to construct phase diagrams with the translucent ME regions inside the triangular domain. The MEs were formulated from 49.5% w/w water, 5.5% w/w oil, 45% w/w S/Cos at a ratio of 3:1 [47].

Lemon oil constituted the largest ME area (88.80%) while oleic made up the smallest ME domain (32.29%) at the same S/Cos weight ratio of 3:1. CTM MEs (M1−M5) were formulated, viscosity, droplet size, refractive index, pH, thermodynamic stability, and in vitro release across cellulose membrane were determined. Among the formulated MEs, M4 (isopropyl myristate/Tween 80/*n*-butanol/water) and M3 (lemon oil/Tween 80/*n*-butanol/water) MEs were optimal based on CTM cumulative percentage release and physical properties. The gel form of M3 and M4 was formulated with 1% Carbopol 940 as the hydrogel. Both preparations were assessed in gel and liquid forms for deposition in mouse skin compared to the commercially available

CTM topical cream. The use of MEs led to substantially higher skin deposition of CTM in comparison with the cream. M4 preparations were more stable than M3 as shown by experiments. Furthermore, the in vitro antifungal activity of M4 against *Candida albicans* was greater compared to a commercially available cream [47].

Zhang and Michniak-Kohn also used Cremophor EL (cosurfactant), Labrasol (surfactant), isopropyl myristate (oil), and water to prepare MEs possessing different microstructures [48]. The authors used sonication to dissolve clotrimazole (CTM) in a mixture of IPM/Labrasol/Cremophor EL, 4/1 (w/w) and subsequently added the correct quantity of water. The dispersion mixed by vortexing to form a transparent and an isotropic solution. Diffusion studies using human skin were carried out for ME and the control formulations with variable CTM concentrations. The skin concentration of the drug was substantially greater for MEs in comparison with the control formulation, as shown by the skin deposition ER of 5.1, 2.8, and 3.0 for the investigated o/w, bicontinuous, and w/o MEs, respectively [48]. The greatest concentration of the drug was obtained from the O/W ME, indicating the importance of the ME microstructure for the promotion of drug delivery into the skin [48]. Significantly, when CMT was incorporated into an ME gel preparation (by adding 1.0% w/w of Carbopol 980) the skin concentration of the drug was similar to what was obtained following the application of MEs, but up to 2.4-fold greater than the marketed CMT cream (Lotrimin) [48]. The authors also investigated a model hydrophobic compound fluorescein isothiocyanate (FITC) and documented significantly greater FITC concentration in every skin layer: dermis, SC, and viable epidermis from o/w ME compared to the bicontinuous and w/o MEs [48].

Skin delivery of the tetrapeptide PKEK with microemulsions

Pro-Lys-Glu-Lys (PKEK) is the cosmeceutical ingredient in the marketed product TEGO Pep 4-Even [9]. When administered topically, this hydrophilic and polar tetrapeptide PKEK can block the pigmentation process and thus decrease effects caused by ultraviolet B radiation [9]. Experiments with human keratinocytes and skin epithelial have indicated that PKEK can reduce UVB-induced mRNA expression of proopiomelanocorticotropin (POMC), TNF-α, and interleukins (IL-6, IL8) but is essential that PKEK penetrates its target in the epidermal basal layer. When this happens, melanocytes are activated at the cellular level [9]. Recently, Neubert et al. studied the effect of microemulsions on the skin delivery of PKEK [9]. 10% of a water-butylene glycol mixture (1:1) (w/w) was used to dissolve PKEK. Next, 65% of oil (TEGOSOFT P) as well as the emulsifiers [TEGO SMO V (8.3%) and TEGO Care PL4 (16.7%)] were added [9]. Then, the dispersion was mixed until all ingredients dissolved. Permeation studies were conducted with finite doses and excised human skin (from breast reduction surgery) was utilized for the experiments [9]. A large quantity of PKEK was delivered from the ME into human skin after a period of 100 min (94%) and 300 min (88%). A significant portion of the compound did not remain in the skin but penetrated the receptor chamber [9]. In contrast, a large fraction of PKEK, which was delivered into the skin from the standard cream, was deposited in the SC and did not diffuse into the deep lying layers of the skin. The results of the experiments demonstrated that MEs are efficient vehicles for the hydrophilic peptides used in cosmeceuticals [9].

Microemulsion for the skin delivery of bee-venom phospholipase A2 (Api m 1)

Recently, an ME with a low concentration of the surface-active agent was recently prepared and utilized for the transport of a model allergen into layers of the epidermis or into dermal dendritic cells and Langerhans cells for allergen-specific immunotolerance induction [49]. Optical density measurement at 600 nm (OD_{600}) was made together with phase diagram by micro plate dilution (PDMPD)-method [49]. Mixtures of the surfactant/cosurfactant phase (SCos; caproylocaproylmacrogol-8 glycerides EP and polyglyceryl-6 dioleate NF 11:8 wt.%), water phase (PBS, glycerol, butylene glycol 83:3:14 wt.%), and the oil phase (cetearyl ethylhexanoate and isopropyl palmitate 7:1 wt.%) were made by the authors [49]. Mixtures of the oil phase and surfactant/cosurfactant phase from 10 up to 90 wt.% SCos were shaken at 25°C [49]. The authors measured OD_{600} after a 30 min equilibration-time and visual evaluation of isotropy was used by the authors to identify MEs. Experiments carried out included the permeation of pig ear skin epidermis by Alexa Fluor-647 labeled bee-venom phospholipase A2 (Api m 1) as well as confocal laser-scanning microscopy [49]. Experimental results using in vivo Api m 1-allergic mouse model showed the beneficial effect of ME in dermal allergen-specific immunotherapy [49].

Transcutaneous delivery of metronidazole with microemulsion

Patients suffering from Rosacea (a chronic skin disorder) usually have inflammatory lesions (telangiectasia, pustules and papules, and erythema) [14]. Three topical drugs are currently used for the management of rosacea: sodium sulfacetamide 10% with sulfur 5%, azelaic acid 15% as well as metronidazole 0.75%, and 1% [14]. Metronidazole (a synthetic derivative of nitroimidazole) possesses antiinflammatory and antimicrobial activities and is utilized for the systemic and local therapy of rosacea [14]. Tirnaksiz et al. formulated a topical w/o type ME loaded with metronidazole and compared its efficacy with a marketed gel product for the pharmacotherapy of rosacea [14]. The authors utilized the water titration method to draw a pseudo-ternary phase diagram.

The mixtures were made using lecithin to butanol at a ratio of 2:1 wt./wt. and with variable ratios of oil to the surfactant/cosurfactant mixture [14]. Oil and surfactant ratios were changed from 9:1 to 1:9. The mixture of cosurfactant, surfactant, and oil were titrated with water drop by drop with magnetic stirring for the establishment of the ME domain border. The mixture was subsequently assessed visually for translucency [14]. A formulation was then selected from the ME domain in the phase diagram. The dosage form was a w/o ME (turbidity: 6.89NTU, conductivity: 1.5 μs/cm, viscosity: 457.3 mPa · s and droplet size: 11.6 nm) [14]. The ME was compared to a gel product in a split-face, baseline-controlled, double-blind, and randomized clinical trial for the management of rosacea. The difference in the abatement of the major symptoms of the disease following the use of the two formulations was statistically significant after a 6-week treatment period [14]. It was reported that 17% of the patients treated with ME had 50% relief from erythema and 100% from inflammatory lesions [14]. The use of ME led to a complete relief in 38% of the patients who suffered from telangiectasia while the marketed product did not grant any relief from the symptoms of telangiectasia [14].

Repaglinide microemulsion gel for percutaneous transport

Repaglinide (RPG) is an oral medication that promotes insulin secretion and is utilized as an antidiabetic agent. It facilitates early-phase insulin release from beta-islet cells in pancreas thus reducing postprandial glucose levels [50]. The drug is marketed as tablets but due to its low solubility, the gastrointestinal (GIT) absorption of RPG is incomplete and consequently oral bioavailability (~50%) is low [51]. In addition, RPG possesses a very short half-life (~1 h) due to fast presystemic metabolism. Increased bioavailability and a sustained therapeutic effect can be attained by utilizing drug delivery systems that are capable of increasing drug dissolution (e.g., microemulsion), circumventing presystemic metabolism (e.g., transdermal systems), and releasing the medication in a controlled fashion for a sustained time frame (e.g., gels). Recently, Shinde and coworkers investigated the influence of ME on the percutaneous transport of RPG [51]. Pseudo-ternary phase diagrams were drawn via the water titration method to acquire the concentration range of ME constituents. The surfactant to cosurfactant (K_m) weight ratio varied as 1:1, 2:1, or 3:1 [51]. Oily mixtures prepared from surfactant, oil, and cosurfactant were formulated in which the weight ratio of oil to the surfactant–cosurfactant mixture (S_{mix}) was varied and at a specific K_m ratio, a pseudo-ternary phase diagram was drawn. The authors added water dropwise to each of the oily mixtures at 37°C until the formulations turned turbid.

The concentrations of ME excipients were documented, and a pseudo-ternary phase diagram was drawn [51]. To increase the residence time and skin penetration of RPG, rationally designed MEs with mean globule size of

36.15 ± 9.89 nm were formulated into a gel with xanthan gum. Ex vivo transport studies across rat skin showed higher steady-state permeation rate for RPG ME as compared to an ME gel loaded with the drug [51]. After 24 h, the cumulative drug transport values from ME and ME gel were 229.19 ± 24.34 and 180.84 ± 17.40 μg/cm^2 respectively [51]. The use of the ME formulation and ME gel led to a 12.30- and 10.97-fold increase in transdermal flux in comparison with the drug suspension [51]. Overall, the use of a transdermal microemulsion gel loaded with RPG led to considerable drug delivery benefit compared to orally administered dosage form [51].

The influence of microemulsion on the transcutaneous delivery of cyclosporine

Cyclosporine is an immunosuppressant cyclic peptide used for the management of psoriasis [27]. The drug inhibits interleukin (IL)-2 and T-cell function [52]. The topical application of this drug can reduce or avoid problems associated with systemic immunosuppression [27]. But less than optimal physicochemical properties (Log $P \approx 3$; MW: 1202 Da) of this compound hinder its transport across the skin. Recently, Benigni et al. prepared MEs using either a soluble derivative of vitamin E (TPGS) or Tween 80 as surfactants, 1,3-propanediol, propylene glycol or Transcutol as cosurfactants and oleic acid as oil phase [27]. The authors constructed pseudo-ternary phase diagrams using the aqueous titration method and after each addition, the mixture was vortexed and left to rest for 1 min [27]. The translucence and viscosity of the system were then examined by visual observation. A formulation is typically viscous and clear in the microgel region but clear with low viscosity in the ME domain. OriginPro software was used to construct the diagrams. Four TPGS-based and five Tween 80-based formulations were selected, described in terms of rheological properties (high-viscosity systems) or droplet size (low-viscosity systems), loaded with 6 mg/g of the drug and administered ex vivo on pig skin for 22 h. Optimal skin deposition profiles were observed either with a high-viscosity TPGS-based ME (18.3 ± 5.69 μg/cm^2) or a low-viscosity Tween 80-based ME (9.78 ± 3.86 μg/cm^2), with approximately three and sixfold enhancement respectively when compared with a control drug solution in propylene glycol [27].

Transcutaneous delivery of lapachol with microemulsion

Lapachol is a naphthoquinone that is isolated from the bark of *Tabebuia avellanedae* [53]. The compound has immunosuppressive, contraceptive, antimicrobial, antiulcer, anticancer, antimalarial, antiinflammatory, trypanocidal, leishmanicidal, molluscicidal, and antifungal activities [53]. It is a good transdermal drug delivery candidate due to a relatively low molecular weight (242 g/mol), moderate lipophilicity (log $P_{o/w} = 2.69$; water solubility = 2 mg /L at 25°C), and low oral bioavailability [53]. In an interesting study, Tabosa and colleagues prepared and characterized a transdermal ME loaded with lapachol [53]. To achieve this objective, the authors constructed pseudo-ternary phase diagrams to determine the ME domains. The selected formulations were characterized by physicochemical properties and skin transport studies [53]. From the screening of surfactants and oils, a range of microemulsions were developed using oleic acid, a mixture of Cremophor EL, Tween 20, and water [53]. The MEs were characterized by cross-polarizing light microscopy, electrical conductivity, pH, zeta potential, and rheology; SAXS and DSC ex vivo studies were carried out with pig ear skin to evaluate the permeation and retention of lapachol. Systems containing different concentrations of Cremophor EL (8.4%–41.6%), Tween 20 (5.4%–41.6%), and oleic acid (12%–31.9%) are able to form microemulsions and lapachol was delivered more effectively through the skin from all of the microemulsions tested than by the control (oleic acid) [53].

Microemulsion for the skin transport of zidovudine

Zidovudine (AZT) is approved by regulatory authorities as an anti-HIV drug [29]. AZT possesses a short half-life (1 h) in combination with low bioavailability because of presystemic metabolism. Thus, AZT is a suitable candidate for transdermal delivery [29]. Recently, Carvalho et al. compared liquid crystal and ME systems loaded with AZT for transdermal administration [29]. Suitable ratios of aqueous phase, surfactant/cosurfactant (Labrosol and Oleic Plurol), and the oil phase (isopropyl myristate) were mixed at room temperature [29]. The authors used pseudo-ternary diagrams to identify the ME region. The ME displayed considerable penetration enhancing influence (ER = 1.98). In vitro permeation experiments (using porcine ear skin) demonstrated that the quantity of the drug that was transported across the skin was significantly higher for the ME in comparison with LP and control formulations [29]. The results from the study were comparable with published reports which indicate that MEs can destabilize SC lipid bilayer due to the high ratio of surfactants [29]. As a result, skin permeability is enhanced and poorly permeable compounds such as AZT can be transported across the skin in greater amounts [29].

Percutaneous transport of ropivacaine-loaded microemulsion

Ropivacaine (1-propyl-20,60-pipecoloxylidide) (RPC) is a local anesthetic agent utilized for the management of postoperative pain and labor analgesia [54]. The need for a longer acting formulation and improved compliance has spurred research for other routes of RPC delivery including transdermal [54]. RPC is a good candidate for transdermal delivery because it possesses a $\log P$ value of 2.9 and a low molecular weight (MW = 274.41) [54].

An RPC-loaded ME and ME gel were recently investigated. Simplex lattice experiment design (Design Expert software) was used for formulation design and optimization while ternary phase diagrams were used to identify the ME domain [54]. Pharmacodynamic activity, skin irritation, and transdermal drug delivery studies were carried out to assess the potential of using ME for percutaneous RPC transport [54].

To determine the concentration of constituents like water, cosurfactant, oil, and surfactant for the ME, pseudo-ternary phase diagrams were drawn by the authors [54]. The water titration method was used for experiments. Several self-emulsifying systems comprising surfactant/cosurfactant/oil were formulated. At a defined Km, freshly formulated self-emulsifying systems were titrated with distilled water under magnetic stirring [54]. Particle size and drug solubility were evaluated as dependent variables while Capryol 90 (X1), Smix (X2, Labrasol1: absolute ethanol = 1:2 w/w), water (X3) were considered as independent variables [54]. The optimal ME formulation comprising 32% water, 53% Smix, and 15% Capryol 90 respectively was selected [54]. In vitro transport studies revealed that RPC had a significantly greater cumulative amount from ME than that obtained from ME gel [54]. Intriguingly, both ME and ME-gel exhibited considerable analgesic action on writhing (engendered by acetic acid) in mice [54].

Celecoxib microemulsion-based gel for transdermal delivery

Celecoxib (CXB) selectively blocks cyclooxygenase-2 and possesses antipyretic, antiinflammatory, and analgesic effects [55]. The drug has poor aqueous solubility and therefore the formulation of CXB as a microemulsion-based gel to improve permeation through the skin and reduce side effects is desirable [55]. The investigators utilized orthogonal experimental design to determine CXB solubility in Transcutol P (cosurfactant), triacetin (oil phase), and Tween 80 (surfactant) with the goal of formulating an appropriate ME [55]. The concentration and Km value of water, Smix, and oil were verified by central composite design and pseudo-ternary phase diagram. The authors then used 1% carbopol 934 to prepare the CXB ME gel. Ex vivo skin penetration and in vivo pharmacokinetics were also examined. Ex vivo transdermal delivery studies in mice were conducted to compare ME with a traditional gel. The results showed that the use of an ME gel led to a higher transdermal flux possibly due to a smaller globule size and high entrapment in the ME.

Skin delivery of imiquimod with microemulsion

Imiquimod (IMQ) is used clinically as an immunostimulant for the management of basal cell carcinoma, skin infections, and actinic keratosis [56]. The pharmacological action of IMQ is thought to be induced by binding to Toll-like receptors 7 and 8, resulting in the release of pro-inflammatory chemokines, cytokines, and other mediators [56]. Pescina et al. prepared viscous MEs from isostearic (ISO) acid (oil phase) and D-α-Tocopheryl polyethylene glycol 1000 succinate (surfactant) and used the formulation for the skin delivery of IMQ [56]. D-α-Tocopheryl polyethylene glycol 1000 succinate (TPGS) is normally synthesized via esterification of vitamin E succinate with PEG 1000. ISO acid is made up primarily of methyl branched isomers of octadecanoic acid [56]. ISO acid is liquid at room temperature (melting point $< 10°C$), exhibits solubilization properties comparable to oleic acid, but is more resistant to oxidation. The authors constructed pseudo-ternary phase diagrams to identify the gel, gel-microemulsion, and ME domains [56]. ISO acid or oleic acid were used as the oil phase while 1/1 (w/v; g/mL) mixture of TPGS and cosurfactant (either 1,2-propanediol or Transcutol) was utilized as the surfactant system (S_{mix}) [56]. Water titration technique was utilized for the construction of the pseudo-ternary phase diagrams and this entailed adding increasing amounts of water (between 5% and 95%) to fixed proportions of oil/S_{mix} [56]. Following every addition, the mixture was vortexed and left to rest for 2 min before undergoing visual examination to assess translucence and viscosity. The authors identified a particular domain in the diagram as ME if it exhibited low viscosity and was clear whereas the microemulsion-gel region was viscous and clear [56]. SAXS and rheology were also used to characterize the systems; furthermore, the ability of the systems to boost IMQ skin uptake was also examined in vitro using a pig skin model [56]. The most optimal drug delivery system was the gel-like ME made up of about $\approx 27\%$ of Transcutol, $\approx 26\%$ of TPGS, $\approx 21\%$ of ISO acid, and 26% of water. The amount of IMQ that was deposited in the skin after 6 h was 3.0 ± 1.1 $\mu g/cm^2$ [56]. The quantity deposited was greater than what was reported for a marketed cream Imunocare (1.9 ± 0.8 $\mu g/cm^2$), despite the lower concentration of the vehicle (13 mg/g) used for the ME compared to Imunocare cream (50 mg/g) [56].

References

[1] Ita K. Progress in the use of microemulsions for transdermal and dermal drug delivery. Pharm Dev Technol 2016;22(4):467–75.

[2] Shukla T, et al. Biomedical applications of microemulsion through dermal and transdermal route. Biomed Pharmacother 2018;108:1477–94.

[3] Lawrence MJ, Rees GD. Microemulsion-based media as novel drug delivery systems. Adv Drug Deliv Rev 2012;64(Supplement):175–93.

[4] Mittal KL. Handbook of microemulsion science and technology. Routledge; 2018. 864 pages.

[5] Kelchen MN, Brogden NK. In vitro skin retention and drug permeation through intact and microneedle pretreated skin after application of propranolol loaded microemulsions. Pharm Res 2018;35(12):228.

[6] Naoui W, et al. Microemulsion microstructure influences the skin delivery of an hydrophilic drug. Pharm Res 2011;28(7):1683–95.

[7] Hoar TP, Schulman JH. Transparent water-in-oil dispersions: the oleopathic hydromicelle. Nature 1943;152:102.
[8] Boonme P, et al. Characterization of microemulsion structures in the pseudoternary phase diagram of isopropyl palmitate/water/Brij 97:1-butanol. AAPS Pharm Sci Tech 2006;7(2):E45.
[9] Neubert RHH, et al. Dermal peptide delivery using enhancer moleculs and colloidal carrier systems. Part II: tetrapeptide PKEK. Eur J Pharm Biopharm 2018;124:28–33.
[10] Amiri-Rigi A, Abbasi S. Extraction of lycopene using a lecithin-based olive oil microemulsion. Food Chem 2019;272:568–73.
[11] Callender SP, et al. Microemulsion utility in pharmaceuticals: implications for multi-drug delivery. Int J Pharm 2017;526(1–2):425–42.
[12] Patil NH, Devarajan PV. Chapter 20—Colloidal carriers for noninvasive delivery of insulin. In: Ohshima H, Makino K, editors. Colloid and interface science in pharmaceutical research and development. Amsterdam: Elsevier; 2014. p. 411–42.
[13] Lu GW, Gao P. Chapter 3—Emulsions and microemulsions for topical and transdermal drug delivery. In: Kulkarni VS, editor. Handbook of non-invasive drug delivery systems. Boston: William Andrew Publishing; 2010. p. 59–94.
[14] Tirnaksiz F, et al. Preparation and evaluation of topical microemulsion system containing metronidazole for remission in rosacea. Chem Pharm Bull (Tokyo) 2012;60(5):583–92.
[15] Hsieh CM, et al. Oil-in-water microemulsions stabilized by 3-(N,N-dimethylalkylammonio)propanesulfonate surfactants of varying alkyl chain length: solubilisation of testosterone propionate. Int J Pharm 2017;525(1):1–4.
[16] Narasimha Murthy S, Shivakumar HN. Chapter 1—Topical and transdermal drug delivery. In: Kulkarni VS, editor. Handbook of non-invasive drug delivery systems. Boston: William Andrew Publishing; 2010. p. 1–36.
[17] Kreilgaard M. Influence of microemulsions on cutaneous drug delivery. Adv Drug Deliv Rev 2002;54(Supplement):S77–98.
[18] Lopes LB. Overcoming the cutaneous barrier with microemulsions. Pharm 2014;6 (1):52–77.
[19] Lipfert F, et al. Stability of near-surface ordering of bicontinuous microemulsions in external shear-fields. J Colloid Inter Sci 2019;534:31–6.
[20] Bera A, et al. Screening of microemulsion properties for application in enhanced oil recovery. Fuel 2014;121:198–207.
[21] Winsor PA. *Hydrotropy, solubilisation and related emulsification processes*. Trans Faraday Soc 1948;44(0):376–98.
[22] Niu Z, et al. Lipid-based nanocarriers for oral peptide delivery. Adv Drug Deliv Rev 2016;106(Pt B):337–54.
[23] El Khayat NW, et al. Optimization of eugenol microemulsion for transdermal delivery of indomethacin. J Drug Deliv Sci Technol 2018;48:311–18.
[24] Gupta M, Sharma V, Chauhan NS. Chapter 11—promising novel nanopharmaceuticals for improving topical antifungal drug delivery. In: Grumezescu AM, editor. Nano- and microscale drug delivery systems. Elsevier; 2017. p. 197–228.
[25] Patel G, Misra A. 10—Oral delivery of proteins and peptides: concepts and applications. In: Misra A, editor. Challenges in delivery of therapeutic genomics and proteomics. London: Elsevier; 2011. p. 481–529.
[26] Sintov AC. Transdermal delivery of curcumin via microemulsion. Int J Pharma 2015;481 (1–2):97–103.
[27] Benigni M, et al. Development of microemulsions of suitable viscosity for cyclosporine skin delivery. Int J Pharm 2018;545(1–2):197–205.

[28] Hathout RM, Elshafeey AH. Development and characterization of colloidal soft nano-carriers for transdermal delivery and bioavailability enhancement of an angiotensin II receptor blocker. Eur J Pharm Biopharm 2012;82(2):230–40.
[29] Carvalho AL, et al. Evaluation of microemulsion and lamellar liquid crystalline systems for transdermal zidovudine delivery. J Pharm Sci 2016;105(7):2188–93.
[30] Lopes LB, et al. Overcoming the cutaneous barrier with microemulsions. Pharmaceutics 2014;6(1):52–77.
[31] Kim C-K, et al. Preparation and physicochemical characterization of phase inverted water/oil microemulsion containing cyclosporin A. Int J Pharma 1997;147(1):131–4.
[32] Valoppi F, Frisina R, Calligaris S. Fabrication of transparent lemon oil loaded microemulsions by phase inversion temperature (PIT) method: effect of oil phase composition and stability after dilution. Food Biophysics 2017;12(2):244–9.
[33] Mayer S, Weiss J, McClements DJ. Vitamin E-enriched nanoemulsions formed by emulsion phase inversion: factors influencing droplet size and stability. J Colloid Inter Sci 2013;402:122–30.
[34] Wang Y. Preparation of nano- and microemulsions using phase inversion and emulsion titration methods: a thesis presented in partial fulfilment of the requirements for the degree of Master of Food Technology at Massey University. Auckland: Massey University; 2014.
[35] Freemantle M. An introduction to ionic liquids. RSC Pub; 2010. p. 281.
[36] Poh Y, Ng S, Ho K. Formulation and characterisation of 1-ethyl-3-methylimidazolium acetate-in-oil microemulsions as the potential vehicle for drug delivery across the skin barrier. J Mol Liq 2019;273:339–45.
[37] Syed HK, Peh KK. Identification of phases of various oil, surfactant/co-surfactants and water system by ternary phase diagram. Acta Pol Pharm 2014;71(2):301–9.
[38] Wang C, et al. Ionic liquid—microemulsions assisting in the transdermal delivery of dencichine: preparation, in-vitro and in-vivo evaluations, and investigation of the permeation mechanism. Int J Pharm 2018;535(1–2):120–31.
[39] Tashtoush BM, Bennamani AN, Al-Taani BM. Preparation and characterization of microemulsion formulations of nicotinic acid and its prodrugs for transdermal delivery. Pharm Dev Technol 2013;18(4):834–43.
[40] Szumała P, et al. Transdermal transport of collagen and hyaluronic acid using water in oil microemulsion. Int J Pharma 2019;118738.
[41] Dave K, et al. Chemoprevention of breast cancer by transdermal delivery of alpha-santalol through breast skin and mammary papilla (nipple). Pharm Res 2017;34(9):1897–907.
[42] Lahrichi A, et al. Effects of propranolol therapy in Moroccan children with infantile hemangioma. Arch Pediatr 2018;25(8):449–51.
[43] Hu X, et al. Percutaneous absorption and brain distribution facilitation of borneol on tetramethylpyrazine in a microemulsion-based transdermal therapeutic system. Asian J Pharm Sci 2018;14(3):305–12.
[44] Hathout RM, et al. Microemulsion formulations for the transdermal delivery of testosterone. Eur J Pharm Sci 2010;40(3):188–96.
[45] Yehia R, et al. Anti-tumor efficacy of an integrated methyl dihydrojasmonate transdermal microemulsion system targeting breast cancer cells: in vitro and in vivo studies. Colloids Surf B Biointerfaces 2017;155:512–21.
[46] Spiekermann PH, Young MD. Clinical evaluation of clotrimazole. A broad-spectrum antifungal agent. Arch Dermatol 1976;112(3):350–2.
[47] Hashem FM, et al. Formulation, characterization, and clinical evaluation of microemulsion containing clotrimazole for topical delivery. AAPS Pharm Sci Tech 2011;12(3):879–86.

[48] Zhang J, Michniak-Kohn BB. Investigation of microemulsion and microemulsion gel formulations for dermal delivery of clotrimazole. Int J Pharm 2018;536(1):345–52.

[49] Kiselmann C, et al. Development of a skin-friendly microemulsion for dermal allergen-specific immunotherapy. Int J Pharm 2018;550(1–2):463–9.

[50] Xiao ZX, et al. Identification of repaglinide as a therapeutic drug for glioblastoma multiforme. Biochem Biophys Res Commun 2017;488(1):33–9.

[51] Shinde UA, Modani SH, Singh KH. Design and development of repaglinide microemulsion gel for transdermal delivery. AAPS Pharm Sci Tech 2018;19(1):315–25.

[52] Rosmarin DM, et al. Cyclosporine and psoriasis: 2008 National Psoriasis Foundation Consensus Conference. J Am Acad Dermatol 2010;62(5):838–53.

[53] Tabosa MAM, et al. Microemulsion formulations for the transdermal delivery of lapachol. AAPS PharmSciTech 2018;19(4):1837–46.

[54] Zhao L, et al. Ropivacaine loaded microemulsion and microemulsion-based gel for transdermal delivery: preparation, optimization, and evaluation. Int J Pharm 2014;477(1–2):47–56.

[55] Cao M, Ren L, Chen G. Formulation optimization and ex vivo and in vivo evaluation of celecoxib microemulsion-based gel for transdermal delivery. AAPS Pharm Sci Tech 2017;18(6):1960–71.

[56] Pescina S, et al. Microemulsions based on TPGS and isostearic acid for imiquimod formulation and skin delivery. Eur J Pharm Sci 2018;125:223–31.

Chapter 7

Prodrugs

A prodrug is a precursor of a drug that is biotransformed into an active pharmacological agent inside the body, either through a biocatalytic process or through a spontaneous mechanism such as hydrolysis [1]. Normally, a molecule (termed "promoiety") is grafted onto an active pharmaceutical ingredient (API) that will facilitate transport to a pharmacological target, after which the promoiety is eliminated to form the pharmacologically active molecule [2]. Using prodrugs can improve pharmaceutical properties such as odor, taste, chemical stability, solubility and can reduce irritation and pain as well as challenges in the formulation and production of the active pharmaceutical ingredient [3]. Furthermore, the use of prodrugs can result in the optimization of pharmacokinetic profile including the reduction or elimination of the first pass effect [3]. Significantly, therapeutic index (lower toxicity) can also be enhanced when prodrugs are utilized [3]. Prodrugs are frequently used to increase the permeability and/or solubility of a compound leading to increased transdermal permeation [4]. Reactions with sugars, polymers, amino acids, sulfuric acid, and phosphoric acid have been used to boost oral bioavailability and aqueous solubility [5].

It has been documented that 7 out of 32 molecules of the drugs that were approved for clinical use in the United States in 2015 were prodrugs. An important prodrug is sofosbuvir, the API in Harvoni, the second most selling drug in 2015 [1]. Tedizolid phosphate (Sivextro) and isavuconazonium sulfate (Cresemba) are also prodrugs that were equally approved for use [6]. The principal goal of creating a prodrug is to alter the chemical structure of a drug molecule with the aim of imparting desirable physicochemical and/or pharmacokinetic properties [4]. Albert first used the term "prodrug," but regarded the term "predrug" as more accurate [3]. Over the past several decades, numerous prodrugs have been developed, with some of them approved by regulatory authorities for clinical use. Frequently, the prodrug approach is less difficult and more feasible than creating an entirely new drug molecule with optimal properties or reformulating an existing API [6]. Prodrugs can be synthesized via bioprecursor-based or carrier-linked methods [7]. When the carrier-linked approach is used, the API is bound to a carrier moiety using a transient covalent bond. Cleavage of a carrier prodrug subsequently creates a molecule with enhanced biological activity and at least one side

Transdermal Drug Delivery. DOI: https://doi.org/10.1016/B978-0-12-822550-9.00007-7

product, the carrier, which may possess targeting properties (for instance antibodies) or are pharmacologically inert (e.g., polyethylene glycol) [7]. Carriers-linked prodrugs may be bipartite (the carrier is directly attached to the API) or tripartite (the carrier is linked to the drug through a linker) [8]. Codrugs are a subset of prodrugs comprising two drugs that are linked in a single molecule, so that each drug acts as a carrier for the other [9]. There are certain rules that guide the synthesis of carrier-linked prodrugs: the bond between the API and the carrier is normally covalent; the prodrug should be less active or inactive compared to the parent compound; the bond between the API and the carrier must disintegrate in vivo; the carrier that is liberated in the body as well as the initial prodrug itself must not be harmful; and the formation of the API must occur swiftly to ensure effective drug levels at the drug target and to keep either API inactivation or alternate prodrug metabolism pathways to the barest minimum [7].

There is no carrier group in bioprecursors (BPs). Instead, they are activated by the enzymatic biotransformation of a functional group. There is normally a molecular modification of the API. This creates a new compound that can become a substrate of the enzymes leading to the formation of metabolite (API). As an illustration, if the drug molecule possesses a carboxyl functional group, the bioprecursor may have an alcoholic functional group that is biotransformed via oxidation to form an aldehyde [7]. Subsequently the drug molecule containing a carboxylic acid group is formed. Even though biologically active metabolites are typically created via phase I reactions (oxidation, reduction, or phosphorylation), biologically active compounds can also be formed through phase II conjugation reactions. Parameters that can be changed include partition coefficient, solubility in both aqueous as well as oily phases, ionization, molecular weight, hydrogen bonding (HB), and melting point [4]. Bioprecursor-based prodrugs are usually transformed chemically into the active therapeutic agent via oxidation (e.g., dexpanthenol, nabumetone), hydration (an example is the lactone functional group in certain statins), or reduction [e.g., platinum(IV) complexes, sulindac] [10].

Sloan et al. highlighted two methods for making prodrugs—the synthesis of either a simple acyl-type derivative or a soft alkyl derivative [11]. The first type of derivative has a heteroatom, X (S, O, or N) with a hydrogen attached to it: drug–X–H. In the case of the acyl-type prodrug, drug X–H is modified to drug-X-(C=X′)R by substituting H with (C=X′)R, where R is an X-alkyl, alkyl, or aryl group and X′ is also a heteroatom (O, S, or N) [11]. A classic illustration is an ester derivative where X′=O, X–H is a hydroxyl functional group (O–H) and R is an alkyl group as observed in glucocorticoid steroid esters [11]. Alternatively, X–H may be a carboxylic acid group ([C=O]O–H), leading to the formation of an ester that is simply drug–X–R; Let us consider the case of angiotensin-converting enzyme inhibitor ester derivatives [11]. It was shown that a nucleophilic attack on the carbon of the polarized C=O (or C=X′) results in the formation of a tetrahedral intermediate that releases drug−X−, which is in a balance with drug−X−H at the pH of 7.4. The next type of derivative is a soft alkyl molecule. Soft alkyl derivatives feature a CHR′−X″ functional group between drug−X and an acyl group ([C=O]R): drug−X−CHR′−X″(C=X′)R where R′ is defined as R and X″ has similar definition as X or X′[11].

The soft alkyl derivative is subjected to hydrolysis/metabolism like simple acyl derivatives do, the difference being that a drug−X−CHR′X″− intermediate is released after nucleophilic attack on the polarized C=X′. The intermediate spontaneously breaks down into CHR′=X″ and drug−X−, which is in equilibrium with drug−X−H at pH 7.4 [11]. N′Da has also described two derivatization routes for making prodrugs: (1) synthesis of ethers, carbamates, esters, and carbonates via PEGylation. These derivatives are imbued with more optimal physicochemical features and can easily permeate the skin in comparison to the parent drug (2) boosting lipophilicity via the lengthening of the alkyl chain [12]. Certain functional groups such as carbonyls, phosphates/phosphonates, carboxylic acids, amines, and hydroxyls can easily be used to create prodrugs [13]. The groups typically used to protect these functional groups are esters, carbonates, carbamates, amides, phosphates, and oximes [13]. Thioethers and thioesters have also been utilized for the protection of imines and thiols while *N*-Mannich bases can protect amines [13]. Several polar groups are required for drugs to bind to receptors but these functional groups may also restrict the drug from crossing membranes [7]. This phenomenon is observed with carboxylic acid groups. One method of solving this problem is to mask the acid group through the creation of a less polar ester [7]. An ester can permeate lipophilic membranes and when it reaches the bloodstream, hydrolysis of the molecule into the parent acid drug will occur. There is a vast array of ester prodrugs in the scientific literature and these molecules can be utilized to mask phosphate, carboxylate, and tetrazole groups [7]. Esters are normally used because of the simplicity of synthesis as well as their ability to mask the charge on phosphates, carboxylic acids, and other functional groups [13]. Once in the body, esters are readily hydrolyzed by esterases to a carboxylic acid and an alcohol. Human carboxylestrase I (hCE1) is reported to have an impact on the hydrolysis of ester prodrugs. The synthesis of ester derivatives represents an important method of increasing drug permeation through the skin, as esters tend to possess optimal membrane permeability due to their higher lipophilicity [14].

There are several serine-type esterases in the human skin and these enzymes act on a variety of exogenous substrates such as 4-methyl umbelliferyl heptanoate, ketoprofen ethyl ester, and diester prednicarbate [15]. The capacity of stratum corneum (SC) to hydrolyze xenobiotics has a marked influence on the half-life of esters. Prodrugs crossing the SC may be subject to enzymatic reactions such as epoxidation and hydroxylation within the dermis and the viable epidermis [15]. Esters can be used either as antedrugs or prodrugs [14]. Ester derivatives that are employed as prodrugs are essentially chemically altered drug substances with less potent therapeutic action. On the contrary, antedrugs are therapeutically active molecules that are transformed to less active or inactive end-products in the bloodstream, thereby circumventing adverse effects [14]. An example of an ester-type prodrug is the drug oseltamivir that is a neuraminidase inhibitor used for the management of influenza [16,17]. Ester-type prodrugs can be easily designed and synthesized cost effectively since they possess good chemical stability and simple structures. A significant limitation is that certain esters are not subject to enzymatic breakdown in vivo by esterases, or the rates of disintegration are exceedingly slow [16]. One way of tackling this challenge is to use enzyme-activated prodrug with a breakable bond, as exemplified by candesartan cilexetil (a prodrug of candesartan), pivampicillin (a prodrug of ampicillin), and olmesartan medoxomil (a prodrug of olmesartan) [16]. They can be quickly biotransformed into parent drugs in two stages: initial esterase-driven hydrolysis and then a spontaneous breakdown of the linker [16]. These esters possess increased oral bioavailability due to high lipophilicity.

The second approach entails changing the hydroxyl functional group that is present in many drug molecules. Certain prodrugs have cleavable moieties like organic acids, amino acids, sugars, and phosphates that are covalently linked to the hydroxyl functional group of parent drugs; these derivatives can then be easily metabolized by esterase, alkaline phosphatase, peptidase, sugar digesting, and other enzymes [16]. Drug solubility can be improved via the prodrug approach. A common approach entails the incorporation of certain ionizable groups, such as hemisuccinate, phosphate, or amino acid esters into a poorly water-soluble drug or conjugation to neutral molecules like polyethylene glycol [7]. Several phosphate or phosphate-based prodrugs, incorporated through linkers or directly conjugated to a molecule, have been utilized to increase aqueous solubility of numerous compounds [7].

Earlier prodrug approaches were based on the postulate that the skin, and more specifically the SC, constitutes a lipid barrier and that dermal and transdermal drug delivery can be enhanced by making increasingly more lipophilic prodrugs (analogs or homologs) [18]. The current thinking is that the intercellular multilamellar bilayers that constitute that skin barrier comprise alternating aqueous and lipid phases even though the SC is principally a lipid barrier [18]. A skin permeant must cross both phases and so a prodrug must be imbued with adequate lipid and water solubilities, or a balance of the two [18].

Skin delivery of siRNA with prodrugs

There are many benefits associated with the skin delivery of siRNA such as the powerful knockdown of disease symptoms, direct access to the diseased site, and limited off-target effects [19]. Nonetheless, transporting siRNA into skin is challenging. Over the years, several attempts have been made to facilitate an efficient transport of topical siRNA. Recently, Zakrewsky et al. suggested the use of RNAi conjugated to ionic liquid moieties (robed-siRNA) [19]. The authors prepared robed-siRNA via a scalable and simple, two-step method that can be used to fine-tune biocompatibility, cell internalization, skin penetration, and other physicochemical properties [19]. The authors synthesized the ionic liquid-based prodrugs from benzyl dimethyl alkyl ammoniums with three different alkyl chains: tetradecyl (BDTA), octyl (BDOA), and stearyl (BDSA) [19]. Various siRNA sequences were utilized including a matrix metalloproteinase-12 (MMP-12) knockdown sequence (siRNA3), two glyceraldehyde-3-phosphate dehydrogenase (GAPDH) knockdown sequences (siRNA1 and siRNA2) as well as a nonsilencing control siRNA sequence (siRNA4) [19]. Using this approach, the authors detected one robed-siRNA [benzyl dimethyl octyl ammonium (BDOA)-siRNA] with good skin penetrability as well as the capacity to increase cell internalization in comparison with naked siRNA [19].

Significantly, the transcutaneous permeation of siRNA1 increased significantly when it was robed with ionic liquid moieties [19]. The percentage of the administered dose transported into the viable epidermis was 9.60 ± 2.85, 9.85 ± 2.64, and 7.33 ± 0.24 for BDTA-, BDOA-, and BDSA-siRNA1 in comparison with 2.06 ± 0.15 for unrobed siRNA1 [19]. In the same manner, the percentage of administered dose transported into the dermis was 8.89 ± 0.77 and 12.94 ± 2.56 for BDSA- and BDOA-siRNA1 in comparison with 2.26 ± 1.16 for naked siRNA1 [19]. Intriguingly, the percentage of the administered dose transported into the dermis was less (0.49 ± 0.18) when siRNA1 was conjugated to BDTA [19]. It is noteworthy that BDOA-siRNA induced significant protein knockdown in human skin tissues and cell culture [19]. BDOA-siRNA also prevented the breakdown of elastin in the skin after exposing the tissue to ultraviolet B rays. All in all, the data from these authors showed that therapeutic siRNA protected with ionic liquids may be beneficial for the management of skin diseases [19].

Skin transport of bioengineered carboxymethyl cellulose-doxorubicin prodrugs

Globally, about 17.5 million new cases of cancer were recorded in 2015 and the disease is characterized by high mortality and morbidity rates [20]. It has been estimated that the number of new cases of cancer may increase by 70% during the next 20 years [20]. Doxorubicin (Dox) is an anthracycline antibiotic with a broad antitumor spectrum and it has been utilized either for monotherapy or in conjunction with other antitumor medications for the management of different types of tumors [20]. Regrettably, the use of Dox for therapy is hampered by its less than optimal pharmacokinetic profile

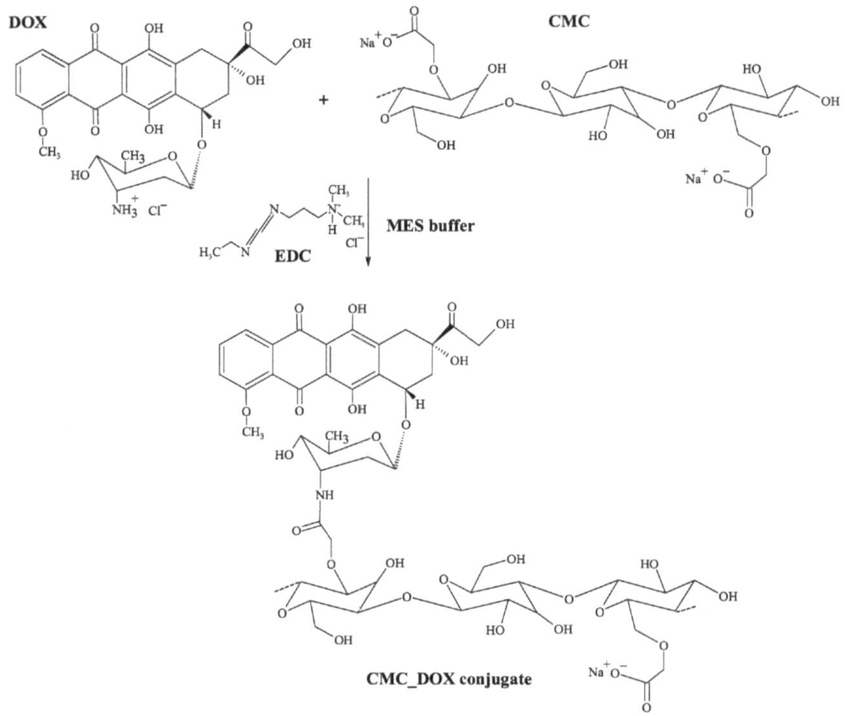

FIGURE 7.1 The precursors, reaction, and carboxymethyl cellulose-doxorubicin conjugate product. *Reproduced with permission from Capanema NSV, et al. Bioengineered carboxymethyl cellulose-doxorubicin prodrug hydrogels for topical chemotherapy of melanoma skin cancer. Carbohydr Polym 2018;195:401–12.*

including short half-life, high volume of distribution, low bioavailability, rapid distribution, and excretion [20]. Recently, Capanema and coworkers synthesized a novel prodrug from carboxymethylcellulose (CMC) and doxorubicin hydrochloride (DOX) by linking both moieties via covalent amide bonds [21]. DOX was linked to CMC via 1-ethyl-3-[3-dimethylamino-propyl] carbodiimide hydrochloride (EDC) that served as the coupling agent [21]. The authors used citric acid (CA) as a cross-linker to create CMC-DOX bioconjugates that were ultimately used to form two-dimensional hydrogels against skin cancer cells [21]. The release profiles of the two CMC-DOX conjugates with the degree of substitution 1.22 (CMC-1.22_DOX_CA) and 0.77 (CMC-0.77_DOX_CA) were characterized by an initial burst in the first 60 min followed by a continuous release up to 24 h (1440 min) [21]. The cumulative release of the drug from the prodrug hydrogels CMC-1.22_DOX_CA and CMC-0.77_DOX_CA was 25% ± 2% and 18% ± 2%, respectively [21]. The precursors, reaction, and carboxymethyl cellulose-doxorubicin conjugate product are shown in Fig. 7.1.

Remarkably, there was no statistically significant difference between the cell viability response for free DOX in normal or cancer cells [21]. Nonetheless, cell viability response was 3.3-fold and 4.5-fold delayed for CMC-DOX with DS 1.22 and 0.77, respectively, for A375 melanoma cells, 5.0-fold (CMC-1.22_DOX_AC) and 6.9-fold delayed (CMC-0.77_DOX_AC) for HEK 293 T cells [21]. The authors ascribed the delayed effect of toxicity documented for CMC-DOX conjugate hydrogels to the physicochemical properties (the presence of amide bonds between DOX and CMC) of the conjugates. This necessitates cleavage inside each specific cell line for the release of the parent compound [21].

The effect of ester promoieties on the percutaneous transport of ketorolac

Ester promoieties can impact the skin transport profiles of drugs [22]. Liu et al. investigated heptyl (KH), diketorolac heptyl (DKH), benzyl (KB), and tert-butyl (KT) prodrugs of ketorolac [22]. The carboxylic acid functional group in the molecule of the parent drug was used to form esters. The transport of ketorolac and its prodrugs across nude mouse skin was determined by the authors. Log K values followed the order: ketorolac < KT < KB < KH < DKH. Molecular modeling was also utilized for the prediction of partition coefficients (A log P) of ketorolac and its prodrugs. Predictably, the ester derivatives were more lipophilic than ketorolac [22]. Because there was prodrug hydrolysis during skin transport studies, the flux was calculated as the sum of the prodrug and ketorolac molecules in the receptor chamber. The transdermal flux of ketorolac was 3.24 $nmol/cm^2/h$ while a low skin accumulation of 0.36 nmol/mg was also observed. Of all the compounds investigated, KT had the highest permeation. The transdermal flux of KT was 8.21 $nmol/cm^2/h$ with an enhancement ratio of 2.5 in comparison with the parent compound [22]. The flux of KB was 6.63 $nmol/cm^2/h$ and this was slightly less compared to KT. KH and DKH displayed decreased skin transport that was 4-fold and 12-fold less compared to ketorolac, respectively. The proportion of the parent compound in the receptor compartment was 40%, 21%, 37%, and 23% for KT, KB, KH, and DKH, respectively. As observed for their flux values, KT and KB displayed the highest deposition in the skin. The skin uptake of all the ester derivatives was higher compared to the parent drug [22].

Percutaneous penetration of apomorphine prodrugs

Apomorphine is a β-phenylethylamine that structurally resembles the neurotransmitter dopamine because of the presence of a catechol moiety in both molecules [23]. The drug is a chiral molecule with the S-form of the molecule possessing antidopaminergic activity and the R-form being a dopamine agonist [23]. The clinical efficacy of apomorphine has been linked to its action on D1, D5, D2, D3, and D4 dopamine receptors [24]. Motor fluctuations that are refractory to conventional drug therapy are one of the most challenging features of advanced stages of Parkinson's disease [25]. These fluctuations can be managed with apomorphine administered in the form of bolus or subcutaneous injections [25,26]. But administering apomorphine orally to patients with advanced Parkinson's disease is often unsuccessful because high doses that are needed due to presystemic metabolism and high oral doses of apomorphine can lead to nephrotoxicity and gastrointestinal complications [27]. To address these challenges, Liu et al. synthesized diisobutyryl apomorphine (DIA) and diacetyl apomorphine (DAA)—diester prodrugs of apomorphine [27]. Apomorphine esters were synthesized via two hydroxyl groups present in the apomorphine molecule. Isobutyryl and acetyl moieties were used to create the prodrugs.

The transdermal delivery of apomorphine and its prodrugs across nude mouse dorsal skin was studied [27]. The authors investigated the percutaneous transport of DIA, DAA, apomorphine base, and apomorphine HCl. Mineral oil, 30% aqueous solution of glycerol, and 30% PEG400 in water were the vehicles used for the experiments. The authors found intact ester in the receptor compartment together with different quantities of the parent compound. The cumulative amounts of apomorphine and the prodrug were combined in molar units since prodrug degradation occurs during transport into and through the skin. It was reported that transdermal delivery was enhanced in the following order: DIA > DAA > apomorphine HCl > apomorphine base [27]. The transcutaneous transport following the use of these prodrugs was ascribed to their lipophilicity and modest water solubility [27]. DIA was used as an aqueous suspension due to its low solubility. DIA had a transdermal flux of 51 nmol/cm^2/h in water and this was 10-fold higher compared with apomorphine HCl. When other vehicles such as PEG400 and glycerol were used for the experiments, a similar trend was documented. The authors did not find any compound in the receptor solution following the transport of apomorphine base and apomorphine HCl from PEG400 [27].

Skin delivery of polymer conjugated prodrug of all-trans retinoic acid

All-trans retinoic acid (ATRA) modulates cytokine production and blocks NOS2 expression thus downregulating in vitro NO production [28]. Castleberry and colleagues recently reported a prodrug approach based on the covalent bonding of the drug to polyvinyl alcohol (PVA) that leads to the synthesis of an amphipathic nanomaterial that is soluble in water [29]. The PVA-ATRA prodrug (PATRA) accumulates in the skin leading to a prolonged delivery of ATRA [29]. The authors studied the retention, uptake, and permeation of ATRA in porcine skin via Franz diffusion cell experiments. The concentration of ATRA was measured in both the deposition and penetration every 4 h using a UV absorbance analytical technique. Sustained release of the compound was shown in vitro for over 10 days without decreased pharmacological activity over that period. Following hydration, PATRA nanofibers are formed and these subsequently self-assemble into nanoparticles [29]. Retention and uptake of the prodrug increased remarkably compared with the free ATRA in experiments with porcine skin, and PATRA also accumulated within skin epidermis [29]. There was a markedly higher deposition of PATRA within porcine skin compared to the free ATRA. Following 12 h of experiments, about 8.2% ± 1.1% of PATRA was deposited in the treated skin in comparison to 1.9% ± 0.9% when free ATRA was used. Furthermore, the use of PATRA in animal experiments resulted in a significant decrease in gross inflammation as well as a decrease in histological symptoms of inflammation in comparison with the free ATRA [29].

Skin delivery of naproxen prodrugs

Skin transport of nonsteroidal antiinflammatory drugs (NSAIDs) is hampered by the efficient barrier properties of the skin and poor physicochemical properties of most drugs leading to inadequate transdermal flux [9]. Several approaches have been made to enhance skin transport one of which is the prodrug method [9]. Rautio and coworkers investigated piperazinyl and morpholinyl prodrugs of naproxen for skin delivery [30]. The parent compound was formed following enzymatic hydrolysis of the prodrugs. In transport experiments carried out with human skin in vitro, the transdermal flux of the parent drug was 6.5 and 1.6 $nmol/cm^2/h$ from a saturated aqueous buffer with the pH of 7.4 and 5.0, respectively [30]. The use of two piperazinyl prodrugs (2-(4-methyl-1-piperazinyl)ethyl-2-(6-methoxy-2-naphthyl)propanoate and 4-(4-methyl-1-piperazinyl)butyl-2-(6-methoxy-2-naphthyl)propanoate) led to a nine and fourfold increase in percutaneous transport at pH 7.4, respectively, in comparison with naproxen. When 2-(4-methyl-1-piperazinyl)ethyl-2-(6-methoxy-2-naphthyl)propanoate was used, there was a significant (fourfold) increase in transdermal delivery at pH 5.0 in comparison with naproxen [30].

Transdermal delivery of natrexone prodrugs

Naltrexone is used for the therapy of a variety of inflammatory disorders in many organ systems [31]. The drug is also used for the therapy of opioid use disorder, a chronic, relapsing condition that affects many people globally [32]. Naltrexone binds to the brain's receptors thus inhibiting the effect of opioids [32]. Thus the drug can be used to prevent relapse following opioid withdrawal [32]. Orally administered NTX is subject to substantial presystemic metabolism (60%–95%) leading to a lower proportion of the active pharmaceutical ingredient in the bloodstream for pharmacological action

[33]. *N,N*-dialkyl carbamate and *N*-monoalkyl prodrugs of naltrexone (NTX) were prepared and in vitro transport studies of these compounds across human skin were conducted [33]. All *N*-monoalkyl carbamates displayed higher transdermal delivery rates in comparison to the parent compound while *N,N*-dialkyl carbamates displayed comparable or less flux than the parent drug [33]. The permeation rate increase for *N*-monoalkyl carbamates declined marginally with increased alkyl chain length and that was comparable to trends documented in studies involving straight-chain carboxylate ester prodrugs of NTX [33]. A larger proportion of prodrug biotransformation to the parent compound within the skin seemed to be associated with enhanced skin flux. *N*-monoalkyl carbamate prodrugs were less stable in a buffer and in plasma compared to *N,N*-Dialkyl carbamate prodrugs [33].

Transcutaneous permeation of haloperidol prodrugs

About 21 million people suffer from schizophrenia globally and it constitutes the third most disabling disease of the central nervous system with a global cost of 23.7 million disability-adjusted life years [34]. Haloperidol is synthesized from butyrophenone and utilized for management of schizophrenia [35]. The drug possesses affinity to several cerebral and extracerebral receptors such as sigma, muscarinic M1, histamine H1, alpha adrenergic, serotonin 5HT2, and dopamine D2 receptors [35]. Morris and coworkers synthesized decyl (HD), octyl (HO), butyl (HB), propyl (HP), Ethyl (HE) O-acyl esters of haloperidol (HA) and investigated their transport across guinea pig and full-thickness human skin [36]. The penetration of HA across guinea pig skin was reported to be higher than that of its prodrugs [36]. Only the derivative with the least molecular weight (HE) was transported across the skin considerably. Low concentrations of HB and HP were found in the receptor solution, whereas HD and HO transport was not detectable [36]. The HA penetration curve was flat toward the end of the transport study as the drug concentration was close to 40% of the saturation solubility. The permeation rate of HA was thus computed by utilizing data from the first 24 h only [36].

Skin delivery of fexofenadine prodrugs

Imai et al. used the prodrug approach to investigate the percutaneous penetration of fexofenadine (FXD), a lipophilic and nonsedating antihistamine medication [14]. The drug has a molecular weight of 502, which points to the possibility of slow transport into and across the skin. FXD is an amphiphilic molecule with piperidino (pKa 9.53) and carboxyl (pKa 4.25) groups with an isoelectric point of 6.9. The solubility of the drug is 294 mM in pH 7.4 phosphate buffer and log PC is 0.31 [14]. To enhance the partition of FXD into the SC, the authors synthesized a prodrug (ethyl-FXD) in which an ethyl group was used to substitute the carboxyl group of FXD. The in vitro transdermal delivery across rat-stripped and full-thickness skin was conducted at 32°C. The authors determined the steady-state flux and lag time of FXD and the values were 11.1 ± 3.84 pmol/(h cm^2) and 3.73 ± 0.135 h, respectively. The cumulative quantity of FXD that was transported over 12 h was 74.5 ± 27.7 pmol/cm^2 [14].

The concentrations of the drug were 292 ± 73.4 and 5160 ± 389 nmol/g tissue in the viable skin and SC, respectively. When stripped skin was used for experiments, the percutaneous transport of FXD was significantly enhanced. The cumulative quantity that was transported in 12 h was $16{,}000 \pm 2300$ pmol/cm^2, which was 215 times higher than the quantity detected in full-thickness skin while the steady-state flux of FXD was 1920 ± 590 pmol/(h cm^2) [14]. Intriguingly, ethyl-FXD was not found in the receptor solution during the percutaneous penetration study; only FXD formed via enzymatic hydrolysis was detected in the receptor solution when stripped and full-thickness skin samples were used. FXD was not found in the donor solution after 12 h of the penetration through either stripped or full-thickness skin. The cumulative amount of FXD that was transported across the skin and steady-state flux values were 269 ± 54.4 pmol/cm^2 and 36.2 ± 8.29 pmol/(h cm^2), respectively [14]. The permeability coefficient (Kp) was $652 \pm 201 \times 10^{-5}$ cm/h in stripped skin, and that was 180 times higher compared to full-thickness skin ($3.60 \pm 1.21 \times 10^{-5}$ cm/h) [14].

Even though the concentration of ethyl-FXD suspension was approximately 1/40 compared to that of the FXD solution because of low drug solubility, the steady-state flux and cumulative amount of the drug in the receptor solution were 3.2 and 3.6 times higher, respectively, when ethyl-FXD rather than the parent compound was used for the experiments [14]. The Kp value of ethyl-FXD was $419 \pm 83.0 \times 10^{-5}$ cm/h, and that was similar to that of the parent compound administered to stripped skin. The concentrations of FXD and ethyl-FXD were 11.8 ± 3.64 380 ± 114 nmol/g tissue, respectively, in viable skin. The concentration of the parent drug found in the SC (421 ± 74.1 nmol/g tissue) was 35-fold higher than in viable skin [14]. The cumulative amount found after 12 h (671 ± 121 pmol/cm^2) and the steady-state flux (82.3 ± 8.66 pmol/(h cm^2)) in stripped skin were 2.5 times and 2.3 higher, respectively, than the corresponding values achieved with full-thickness skin. Be that as it may, the concentrations of ethyl-FXD and the parent compound in viable skin were not significantly different from those in full-thickness skin [14]. The lag times reported following the application of ethyl-FXD to full-thickness skin and stripped skin were 4.58 ± 1.03 and 3.95 ± 0.68 h, respectively. The data demonstrated that the influence of SC stripping was significantly less when ethyl-FXD was administered compared to the parent drug [14].

Prodrugs of phenolic compounds

Plant phenolics are antioxidants that can be incorporated into dermatological formulations [15]. Tyrosol hydroxytyrosol esters were prepared from decanoic and lipoic acids. Correspondingly, several ferulic acid esters (a long-chain acyl ester or glycerides) were utilized to study the likelihood that these molecules will undergo enzymatic hydrolysis. Hydroxytyrosol and tyrosol possess a side primary alcohol functional group as well as phenolic hydroxyl groups [15]. Either of two medium-chain length fatty acids (lipoic acid or decanoic acid) was used to esterify the primary alcohol group. The thiolane group of lipoic acid creates a bulky component at the end of the acyl group [15]. Solutions of the investigated compounds were placed on top of skin samples and incubated for 4 h at 34C [15]. Hydrolysis products and substrates were recovered from treated pig skin explants with chloroform/methanol extracts. Pig skin homogenate, microemulsions of tyrosol, and hydroxytyrosol derivatives as well as soy phosphatidylcholine liposomes were used to study skin homogenate and intact skin hydrolytic activities [15]. It was reported that extracted esterases hydrolyzed the esters in the microemulsion in the following order: tyrosyl lipoate > tyrosyl decanoate > hydroxytyrosyl lipoate > hydroxytyrosyl decanoate. Furthermore, tyrosyl decanoate underwent relatively moderate hydrolysis (10%–30% after 24 h) when loaded into liposomes, whereas hydroxytyrosyl decanoate in liposomes did not undergo hydrolysis at all in the skin extract. The esters synthesized from ferulic acid did not undergo hydrolysis by the extract in aqueous buffer, liposome, or microemulsion [15]. The authors concluded that the rate at which phenolic esters underwent hydrolysis by skin esterases was a function of the structure of the ester as well as the composition of the formulation utilized to transport the derivatives into the skin. Alkanoic esters of hydroxytyrosol and tyrosol underwent hydrolysis by skin esterases when formulated as an anionic microemulsion, but remained mostly unchanged when formulated into cationic liposomes [15].

Polyoxyethylene esters as prodrugs of selected nonsteroidal antiinflammatory drugs for transdermal delivery

Polyoxyethylene esters of naproxen, ketoprofen, and diclofenac were synthesized by using a succinic acid spacer to conjugate these drugs to polyoxyethylene glycols [37]. The percutaneous permeation of these esters across human skin was investigated in vitro. In addition, the authors studied the topical antiinflammatory effect of these esters, by examining the capacity of these molecules to suppress methyl nicotinate (MN)-engendered skin erythema in healthy humans [37]. The authors observed that all the esters substantially enhanced the cumulative quantity of the parent drug that was transported across the skin [37]. Moreover, a greater cumulative amount of drug that crossed the skin was documented only for naproxen, ketoprofen, and diclofenac esters compared to the parent drug [37]. The reported solubilities and fluxes demonstrated that the most permeable derivatives were those that possessed both an adequate lipophilicity and aqueous solubility compared to the parent compound. Some of the esters exhibited a significant and prolonged antiinflammatory activity in humans in comparison to the parent drugs [37].

Transdermal delivery of phenylalanyl-glycine prodrugs

Several researchers have studied the influence of prodrugs on the transcutaneous delivery of peptides. Yamamoto and coworkers prepared three lipophilic prodrugs of phenylalanyl-glycine (C6-Phe-Gly, C4-Phe-Gly, C8-Phe-Gly) by conjugating the peptides with caproic acid (C6), butyric acid (C4), and octanoic acid (C8) [38]. The influence of acylation on the permeability, stability, and deposition of Phe-Gly in the skin was evaluated. The authors conducted transport studies with Phe-Gly and its acyl derivatives. Phe-Gly broke down rapidly in the skin homogenate. Conversely, acyl-Phe-Gly prodrugs exhibited more chemical stability compared to Phe-Gly. Nonetheless, the study did not reveal any significant difference in the stability of acyl-Phe-Gly derivatives. Phe-Gly itself was not found in the receptor chamber across intact skin. However, C6-Phe-Gly, C4-Phe-Gly, and C8-Phe-Gly were transported across intact skin, and C6-Phe-Gly displayed the highest permeability.

The cumulative quantities of C6-Phe-Gly, C4-Phe-Gly, and C8-Phe-Gly transported after 24 h were approximately 4%, 2.5%, and 2% of the applied dose, respectively [38]. The transport of these compounds through stripped rat skin was also evaluated. In general, the transport of Phe-Gly and its acyl derivatives across stripped skin was significantly greater compared to intact skin. The transport of acyl derivatives was lower than that of Phe-Gly during the initial phase of the transdermal experiments, but was higher than that of Phe-Gly during the later phase of the study [38]. Conversely, a metabolite of Phe-Gly (phenylalanine) was found in stripped skin experiments. The cumulative quantity of each of the acyl-Phe-Gly derivatives that permeated stripped skin after 6 h was approximately 50% [38]. Conversely, the cumulative amount of native Phe-Gly that permeated stripped skin after 6 h was approximately 30%. Interestingly, when the authors used ethanol to pretreat the skin, the percutaneous transport of native Phe-Gly was greater compared to the acyl derivatives. This was attributed by the authors to the inactivation of the skin peptidases responsible for Phe-Gly degradation [38].

Skin permeation of atenolol and propranolol esters

Anroop et al. synthesized and evaluated the transdermal delivery of esters of propranolol and atenolol [39]. Propanolol caproate and propanolol capriate, atenolol capriate, and atenolol caproate were prepared by adding alkyl pendant chains to the β-hydroxy functional group of the drugs with the aim of increasing their log P values [39]. In vitro transdermal drug delivery experiments in excised mice skin demonstrated that the prodrugs are easily transported transdermally compared to the respective parent drugs and marked flux increase (6.2-fold) was reported for both drugs. Atenolol capriate (C10 side chain) displayed the highest permeability coefficient while propranolol caproate ester (C6 side chain) showed the highest permeability coefficient. The authors postulated that the dissimilarity in permeability may be due to intrinsic lipophilicity differences [39].

For a prodrug to be therapeutically useful, it has to be converted into the parent compound. In another study by Anroop et al., minimal amount of prodrugs were detected in the receiver compartment (physiological saline) in permeation experiments [40]. As enzyme activity is considerably high in viable epidermis and dermis layers of the skin, accelerated breakdown in the receiver fluid and enzymatic conversion was observed as a plausible explanation [40]. The authors carried out permeation studies by delivering the drug and prodrugs from a donor vehicle consisting of 20% ethanol-acetate buffer (pH 4). In general, permeation rate increased proportionally with increase in the length of alkyl side chain (addition of up to five carbon units). The addition of more carbon units did not lead to the exhibition of any specific pattern [40]. The cumulative amount permeated after 6 h decreased in the following pattern: atenolol valerate > butyrate > capriate > propionate > caproate > acetate > atenolol [40]. Atenolol capriate the prodrug with highest lipophilicity showed moderate benefit in terms of flux. Atenolol valerate (20 mM) recorded the highest flux (1.36 $\mu mol/cm^2/h$) and caused a fourfold flux enhancement in going from a donor concentration of 5–20 mM [40].

The transcutaneous penetration of theophylline prodrugs

Majumdar and coworkers synthesized two classes of theophylline (Th-H) derivatives with ethyleneoxy functional groups [41]. The first was an acyl derivative in which methoxyethyleneoxycarbonyl chlorides were employed to acylate Th-H [41]. In the second type, *N*-methyl-*N*-methoxyethyleneoxycarbonylaminomethyl chlorides were used to alkylate Th-H [41]. These derivatives were more soluble in isopropyl myristate (IPM) than the parent compound, and three of the prodrugs displayed more aqueous solubilities than Th-H [41]. When the prodrug with the highest aqueous solubility was used for permeation experiments, the authors recorded the maximum transport of all chemical species containing Th-H through hairless mouse skin from IPM (maximum flux, J_{MMIPM})—more than seven times that of the parent compound whereas the other two prodrugs produced a maximum flux that was more than three times that of Th-H [41]. The acyl-type prodrugs transported only Th-H, whereas the soft alkyl Th-H transported 60%–70% of Th-H and the unchanged prodrug. The introduction of ethyleneoxy groups into both acyl-type and soft alkyl prodrugs enhanced water and lipid solubilities particularly when two ethyleneoxy groups were introduced into the molecules [41].

Transdermal delivery of acyclic nucleoside phosphonates

Acyclic nucleoside phosphonates display broad-spectrum antiviral activity; examples are adefovir, cidofovir, and tenofovir [42]. 9-[2-(phosphonomethoxy) ethyl]guanine (PMEG) is a nucleoside phosphonate with antiproliferative effect but its therapeutic value is constrained by significant toxicity and low cellular permeability [42]. These limitations were partially circumvented by using the prodrug N^6-cyclopropyl2,6-diamino-9-[2-(phosphonomethoxy)ethyl]purine (cPr-PMEDAP) [42]. The properties of cPr-PMEDAP were initially investigated through pig skin, which is a widely accepted model of the human skin. The transdermal flux of 1% cPr-PMEDAP through full-thickness pig skin was low, with values ranging from 0.3 ± 0.1 μg/cm^2/h at pH 4 to 1.6 ± 0.8 μg/cm^2/h at pH 8 [42]. The amount of cPr-PMEDAP deposited in the skin ranged from 180 ± 39 μg/g of the tissue at pH 3 to 346 ± 64 μg/g at pH 7. When the pH was increased to 8, the dermal content of cPr-PMEDAP declined, but these differences were not statistically significant [42]. When human skin was utilized in subsequent experiments, the transport of cPr-PMEDAP into the receptor chamber decreased [42]. The human SC was a more efficient barrier against the transport of hydrophilic phosphonate compared to pig skin, with percutaneous flux values ranging from 38 to 44 ng/cm^2/h, which correlates with 32 μg of cPr-PMEDAP being transported from a 30 cm^2 patch during 24 h period [42]. The authors incorporated chemical penetration enhancers to increase percutaneous flux values [42].

Percutaneous transport of thalidomide prodrugs

Thalidomide (TDE) blocks the synthesis and expression of several cytokines like granulocyte macrophage colony-stimulating factor (GM-CSF), tumor necrosis factor-α, interleukin-6 (IL-6), and interleukin-1β (IL-1β) [43]. TDE displays antiangiogenic, immunomodulatory, antiinflammatory, and anti-vascular endothelial growth factor (VEGF) effects [44]. The drug has been used for the management of Crohn's disease, rheumatoid arthritis, and multiple myeloma [44]. Goosen et al. investigated the transcutaneous permeation of thalidomide and three of its *N*-methyl, *N*-propylyl, and *N*-pentyl analogs across human skin [45]. The authors used vertical Franz diffusion cells to perform in vitro transport studies. The steady-state flux values showed that the delivery of *N*-methyl thalidomide across human skin was higher compared to the parent molecule. However, transcutaneous fluxes skin reduced significantly from that of the methylated compound when the chain length was extended to propyl and pentyl. However, the flux values were higher than those of thalidomide, which was less than 0.025 μg/cm^2/h [45]. The *N*-methyl thalidomide also exhibited the highest water (buffer) solubility compared to thalidomide, the *N*-pentyl, and *N*-propyl derivatives. The *N*-propyl and *N*-pentyl derivatives were more lipid soluble and exhibited higher partition coefficient values than the *N*-methyl analog. Intriguingly, the *N*-methyl thalidomide, the prodrug with the highest aqueous solubility exhibited the highest skin permeability [45].

Transdermal delivery of cytarabine prodrugs

Cytarabine (Cyt) is commonly used for the management of acute lymphoblastic leukemia, acute myeloid leukemia, and other hematological tumors [46]. Legoabe et al. synthesized and investigated the skin permeability of *N*4-carbamate prodrugs of cytarabine [47]. A two-stage procedure was used for the synthesis of these derivatives. Initially, the authors activated methoxypoly(ethylene glycol) using *p*-nitrophenyl chloroformate. Subsequently, reactions of the activated intermediates with cytarabine and *N*-hydroxysuccinamide yielded *N*4-methoxypoly(ethylene glycol) carbamate prodrugs [47]. The first member of the series (cytarabine *N*4-methoxyethyleneoxycarbamate)(1) was found to have a higher flux than others [47]. Cyt *N*4-methoxydiethyleneoxycarbamate(2) and cytarabine *N*4-methoxytriethyleneoxycarbamate(3) were not found in the receiver. The skin permeability of cyt *N*4-methoxyoctaethyleneoxycarbamate (4), cyt *N*4-methoxydodecaethyleneoxycarbamate(5), and cyt *N*4-methoxyheptadecaethyleneoxycarbamate(6) was higher compared to cyt *N* 4-methoxydiethyleneoxycarbamate and cyt *N*4-methoxytriethyleneoxycarbamate even though compounds 4, 5, and 6 had higher molecular weights [47]. This report was in agreement with the findings of Bonina et al. [48] who observed that some higher molecular weight compounds of a homologous series permeated the skin in higher amounts compared to compounds with lower molecular weights [47]. Cytarabine and its carbamate prodrugs investigated in the research project by Legoabe et al. were polar with HB groups. HB groups have the tendency to reduce percutaneous transport due to interactions with the polar head groups of the intercellular lipids localized in the skin [47]. Even though the apparent molecular weights of *N*4-oligomeric ethylene carbamates (243.2−433.4 g/mol) were within the optimal range for percutaneous transport, no significant increase in transcutaneous transport of the drug was documented. This was ascribed to the fact that polyethylene glycol (PEG) moieties in solution have higher effective molecular weight (MW) due to the bonding of the oxyethylene chain with water molecules [47].

Transdermal permeation of acetylsalicylic acid prodrugs

Gerber and colleagues studied the percutaneous transport of acetylsalicylic acid (ASA) prodrugs [49]. An attempt was made to establish a correlation between flux values and certain physicochemical properties with the objective of finding out if the transdermal administration of ASA or its prodrugs will lead to the achievement of therapeutic concentrations [49]. The authors synthesized ASA derivatives by using various alcohols for the esterification of acetylsalicyloyl chloride. The distribution coefficient (log D), aqueous solubility, and transcutaneous permeation rates were measured for ASA and its derivatives. The authors also studied ex vivo transport across female human abdominal skin [49]. The water solubility of ASA (6.56 mg/ml) was greater than that of the prepared prodrugs and the log D of ASA (−0.85) was less than that of its prodrugs (ranging from −0.25 to 1.95) [49]. An inverse correlation between the log D values and aqueous solubility data was demonstrated. The experimental permeation rate of ASA (263.83 nmol/cm^2 h) was significantly greater compared to its prodrugs (from 0.12 to 136.02 nmol/cm^2 h) [49].

References

[1] Walther R, Rautio J, Zelikin AN. Prodrugs in medicinal chemistry and enzyme prodrug therapies. Adv Drug Deliv Rev 2017;118:65–77.

[2] Bildstein L, Dubernet C, Couvreur P. Prodrug-based intracellular delivery of anticancer agents. Adv Drug Deliv Rev 2011;63(1–2):3–23.

[3] Ghawanmeh AA, et al. Colchicine prodrugs and codrugs: chemistry and bioactivities. Eur J Med Chem 2018;144:229–42.

[4] Ita KB. Prodrugs for transdermal drug delivery—trends and challenges. J Drug Target 2016;24(8):671–8.

[5] Zhou M, et al. Prodrugs of triterpenoids and their derivatives. Eur J Med Chem 2017;131:222–36.

[6] Rautio J, Karkkainen J, Sloan KB. Prodrugs—recent approvals and a glimpse of the pipeline. Eur J Pharm Sci 2017;109:146–61.

[7] Abet V, et al. Prodrug approach: an overview of recent cases. Eur J Med Chem 2017;127:810–27.

[8] Lesniewska-Kowiel MA, Muszalska I. Strategies in the designing of prodrugs, taking into account the antiviral and anticancer compounds. Eur J Med Chem 2017;129:53–71.

[9] Peesa JP, et al. A perspective review on role of novel NSAID prodrugs in the management of acute inflammation. J Acute Dis 2016;5(5):364–81.

[10] Zawilska JB, Wojcieszak J, Olejniczak AB. Prodrugs: a challenge for the drug development. Pharmacol Rep 2013;65(1):1–14.

[11] Sloan KB, Devarajan-Ketha H, Wasdo SC. Dermal and transdermal delivery: prodrugs. Ther Deliv 2011;2(1):83–105.

[12] N'Da DD. Prodrug strategies for enhancing the percutaneous absorption of drugs. Molecules 2014;19(12):20780–807.

[13] Vytla D, et al. Prodrug approaches to reduce hyperexcitation in the CNS. Adv Drug Deliv Rev 2012;64(7):666–85.

[14] Imai T, et al. Expression of carboxylesterase isozymes and their role in the behavior of a fexofenadine prodrug in rat skin. J Pharm Sci 2016;105(2):714–21.

[15] Laszlo JA, et al. Phenol esterase activity of porcine skin. Eur J Pharm Biopharm 2015;89:175–81.

[16] Hamada Y. Recent progress in prodrug design strategies based on generally applicable modifications. Bioorg Med Chem Lett 2017;27(8):1627–32.

[17] Martinot M, et al. Analysis of delays in the prescription of oseltamivir in hospitals and potential for improvement. Med Mal Infect 2019;49(1):59–62.

[18] Sloan KB, Wasdo SC, Rautio J. Design for optimized topical delivery: prodrugs and a paradigm change. Pharm Res 2006;23(12):2729–47.
[19] Zakrewsky M, Mitragotri S. Therapeutic RNAi robed with ionic liquid moieties as a simple, scalable prodrug platform for treating skin disease. J Control Release 2016;242:80–8.
[20] Darwish S, et al. Synthesis and antiproliferative activities of doxorubicin thiol conjugates and doxorubicin-SS-cyclic peptide. Eur J Med Chem 2019;161:594–606.
[21] Capanema NSV, et al. Bioengineered carboxymethyl cellulose-doxorubicin prodrug hydrogels for topical chemotherapy of melanoma skin cancer. Carbohydr Polym 2018;195:401–12.
[22] Liu KS, et al. Impact of ester promoieties on transdermal delivery of ketorolac. J Pharm Sci 2014;103(3):974–86.
[23] Borkar N, Mu H, Holm R. Challenges and trends in apomorphine drug delivery systems for the treatment of Parkinson's disease. Asian J Pharm Sci 2018;13(6):507–17.
[24] Jenner P, Katzenschlager R. Apomorphine—pharmacological properties and clinical trials in Parkinson's disease. Parkinsonism Relat Disord 2016;33(Suppl 1) S13–S21.
[25] Menon R, Stacy M. Apomorphine in the treatment of Parkinson's disease. Expert Opin Pharmacother 2007;8(12):1941–50.
[26] Djamshidian A, Poewe W. Apomorphine and levodopa in Parkinson's disease: two revolutionary drugs from the 1950. Parkinsonism Relat Disord 2016;33(Suppl 1):S9–s12.
[27] Liu K-S, et al. Enhancement of transdermal apomorphine delivery with a diester prodrug strategy. Eur J Pharm Biopharmaceutics 2011;78(3):422–31.
[28] Behairi N, et al. All-trans retinoic acid (ATRA) prevents lipopolysaccharide-induced neuroinflammation, amyloidogenesis and memory impairment in aged rats. J Neuroimmunol 2016;300:21–9.
[29] Castleberry SA, et al. Polymer conjugated retinoids for controlled transdermal delivery. J Control Release 2017;262:1–9.
[30] Rautio J, et al. Piperazinylalkyl prodrugs of naproxen improve in vitro skin permeation. Eur J Pharm Sci 2000;11(2):157–63.
[31] Lee B, Elston D. The uses of naltrexone in dermatological conditions. J Am Acad Dermatol 2018;80(6):1746–52.
[32] Tompkins CNE, et al. Factors influencing recruitment to a randomised placebo-controlled trial of oral naltrexone and extended release implant naltrexone: qualitative study. JSAT 2019;99:52–60.
[33] Vaddi HK, et al. Human skin permeation of 3-O-alkyl carbamate prodrugs of naltrexone. J Pharm Sci 2009;98(8):2611–25.
[34] Ita K. Percutaneous transport of psychotropic agents. J Drug Deliv Sci Technol 2017;39:247–59.
[35] Vesely P, et al. Haloperidol affects coupling between QT and RR intervals in guinea pig isolated heart. J Pharmacol Sci 2019;139(1):23–8.
[36] Morris AP, Brain KR, Heard CM. Skin permeation and ex vivo skin metabolism of O-acyl haloperidol ester prodrugs. Int J Pharm 2009;367(1–2):44–50.
[37] Bonina FP, et al. In vitro and in vivo evaluation of polyoxyethylene esters as dermal prodrugs of ketoprofen, naproxen and diclofenac. Eur J Pharm Sci 2001;14(2):123–34.
[38] Yamamoto A, et al. Enhanced transdermal delivery of phenylalanyl-glycine by chemical modification with various fatty acids. Int J Pharm 2003;250(1):119–28.
[39] Anroop B, et al. Synthesis and comparative skin permeability of atenolol and propranolol esters. J Drug Deliv Sci Technol 2005;15(2):187–90.

[40] Anroop B, et al. Transdermal delivery of atenolol: effect of prodrugs and iontophoresis. Curr Drug Deliv 2009;6(3):280–90.
[41] Majumdar S, Mueller-Spaeth M, Sloan KB. Prodrugs of theophylline incorporating ethyleneoxy groups in the promoiety: synthesis, characterization, and transdermal delivery. AAPS PharmSciTech 2012;13(3):853–62.
[42] Vavrova K, et al. Enhanced topical and transdermal delivery of antineoplastic and antiviral acyclic nucleoside phosphonate cPr-PMEDAP. Pharm Res 2011;28(12):3105–15.
[43] Guo P, Hu S-P. Thalidomide alleviates postoperative pain and spatial memory deficit in aged rats. Biomed Pharmacother 2017;95:583–8.
[44] Sun S, et al. Local delivery of thalidomide to inhibit neointima formation in rat model with artery injury. Pathol Res Pract 2018;214(9):1303–8.
[45] Goosen C, et al. Percutaneous delivery of thalidomide and its N-alkyl analogs. Pharm Res 2002;19(4):434–9.
[46] Liu R, et al. A preclinical evaluation of cytarabine prodrug nanofibers assembled from cytarabine-lauric acid conjugate toward solid tumors. Int J Pharm 2018;552(1):111–18.
[47] Legoabe LJ, et al. Synthesis and transdermal permeation of novel N4-methoxypoly(ethylene glycol) carbamates of cytarabine. Drug Dev Ind Pharm 2010;36(12):1477–85.
[48] Bonina FP, et al. In vitro and in vivo evaluation of polyoxyethylene indomethacin esters as dermal prodrugs. J Control Release 1995;34(3):223–32.
[49] Gerber M, et al. Synthesis and transdermal properties of acetylsalicylic acid and selected esters. Int J Pharm 2006;310(1–2):31–6.

Chapter 8

Microneedles

Microneedles (MNs) are ultra-small needles (usually less than 1000 μm) that are used to create pores in the skin and facilitate the transcutaneous delivery of medications into the bloodstream [1–4]. These micro-scaled projections are able to painlessly disrupt the stratum corneum (SC) and reach the epidermal and dermal layers facilitating drug release [5]. MN penetration into the skin has been described as a series of sequential penetrations until a maximum force is applied [6]. The human skin is viscoelastic with fluidic and fibrous segments [7]. Alterations in viscoelasticity can be caused by aging, scarring, swelling, genetic conditions affecting connective tissues, dehydration, rehydration therapy, sun exposure, and impaired heart function [7]. These changes in skin viscoelasticity can exert considerable influence on percutaneous drug transport. Mechanical loading devices are normally used to perform fracture and insertion experiments [8]. For MNs to pierce the skin without breaking, the MN fracture force must be greater than the insertion force [9]. It has been estimated that when MN tip radius is less than 12 μm, an insertion force of 0.045 N is required for one MN to penetrate the skin [10]. A displacement-force test device is typically used to measure MN insertion force while fracture force can be determined by using an axial load test station [11]. Microindenters can also be used for fracture force measurements [9]. As an example, Hartmann and coworkers utilized a spherical indenter to administer load directly onto the tip of a single MN [10]. The authors reported average initial crack fracture forces between 1.341 ± 0.443 and 1.823 ± 0.455 N [10]. The theoretically estimated insertion pressure needed to pierce the skin is 3.183×10^6 Pa [2,9]. It has also been reported in the literature that metal MNs possessing a tip radius of approximately 30 and 80 μm require insertion forces of 0.08 and 3.04 N, respectively, for effective skin piercing [9,11,12]. Indeed, there is an equation which shows the relationship between insertion force and the MN tip area [9,13]:

$$F_i(N) = 0.00012 \times A\left(\mu\text{m}^2\right) \tag{8.1}$$

where A is the cross-sectional area of the MN tip in μm^2 and F_i is the insertion force in Newton.

An MN-based transdermal drug delivery approach combines the traditional transdermal patch application experience with injection-like drug

Transdermal Drug Delivery. DOI: https://doi.org/10.1016/B978-0-12-822550-9.00008-9

delivery [14]. Considered as a hybrid between the transdermal patch and the hypodermic needle, MNs have transformed transdermal and intradermal drug delivery research [15]. MNs with their peculiar features have the potential to enhance the range of transdermally administered medications currently delivered via other routes of administration [16]. MNs can be fabricated from various materials including stainless steel, ceramic, polymers, silicon, titanium, glass, silk, or sugars [4,17,18]. The obvious benefit of MNs is that they possess adequate length to cross the SC but are too short to stimulate nociceptors in the dermis [18–20]. Besides painlessness [21] and minimal invasiveness [22], the use of MNs can lead to improved patient compliance [23,24], increased drug bioavailability [22], the potential for self-vaccination [25], reduced risk of infection [26], and the ease of disposal [27]. Despite this array of benefits, there are also several disadvantages associated with the utilization of MNs for drug delivery. Problems with dosing accuracy may be encountered as the drug may escape or may penetrate the skin at different rates if the device is not properly held [28]. In addition, there is interindividual variability in the thickness of the SC and other skin layers and this can affect transdermal delivery rates following the application of MNs [28]. Furthermore, hydration can impact transcutaneous drug penetration and the MN tip may break off under certain circumstances [28]. MNs also need to be administered with adequate force to avoid breaking or bending before insertion [29]. Another disadvantage is that MNs can cause skin irritation and in some cases allergy [29]. Nevertheless, there is tremendous enthusiasm in the utilization of MNs for transcutaneous flux enhancement over the last 20 years. There are five categories of MNs [4]: solid MNs [30,31], hollow microneedles (HMNs) [32,33], hydrogel-forming microneedles (HFMNs) [34,35], DMNs [1,36–38], and coated microneedles (CMNs) [39,40]. Distinct types of MNs are shown in Fig. 8.1 and Table 8.1 depicts MN-assisted percutaneous drug delivery.

Solid microneedles

Fabrication

The main advantage of solid MNs is the mechanical robustness [26] that makes skin penetration easier compared to other types of MNs. But a limitation of this mode of administration is that it entails two stages—first piercing the skin and then administering a patch or solution [24]. Solid MNs can be produced from a variety of materials including stainless steel [42], silicon [43], ceramic [44], and titanium [31]. Technologies used in fabricating stainless steel MNs include infrared laser electromachining [45] and wire electrical discharge machining [46]. Martanto and coworkers first drafted the shape and orientation of microneedle arrays (MNAs) in a computer-aided design (CAD) file and then used infrared laser to cut the MNs from stainless steel

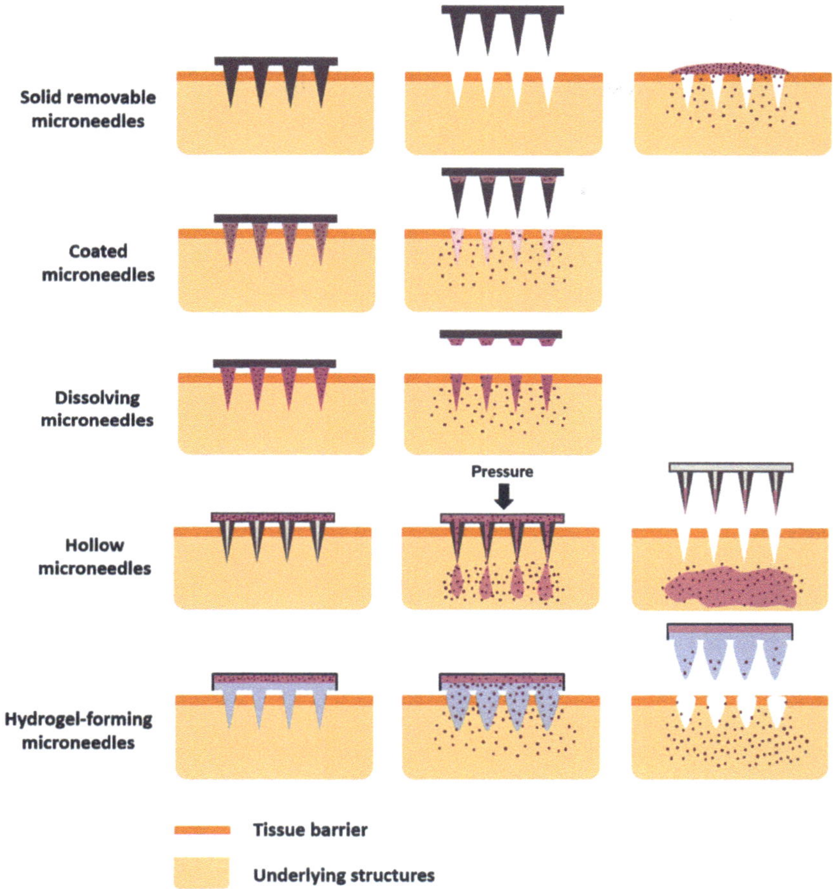

FIGURE 8.1 Types of microneedles, step-by-step process of their application, and corresponding mechanisms of drug delivery across a tissue barrier. *Reproduced with permission from Rzhevskiy AS, et al. Microneedles as the technique of drug delivery enhancement in diverse organs and tissues. J Control Release 2018;270:184–202.*

sheets [45]. The 1000 Hz laser beam was used to trace the needle shape, ablate the metal, and create the MNs [45]. The needles were subsequently bent at 90-degree angle out of the stainless steel sheet plane. Electropolishing was carried out with a 6:3:1 mixture of glycerin, phosphoric acid, and water [45]. Gill and Prausnitz described an electropolishing process that involved the use of this mixture maintained at a stirring rate of 150 rpm and a temperature of 70°C [39]. The authors used MNs as the anode and a copper plate as the cathode [39]. After electropolishing, the researchers dipped MNs alternately three times in 25% nitric acid and deionized water

TABLE 8.1 Microneedle-assisted percutaneous drug delivery.

Therapeutic agent(s) or model compound(s)	Skin model	Microneedle type	References
Calcein	Human skin	Silicon microneedles	[2]
Galantamine	Human skin	Silicon microneedles	[43]
(Gapdh) siRNA	Mouse skin	Silicon microneedles	[61]
Tiagabine hydrochloride	Pig skin	Stainless steel microneedles	[59]
Potassium chloride	Pig skin	Stainless steel microneedles	[63]
Sumatriptan	Pig skin	Polyvinylpyrrolidone dissolving microneedles	[71]
Measles vaccine	Rhesus macaques skin	Dissolving microneedles prepared from carboxymethyl cellulose, sucrose, threonine	[3]
Doxorubicin	Human skin	Poly(vinyl alcohol) dissolving microneedles	[75]
Iron pyrophosphate	Rat skin	Hyaluronic acid dissolving microneedles	[36]
Plasmid DNA vaccine	Mouse skin	Sodium hyaluronate dissolving microneedles	[87]
FITC-dextran	Pig skin	Silk fibroin dissolving microneedles	[92]
Itraconazole	Human skin	Polyglycolic acid microneedle	[91]
Ovalbumin	Mouse skin	Stainless steel hollow microneedles	[109]
Synthetic mRNA	Pig skin	MicronJet600 hollow microneedles	[111]
Metformin hydrochloride	Pig skin	Hydrogel-forming microneedles prepared from poly(methylvinylether-*co*-maleic acid) cross-linked with poly(ethylene glycol)	[161]

(*Continued*)

TABLE 8.1 (Continued)

Therapeutic agent(s) or model compound(s)	Skin model	Microneedle type	References
Bleomycin	Pig skin	Polylactic acid (L-PLA) microneedles coated with trypan blue, carboxymethyl-cellulose sodium, Tween 80	[126]
Caffeine	Pig skin	Hydrogel-forming microneedles fabricated from poly(methylvinylether-*co*-maleic acid) and polyethylene glycol	[34]
Tetanus toxoid and diphtheria toxoid subunit vaccines	Mouse skin	Ceramic nanoporous microneedle arrays	[65]
Curcumin, cisplatin, and 5-fluororacil	Pig skin	Stainless steel microneedles coated with Soluplus (polyvinyl caprolactam–polyvinyl acetate–polyethylene glycol grafted copolymer)	[133]

for 30 s each [39]. An interesting adaptation of the electropolishing technique was reported by Zhao et al. [47]. The researchers applied 1.8 mA/mm^2 electric current to individual MNA for 15 min and mechanically agitated the MNs to remove air [47].

MN rollers have found increasing application in transdermal drug delivery research [48–50]. The rollers are essentially solid MNs mounted on cylinders. The rationale for using rollers is that MN systems arranged on flat surfaces are difficult to administer to large areas of the human skin because the skin tends to deform in response to MN application [49]. Furthermore, the management of psoriasis and other dermatological disorders requires transcutaneous drug administration into broad areas of the skin [49]. MN rollers can overcome these challenges by rolling over large areas of skin. In addition, less insertion force is required because MNs pierce the skin sequentially, row by row, rather than all at once, as done with traditional microneedle patches (MNPs) [49]. MN rollers are usually made by alternately stacking needle disks (prepared by laser machining, etching, or other methods) [49]. Park and coworkers have also fabricated MN rollers from polymers by using deposition, photolithographic, and micromolding techniques [49]. The authors initially made a female master mold from SU-8 epoxy photoresist and silicon wafer [49]. The next step of the manufacturing process involved the production of a male master structure followed by the making of a polydimethylsiloxane (PDMS) female master mold [49]. Subsequently, the authors covered the female molds with polylactic acid in vacuum oven [49]. In the final step of the fabrication process, the researchers created glued MNs to aluminum cylinders to create polylactic acid (PLA) MN rollers [49]. IN another set of experiments, Nalluri and coworkers studied the influence of Dermaroller (DR) on the transcutaneous flux of sumatriptan [51]. These researchers studied the in vitro skin penetration of sumatriptan using propylene glycol/normal saline (PG:S) [70:30] %v/v) as the donor vehicle and also studied the influence of MN length (0.5 and 1 mm). The authors observed a statistically significant enhancement in the cumulative amount of the drug that penetrated the skin, steady-state flux, diffusion coefficient, and permeability coefficient following MN pretreatment, and the values were in the order of 1 mm DR > 0.5 mm DR > passive permeation [51].

Glass MNs were also fabricated by researchers using conventional drawn-glass micropipette techniques [52]. The manufacturing procedure entailed the pulling of glass capillary tubing that led to the fabrication of glass needles with desired programmable geometries [52]. Silicon MNs form an important category of solid MNs. Wei-Ze and coworkers used reactive-ion etching, thin-film deposition, and photolithography to make silicon MNs [43]. The authors first used low-pressure chemical vapor deposition technique to place nitride on a pad oxide layer and then carried out patterning. After forming square oxide patterns on a silicon substrate, the authors used an isotropic reactive-ion etching technology to remove the uncovered portion of the wafer [43]. Subsequently, the researchers positioned the MNs an adhesive patch made from a low-density polyethylene backing with a polyisobutylene adhesive [43]. Yan and colleagues used a different technique to make silicon MNs [53]. The authors cut silicon wafers into tapered MNs with a dicing saw. Next, tapered and sharp MNs were fabricated with a chemical etching approach [53]. The MNs can breach artificial skin with insertion force values spanning from 0.1 to 10 N [53].

Ceramics are typically created between nonmetallic and metallic elements between which the interatomic bonds are either mostly ionic with some covalent properties or totally ionic [32,54]. Ceramics are FDA-approved materials and are increasingly being used by researchers for percutaneous drug administration due to their excellent molding capabilities, biocompatibility, and mechanical properties [55]. They are used as alternative fabrication materials for MNs because they do not have some of the limitations of polymers and sugars [55]. The porosity of ceramics can be adjusted and the electrostatic interaction between the drugs and the ceramic surface can be used to enhance transdermal drug delivery [32]. However, under tensile stress, ceramic becomes brittle [29]. Micromolding and two-photon polymerization are some of the commonly used techniques for fabricating ceramic MNs [32]. The main type of ceramic is alumina and the major advantage of this material is high resistance and good biocompatibility [29]. Recently, ceramic MNs were fabricated by mixing calcium sulfate hemihydrate with water and subsequent compression of the mixture in polydimethylsiloxane (PDMS) molds [55]. The authors used a vacuum to improve the mold filling step and the ceramic MNs were cured at room temperature for 24 h [55]. Sometimes, titanium is employed for the fabrication of MNs. Zhao and colleagues utilized isotropic wet etching technology to prepare titanium MNs [56]. The authors investigated different mask materials, substrate materials, and etchants for process optimization and a steady etch rate with sputtered nickel mask was achieved [56].

Thermotropic liquid crystalline polymers possess excellent physical properties, particularly strength, high chemical resistance, and stiffness, as well as excellent dimensional and thermal stability [57]. Recently, MNAs were molded from a thermotropic liquid crystal polymer (Vectra MT-1300) [58]. The MNAs had three-sided pyramidal-shaped MNs in a pattern of 14 rows × 14 columns with MN heights of 700 microns and tip-to-tip distance between neighboring MNs of 500 microns [58].

Transdermal drug delivery with solid microneedles

In the last two decades, there has been a surge in the number of research publications dedicated to solid MNs [2,48,59]. Henry et al. were the first to demonstrate an increased transcutaneous flux of calcein following the application of silicon MNs [2]. The MNs were produced via reactive-ion etching that entailed the deposition of chromium on silicon wafers and subsequent patterning into dots [2]. The authors then etched patterned wafers in a reactive-ion etcher using O_2 and SF_6 at a power setting of 150 W and pressure of 150 mTorr for a run time of about 250 min [2]. The transdermal penetration rate of calcein across human skin increased significantly in vitro following the use of these MNs [2]. Wei-Ze also investigated the influence of super-short (70−80 μm) silicon MNs on the transdermal transport of galantamine (GAL) [43]. The authors used wet etching technology to make the MNs and reported an enhanced transdermal delivery of the GAL [43]. The authors also observed an increased skin permeability of GAL in direct proportion to insertion force and the number of MNs (within a certain range) [43].

Vucen et al. studied the percutaneous penetration of ketoprofen by combining nanospheres with solid silicon MNs [60]. ImmuPatch silicon MNs (Tyndall National Institute, Cork, Ireland) were used in this study [60].

Permeation experiments were carried out and the authors reported that the transdermal flux of ketoprofen from nanospheres across MN-treated skin was $2.14 \pm 0.11\ \mu g/cm^2/h$. The drug flux across untreated skin was $0.93 \pm 0.07\ \mu g/cm^2/h$ [60]. In another study, Yan and coworkers documented the capacity of a 7×7 MNA silicon MNs to increase the permeation rate of a model compound through treated rat skin 36-fold in comparison with untreated skin [53]. The efficient use of siRNA-based therapeutic systems is important for the management of dermatological disorders caused by aberrant gene expression, including alopecia, allergic skin diseases, hyperpigmentation, psoriasis, and others [61]. Recently, Deng et al. evaluated the influence of solid silicon MNs on the skin transport of cholesterol-modified housekeeping gene (Gapdh) siRNA [61]. After applying MNs on mouse ear skin, there was enhanced penetration of siRNA into the skin and the reduction of Gapdh gene expression by up to 66% in the skin with no buildup in critical body organs [61].

Other materials have also been used to fabricate MNs for transdermal drug delivery. Martanto and coworkers inserted arrays of stainless steel MNs into the skin of diabetic rats with and applied a solution of insulin to the skin of the rodents [45]. The researchers reported a decrease in glucose concentration to a level obtained following the subcutaneous administration of 0.05−0.5 IU insulin [45]. Nguyen and colleagues also studied the transport of metoprolol and captopril across pig ear skin following the application of stainless steel MNAs [62]. Experimental results by these authors demonstrated that percutaneous flux values for metoprolol tartrate and captopril rose from 62.28 to $290.93\ \mu g/cm^2/h$ and 75.04 to $608.2\ \mu g/cm^2/h$, respectively, following the application of the MNs [62]. In a different study using MN rollers, Nguyen et al. demonstrated enhanced transdermal permeation of tiagabine hydrochloride (TH) across MN-treated pig skin [59]. In this set of experiments, there was a 6.74-fold enhancement in the transdermal delivery of TH ($86.42 \pm 25.66\ \mu g/cm^2/h$) following the use of MN rollers in comparison with untreated pig skin ($12.83 \pm 6.30\ \mu g/cm^2/h$) [59]. Abiandu and Ita studied the effect of solid MNs on the delivery of potassium chloride across pig skin in vitro [63]. Transport experiments were conducted with Franz diffusion cells. Potassium chloride concentration in the receptor chamber was quantified via inductively coupled plasma optical emission spectrometry [63]. Microconduits were probed with confocal laser scanning microscopy, brightfield stereomicroscopy, and digital microscopy. The average transdermal flux of potassium chloride following passive transport was $0.637 \pm 0.02\ mg/cm^2/h$, while the mean transdermal flux of potassium chloride across MN-treated skin was $6.33 \pm 18.70\ mg/cm^2/h$ [63]. This increase in transdermal flux was found to be statistically significant with $P < .05$. The depth of the micro channels formed by the MN rollers was $173 \pm 26.94\ \mu m$ [63]. The passive delivery of amlodipine besylate and verapamil hydrochloride across porcine skin is low [48]. Kaur et al. studied the transdermal delivery of amlodipine besylate across MN-treated porcine ear skin in vitro using vertical static Franz diffusion cells [48]. The receptor compartment contained 5 mL of phosphate-buffered saline (PBS) and this was kept at a temperature of 37°C. The donor compartment was covered with parafilm to prevent evaporation. Passive transport across untreated pig skin was employed as the control. Aliquots were taken every 2 h for 12 h and analyzed by liquid chromatography-mass spectrometry [48]. The transdermal delivery of verapamil went up significantly from 8.75 to 49.96 μg/cm^2/h across MN-roller treated porcine skin [48]. The permeation rate of amlodipine following the use of MN roller was 1.05 μg/cm^2/h in comparison with the passive flux was 0.19 μg/cm^2/h [48]. The transdermal flux of amlodipine besylate following the use of stainless steel MNs was 22.39 μg/cm^2/h, while the passive permeation rate for the drug was 1.57 μg/cm^2/h [48].

Badran and coworkers also evaluated the effect of MN-roller pretreatment on the magnitude of transepidermal water loss, skin surface morphology, and the transcutaneous flux of mannitol across excised human full-thickness skin [50]. The authors investigated the combined influence of invasomes (highly flexible phospholipid vesicles loaded with ethanol and terpenes) and DRs (needle lengths of 150, 500, and 1500 μm) on the transport of radiolabeled mannitol [50]. The authors found out that the simultaneous application of the DR (150 μm needles) and invasomes led to increased drug concentration in the SC (1.4-fold) and in the stripped skin (3.1-fold) as well as in the receptor compartment (13.6-fold) in comparison to the use of invasomes without the concomitant use of the DR [50]. Sivaraman and Banga recently documented an interesting approach utilizing solid maltose MNs to create pores in the skin and then applying in situ-forming hydrogel MNs [64]. The rationale is that the thermosensitive and amphiphilic nonionic triblock copolymer Pluronic F127 usually changes from a solution phase at room temperature to a gel phase in the skin [64]. The authors first pierced porcine and human skin using 500-μm length maltose MNs and then administered the poloxamer-based methotrexate-loaded formulation [64]. The solution changed into a gel in the skin (32°C) and then acquired an MN shape [64]. The authors investigated methotrexate-loaded poloxamer and nonpoloxamer-based systems and found out that the Pluronic F127-based 0.2% and 0.4% w/w systems delivered a mean cumulative methotrexate amount of 32.2 ± 15.76 and 114.54 ± 40.89 μg/cm^2 when administered in the form of in situ-formed hydrogel MNs. In comparison, the nonpoloxamer-based formulations delivered 17.19 ± 5.68 and 119.56 ± 43.72 μg/cm^2 via maltose MN−treated skin [64]. The poloxamer and nonpoloxamer-based 0.2% w/w and 0.4% w/w dosage forms transported comparatively lesser amounts of methotrexate than the MN-treated skin. The 0.2% w/w poloxamer and nonpoloxamer-based formulations delivered 1.95 ± 1.87 and 7.65 ± 9.60 μg/cm^2 of the drug, respectively, whereas the 0.4% w/w poloxamer and nonpoloxamer-based formulations delivered 4.15 ± 1.20 and 60.94 ± 48.81 μg/cm^2 of methotrexate, respectively, via passive transport [64]. The authors also studied methotrexate transport across dermatomed human skin and found out that the poloxamer-based 0.2% and 0.4% w/w methotrexate systems transported 3.89 ± 0.60 and 10.27 ± 6.98 μg/cm² of the drug, respectively, within 72 h [64].

Ceramic MNs have also been employed for drug and vaccine delivery. The effect of ceramic nanoporous microneedle arrays (npMNAs) on the intradermal transport of tetanus toxoid (TT) and diphtheria toxoid (DT) subunit vaccines was recently studied [65]. The researchers tested ceramic (alumina) npMNAs, with over 100 MNs per array, an average pore of 80 nm, and a length of 475 μm [65]. Imiquimod DT and TT were loaded into the npMNAs [65]. The authors showed that DT and TT were released into ex vivo murine skin following piercing by npMNAs [65]. Remarkably, the use of DT and TT-loaded npMNAs on mouse skin in vivo induced the formation of antigen-specific antibodies, with titers comparable to those obtained following subcutaneous vaccine administration [65]. In another experiment, Shirkhanzadeh et al. coated stainless steel acupuncture needle tips with calcium phosphate and loaded them with solid trehalose [66] These MNs effectively pierced the SC and provided direct port of entry into the epidermis without stimulating nociceptors or breaking [66].

Several novel MN-based delivery systems have also been developed for the administration of vaccines [67]. With this approach, it is possible to achieve dose sparing, reduced costs, and ease of administration, and there is no need for a cold chain [67]. Recently, unique MNAs (Nanopatch) were fabricated for vaccine delivery [68,69]. The authors deployed a methodology to make high aspect ratio and high-density micro-nanoprojections [69]. The uncommon high projection density ($>$ 20,000 per cm²) was achieved through the utilization of a controlled mixed plasma in a deep reactive-ion etching process, leading to the manufacture of long, tapered tips without limiting the overall density [69]. With a tailored process, the authors were able to produce structures of tunable height and shape, with enhanced uniformity across the face of silicon wafers [69]. The suitability of these devices for transdermal vaccine delivery was demonstrated. The Nanopatch (NP) was manufactured from silicon wafer via dry etching [68]. Using SU-8 photoresist and silicon wafers in combination with dry etching, the authors fabricated high-density MNs (more than 20,000 projections per cm²) [68,69].

Dissolving microneedles

Dissolving microneedles (DMNs) are fabricated, predominantly, from polymers or polysaccharides and typically pierce the skin before releasing the incorporated medication(s) [1,24,70–72]. DMNs consist of needles less than 1000 μm in length that can painlessly cross the SC and deliver their drug payload into the bloodstream [73]. Following the administration of DMNs, these microscopic needles breach the epidermis creating microconduits into the dermis allowing medications to be absorbed into the bloodstream [74]. Subsequently, the interstitial fluid of the skin will dissolve the DMNs [36]. Micromolding, thermal drawing, droplet-born air blowing (DAB), and centrifugal lithography (CL) techniques are commonly used for the fabrication of DMNs [1,3,75–77]. The following steps are usually taken when preparing DMNs via the micromolding technique [78]: (1) female mold fabrication, (2) mold cavity filling with a drug-loaded polymer, (3) medication-loaded polymer curing, and (4) DMN peeling from the mold [78]. Some DMNs consist of tips and pedestals [79]. The tips have to be strong enough for insertion into the SC, while the pedestal makes it easier for the MNs to adhere to the skin [79]. Subsequently, force is transmitted to the tips [79]. DMNs undergo complete dissolution in the skin leaving behind no harmful waste [70]. Another advantage of this class of MNs is that a one-step administration is required, which is convenient for patients [24]. Furthermore, patients can self-administer DMNs safely without the assistance of trained personnel [80]. However, due to skin elasticity and the uneven nature of the skin surface, total skin insertion of DMNs may not always occur, resulting in incomplete transport of the encapsulated drugs [80]. One of the ways this problem can be addressed is to use a nanomaterial-strengthened DMN patch [81].

Layered double hydroxides (LDHs) are anionic clay materials with high anionic exchange capabilities (2–3 m_{eq}/g) and large surface areas [82–84]. LDHs can be synthesized from a variety of compositions and metal-anion combinations [83]. In addition, these anionic clays are chemically stable and biocompatible and possess pH-dependent solubility [83]. Hydrotalcite, $[Mg_6Al_2(OH)_{16}](CO_3)\cdot 4(H_2O)$, is an example of an LDH [83]. LDHs have a general formula, which is $[MII_{1-x}MIII_x(OH)_2]^{x+}[A^{(n-)}_{(x/n)}\cdot y\text{-}H_2O]^{x-}$, where A^{n-} is an n-valent anion and M(II) and M(III) are divalent and trivalent metal cations, respectively [83]. LDHs possess layered crystal structure that varies depending upon the nature of the anions, the type of cations, and the M(II)/M(III) molar ratios [83]. In an interesting study, Yan et al. prepared MNs comprising nanomaterials, dissolving polymers, and drug/biomolecules [81]. The authors used a nanocomposite prepared from sodium carboxymethyl cellulose (CMC) nanoparticles and LDHs. This composite enhanced the mechanical strength of the DMNs [81]. After the nanoparticles were dried, their elastic modulus and hardness were determined via nanoindentation [81]. Three periods: loading-holding-unloading made up the nanoindentation cycle [81]. The researchers increased loading forces at constant speed and the nanoindenter tip sank into materials during the loading period, which caused both elastic and plastic deformation [81]. Robust materials require a higher force for the same depth of penetration during the loading period [81]. Pure CMC has an elastic modulus of 0.993 ± 0.065 GPa, while that of 5 wt.% of LDH-loaded CMC is 2.878 ± 0.123 GPa [81]. On the other hand, the hardness of pure CMC polymer is 0.067 ± 0.001 GPa, while the addition of 2, 5, and 10 wt.% of LDH nanoparticles to CMC increased the hardness

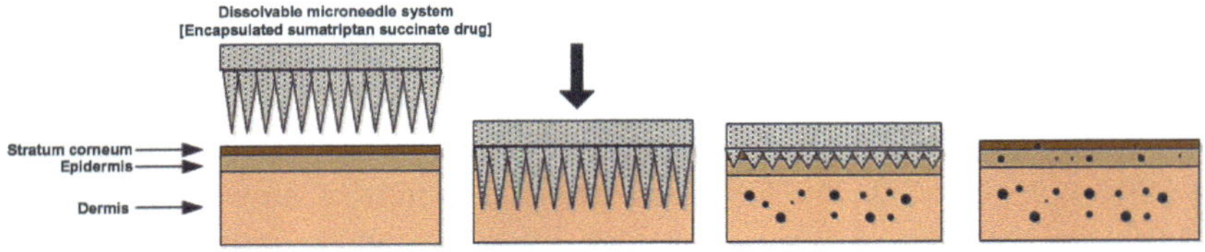

FIGURE 8.2 The schematic representation of sumatriptan-loaded dissolvable microneedles. *Reproduced with permission from Ronnander P, et al. Dissolving polyvinylpyrrolidone-based microneedle systems for in-vitro delivery of sumatriptan succinate. Eur J Pharm Sci 2018;114:84–92.*

of the nanocomposites to 0.080 ± 0.001, 0.111 ± 0.004, and 0.118 ± 0.001 GPa, respectively [81].

It was demonstrated that CMC-LDH MNs prepared from these reinforced nanoparticles penetrated porcine and human skin more reliably than pure CMC MNs [81]. More importantly, the MNs prepared from nanocomposites dissolved in the skin and released their contents within 1 min [81]. The authors also investigated the influence of the obtained MNs on vaccine transport and the results provided evidence of a more potent antibody response compared with subcutaneous administration [81]. Another approach to strengthen DMNs entails drug encapsulation into DMN tip, while a stronger material is used for the fabrication of the pedestal of a two-layered DMN [80]. Yang and coworkers used fibrous sheet produced by electrospinning hydrophobic and hydrophilic polymer solutions to make DMNs [80]. The fibrous sheet was used to cover DMN pillar arrays [80]. The researchers used different flow rates (0.2-2 mL/h) and voltages (6.0-12.0 kV) to electrospin polymer solution at room temperature [80]. Insulin-loaded DMNs fabricated with this technique had a hypoglycemic effect in a healthy mouse mode [80].

Ronnander et al. recently prepared sumatriptan-loaded DMNs from polyvinylpyrrolidone (PVP) [71]. The MNs had 600 needles with each needle measuring 300 μm in width, 500 μm in height, and a pitch of 350 μm [71]. A schematic representation of the sumatriptan-loaded dissolvable MNs is shown in Fig. 8.2.

Micromolding fabrication technique was employed with platinum-cured silicon MNA used as the negative mold [71]. A solution containing PVP, glycerin, polysorbate 80, and sumatriptan succinate was used to fill the molds [71]. The authors studied the transdermal penetration of sumatriptan succinate from DMNs across the Göttingen minipig skin and reported an enhanced transdermal flux of sumatriptan succinate compared to passive diffusion [71]. The permeation profiles of sumatriptan succinate–loaded MNs after 32 h are shown in Fig. 8.3.

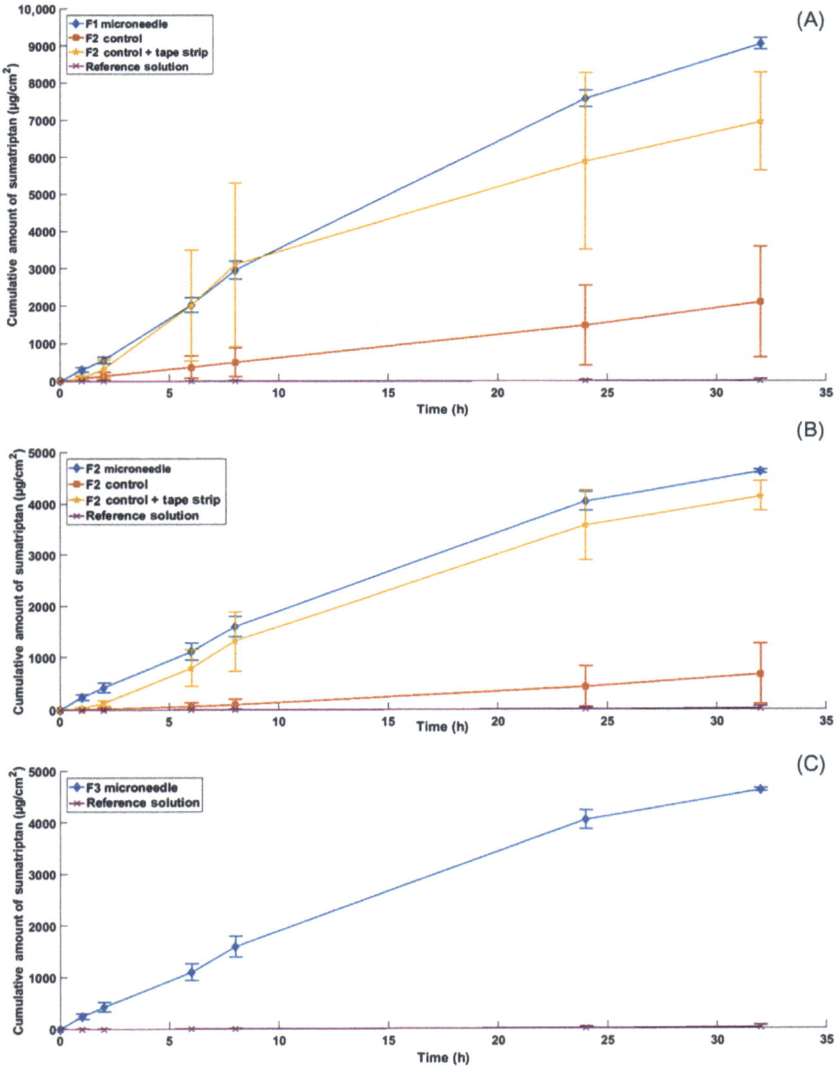

FIGURE 8.3 Permeation profiles of sumatriptan succinate–loaded microneedles after 32 h: (A) F1 microneedles, F1 control (microneedle inverted on skin), F1 control + tape strip (15 ×), and reference solution (5 mg/mL sumatriptan succinate); (B) F2 microneedles, F2 control, F2 control + tape strip (15 ×), and reference solution; (C) F3 microneedles and reference solution. *Reproduced with permission from Ronnander P, et al. Dissolving polyvinylpyrrolidone-based microneedle systems for in-vitro delivery of sumatriptan succinate. Eur J Pharm Sci 2018;114:84–92.*

The administration of a formulation prepared from 30% PVP and loaded with 8.7 mg of sumatriptan, resulted in a permeation rate of 395 ± 31 μg/cm^2/h over 7 h compared to a passive transcutaneous drug flux of 30 ± 24 μg/cm^2/h [71]. Edens and colleagues also prepared DMNs from a mixture of 15% w/v sucrose, 300 mM threonine, and 2% w/v carboxymethyl cellulose using PDMS micromolds [3]. The DMNs were loaded with measles vaccine (1000 $TCID_{50}$) and administered to rhesus macaques [3]. Subcutaneously administered vaccine served as the control. The authors showed the protective neutralizing antibody titers generated in both groups of macaques were equivalent [3].

The amount of medication that can be loaded into DMNs is somewhat limited and considerable research effort has been directed toward increasing loading. Recently, DMNs containing a high dose of lidocaine hydrochloride were prepared with a composite material [85]. The researchers mixed a dispersion containing the a brittle material poly(methyl vinyl ether-*co*-maleic anhydride) copolymer (Gantrez S-97), a ductile material (hydroxymethylcellulose), the drug lidocaine and water at a mass ratio of 12% Gantrez S-97, 3% HPMC, 50% deionized water, and 35% lidocaine hydrochloride to obtain optimal mechanical properties [85]. The authors centrifuged the solution at 3500 rpm for 5 min for bubble removal and uniformly applied it to a PDMS female mold. This was again centrifuged at 3500 rpm for 5 min [85]. Lidocaine hydrochloride constituted 70% of the weight of the MN tip and the drug amount was 3.43 ± 0.12 mg [85]. The MNs permeated rat skin with an MN fracture force of 5.442 ± 0.412 N, which was adequate for the skin piercing [85]. Although lidocaine hydrochloride–loaded DMNs dissolved inside the skin of a rat in 5 min (in comparison, the onset of a marketed lidocaine cream was 100 min), local anesthesia following the administration of DMNs was sustained for 16 min, which was shorter than that of a marketed cream with an efficacy lasting for approximately 130 min [85].

Nguyen et al. also utilized micromolding to fabricate poly(vinyl alcohol) (PVA) MNs and studied the percutaneous transport of doxorubicin from the DMNs [75]. A PDMS mold was filled with PVA solution and then centrifuged at 4000 rpm at 40°C for 20 min [75]. Subsequently, the authors prepared doxorubicin-loaded MNs. The PVP DMNs were used for drug transport studies across dermatomed human skin, and it was revealed that there was a higher transdermal flux (4351.55 ± 560.87 ng/cm^2) in comparison with the untreated group (0.00 ± 0.00 ng/cm^2, $n = 4$, $P < .01$) [75]. Maurya and colleagues also used the mold casting method to fabricate hyaluronic acid-based DMNs containing iron pyrophosphate [36]. The goal of the research project was to assess the potential of providing iron replacement therapy with DMNs as iron deficiency anemia (IDA) can influence cognitive functions and physical activity especially in women and children [36]. Iron pyrophosphate–loaded DMNs were prepared by using an aqueous ferric pyrophosphate solution (250 mg/mL) to make a 50% w/w hyaluronic acid

(HA) solution [86]. The HA-FPP mixture was then used to fill a polydimethylsiloxane mold [36]. The micromold was dried overnight and the MNs removed from the molds [36]. The MNs were placed on the backing layer at a distance of 464.31 ± 12.822 μm from each other. The measurements were 467.59 ± 15.23 μm in height, a tip diameter of 6.48 ± 1.22 μm, and 183.29 ± 18.68 μm in base width (the aspect ratio was 2.5). Approximately 130 μg of ferric pyrophosphate (FPP) which is equivalent to 5 μg of elemental iron was transported across excised rat skin [36]. The authors estimated that four MNPs per day per rat were needed to achieve target iron levels in rats [36]. Noteworthy is the fact that IDA was successfully managed with a 1.5 g/dL recovery in the hemoglobin levels within 7 days following the administration of FPP-loaded MNs [36]. There was a subsequent increase in hematocrit level and red blood cell count [36]. Another important point worthy of emphasis is that the quantity of iron recovered from the skin following 5 min of DMN administration was 130.54 ± 18.64 μg, which represented approximately 66% of the total drug content in the MNs [36].

An interesting approach is the use of DMNs for plasmid DNA vaccination with the aim of providing antigen-specific cellular immunity [87]. In a publication by Yan and colleagues, the researchers reported that they prepared DMNs using PDMS molds filled with a 15% sodium hyaluronate solution mixed with a plasmid DNA vaccine [87]. The plasmid DNA vaccine was loaded with the plasmid vector pVAX1 encoding the secreted protein Ag85B derived from *Mycobacterium tuberculosis* [87]. The authors compared vaccine delivery from DMNs and vaccine administration using intramuscular injection. At a low dose (4.2μg), drug transport following intramuscular immunization and microneedle patch (MNP) were similar [87]. However, at a higher dose (12.6 μg), immunization with MNP provided a higher antibody response than intramuscular administration [87]. In addition, lymphocytes in the spleen apparently produced higher levels of interferon-γ and TNF-α following the administration of higher vaccine doses from the MNP compared to intramuscular administration [87]. In a separate study, Tas et al. fabricated DMNs from polyvinylpyrrolidone (PVP) using micromolding and loaded the needles with dihydroergotamine mesylate (DHE) [38]. The drug-loaded MNs had a content uniformity of 108% ± 9% pig skin ex vivo and these DMNs dissolved within 2 min [38]. The authors evaluated pharmacokinetic parameters of DHE and reported a relative bioavailability of 97% [38]. In addition, the area under curve following the administration of DHE-loaded microneedles (1259 ± 917 ng/mL min) was comparable to subcutaneous injection [38].

The fabrication of certain DMNs requires the use of complicated microfabrication procedures in a clean-room setting leading to high costs [88]. Nejad et al. published a report in which an inexpensive, clean room–free technique was used for the fabrication of DMNs [88]. Commercially available CO_2 laser cutters were used to fabricate MN molds [88]. The authors made a sharp conical shape in an acrylic sheet [88]. Subsequently, the authors utilized the molds to produce PVA MNs [88]. An alternative microfabrication procedure involves the use of drawing lithography (DL) [89–91]. Using this technique, a three-dimensional (3D) microstructure is directly extended from a two-dimensional (2D) viscous polymer material [89]. The rationale for using this technique is that conventional subtractive micromanufacturing methods based on planar 2D geometries may not always be effective in making MNs [1]. On the other hand, DL is an MN fabrication method that entails drawing a thermosetting polymer from a 2D solid surface without utilizing light irradiation or a mask [1]. In DL, there is an elastic deformation of polymers during the glass transition state and subsequent fabrication of 3D MNs by stretching deformation [1].

Hydrogels are 3D porous structures prepared from polymers capable of swelling in water. Hydrogels can be used to incorporate medications [92] but are not mechanically robust enough to penetrate the epidermis. An example of this type of material is silk fibroin (SF), which is biocompatible but can only produce MNs that are soluble, causing burst release of entrapped drugs. As a result, hydrogels are not optimal for use as sustained release transdermal drug delivery systems [92]. Recently, Yin modified SF MNs with 2-ethoxyethanol (ECS) and showed that these microprojections can be easily inserted into pig skin at a depth of about 200 μm [92]. The authors mixed 2-ethoxyethanol (ECS), urea (URE), glycine (GLY), *N*-dimethylformamide (DMF) with aqueous SF and poured the modified aqueous silk solution into polydimethylsiloxane (PDMS) mold (15×15 pore array, 150–1000 μm intervals and 300–700 μm depth), followed by numerous drying (25°C, 55% humidity) and degassing (>0.09 MPa) operations [92]. The authors demonstrated that the swelling properties of SF MNs can be optimized to enhance transdermal transport [92].

An emerging body of in vivo, in vitro, and clinical evidence has confirmed that itraconazole (ITC) possesses antineoplastic activities [93]. The drug significantly upregulates Axin-1 and Gli-3, while downregulating Wnt3A, Gli-1, cyclin D1, Gli-2, and β-catenin leading to potent inhibitory effects of ITC on Wnt and Hedgehog (Hh) signaling pathways [94]. In addition, it has been shown that itraconazole can block the growth of basal cell carcinoma (BCC) by suppressing the Sonic Hedgehog (SHH) signaling pathway [91]. DL was used to fabricate ITC-loaded polyglycolic acid MNAs, and the authors investigated the percutaneous transport of ITC from the MNA to a human BCC model [91]. Skin grafts with devitalized split-thickness human dermis that had been seeded with human keratinocytes transduced to express human SHH protein were sutured to the skin of immunodeficient mice [91]. The authors then prepared polyglycolic acid MNAs (642 μm long, 1×4 arrays) with sharp tips and found out that when they used polyglycolic acid MNs on skin graft tissues, the latter were significantly thinner than the untreated tissues [91]. In another study, Chen deployed magnetorheological DL to produce unmolded MNAs, MNs, and bio-inspired MNs [8]. The authors drew MN 3D structure from a droplet of curable magnetorheological fluid by using an external magnetic field [8]. MN preparation comprised two main steps: magneto-capillary self-shrinking and elasto-capillary self-thinning, and MN height and tip radius were significantly affected [8].

In an interesting study, 3D printing (3DP) technology [22] was utilized for the production of DMNs [22,95]. With 3D modeling software, Lazuriaga and colleagues designed several MNs with varying shapes, lengths, and needle densities from polylactic acid, and these were made rapidly via 3DP [95]. The authors developed a chemical etching procedure, which made it possible to produce MNs with small tip sizes (approximately 1 μm) [95]. Scanning electron microscopy was used to confirm that this method produced needles with tip sizes from 1 to 55 μm, and these tips were adequate for pig skin penetration [95].

Lee and coworkers formulated DMNs by using centrifugal force to cast carboxymethyl cellulose (CMC) into molds [96]. One of the disadvantages of casting methods of MN fabrication is that these technologies may not be effective with labile drugs (e.g., proteins and peptides) [97]. Several researchers have used the DAB process to fabricate MNs by first stretching polymer droplets and then air blowing [97]. The DAB technology is advantageous since long drying time and master structures are not needed and MN production is carried out promptly in a cost-effective manner [97]. Recently, Kim and coworkers fabricated obelisk-shaped multilayer MNs, by the simultaneous application of spray deposition and micro-milling methods [97]. The researchers used micro-milling as a cost-effective and an environmental-friendly technology to produce primary metal MN masters, while obelisk-shaped multilayer MNs were then fabricated with the spray deposition technique via the sequential filling of MN molds with poly(lactic-*co*-glycolic acid) and polyvinylpyrrolidone dispersions [97]. The authors tested the obelisk-shaped MNs and found out that they were more robust than pyramid-shaped MNs [97]. The highest resistance against compressive force was displayed by beveled circular obelisk-shape MNs and this value was about 2.12 times larger than that of the pyramid-shaped MNs [97].

The DAB technique of DMN fabrication involves shaping polymer droplets into MNs via air blowing [78]. The major advantage of DAB is that there is no need to use heat or ultraviolet (UV) radiation for curing the drug-loaded polymer during the fabrication process because air blowing is directly applied to the polymer droplet [78]. Furthermore, the tendency for drug loss is minimized since each DMN is formed from a single droplet [78]. Another advantage is that DMNs can be produced in about 10 min using DAB, hence the fabrication cost is reduced [78]. Using this technique, the activity of biologicals can also be maintained [78]. Huh and colleagues recently formulated DMNs using the DAB and compared them with those fabricated via CL [98].

In CL, viscous polymer drops self-shape into DMNs via centrifugal forces without the use of a drawing system or a mold [77]. When employing CL, a centrifugal force is deployed on polymer drops [77]. The drops are self-shaped into two DMNs under the influence of the following processes: elongation, necking, head-rising, contact hourglass shaping, and separation [77]. In contrast, DAB entails dispensing a polymer via a dispenser over a stage [99] located on a pulling and pushing device [99]. The upper stage of the rate-controllable device is typically driven down until the droplets come in contact with the surface of the upper stage. Next, the stages are separated, and the polymer drops are processed into solids to create DMNs [99].

Ascorbic acid is a low molecular−weight compound that easily undergoes oxidation, while epidermal growth factor is not a stable peptide [98]. Huh et al. incorporated the two compounds into the DMNs using CL and DAB [98]. The authors reported that the physical properties and appearance of DMNs made via the two techniques were comparable. In contrast, epidermal growth factor immunoreactivity in DMNs made by DAB and CL was $80.67\% \pm 8.00\%$ and $92.08\% \pm 2.86\%$, respectively, at baseline and declined to $41.75\% \pm 16.17\%$ and $75.32\% \pm 19.40\%$, respectively, 24 h after they were loaded with medications [98]. Furthermore, the pharmacological activity of ascorbic acid as exhibited by free-radical scavenging activity remained steady at $88.24\% \pm 0.78\%$ in DMNs manufactured by CL but diminished over time to $67.02\% \pm 1.11\%$ in DMNs produced by DAB [98]. The authors concluded that CL conditions had less impact on the DMNs, leading to reduced pharmacological activity loss in comparison with what was obtained when DAB technique was utilized [98].

Hollow microneedles

HMNs have lumens like the conventional hypodermic needles but are shorter (less than 1000 μm) and can deliver drug solutions into the skin or through the skin into the bloodstream [32,100]. The use of HMNs is based on the "poke and flow" principle [70]: the needles first pierce the skin ("poke") and then the liquid drug formulation is transported into the skin or transdermally into systemic circulation ("flow"). Because the needles are shorter, a reduced insertion pain has been reported in the literature [100]. The flow rate of a medication can also be regulated in HMNs by using micropumps and syringes [32]. The control devices allow HMNs to regulate the rate and quantity of drug transport [100]. An HMN can be viewed as a mechanical mode of transport and because there is no need to integrate the medication into the needle structure, it is easier to adjust the shape and these devices can be used to administer existing drug formulations currently given to patients via hypodermic injections [101]. An additional advantage is that researchers can use HMNs to deliver macromolecules as well as larger volumes of drug solution in comparison with other types of MNs [101]. However, HMNs also have disadvantages:

sometimes, the channels of HMNs can sometimes be blocked and this leads to a reduction in drug delivery efficiency [102]. Another disadvantage is that certain HMNs are not sharp enough to pierce the skin and may require refinements in microfabrication procedures [103]. HMNs can be fabricated via several techniques including the modified syringe [104], drawn-glass micropipette [105], modified-LIGA process [106], sacrificial micromolding [107], and etching [33,107]. An interesting approach is to make HMNs from 34-gauge needles [104]. Using this approach, Jun et al. altered a 34-gauge beveled needle (NanoFil) to create an HMN [104]. The adapted syringe was subsequently attached by tubing to a Hamilton syringe [104]. McAllister has documented the fabrication of glass MNs using conventional drawn-glass micropipette techniques [105]. Glass capillaries were pulled in a micropipette puller and then beveled [105]. Davis et al. reported the production of HMNs using a modified-LIGA process [106]. LIGA (derived from the German words lithographie, galvanoformung, abformung) refers to lithography, electroplating, and molding. The technique is widely used in microfabrication [108]. Davis and coworkers utilized a UV laser to fabricate polyethylene terephthalate molds and then used electrodeposition to coat the molds. The researchers selectively etched the polymer mold to create MN MNs [106].

A different approach was used by Norman and colleagues for HMN fabrication [107]: (1) The researchers used a laser micromachine to produce a master structure with a cavity [107], (2) they subsequently fabricated a micromold from the master structure, (3) the micromold was used to replicate the master structure, (4) a gold seed layer was sputtered onto the replicas, (5) the HMN structure was created via selective electrodeposition, (6) the sacrificial replicate structure was dissolved to form a hollow-metal MN, and (7) the MN was integrated with a source of pressure for fluid delivery [107]. In another study, Du and coworkers etched fused silica capillaries to make HMNs [33]. The authors filled 4-cm silica capillaries with silicone oil in a vacuum oven (100°C) overnight [33]. The ends of the capillaries were subsequently dipped into $\geq 48\%$ hydrofluoric acid (etching) for 4 h at room temperature to form HMNs [33]. As a final step, the MNs were dipped into sulfuric acid (250°C) for 5 min to remove polyimide coatings [33]. Gardeniers et al. have described a method of making hollow out-of-plane microneedles from silicon using a combination of thin film deposition, anisotropic wet etching and deep-reactive ion etching [86]. The authors used lithography to define the curvature of the needle tips. The HMNs were tested and it was shown that they were robust and capable of piercing the skin without breaking [86]. The authors also measured transdermal water loss before and after MN skin penetration. There was a 2.3-fold increase in transepidermal water loss (TEWL) following needle penetration but after the MNs were removed, the TEWL returned to normal within a short period of time [86]. More importantly, there was about a 750-fold enhancement in the transport of diclofenac following the use of HMNs [86].

Lyon and colleagues have also described a different technology of making HMNs by deploying polyimide and vertically aligned carbon nanotubes (VA-CNTs) [101]. The rationale for using polyimide as the composite matrix is that it possesses a high intrinsic stiffness (about 2.5 GPa), which is enough to pierce the skin [101]. This microfabrication approach is also feasible because different patterns of VA-CNTs can be made by utilizing catalyst patterning techniques [101]. Initially, VA-CNTs are utilized as a porous platform for designing the shape of the microneedles with the added benefit of a one-step definition of the geometry of the microneedle, including the lumen [101]. The authors added polymer resin to the VA-CNTs to obtain composite MNs, with the simultaneous creation of a polymeric base to keep the MNs together [101]. In a related set of studies, Lyon et al. used spin coating to make nanotube-polyimide composite and at the same time create a polyimide base on top of the silicon wafer [101]. After that, a polyimide resin was used to cover the carbon nanotubes. The authors then spin-coated and thermally cured the polyimide using a four-stage temperature increase from 100°C to 250°C. The last stage of the microfabrication process entailed detaching the MN device from silicon wafer by utilizing tweezers or a razor blade [101].

Ovalbumin fluorescein (OVA-F) conjugate induces an immune response but has a low skin permeability [109]. Thus this compound is often utilized as a model for the study of the efficacy of HMN drug/vaccine administration. Pamornpathomkul and coworkers studied the influence of OVA antigen doses and MN type on in vitro skin transport and immunization in mice [109]. Stainless steel acupuncture needles (32-gauge and measuring 0.25×30 mm) were used for vertical puncturing of a silicone sheet ($15 \times 15 \times 2$ mm) [109]. The opposite ends of the needles were then bent to attain a perpendicular shape for needle anchoring in the silicone sheet [109]. The HMN patch had 25 needles and was fixed to an adhesive tape. Confocal laser scanning microscopy and in vitro skin transport experiments demonstrated that the employment of HMNs resulted in the enhanced transcutaneous flux of OVA-F in comparison with solid MNs and the control group [109]. It is worthy to note that when the researchers used HMNs for the transport of OVA into mouse skin, there was a stronger immunoglobulin G immune response compared to subcutaneous injection [109]. In another study, researchers delivered insulin into diabetic hairless rat skin with HMNs and measured blood glucose concentration over 4.5 h [52]. The authors found out that the glucose concentration decreased sharply and then stabilized at about 25% below pretreatment values over the course of 4.5-h following infusion [52]. The drop in glucose level was significantly less than glucose concentration observed in the control group (saline delivered with HMNs) [52].

Rad and coworkers used replication, 3D modeling, and microscale printing to fabricate HMNs [110]. The fabrication procedure entailed the making of microstructures directly from CAD drawings via 3D stereolithography and then carrying out replication by soft embossing [110]. A system comprising two nanoliter reservoirs and 4 × 4 array of open-channel microneedles was created [110]. Subsequently, the researchers used multiphoton fluorescence microscopy to monitor the transport of a fluorescein tracer into excised rabbit ear skin [110]. When fluorescein solution was administered to rabbit skin without MN pretreatment, the fluorescein signal disappeared at 66 μm below the skin surface [110]. However, when the rabbit skin was pretreated with the MNP, fluorescein was tracked to a depth of at least 160 μm [110].

Synthetic mRNA is increasingly being used in gene therapy because of numerous advantages such as the transient presence of exogenously expressed proteins, the elimination of insertional mutagenesis, and the direct translation of synthetic mRNA [111]. Nevertheless, systemic delivery of synthetic mRNA can result in poor cellular targeting as well as unspecific uptake into cells or organs [111]. Golombek and coworkers recently used the MicronJet600 HMNs for the skin transport of synthetic mRNA [111]. The authors detected high levels of secretable humanized Gaussia luciferase protein that was ascribed to a more efficient delivery of synthetic mRNA [111].

Coated microneedles

CMNs are formed from substrates coated with drug-loaded formulations [40,102]. Although it is difficult to deposit a known amount of drug on a needle [112], CMNs have attracted tremendous interest because of the rapidity with which medications are delivered into the skin and the capacity of these devices to increase the long-term stability of active pharmaceutical ingredients [102]. CMNs are useful for the transcutaneous delivery of labile biologics because these are dry-coated and stable devices integrated with formulations [47]. The major shortcomings of CMNs are the difficulty in incorporating larger doses of medications [40], poor coating efficiency [41], and immunogenicity [41]. Nevertheless, these MNs are utilized for the administration of low-dose drugs and vaccines [40]. The advantage of using CMN array for vaccine delivery is that it crosses the SC barrier to target dendritic cells, inexpensive, and can be self-administered by patients [113]. Stainless steel, silicon, and polymers are often used for the manufacturing of CMNs [102]. Surfactants are frequently added to the coating dispersion to reduce contact angle and improve coating uniformity, while viscosity enhancers are added to increase coating thickness [40,113]. Kim and coworkers have also shown that including trehalose in the coating formulation can prevent antigen aggregation [113]. Indeed, the authors prepared the coating solution from a wide range of excipients including carboxymethyl cellulose (CMC), Lutrol F-68, sucrose, glucose, inulin, and dextran [113]. To assess the coating deposition on MNs, Shakya et al. mixed OVA with *N*-hydroxysuccinimide (NHS)-activated fluorescein dye and amine-reactive 1-ethyl-3(3-dimethylaminopropyl) carbodiimide (EDC) [114]. The FITC-conjugated OVA was then coated on MNs and stereomicrography was subsequently carried out before and after the CMNs were inserted into mouse skin [114].

CMNs are typically obtained using a two-step process: the fabrication of solid MN substrate followed by coating. Serpe et al. used wet etching technology to make stainless steel MNs measuring 700 μm in length and 200 μm in width [115]. A microscope was used to manually bend each MN "out of plane" [115]. The final phase of the CMN fabrication process involved immersing the MNs into a coating solution via the use of a computer-controlled apparatus [115]. Sulforhodamine, 0.5% (w/v) Lutrol F-68 NF, and carboxymethyl cellulose sodium salt were used to make the coating solution [115]. Peters and colleagues fabricated titanium MNAs by photochemical etching and made a 100 μm thin drug film by using a roller drum and a drug formulation reservoir [116]. The coating formulation consisted of 15% w/w recombinant human erythropoietin alfa, 0.2% w/w polysorbate 20, and 15% w/w sucrose [116]. There are different methods of preparing CMNs: dip coating [41,117,118], electrohydrodynamic atomization (EHDA) [119], inkjet printing [120,121], spray coating [122], and brushing [123].

Dip coating

Dip coating is a fast, low cost, and simple mode of coating that makes it possible to regulate film thickness and deposition rate and by controlling the number of dips and dipping time [124,125]. Researchers can also vary other deposition parameters such as the withdrawal speed, dip speed, and drying time [125]. Dip coating entails the dipping and withdrawing of MNs from a solution that contains the coating material; upon drying, a coating is obtained on the MN surface [120]. Once the CMNs pierce the skin, the coating dispersion is rapidly dissolved by the skin's interstitial fluid, and the drug is delivered [41]. There are numerous approaches for dip-coating MNs [117]: the utilization of micropositioning devices to immerse MNs into coating solution reservoirs, using a high-viscosity coating solution to decrease the influence of capillary action [117] and MN dip-coating approach that uses a microstructure well [126]. The microstructure approach entails the fabrication of poly-L-lactic acid s via micromolding, treatment of MN surfaces by an UV/Ozone process, loading the coating formulation into the UV/Ozone processed microstructure, submerging the MNs in the coating solution placed in the microstructure well, immersing MNs into the coating solution once, and then dip-coating thrice [126].

Lee et al. recently developed coated MNs for the skin transport of bleomycin [126]. The authors prepared poly-l-lactic acid (PLLA) MNs via a molding process and then used a dip-coating method based on a microstructure well to partly coat the MN tips [126]. The MNs were dip-coated three times with solutions of carboxymethyl-cellulose sodium salt [4%, 8%, 11%, 14% (w/w)] [126]. The authors showed that more than 80% of the drug dissolved into the skin in vitro within 15 min when these CMNs were used [126]. Tip-coated MNs were more effective in transporting bleomycin into the skin in comparison with intralesional injection. A T_{max} of 50 min was achieved [126].

In another set of experiments, PLLA MN tips were coated with a lidocaine-loaded formulation using a dip-coating device [127]. The device consisted of a plate that holds an MNA and a reservoir that contains a coating solution [127]. The MNs were fixed onto the plate using a double-sided foam tape and the reservoir was gently filled with a coating solution using a micropipette [127]. The dip-coating process was conducted by dipping and withdrawing the MNs from the coating solution in the reservoir [127]. Micromolding was deployed for MN fabrication with subsequent coating of the needle tips with the lidocaine [127]. There was a timely release of the drug from the coated MNs into PBS within 2 min. In addition, lidocaine was stable at 37°C, 4°C, and 25°C for 3 weeks [127]. The authors documented the delivery of 200.8 ± 43.9, 224.2 ± 39.3, and 244.1 ± 19.6 μg of lidocaine into the skin 1, 2, and 5 min after application with a delivery efficiency of 69%, 77%, and 84%, respectively [127]. The transport efficiency of the drug from the coated MNs was 22.0, 13.6, and 14.0 times higher compared to a currently marketed topical anesthetic EMLA cream [127].

Micropositioning devices are typically used to dip MNs into solutions [117]. An advantage of this approach is that there is a physical barrier between the coating solution and the MN base, leading to reduced drug loss [117]. Caudill et al. utilized such devices [117]. Continuous liquid interface production entails subjecting a pool of liquid resin to UV radiation through a window that allows oxygen permeation [117]. There is selective polymerization of the resin by UV light exposure [117]. The authors used mask devices to coat polyethylene glycol-based microneedles with lysozyme, bovine serum albumin (BSA) and ovalbumin (OVA) [117]. The microneedles were fabricated via continuous liquid interface production (CLIP) [117]

Electrohydrodynamic atomization

EHDA entails the use of electricity to generate very fine droplets from a liquid [128]. A syringe pump, a high-voltage power source, a metal needle serving as nozzle, a collector, and a syringe are components of an EHDA system [128]. The flow rate and other physical properties of the liquid determine the drop size [129]. A charged liquid jet is normally discharged from the nozzle tip and deposited in a collector following the application of a high voltage to a polymer dispersion and the achievement of the required voltage [40,130,131]. Several EHDA methods have been reported in the literature [121]: multiplexed EHDA (liquid formulation delivered via a single or coaxial nozzle array), single needle (the formulation is injected via a single-precision syringe pump into a single nozzle), and coaxial EHDA (separately enveloped nozzles are used to feed two or more immiscible liquids). Different spraying modes (simple-jet, microdripping, dripping, multiple cone spraying, and stable cone-jet) can be obtained through the effect of surface tension stress and electric stress on the liquid-gas interface [128]. Another factor that influences spraying is the nozzle liquid kinetic energy [128]. Khan et al. used EHDA to deposit particles (100 nm to 3 μm) and fibers (400 nm to 1 μm) directly on MNs in a controlled and selectable manner (applied voltage variable 6–19 kV and flow rates variable approximately 5–50 μL/min) using fluorescein dye as a disease-state marker or a potential drug and polyvinylpyrrolidone as the coating solution [119].

Inkjet printing

Inkjet printing refers to a noncontact, precisely controlled deposition and additive printing technique [132] that is being increasingly utilized for coating MNs [133]. The technique involves the placing of 1–100 pL droplets of liquid into devices in a digitally controlled and noncontact way [40]. It is possible to deposit thin layers (<1 μm) of different types of materials due to the small volume of droplets used for coating (approximately 10^{-12}–10^{-9} L), [134]. The mature state of the inkjet printing technology has led to the use of drug solution in very low volumes (pL) with high precision without the need for bulky or expensive equipment [135]. Drop on demand (DoD) and continuous inkjet (CIJ) are the most commonly used modes of the inkjet printing [40]. In CIJ printing, an unbroken liquid stream is removed via a nozzle [136]. A stream of drops is subsequently formed when the liquid stream breaks up under surface tension [136]. When using DoD inkjet printing, researchers can dispense small volumes of liquids in a drop-wise and contactless manner [137]. With a piezoelectric microdispenser, droplets are created in a DoD fashion via the triggering of a ceramic actuator [133]. Investigators typically control droplet size by adjusting excitation frequency, pulse width, and amplitude [133].

Recently, Boehm and colleagues used piezoelectric inkjet printing to prepare voriconazole-loaded polyglycolic acid MNs [138]. The investigators prepared polyglycolic acid (PGA) MNs with sharp tips (mean tip radius = 25 ± 3 μm) by utilizing DL and injection molding [138]. The hardness (588.2 ± 33.8 MPa) and elastic modulus (9.9 ± 0.3 GPa) of the PGA material were measured by nanoindentation [138]. MNs loaded with voriconazole were effective against *Candida albicans* unlike the unmodified and vehicle-modified MNs [138]. However, no activity against *Staphylococcus aureus, Pseudomonas aeruginosa*, or *Escherichia coli* was observed when vehicle-modified, voriconazole-modified, and unmodified MNs were utilized [138]. Uddin and coworkers also used inkjet printing technology to coat CMNs with three anticancer agents—curcumin (CRC), cisplatin (CPT) and 5-fluorouracil (5FU) [133]. The investigators fabricated solid MNs from stainless steel sheets via laser micromachining and then coated the MNs with dispersions comprising Soluplus (polyvinyl caprolactam–polyvinyl acetate–polyethylene glycol-grafted copolymer) and different classes of drugs [133]. The polymer was chosen because of its ability to increase drug solubility [133]. MNs were placed on a holder at 45 degrees relative to a piezoelectric dispenser [133]. The dispenser is equipped with a piezoelectric ceramic that deforms when voltage is applied leading to droplet ejection from the nozzle at a velocity of 1–5 m/s ("DoD") [133]. The drug/polymer dispersion was applied through the dispenser (PicPip 300) onto the MN surface in the form of 300 pL droplets. Fast release rates were achieved for the water-insoluble CPT and CRC (1 h) as well as the hydrophilic 5FU (3 h) [133].

Three-dimensional printing

In 3DP (also called additive manufacturing technologies), researchers use CAD to produce physical objects by consecutively creating different layers [6]. The technologies, also called "rapid prototyping" or "solid free-form," entail fusing or depositing materials in layers [139]. A digital design is made, sliced in layers, and sent to a printer for fabrication [139]. 3DP has elicited significant interest in manufacturing because it facilitates the fabrication of parts that were previously challenging to produce [139]. 3DP technologies can be categorized into: vat polymerization, material jetting (MJ), powder bed fusion (PBF), material extrusion (ME), and direct energy deposition (DED) [112]. Vat polymerization requires the selective polymerization and curing of photosensitive polymers through laser emissions or projections of light [22]. Powder bed fusion (PBF) and direct energy deposition (DED) are comparable because both administer high energy onto a powder bed. PBF uses high temperature to fuse powder particles, whereas DED entails the use of melting with the subsequent material deposition [112]. In material jetting (MJ), a solution of the binding agent is pushed through very tiny nozzles at high speed. The binder liquid is subsequently deposited them onto a substrate in accordance with a CAD-generated model [112]. When utilizing ME, researchers deploy either a low melting – point paste (pneumatic or syringe extrusion) or a high melting – point thermoplastic polymer [112]. In DED, a high energy source is applied onto a powder bed to pull particles together using a CAD-defined image [112]. The major steps involved in 3DP are designing the drug product or device in the computer, and slicing the design (i.e., translating the 3D model into multiple individual layers) printing [140]. A CAD and draft software is normally used to create the design. After that, slicing is carried out to input the speed of printing, infill percentage, temperature, nozzle movement, or extrusion speed [140,141]. Following slicing, researchers conduct 3D printing to obtain the final product [140].

Recently, Pere et al. used 3D printing to produce polymeric MNs from Dental SG (a biocompatible Class I resin) [6]. The authors first used stereolithography to produce the MNs and then excess resin was removed with isopropyl alcohol [6]. UV radiation for 60 min at 40°C was then used to cure the MNs to confer greater mechanical strength [6]. The authors utilized ink-jet printing to coat the MNs with insulin solution through a piezo-driven dispenser (PicPip 300). The investigators positioned the MNs at 45 degrees relative to the dispenser and placed two droplets of the coating formulation longitudinally to the axis of each MN [6]. Three coating formulations [xylitol (5:1 wt./wt.), insulin:mannitol (5:1 wt./wt.), and insulin:trehalose (5:1 wt./wt.)] were used for experiments [6]. Using Franz diffusion cells for transport studies, the investigators reported that insulin was released rapidly within 30 min irrespective of the MN design (pyramids or cones) [6].

Spray coating

Spray coating is commonly utilized to coat MNs [40,121]. The liquid feed is typically atomized by means of pressure, ultrasound, or piezoelectric-actuated apertures (vibrating-mesh nozzles) [142]. Spray coating can be broken down into three stages: (1) atomization which is essentially the generation of fine droplets, (2) substrate deposition, and (3) coalescence of droplets on the substrate [143]. Spray density and spray velocity have considerable influence on the deposition of droplets on a surface [143]. Spray velocity is a function of the nozzle-to-surface distance and atomization air pressure [143]. Higher air-cap setting, higher atomization level, and lower gun-to-surface distances can enhance spray velocity [122]. When an ultrasonically atomized solution of a drug, polymer, and solvent are applied onto a device, the polymer/drug dispersion flows onto the surface of a vibrating nozzle causing the liquid to create standing capillary waves [144]. There is a proportionality between the power of the vibrations and the height of the capillary waves. At a certain critical amplitude, small droplets of liquid are ejected from the tops of the waves and this critical frequency is a constant for each nozzle mass and design [144]. McGrath and coworkers recently spray-coated silicon MNs with two film-coating materials—carboxymethyl cellulose (CMC) and hydroxypropylmethylcellulose (HPMC) [122]. Interestingly, a surfactant (1%, w/w Tween 80) was included in the CMC films to facilitate droplet coalescence on the silicon substrate [122]. In another set of experiments, Vrdoljak et al. spray-coated solid MNs with sugar-based formulations containing modified vaccinia virus Ankara and live adenovirus [143]. The authors prepared suitable sugar-based formulations and utilized them for spray coating each MN [143]. It is important to note that these live virus-coated MNAs elicited a CD8 + T cell response or antibody in mice that was similar to that achieved by intradermal vaccination [143].

Partial immersion

Commier and colleagues coated titanium MNs via partial immersion [145]. The hexagonally patterned MNs (Macroflux) measured 2 cm^2 with 321 microneedles/cm^2 [145]. The coating solutions were loaded with 0.2 wt.% polysorbate and 24 or 40 wt.% desmopressin [145]. The researchers carried out the coating under room conditions (22°C, 45% relative humidity) using a device that restricts the drug to MN tips. The MN tips were then coated with desmopressin and administered to hairless guinea pig skin for 5 or 15 min [145]. Therapeutic concentrations of the drug were obtained after 5 min and the bioavailability went up to 85% [145].

Nitrogen gas jet coating

Jets (i.e., collimated streams of matter) [146] are being increasingly utilized for coating MNs [147]. Gas jet drying can be used to evenly wet MNs with coating solutions [148]. This technique is beneficial because (1) excess coating solution can be promptly discarded by a gas-jet (N10 m/s), averting the use of thick coatings on the needles (2)The coating solution can be uniformly spread on the MNs (3) coating solution viscosity rises rapidly, making it possible for the solution to dry onto the MNs and (4) the coating solution flows over MN base and the bottom layer viscosity of the coating solution is not significantly altered [148]. Chen and coworkers fabricated MNs from silicon using deep reactive ion etching [149]. The MNs were coated with the vaccine by deploying nitrogen gas-jet (approximately 10 m/s) [149]. MNs were treated with a gas-jet at an incident angle (α) of 20° [149]. MN patch comprised 3364 densely packed MNs and the patch size was 5×5 mm [148]. The MN pitch was 70 μm, while the MN base diameter was 25–30 μm [148].

Chen et al. coated MNs with a solution made up of Fluvax 2008 and methylcellulose [149]. The CMNs were administered to mice and the authors revealed that the time to peak serum antibody response was 2 weeks [149]. In addition, about 75% and 90% of the influenza vaccine diffused within 2 and 7 days, respectively [149]. This result compares favorably with the result obtained following intramuscular liquid vaccine injection [149]. In another study, the same research group varied coating parameters and removed the patch edge. This led to an enhanced delivery efficiency from 6.5% to 32.5% [147]. An important fallout of this research was the demonstration by the authors that the dry coating with nitrogen jet can potentially bypass the need for a cold chain, which is a critical bottleneck for vaccine supplies especially in developing countries [147]. The same research laboratory also documented a study in which hemagglutinin inhibition assay titer and antiinfluenza IgG antibody response generated by the coated MNs were similar to that achieved by intramuscular injection [150].

Polyelectrolyte multilayer assembly

A layer-by-layer technique was used to deposit polyelectrolytes on MNs [151]. Kim et al. coated polycarbonate MNs were with polydopamine (pDA) and immersed the microscopic needles in a dopamine coating solution [151]. Heparin/albumin multilayered films were deposited on the pDA-coated MNs by alternatively dipping the MNs into albumin and heparin solutions [151]. Before changing the dipping solution, the MNs were washed twice with a buffer [151]. This process was iterated until the deposition of 16 bilayers was completed [151]. Coating ended with heparin deposited on the outer MN layer [151]. Subsequently, the MNs were immersed in a DNA polyplex solution, washed, and dried [151]. Cationic polymers (Man-DA3) and plasmid DNA (pTarget-Ig-Aβ-Fc) were used to formulate the polyplex coating solution [151]. When applied to mouse skin, there was a rapid release of the polyplex. In addition, a DNA vaccine encoding a secretable fusion protein containing amyloid beta monomer (Aβ1−42), as well as a polymer directed at antigen-presenting cells was also developed. The formulated vaccine induced a potent immune response similar to subcutaneous injection [151]. Furthermore, a strong and immediate recall immune response was achieved, following an antigen challenge postimmunization [151].

Hydrogel-forming microneedles

HFMNs imbibe the skin's interstitial fluid creating channels between and an attached drug reservoir and the skin [15,24,152]. These MNs can be taken from the skin intact from skin, leaving behind no polymer [153]. One of the advantages of HFMNs is that the delivered doses of medications are not restricted by what can be loaded into the needles themselves (the drugs are loaded into the reservoir) making it possible to administer high-dose medications [35]. Another benefit of this class of MNs is that the systems adhere to the skin via a backing layer, improving patient compliance because patch administration only entails one step [154]. In addition, HFMNs function as rate-controlling membranes because upon insertion, they allow prolonged delivery of medications at a rate that can be adjusted via cross-link density, which determines swelling rate [153]. HFMNs are soft following skin insertion, thus reducing the risk of infection transmission [35].

Gantrez AN-139, a linear methyl vinyl ether/maleic anhydride copolymer is often used to fabricate HFMNs [155]. Poly(methyl vinyl ether-co-maleic anhydride) (PMVE/MA) hydrogels can be cross-linked with polyethylene glycol (PEG) and other plasticizers [156] Aqueous blends of PEG-PMVE/MA gels (15%, w/w PMVE/MA and 7.5%, w/w polyethylene glycol [PEG] 10,000) have been used to fabricate HMNs [35]. The authors first prepared silicon master templates by a combination of deposition, lithography, and etching [157]. Low-pressure chemical vapor deposition was employed to coat a silicon wafer with a nitride and oxide layer and then the investigators deployed plasma etching to lithographically pattern this layer [157]. Next, 29% (w/v) potassium hydroxide solution was used to etch the patterned wafer under constant agitation at a temperature of 79°C [157]. The silicon MNs had an aspect ratio of 3:2 (height:base diameter), an interspacing of 750 μm between MN rows, an MN height of 280 μm, and a base diameter of 240 μm [35]. These silicon MNAs were subsequently used to fabricate Silastic 9280/60E silicon elastomer molds [35]. To produce MNs, blends of PEG-PMVE/MA gels (7.5%, w/w polyethylene glycol [PEG and 15%, w/w PMVE/MA] 10,000 in water) were placed in the silicon molds, sealed with an aluminum lid, and centrifuged [35]. Subsequently, the investigators dried the PEG-PMVE/MA MNs at room temperature for 48 h [35]. In a recent study, Kearney et al. formulated and evaluated an integrated MNP containing donepezil hydrochloride [158]. Components of the transdermal patch included a film loaded with donepezil hydrochloride as well as HFMNs [158]. The plasticized films were prepared from either poly(methyl vinyl ether-*co*-maleic anhydride/acid) or poly(vinylpyrrolidone) [158]. The authors studied the in vitro penetration of donepezil hydrochloride from an HFMN patch across stillborn piglet skin and showed that 854.71 ± 122.71 μg of the drug was transported after 24 h [158]. The blood level of drug was 51.8 ± 17.6 ng/mL following the administration of the patch to male Sprague-Dawley rats [158]. The authors showed that HFMNs can be utilized for the achievement of therapeutic blood concentration of an important medication (donepezil) [158].

HFMNs can be fabricated from synthetic and natural polymers [156]. Synthetic polymers are usually prepared to provide the desired degradation properties, while the major advantages of natural polymers are their biocompatibility and biodegradability [156]. Pectin is a natural polymer and a gelling agent used for the preparation of fruit juice, jams, and jellies [156]. The compound is a negatively charged polysaccharide, made from β-1,4-linked α-d-galacturonic acid residues with a part of the carboxyl group being methoxylated [156]. Recently, Demir et al. prepared HFMNs from PMVE/MA-pectin (PMVE/MA-PE) hydrogel systems [156]. The bioadhesive and swelling properties of the PMVE/MA-PE hydrogel were studied and a carbonyl group band shift was found from 1706 to 1776/cm, while the glass transition temperature (T_g) of the cross-linked polymer went up from 55.4°C ± 0.9°C to 119.5°C ± 0.3°C confirming the esterification reaction within the cross-linked films [156]. The researchers used spin casting for the microfabrication of these hydrogel MNAs [156]. 3D-printed MNs were first fabricated and then PDMS inverse replicates of the MNs were used as molds. PMVE/MA-PE dispersion was subsequently poured into the PDMS micromolds [161]. These molds were centrifuged at 3500 rpm at 5°C for 20 min and cured at room temperature for 24 h. The authors then carried out high-temperature cross-linking at 82°C for 24 h [156] and found that the obtained HFMNs were clear, rigid, and sharp [156].

Most HFMNs reported in the literature are fabricated from Gantrez AN-139 cross-linked with polyethylene glycol [35,159]. Increasingly, attempts are being made to combine PMVE/MA with other materials. Hyaluronic acid (HA) is a natural linear polysaccharide created from repeating units of *N*-acetyl-D-glucosamine disaccharide and D-glucuronic acid [160]. This polymer is biocompatible, biodegradable, nontoxic, and nonimmunogenic and possesses many hydroxyl and acidic groups in the molecule and these functional groups can be modified [160]. Recently, Larrañeta et al. prepared HA-based hydrogels using varying concentrations of Gantrez S-97 (GAN) (1%, 3%, and 5% w/w) and 5% (w/w) HA and utilized these hydrogels for the preparation of HFMNs [160]. The authors used a microwave technique to prepare hydrogels and micromolding was then used to prepare the HFMNs [160]. The authors poured aqueous blends containing GAN S-97 (3% w/w) and HA (5% w/w) into laser engineered silicon micromolds (19×19), centrifuged them for 15 min at 3500 rpm and dried them under ambient conditions for 48 h [160]. The last stage of the manufacturing process entailed placing the molds inside a convection oven at 80°C for 24 h [160]. The 600 μm high and 300 μm wide MNs with 50 μm interspacing were conical [160].

In another interesting study, Migdadi and colleagues investigated the transdermal delivery of a high-dose medication (metformin hydrochloride) from HFMNs [161]. In the research project, the HFMNs were produced from aqueous blend of 20% w/w poly(methyl vinyl ether-*co*-maleic acid) cross-linked by esterification with 7.5% w/w poly(ethylene glycol) 10,000 Da [161]. The authors investigated the permeation profiles of the drug across dermatomed neonatal pig skin in vitro and showed that the reservoir patch (containing 75 or 50 mg metformin HCl) in combination with the MNs transported 9.71 ± 2.22 and 10.04 ± 1 mg at 6 h, respectively, and 28.15 ± 2.37 and 23.25 ± 3.58 mg at 24 h, respectively [161]. In contrast, only 0.34 ± 0.39 and 0.85 ± 0.68 mg were transported, respectively, at 6 h, while 0.39 ± 0.39 and 1.01 ± 0.84 mg were transported, respectively, at 24 h, from drug reservoirs (no MNs), which were used in the experiments as controls [161].

It has been asserted that the market success of MN systems will be a function of not only their therapeutic efficacy but also of acceptability by patients [34]. Caffarel-Salvador et al. have stated that MNs, when approved for use by regulatory authorities, will also require acceptability by parents who will administer them to their children pediatricians, who will prescribe the products, and the pediatric patients themselves [34]. It is well known that the formulation of drug delivery systems for pediatric use is accompanied by many obstacles, partly because investigators have to take into consideration different age groups with accompanying challenges. Different requirements have to be met in dosage form design to obtain optimal results [34]. Drug administration through the oral cavity is sometimes problematic for this group of patients due to the difficulty of swallowing as well as palatability issues [34]. Trypanophobia (fear of injections) is also a problem with children [34]. Taking these factors into consideration, HFMNs were fabricated and loaded caffeine, which is commonly used in pediatric patients. The HFMNs were fabricated from aqueous blends containing 7.5% w/w PEG and 15% w/w PMVE/MA using 11 × 11 and 19 × 19 molds [34]. In experiments with rats, the researchers quantified caffeine blood levels following application of drug-loaded HFMNs in comparison with the pharmacokinetic profile obtained following the administration of oral caffeine solution [34]. It was shown that the administration of 653.35 ± 14.76 mg of caffeine from eight reservoir patches attached to HFMNs led to a prolonged transport of the drug over 24 h, reaching a peak plasma concentration of 23.87 μg/mL [34]. This is a clinically relevant concentration range as it has been documented that a caffeine blood level of 5–50 μg/mL can be therapeutically efficacious in preterm neonates [34].

HFMNs have also been investigated for therapeutic drug monitoring. Lithium is used for the management of bipolar disorder—a psychiatric disorder characterized by recurrent episodes of depression and mania [162]. The therapeutic blood level of lithium is from 0.4 to 1.2 mmol/L and due to the narrow therapeutic index of the medication, lithium toxicity can occur [163]. Eltayib et al. developed HFMNs for the extraction and monitoring of lithium in vitro and animal experiments [163]. The authors fabricated 600 μm high, 300 μm wide MNs with an interspacing of 50 μm in the form of 19 × 19 arrays [163]. The HFMNs were prepared via micromolding using aqueous blends containing hydrolyzed PEG 10,000 (5.6%) and PMVE/MA (11.1%) [163]. MN-assisted lithium quantification was conducted across dermatomed neonatal porcine skin (300–400 μm thickness), placed on a modified Franz-cell system with either 0.9 or 2 mmol/L of lithium citrate [163]. In vitro, there was no significant difference in the experimentally determined average lithium concentrations following 30 min MN-assisted administration to excised neonatal pig skin for lithium citrate concentrations of 0.9 and 2 mmol/L. On the other hand, the extracted average lithium concentrations were significantly different after 1 h of application, and these depended on concentration. In animal studies, the investigators dosed rats with lithium citrate equivalent to 15 and 30 mg/kg of lithium carbonate, respectively. The HFMNs were administered 1 h after dosing and removed an hour later. There was no significant difference between lithium concentrations between the two groups. Nonetheless, the higher dosed rats showed a drug concentration that was equivalent to a mean rise of 22.5% compared to lower dosed rats [163].

References

[1] Ita K. Dissolving microneedles for transdermal drug delivery: advances and challenges. Biomed Pharmacother 2017;93:1116–27.

[2] Henry S, et al. Microfabricated microneedles: a novel approach to transdermal drug delivery. J Pharm Sci 1998;87(8):922–5.

[3] Edens C, et al. A microneedle patch containing measles vaccine is immunogenic in non-human primates. Vaccine 2015;33(37):4712–18.

[4] Rzhevskiy AS, et al. Microneedles as the technique of drug delivery enhancement in diverse organs and tissues. J Control Release 2018;270:184–202.

[5] Zhang Y, et al. Advances in transdermal insulin delivery. Adv Drug Deliv Rev 2018;139:51–70.

[6] Pere CPP, et al. 3D printed microneedles for insulin skin delivery. Int J Pharm 2018;544 (2):425–32.

[7] Clancy NT, et al. A new device for assessing changes in skin viscoelasticity using indentation and optical measurement. Skin Res Technol 2010;16(2):210–28.

[8] Chen Z, et al. Rapid fabrication of microneedles using magnetorheological drawing lithography. Acta Biomater 2018;65:283–91.

[9] Ita K. Reflections on the insertion and fracture forces of microneedles. Curr Drug Deliv 2017;14(3):357–63.

[10] Hartmann XH, et al. Insertion process of ceramic nanoporous microneedles by means of a novel mechanical applicator design. Pharmaceutics 2015;7(4):503–22.

[11] Davis SP, et al. Insertion of microneedles into skin: measurement and prediction of insertion force and needle fracture force. J Biomech 2004;37(8):1155–63.

[12] Lhernould MS, Deleers M, Delchambre A. Hollow polymer microneedles array resistance and insertion tests. Int J Pharm 2015;480(1–2):152–7.

[13] Lu Y, et al. Microstereolithography and characterization of poly(propylene fumarate)-based drug-loaded microneedle arrays. Biofabrication 2015;7(4):045001.

[14] Milewski M, et al. Stabilization and transdermal delivery of an investigational peptide using MicroCor® solid-state dissolving microstructure arrays. Journal of Pharmaceutical Sciences 2019.

[15] Sabri AH, et al. Intradermal and transdermal drug delivery using microneedles—fabrication, performance evaluation and application to lymphatic delivery. Adv Drug Deliv Rev 2019; [Epub Online ahead of print].

[16] Wolaschka T. Microneedles as a perspective for transdermal therapeutic systems. Ceska Slov Farm 2019;68(1):12–26.

[17] Kim KS, Ita K, Simon L. Modelling of dissolving microneedles for transdermal drug delivery: theoretical and experimental aspects. Eur J Pharm Sci 2015;68:137–43.

[18] Ita K. Transdermal delivery of drugs with microneedles: strategies and outcomes. J Drug Deliv Sci Technol 2015;29(Suppl C):16–23.

[19] Gupta J, et al. Kinetics of skin resealing after insertion of microneedles in human subjects. J Control Release 2011;154(2):148–55.

[20] Kaushik S, et al. Lack of pain associated with microfabricated microneedles. Anesth Analg 2001;92(2):502–4.

[21] Gill HS, et al. Effect of microneedle design on pain in human volunteers. Clin J Pain 2008;24(7):585–94.

[22] Economidou SN, Lamprou DA, Douroumis D. 3D printing applications for transdermal drug delivery. Int J Pharm 2018;544(2):415–24.

[23] Cheung K, Das D. Microneedles for drug delivery: trends and progress. Drug Deliv 2014;23:2338–54.

[24] Ita K. Transdermal delivery of drugs with microneedles-potential and challenges. Pharmaceutics 2015;7(3):90–105.

[25] Norman JJ, et al. Microneedle patches: usability and acceptability for self-vaccination against influenza. Vaccine 2014;32(16):1856–62.

[26] Larrañeta E, et al. Microneedle arrays as transdermal and intradermal drug delivery systems: materials science, manufacture and commercial development. Mater Sci Eng R Reports 2016;104:1–32.

[27] Al-Zahrani S, et al. Microneedle-mediated vaccine delivery: harnessing cutaneous immunobiology to improve efficacy. Expert Opin Drug Deliv 2012;9(5):541–50.

[28] Bariya SH, et al. Microneedles: an emerging transdermal drug delivery system. J Pharm Pharmacol 2012;64(1):11–29.

[29] Serrano-Castaneda P, et al. Microneedles as enhancer of drug absorption through the skin and applications in medicine and cosmetology. J Pharm Pharm Sci 2018;21(1):73–93.

[30] Hoang MT, Ita KB, Bair DA. Solid microneedles for transdermal delivery of amantadine hydrochloride and pramipexole dihydrochloride. Pharmaceutics 2015;7(4):379–96.

[31] Ameri M, et al. Human growth hormone delivery with a microneedle transdermal system: preclinical formulation, stability, delivery and PK of therapeutically relevant doses. Pharmaceutics 2014;6(2):220–34.

[32] Ita K. Ceramic microneedles and hollow microneedles for transdermal drug delivery: two decades of research. J Drug Deliv Sci Technol 2018;44:314–22.

[33] Du G, et al. Immunogenicity of diphtheria toxoid and poly(I:C) loaded cationic liposomes after hollow microneedle-mediated intradermal injection in mice. Int J Pharm 2018;547 (1–2):250–7.

[34] Caffarel-Salvador E, et al. Potential of hydrogel-forming and dissolving microneedles for use in paediatric populations. Int J Pharm 2015;489(1–2):158–69.

[35] Donnelly RF, et al. Hydrogel-forming microneedle arrays exhibit antimicrobial properties: potential for enhanced patient safety. Int J Pharm 2013;451(1–2):76–91.

[36] Maurya A, et al. Rapidly dissolving microneedle patches for transdermal iron replenishment therapy. J Pharm Sci 2018;107(6):1642–7.

[37] Chu LY, Choi S-O, Prausnitz MR. Fabrication of dissolving polymer microneedles for controlled drug encapsulation and delivery: bubble and pedestal microneedle designs. J Pharm Sci 2010;99(10):4228–38.

[38] Tas C, et al. Dihydroergotamine mesylate-loaded dissolving microneedle patch made of polyvinylpyrrolidone for management of acute migraine therapy. J Control Release 2017;268:159–65.

[39] Gill HS, Prausnitz MR. Coated microneedles for transdermal delivery. J Control Release 2007;117(2):227–37.

[40] Ita K. Modulation of transdermal drug delivery with coated microneedles. J Drug Deliv Sci Technol 2018;45:203–12.

[41] Jung D, et al. Nano-patterning of a stainless steel microneedle surface to improve the dip-coating efficiency of a DNA vaccine and its immune response. Colloids Surf B Biointerfaces 2017;159(Suppl C):54–61.

[42] Koutsonanos DG, et al. Delivery of subunit influenza vaccine to skin with microneedles improves immunogenicity and long-lived protection. Sci Rep 2012;2:357.

[43] Wei-Ze L, et al. Super-short solid silicon microneedles for transdermal drug delivery applications. Int J Pharm 2010;389(1):122–9.

[44] Boks MA, et al. Controlled release of a model vaccine by nanoporous ceramic microneedle arrays. Int J Pharm 2015;491(1-2):375–83.

[45] Martanto W, et al. Transdermal delivery of insulin using microneedles in vivo. Pharm Res 2004;21(6):947–52.

[46] Zhao X, et al. Microneedle delivery of autoantigen for immunotherapy in type 1 diabetes. J Control Release 2016;223:178–87.

[47] Zhao X, et al. Formulation of hydrophobic peptides for skin delivery via coated microneedles. J Control Release 2017;265:2–13.
[48] Kaur M, et al. Microneedle-assisted delivery of verapamil hydrochloride and amlodipine besylate. Eur J Pharm Biopharm 2014;86(2):284–91.
[49] Park J-H, et al. A microneedle roller for transdermal drug delivery. Eur J Pharm Biopharm 2010;76(2):282–9.
[50] Badran MM, Kuntsche J, Fahr A. Skin penetration enhancement by a microneedle device (Dermaroller) in vitro: dependency on needle size and applied formulation. Eur J Pharm Sci 2009;36(4–5):511–23.
[51] Nalluri BN, et al. In vitro skin permeation enhancement of sumatriptan by microneedle application. Curr Drug Deliv 2015;12(6):761–9.
[52] Wang PM, et al. Precise microinjection into skin using hollow microneedles. J Invest Dermatol 2006;126(5):1080–7.
[53] Yan X-X, et al. Fabrication and testing analysis of tapered silicon microneedles for drug delivery applications. Microelectron Eng 2013;111:33–8.
[54] William DCJ. Materials science and engineering: an introduction. 7th ed. John Wiley and Sons; 2007. p. 836.
[55] Carracedo-Taboada M, et al. The influence of process parameters on the physical characteristics of ceramic microneedles, evaluated using a factorial design. Procedia Manuf 2017;13:153–60.
[56] Gang Z, et al. Fabrication of bulk titanium out-of-plane microneedles. In: 2009 4th IEEE international conference on nano/micro engineered and molecular systems; 2009.
[57] Oh KH, Kim H, Seo Y. A facile synthetic route to novel thermotropic liquid crystalline polymers and characterization of their mesophases. RSC Adv 2017;7(47):29772–8.
[58] <https://patents.google.com/patent/US20130253446>.
[59] Nguyen J, et al. The influence of solid microneedles on the transdermal delivery of selected antiepileptic drugs. Pharmaceutics 2016;8(4):E33.
[60] Vucen SR, et al. Improved percutaneous delivery of ketoprofen using combined application of nanocarriers and silicon microneedles. J Pharm Pharmacol 2013;65(10):1451–62.
[61] Deng Y, et al. Transdermal delivery of siRNA through microneedle array. Sci Rep 2016;6:21422.
[62] Nguyen KT, Ita KB, Parikh SJ, Popova IE, Bair DA. Transdermal delivery of captopril and metoprolol tartrate with microneedles. Drug Deliv Lett 2014;4:236–43.
[63] Abiandu I, Ita K. Transdermal delivery of potassium chloride with solid microneedles. J Drug Deliv Sci Technol 2019;53:101216.
[64] Sivaraman A, Banga AK. Novel in situ forming hydrogel microneedles for transdermal drug delivery. Drug Deliv Transl Res 2017;7(1):16–26.
[65] de Groot AM, et al. Nanoporous microneedle arrays effectively induce antibody responses against diphtheria and tetanus toxoid. Front Immunol 2017;8:1789.
[66] Shirkhanzadeh M. Microneedles coated with porous calcium phosphate ceramics: effective vehicles for transdermal delivery of solid trehalose. J Mater Sci Mater Med 2005;16(1):37–45.
[67] Wan Y, et al. Development of stabilizing formulations of a trivalent inactivated poliovirus vaccine in a dried state for delivery in the nanopatch microprojection array. J Pharm Sci 2018;107(6):1540–51.
[68] Ng HI, Fernando GJ, Kendall MA. Induction of potent CD8(+) T cell responses through the delivery of subunit protein vaccines to skin antigen-presenting cells using densely packed microprojection arrays. J Control Release 2012;162(3):477–84.

[69] Jenkins D, et al. High density and high aspect ratio solid micro-nanoprojection arrays for targeted skin vaccine delivery and specific antibody extraction. RSC Adv 2012;2(8):3490–5.
[70] Kim YC, Park JH, Prausnitz MR. Microneedles for drug and vaccine delivery. Adv Drug Deliv Rev 2012;64(14):1547–68.
[71] Ronnander P, et al. Dissolving polyvinylpyrrolidone-based microneedle systems for in-vitro delivery of sumatriptan succinate. Eur J Pharm Sci 2018;114:84–92.
[72] Vassilieva EV, et al. Improved immunogenicity of individual influenza vaccine components delivered with a novel dissolving microneedle patch stable at room temperature. Drug Deliv Transl Res 2015;5(4):360–71.
[73] Pamornpathomkul B, et al. Dissolving polymeric microneedle arrays for enhanced site-specific acyclovir delivery. Eur J Pharm Sci 2018;121:200–9.
[74] Ronnander P, et al. Modelling the in-vitro dissolution and release of sumatriptan succinate from polyvinylpyrrolidone-based microneedles. Eur J Pharm Sci 2018;125:54–63.
[75] Nguyen HX, et al. Poly (vinyl alcohol) microneedles: fabrication, characterization, and application for transdermal drug delivery of doxorubicin. Eur J Pharm Biopharm 2018;129:88–103.
[76] Choi CK, et al. Spatially discrete thermal drawing of biodegradable microneedles for vascular drug delivery. Eur J Pharm Biopharm 2013;83(2):224–33.
[77] Yang H, et al. Centrifugal lithography: self-shaping of polymer microstructures encapsulating biopharmaceutics by centrifuging polymer drops. Adv Healthc Mater 2017;6(19):1700326.
[78] Kim JD, et al. Droplet-born air blowing: novel dissolving microneedle fabrication. J Control Release 2013;170(3):430–6.
[79] Lau S, et al. Multilayered pyramidal dissolving microneedle patches with flexible pedestals for improving effective drug delivery. J Control Release 2017;265:113–19.
[80] Yang H, et al. Rapid implantation of dissolving microneedles on an electrospun pillar array. Biomaterials 2015;64:70–7.
[81] Yan L, et al. Nanocomposite-strengthened dissolving microneedles for improved transdermal delivery to human skin. Adv Healthc Mater 2014;3(4):555–64.
[82] Bouaziz Z, et al. Dual role of layered double hydroxide nanocomposites on antibacterial activity and degradation of tetracycline and oxytetracyline. Chemosphere 2018;206:175–83.
[83] Mishra G, Dash B, Pandey S. Layered double hydroxides: a brief review from fundamentals to application as evolving biomaterials. Appl Clay Sci 2018;153:172–86.
[84] Szabados M, et al. Structural reconstruction of mechanochemically disordered CaFe-layered double hydroxide. Appl Clay Sci 2019;174:138–45.
[85] Zhan H, et al. Application of composite dissolving microneedles with high drug loading ratio for rapid local anesthesia. Eur J Pharm Sci 2018;121:330–7.
[86] Gardeniers HJGE, Luttge R, Berenschot EJW, de Boer MJ, Yeshurun SY, Hefetz M, et al. Silicon micromachined hollow microneedles for transdermal liquid transport. J Microelectromech Syst 2003;12:855–62.
[87] Yan Q, et al. Enhancement of Ag85B DNA vaccine immunogenicity against tuberculosis by dissolving microneedles in mice. Vaccine 2018;36(30):4471–6.
[88] Nejad HR, et al. Low-cost and cleanroom-free fabrication of microneedles. Microsyst Nanoeng 2018;4:17073.
[89] Lee K, et al. Drawing lithography: three-dimensional fabrication of an ultrahigh-aspect-ratio microneedle. Adv Mater 2010;22(4):483–6.

[90] Lee K, Jung H. Drawing lithography for microneedles: a review of fundamentals and biomedical applications. Biomaterials 2012;33(30):7309–26.
[91] Zhang J, et al. Use of drawing lithography-fabricated polyglycolic acid microneedles for transdermal delivery of itraconazole to a human basal cell carcinoma model regenerated on mice. JOM 2016;68(4):1128–33.
[92] Yin Z, et al. Swellable silk fibroin microneedles for transdermal drug delivery. Int J Biol Macromol 2017;106:48–56.
[93] Pounds R, et al. Repurposing itraconazole for the treatment of cancer. Oncol Lett 2017;14(3):2587–97.
[94] Liang G, et al. Itraconazole exerts its anti-melanoma effect by suppressing Hedgehog, Wnt, and PI3K/mTOR signaling pathways. Oncotarget 2017;8(17):28510–25.
[95] Luzuriaga MA, et al. Biodegradable 3D printed polymer microneedles for transdermal drug delivery. Lab Chip 2018;18(8):1223–30.
[96] Lee JW, Park JH, Prausnitz MR. Dissolving microneedles for transdermal drug delivery. Biomaterials 2008;29(13):2113–24.
[97] Kim MJ, et al. Fabrication of circular obelisk-type multilayer microneedles using micro-milling and spray deposition. Front Bioeng Biotechnol 2018;6:54.
[98] Huh I, et al. Effects of two droplet-based dissolving microneedle manufacturing methods on the activity of encapsulated epidermal growth factor and ascorbic acid. Eur J Pharm Sci 2018;114:285–92.
[99] Fakhraei Lahiji S, et al. Effects of dissolving microneedle fabrication parameters on the activity of encapsulated lysozyme. Eur J Pharm Sci 2018;117:290–6.
[100] Jin X, et al. Insulin delivery systems combined with microneedle technology. Adv Drug Deliv Rev 2018;127:119–37.
[101] Lyon BJ, Aria AI, Gharib M. Fabrication of carbon nanotube-polyimide composite hollow microneedles for transdermal drug delivery. Biomed Microdevices 2014;16 (6):879–86.
[102] Chen Y, et al. Fabrication of coated polymer microneedles for transdermal drug delivery. J Control Release 2017;265:14–21.
[103] Chaudhri BP, et al. High strength, polymer microneedles for transdermal drug delivery. Procedia Eng 2011;25:1377–80.
[104] Jun H, et al. Use of hollow microneedles for targeted delivery of phenylephrine to treat fecal incontinence. J Control Release 2015;207:1–6.
[105] McAllister DV, et al. Microfabricated needles for transdermal delivery of macromolecules and nanoparticles: fabrication methods and transport studies. Proc Natl Acad Sci USA 2003;100(24):13755–60.
[106] Davis SP, et al. Hollow metal microneedles for insulin delivery to diabetic rats. IEEE Trans Biomed Eng 2005;52(5):909–15.
[107] Norman JJ, et al. Hollow microneedles for intradermal injection fabricated by sacrificial micromolding and selective electrodeposition. Biomed Microdevices 2013;15(2):203–10.
[108] Hruby J. Overview of LIGA microfabrication. AIP Conf Proc 2002;625(1):55–62.
[109] Pamornpathomkul B, et al. Enhancement of skin permeation and skin immunization of ovalbumin antigen via microneedles. AAPS PharmSciTech 2017;18(7):2418–26.
[110] Faraji Rad Z, et al. High-fidelity replication of thermoplastic microneedles with open microfluidic channels. Microsyst Nanoeng 2017;3:17034.
[111] Golombek S, et al. Intradermal delivery of synthetic mRNA using hollow microneedles for efficient and rapid production of exogenous proteins in skin. Mol Ther Nucleic Acids 2018;11:382–92.

[112] Lim SH, et al. 3D printed drug delivery and testing systems—a passing fad or the future? Adv Drug Deliv Rev 2018;132:139–68.
[113] Kim YC, et al. Formulation and coating of microneedles with inactivated influenza virus to improve vaccine stability and immunogenicity. J Control Release 2010;142 (2):187–95.
[114] Shakya AK, Lee CH, Gill HS. Cutaneous vaccination with coated microneedles prevents development of airway allergy. J Control Release 2017;265:75–82.
[115] Serpe L, et al. Influence of salivary washout on drug delivery to the oral cavity using coated microneedles: an in vitro evaluation. Eur J Pharm Sci 2016;93:215–23.
[116] Peters EE, et al. Erythropoietin-coated ZP-microneedle transdermal system: preclinical formulation, stability, and delivery. Pharm Res 2012;29(6):1618–26.
[117] Caudill CL, et al. Spatially controlled coating of continuous liquid interface production microneedles for transdermal protein delivery. J Control Release 2018;284:122–32.
[118] Ullah A, Kim CM, Kim GM. Porous polymer coatings on metal microneedles for enhanced drug delivery. R Soc Open Sci 2018;5(4):171609.
[119] Khan H, et al. Smart microneedle coatings for controlled delivery and biomedical analysis. J Drug Target 2014;22(9):790–5.
[120] Boehm RD, et al. Modification of microneedles using inkjet printing. AIP Adv 2011;1 (2):22139.
[121] Haj-Ahmad R, et al. Microneedle coating techniques for transdermal drug delivery. Pharmaceutics 2015;7(4):486–502.
[122] McGrath MG, et al. Determination of parameters for successful spray coating of silicon microneedle arrays. Int J Pharm 2011;415(1–2):140–9.
[123] Moreno E, et al. Skin vaccination using microneedles coated with a plasmid DNA cocktail encoding nucleosomal histones of Leishmania spp. Int J Pharm 2017;533(1):236–44.
[124] Singh R, et al. Synthesis of active absorber layer by dip-coating method for perovskite solar cell. J Mol Struct 2018;1158:229–33.
[125] Chaki SH, et al. CuAlS2 thin films—dip coating deposition and characterization. J Sci Adv Mater Devices 2017;2(2):215–24.
[126] Lee HS, et al. Bleomycin-coated microneedles for treatment of warts. Pharm Res 2017;34(1):101–12.
[127] Baek SH, Shin JH, Kim YC. Drug-coated microneedles for rapid and painless local anesthesia. Biomed Microdevices 2017;19(1):2.
[128] Xie J, et al. Electrohydrodynamic atomization: a two-decade effort to produce and process micro-/nanoparticulate materials. Chem Eng Sci 2015;125:32–57.
[129] Bocanegra R, et al. Multiple electrosprays emitted from an array of holes. J Aerosol Sci 2005;36(12):1387–99.
[130] Nikolaou M, Krasia-Christoforou T. Electrohydrodynamic methods for the development of pulmonary drug delivery systems. Eur J Pharm Sci 2017;113:29–40.
[131] Lim DJ, et al. Microneedles: a versatile strategy for transdermal delivery of biological molecules. Int J Biol Macromol 2017;110:30–8.
[132] Wang Y, et al. Inkjet printing of δ-MnO2 nanosheets for flexible solid-state micro-supercapacitor. Nano Energy 2018;49:481–8.
[133] Uddin MJ, et al. Inkjet printing of transdermal microneedles for the delivery of anticancer agents. Int J Pharm 2015;494(2):593–602.
[134] Rosa M, Barou C, Esposito V. Zirconia UV-curable colloids for additive manufacturing via hybrid inkjet printing-stereolithography. Mater Lett 2018;215:214–17.

[135] Cheow WS, Kiew TY, Hadinoto K. Combining inkjet printing and amorphous nanonization to prepare personalized dosage forms of poorly-soluble drugs. Eur J Pharm Biopharm 2015;96:314–21.

[136] Daly R, et al. Inkjet printing for pharmaceutics—a review of research and manufacturing. Int J Pharm 2015;494:554–67.

[137] Kollamaram G, et al. Inkjet printing of paracetamol and indomethacin using electromagnetic technology: rheological compatibility and polymorphic selectivity. Eur J Pharm Sci 2018;115:248–57.

[138] Boehm RD, et al. Polyglycolic acid microneedles modified with inkjet-deposited antifungal coatings. Biointerphases 2015;10(1):011004.

[139] Trauner KB. The emerging role of 3D printing in arthroplasty and orthopedics. J Arthroplasty 2018;33(8):2352–4.

[140] Khatri P, Shah MK, Vora N. Formulation strategies for solid oral dosage form using 3D printing technology: a mini-review. J Drug Deliv Sci Technol 2018;46:148–55.

[141] Blok LG, et al. An investigation into 3D printing of fibre reinforced thermoplastic composites. Addit Manuf 2018;22:176–86.

[142] Beck-Broichsitter M, et al. Modified vibrating-mesh nozzles for advanced spray-drying applications. Eur J Pharm Biopharm 2015;92:96–101.

[143] Vrdoljak A, et al. Coated microneedle arrays for transcutaneous delivery of live virus vaccines. J Control Release 2012;159(1):34–42.

[144] McDermott M, et al. Application of quality by design (QbD) approach to ultrasonic atomization spray coating of drug-eluting stents. AAPS PharmSciTech 2015;16 (4):811–23.

[145] Cormier M, et al. Transdermal delivery of desmopressin using a coated microneedle array patch system. J Control Release 2004;97(3):503–11.

[146] Park G, et al. The effect of jet shape on jet injection. Conf Proc IEEE Eng Med Biol Soc 2015;2015:7350–3.

[147] Chen X, et al. Improving the reach of vaccines to low-resource regions, with a needle-free vaccine delivery device and long-term thermostabilization. J Control Release 2011;152(3):349–55.

[148] Chen X, et al. Dry-coated microprojection array patches for targeted delivery of immunotherapeutics to the skin. J Control Release 2009;139(3):212–20.

[149] Chen X, et al. Rapid kinetics to peak serum antibodies is achieved following influenza vaccination by dry-coated densely packed microprojections to skin. J Control Release 2012;158(1):78–84.

[150] Fernando GJ, et al. Nanopatch targeted delivery of both antigen and adjuvant to skin synergistically drives enhanced antibody responses. J Control Release 2012;159(2):215–21.

[151] Kim NW, et al. Polyplex-releasing microneedles for enhanced cutaneous delivery of DNA vaccine. J Control Release 2014;179:11–17.

[152] Kearney M-C, et al. Potential of microneedles in enhancing delivery of photosensitising agents for photodynamic therapy. Photodiagn Photodyn Ther 2014;11(4):459–66.

[153] Donnelly RF, et al. Hydrogel-forming microneedles prepared from "super swelling" polymers combined with lyophilised wafers for transdermal drug delivery. PLoS One 2014;9(10):e111547.

[154] Donnelly RF, et al. Hydrogel-forming microneedles increase in volume during swelling in skin, but skin barrier function recovery is unaffected. J Pharm Sci 2014;103 (5):1478–86.

[155] Migalska K, et al. Laser-engineered dissolving microneedle arrays for transdermal macromolecular drug delivery. Pharm Res 2011;28(8):1919–30.
[156] Demir YK, et al. Poly (methyl vinyl ether-co-maleic acid)—pectin based hydrogel-forming systems: gel, film, and microneedles. Eur J Pharm Biopharm 2017;117:182–94.
[157] Donnelly RF, et al. Processing difficulties and instability of carbohydrate microneedle arrays. Drug Dev Ind Pharm 2009;35(10):1242–54.
[158] Kearney M-C, et al. Microneedle-mediated delivery of donepezil: potential for improved treatment options in Alzheimer's disease. Eur J Pharm Biopharm 2016;103:43–50.
[159] Donnelly RF, et al. Hydrogel-forming microneedle arrays for enhanced transdermal drug delivery. Adv Funct Mater 2012;22(23):4879–90.
[160] Larraneta E, et al. Synthesis and characterization of hyaluronic acid hydrogels cross-linked using a solvent-free process for potential biomedical applications. Carbohydr Polym 2018;181:1194–205.
[161] Migdadi EM, et al. Hydrogel-forming microneedles enhance transdermal delivery of metformin hydrochloride. J Control Release 2018;285:142–51.
[162] Luu B, Rodway G. Lithium therapy for bipolar disorder. J Nurse Pract 2018;14(2):93–9.
[163] Eltayib E, et al. Hydrogel-forming microneedle arrays: potential for use in minimally-invasive lithium monitoring. Eur J Pharm Biopharm 2016;102:123–31.

Chapter 9

Iontophoresis, magnetophoresis, and electroporation

In this chapter, we will examine three distinct types of physical enhancement for transdermal drug delivery: Iontophoresis (ITP), magnetophoresis, and electroporation (ETP). Table 9.1 shows the effect of ITP, magnetophoresis, and ETP on transdermal drug delivery.

Transdermal ITP refers to the use of a mild electric current for the transport of charged drug molecules across the skin [1−5]. The technology uses an external electrical potential gradient to drive charged molecules across the skin [6]. A representation of an in vitro iontophoretic setup is shown in Fig. 9.1.

A force is typically exerted on charged particles within an electric field [7]. If the particles move freely, an electric current is generated [7]. Due to force being applied on conduction band electrons, an electronic current is generated in metals [7]. In ionic solutions, current is created due to the force exerted on ions [7]. During ITP, both ionic and electronic currents are at play [7]. In the presence of an electric potential difference, ions diffuse through the epidermis and the dermis, ultimately reaching systemic circulation [8]. ITP takes place mainly through areas of low electrical resistance (appendageal pathways) [9] and appendages constitute approximately 0.1% of the total surface area of human skin [10]. The physicochemical properties of the drug molecule, formulation characteristics and iontophoretic conditions can impact transdermal flux [11]. The possibility of iontophoretic transport through the intercellular pathway is documented in the literature even though the contribution of this pathway is thought to be relatively small [9]. Pikal has asserted that the force imposed by an electric field on an ion is stronger than the concentration gradient which drives passive diffusion [12]. The result of this phenomenon is that ions are driven through a membrane more efficiently by ITP in comparison with passive drug transport [12]. The routes for iontophoretic transport include not just across the stratum corneum (SC) but also via hair follicles and sweat ducts [8].

From the standpoint of ITP, it is important to note that the SC possesses a high electrical resistance and a negative background charge [4,13]. Furthermore, the electrical resistance of the SC drops significantly when the

Transdermal Drug Delivery. DOI: https://doi.org/10.1016/B978-0-12-822550-9.00009-0

TABLE 9.1 The effect of ITP, magnetophoresis, and ETP on transdermal drug delivery.

Therapeutic agent(s) or model compound(s)	Skin model(s)	Method	References
Ranitidine	Pig skin	ITP	[16]
Methotrexate	Human skin	ITP	[48]
Penbutolol	Pig skin	ITP	[50]
Almotriptan malate	Pig skin	ITP	[53]
3-Fluoroamphetamine	Human skin	ITP	[54]
Acyclovir	Pig skin	ITP	[56]
Granisetron	Pig skin	ITP	[60]
Memantine	pig ear skin	ITP	[64]
Ketoprofen	Human skin, rat skin	ITP	[65]
Dexamethasone	Pig skin	ITP	[13]
Donepezil	Rat skin	ITP	[77]
Lidocaine	Pig skin	Magnetophoresis	[82]
Terbutaline sulfate	Human skin	Magnetophoresis	[83]
Doxepin	Pig skin	ETP	[115]
Fentanyl	Human skin	ETP	[112]
Metoprolol	Rat skin	ETP	[121]
Nalbuphine	Rat skin, mouse skin	ETP	[124]
Doxorubicin	Mouse skin	ETP	[109]
Ferric pyrophosphate	Pig skin	ETP	[125]

administered voltage is more than 2 V [4,13]. ITP circumvents the SC and offers a precise control over the quantity of medication delivered [14]. One of the major objectives of transdermal drug delivery is to achieve predictable, controlled, and reproducible release of the active pharmaceutical ingredient into the patient's bloodstream [15] and the iontophoretic approach provides these benefits. Significantly, ITP can be used to drive medications whose physicochemical properties make them poor candidates for passive transdermal transport (polar and charged medications) [16]. If the patch/device rather than the skin is the rate-controlling factor, then drug delivery is more reproducible, with smaller intra- and intersubject

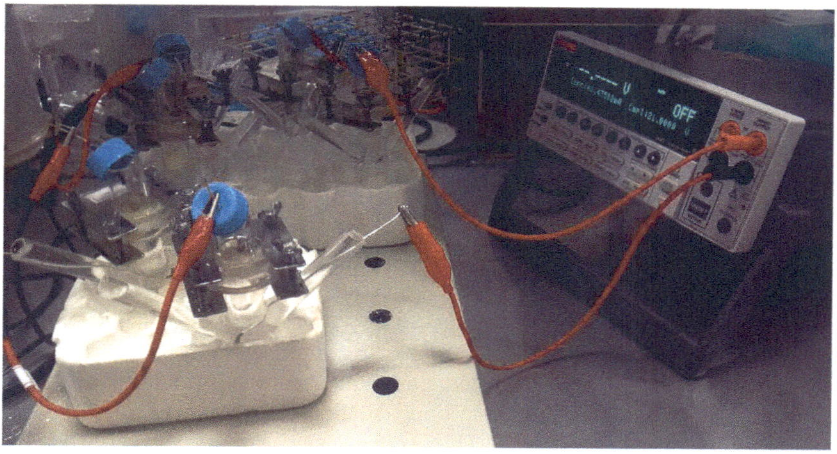

FIGURE 9.1 Representation of an in vitro iontophoretic setup. *Reproduced with permission from Bernardi DS, et al., Effective transcutaneous immunization using a combination of ITP and nanoparticles. Nanomedicine 2016;12(8):2439–48.*

variability [15]. Another benefit of electrotransport is that it can be controlled because drug delivery is proportional to electric current, which can be easily modified [17]. In addition, pharmacotherapy with iontophoretic systems can be individualized for patients [17]. Moreover, when mild current gradient for a short time (generally ≤ 0.5 mA/cm^2 and half-hour for transdermal delivery) is utilized, the risk of infections and tissue trauma can be reduced [18]. Furthermore, ions can be electrostatically bound to ion exchangers prior to administration and these ions are gradually released and delivered across the skin during following the application of a mild electric current [15].

ITP is particularly effective for the transport of ions and the current used in transdermal iontophoretic experiments is usually in the range of 0.5 mA [2,19]. Within the limits of current used (typically less than 0.5 mA), ITP has been postulated to be safe in humans [20]. There is usually neither irritation (beyond mild erythema) nor pain when low-amplitude direct current (DC) is administered to human skin [20]. The Food and Drug Administration has approved transdermal iontophoretic devices for drug delivery (LidoSite®) [2]. The same regulatory authority had also approved GlucoWatch Biographer® for non-invasive glucose sampling but the product has now been withdrawn from the market [21]. The major factors contributing to iontophoretic drug transport include treatment duration, current density, tissue permeability (the skin in this instance), drug concentration, and pH [22,23]. The one-dimensional transdermal flux of a molecule, J_i, in the presence of an applied electric field, E, is a function of both the potential gradient and concentration. J_i can be calculated by using a modified form of the Nernst–Planck equation that also considers convective solvent flow [24]:

$$J_i = -\left[D_i \frac{\partial C_i}{\partial x} + u_i c_i \frac{\partial \varphi}{\partial x}\right] \pm v_w c_i \tag{9.1}$$

and

$$u_i = \frac{z_i D_i F}{RT} \tag{9.2}$$

where z_i, D_i, c_i, and u_i are the valence, diffusion coefficient, concentration, and electrical mobility of ion i, respectively, and v_w is the linear velocity of the convective solvent flow [24]. The electric mobility is the proportionality constant between the flux and the potential gradient, while the diffusion coefficient is the corresponding proportionality constant between flux and concentration gradient [24]. This relationship is described by the Nernst–Einstein equation (Eq. 3.18) [24]. Several investigators have deployed iontophoretic delivery for percutaneous drug delivery of peptides and oligonucleotides (challenging molecules) as well as low molecular–weight compounds [17].

A great deal of effort has been expended toward understanding the physical mechanisms governing ITP [25]. The major mechanisms involved in transdermal iontophoretic transport are electromigration (EM), electroosmosis (EO) and passive diffusion [26,27]. Iontophoretic total solute flux (J_i) is obtained by adding of convective flow (J_{EO}), passive diffusion (J_P), and EM (J_{EM}) [27]:

$$J_i = J_{EO} + J_P + J_{EM} \tag{9.3}$$

In EM, the anode repels positively charged cations and the cathode repels negatively charged anions [28]. Ion migration is the major mode through which electric current is transported across an electrolytic solution [29]. Typically, cations migrate to the cathode, while the anions are attracted to the anode (Fig. 9.2) [29].

The electric field created during ITP drives cationic medications from the anodal chamber and anionic drugs from the cathodal chamber into the skin [28]. ITP provides the external energy that drives drug ions across the skin in consonance with the general principle of electricity which states that opposite charges attract each other, while like charges repel each other [30]. When researchers attempt to drive a positively charged medication across the skin, they place it under a positive electrode, while an anionic drug is placed under a cathode [30]. Indeed, ITP can be either anodal or cathodal [9]. In anodal ITP, the anode is in contact with a solution containing a cationic drug, while the cathode is placed elsewhere on the skin [9]. In the case of cathodal ITP, the cathode is placed in the donor compartment, while the anode is in the receiver compartment of the Franz diffusion cell or an

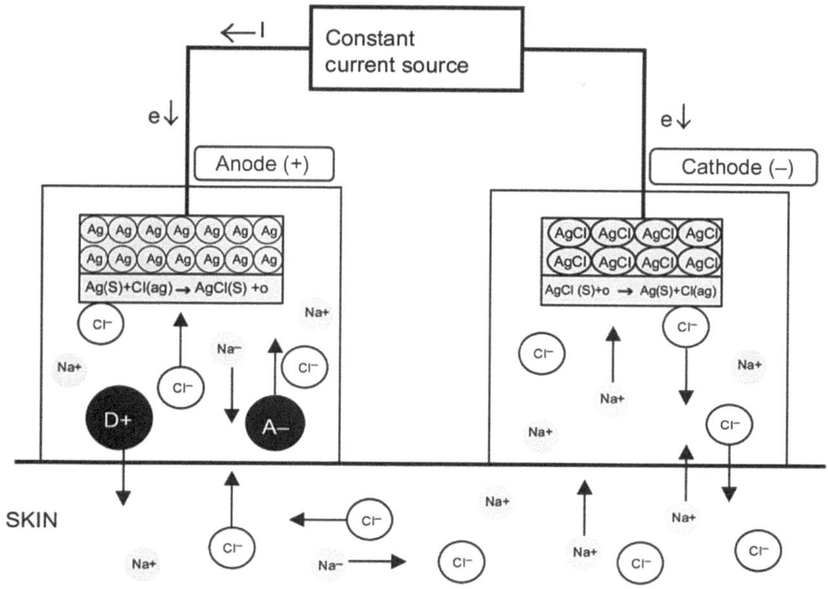

FIGURE 9.2 ITP using an Ag/AgCl electrode system. EM transports the cations, including the drug molecule, from the anodal compartment and into the skin. At the same time, endogenous anions, primarily Cl^-, move into the anodal compartment. *Reproduced with permission from Kalia YN, et al., Iontophoretic drug delivery. Adv Drug Deliv Rev 2004;56(5):619–58.*

analogous experimental system [9]. The iontophoretic movement of an ion is a function of ionic composition of the solutions interacting with the skin [31]. ITP causes ions to compete for a portion of the electric current and the magnitude of each ion's contribution to charge transport is called its transport number. The sum total of transport numbers is unity (1) [27]. In accordance with Faraday's law, the iontophoretic flux (*J*) of a medication delivered by EM is in direct proportionality to the applied current intensity (*I*) [31]:

$$J = \frac{t.I}{F.z_i} \tag{9.4}$$

where J is the flux, t is the transport number, z_i is the valence of an ion i, and F is Faraday's number. The presence of all other ions in an iontophoretic system should be minimized to optimize EM [26]. In an ideal scenario, coions should be eliminated from the dosage form leaving only endogenously encountered counterions [26]. This reduces competition and maximizes the transport number [26]. The transport efficiency of an ionic medication is a function of its physicochemical properties, which determine ionic mobility [31]. In addition, counterion and coion concentration also influences iontophoretic drug transport efficiency [31].

In vitro experiments and calculations based upon Eq. (4.1) are usually used to determine transport number [31]. Mudry and coworkers have emphasized that transport numbers are only valid for each unique set of experimental conditions [31]. The proportion of the total charge flowing in the iontophoretic circuit that is carried by the drug itself is somewhat small and is rarely higher than 10% [32]. Sodium ions are endogenous cations, and these are small, highly mobile species that are more effective charge transporters than drug cations [32]. Alternatively, when a medication is formulated as simply as possible with no competing cations from a buffer or other electrolytes, there is always competition with counterions (mostly the anion chloride) [32]. In a recent study, ITP was used for the transport of an anionic protein across intact skin [33]. The cathodal transport of the anionic protein was adequate to surmount convective solvent flow in the anode-to-cathode direction [33].

Transdermal EO is the convective flow of a solvent transdermally under the influence of an electric field [3,34]. It is the major permeation mechanism of high molecular–weight cations and uncharged molecules [27]. "Volume flow" or bulk fluid flow usually takes place when an electric field or voltage is applied across a porous membrane [12]. This flow represents fluid motion in the absence of a concentration gradient and this is comparable to viscous flow induced by a pressure gradient [12]. Bulk fluid flow is not the same as diffusion [12]. Another point to note is that in EO, pressure difference is absent and fluid flow may either be in the direction of current flow or against it [12]. The isoelectric point (the pH at which the net charge is zero) of the mammalian skin is between 3.5 and 4.8 and at physiological pH, the skin is cation-permselective and negatively charged [28]. Electroosmotic solvent flow that is responsible for the transport of neutral molecules in the anode-to-cathode direction is commonly induced by the preferential passage of counterions [27]. EO can be modulated by altering the formulation in the electrode chambers and changing the permselectivity of the skin [27]. EO is a flow process that reflects solvent velocity and the unit is volume flow per unit area per unit time [2,4,35]:

$$J_{EO} = \upsilon c \tag{9.5}$$

where c is the concentration of drug in the donor solution and υ is the velocity of the current-induced water flow [2,28]. For simplicity and assuming that the contribution to passive flux (J_P) is negligible, Guy and coworkers suggested that the following equation be used to calculate the total iontophoetic flux of a solute [35]:

$$J_t = \frac{z_i u_i c_i I}{F.\sum z_i u_i c_i} + \upsilon c \tag{9.6}$$

Where u_i z_i, c_i are electrical mobility, valence, and concentration of the ion i, while υ is the electroosmotic solvent velocity which is positive when cations are electrophoresed and negative during the ITP of anions, F is Faraday's constant, and I is the current density [35]. All moieties present are under the summation sign while J_t is the total flux of the solute [35]. The average ionic mobility of sodium and chloride ions in the SC is about 1.53×10^{-8} cm^2/V/s and for fast-moving ions of that magnitude of mobility with an acceptable level of current density, the dominant mechanism of ITP is EM [35]. For a slow-moving cationic peptide with a mobility in the range of 10^{-11} cm^2/V/s, the total flux is basically electroosmotic and the value can be 10-fold less than that of the more mobile ions [35]. At intermediate mobilities, the distribution between EO and EM is between the two extremes [35]. The proportion of a charged or neutral molecule transferred by EO or EM is a function of the polarity of the applied current and the physicochemical properties of the molecules [36]. Another point worthy of emphasis is that although Eq. (4.3) shows a linear relationship between drug flux and concentration, transdermal iontophoretic flux may not be enhanced by simply increasing the amount of the medication in the donor compartment [4]. The pH of the solution is equally significant as it determines the ionization of the compound [36]. From the Henderson–Hasselbalch equation, it is known that there is a direct proportionality between ionic fraction and the pH of the solution for weak acids [36]. In contrast, the proportion of undissociated weak base increases with increasing pH and the percentage of ionization can be computed if the pH of the solution and the pKa of the compound are known [36]. Raising the pH of a weak base decreases the ionic fraction of the drug, which decreases iontophoretic transport [37]. Iontophoretic transport depends on current intensity (i.e., the amount of charge expressed in coulombs), time of application of the current, and the cross-sectional skin area in contact with the electrode [36]. In humans, current density can range from 17 μA/cm^2 to 0.5 mA/cm^2, which is ordinarily regarded as a safe current density range [36].

Because electrical mobility declines with increasing molecular weight, researchers have postulated that the iontophoretic delivery of larger molecules such as peptides and proteins occurs mostly via EO [15]. Another perspective links a high charge-to-mass ratio with enhanced electric mobility that should favor protein ITP [33]. Dubey and Kalia have shown that, for an anionic protein, cathodal EM may sometimes be adequate to surmount the opposition due to convective solvent flow in the anode-to-cathode direction [33]. It is also important to emphasize that using a relatively high voltage during ITP enhances the transport of medications by a mechanism of pore formation that reduces the skin's resistance [38]. It is known that a sustained cathodal current may lead to electrochemical polarization of the skin resulting in an increase in skin resistance and decreased drug transport efficiency [38]. DC ITP has been postulated to be an efficient type of transdermal transport because the amount of medication transported is directly proportional to current density [15]. However, constant voltage can lead to skin polarization that ultimately reduces effective current across the skin [15]. The decreased transport efficiency is induced by a voltage drop in the solution caused by the creation of an electric double layer on the electrode surface (electrode polarization). The polarization occurs due to the accumulation of ions whose charge differs from electrode polarity [39]. Transdermal current gradient decay is proportional to a decrease in iontophoretic flux [15]. Furthermore, the uninterrupted use of constant current can reduce the drug ion transport number [15]. Pulsed current ITP (with variable On/Off ratios) can be used to facilitate skin depolarization, allowing the return to steady-state conditions and limiting irritation [38].

In pulsed current ITP, DC is employed periodically [15]. The skin discharges current and depolarizes during the "Off period" of pulse delivery hindering residual charges by the beginning of a new pulse [15]. The SC functions as a parallel resistance/capacitance electric circuit and at fixed applied voltage, the current is initially high because the "capacitor" portion of the circuit is charged but with time, there is a reduction in the current by a value controlled by the "resistor" portion of the circuit [40]. Despite the popularity of DC ITP, the effect of alternating current (AC) ITP on the transport of charged permeants across the human epidermal membrane has also been investigated [41]. A remarkable increase in transdermal flux was documented during AC ITP at the frequency of 2.5–2000 Hz [41]. Two modes of AC ITP were utilized: a constant voltage mode (constant AC voltage across the skin with fluctuating electrical resistance) and a constant conductance method (constant skin resistance with changing applied AC voltage) [41]. During AC ITP, the skin electrical resistance is reduced by the AC electric field [41].

Several iontophoretic systems have been approved by regulatory authorities. LidoSite used ITP to deliver lidocaine and epinephrine [2] and it was approved by the Food and Drug Administration (FDA) as a transdermal iontophoretic system for fast dermal anesthesia [42]. Ionsys was a transdermal iontophoretic system for the administration of fentanyl for the alleviation of pain [42]. Zecuity was loaded with the antimigraine drug sumatriptan and was also approved by the FDA as an iontophoretic drug delivery system [42]. The sale of the product was discontinued by Teva Pharmaceuticals [43] in 2016 due to reports of "scars" and/or "burns" in patients [42]. The use of Ionsys was discontinued in 2009 due to patch corrosion, while the sale of Lidosite was suspended in 2008 [42].

The wearable electronic disposable drug (WEDD) system is a portable, disposable, and noninvasive patch that uses low-level current to transport drugs across the skin [42]. The patch is less than 2 mm wide and it is fabricated from a flexible fabric. The device has screen-printed and planar electrodes as well as a circuitry with a fixed charge capacity [42]. With WEDD, it is possible to obtain different energy profiles without the need for a microprocessor to regulate the charge [42].

Transdermal iontophoretic delivery of therapeutic agents

Ranitidine

Ranitidine curbs meal-stimulated and basal acid secretion by competitively blocking histamine H2 receptors that are on parietal cells [44]. The drug is utilized for the therapy of peptic ulcer, nonulceral dyspepsia, and gastroesophageal reflux disease (GERD) [44]. Ranitidine (free base) is freely soluble in water with a molecular weight of 314.4 Da and a log P that is approximately 0.3 [45]. Noteworthy is the fact that the drug exists mainly as a monovalent cation between pH 4 and 7 due to the presence of two basic groups with pKa values of 2.3 and 8.2 [45]. This property makes ranitidine particularly attractive for anodal ITP [45]. Recently, Djabri et al. examined the feasibility of utilizing ITP for the delivery of ranitidine in pediatric patients [45]. The authors used dermatomed pig skin to investigate anodal ITP of the drug in vitro and found out that ranitidine transport was less at pH 5.6 (donor: water) than at pH 7 (donor: 5 mM Tris) [45]. A direct proportionality was observed between ranitidine transport and the applied current. This increase in drug delivery did not depend on the donor drug concentration when low levels of background electrolytes were present [45]. In another set of experiments, the authors documented an insignificant effect in the transdermal ITP of ranitidine when the drug was transported from aqueous solutions in comparison with gels [45]. Significantly, the authors determined that transdermal iontophoretic gel patches having a surface area between 0.2 and 1.5 cm^2/kg can be used to deliver therapeutic doses of ranitidine to pediatric patients [45].

Methotrexate

Methotrexate (MTX) inhibits DNA synthesis by competitively blocking the enzyme dihydrofolate reductase [46]. The drug is used for the pharmacotherapy of recalcitrant psoriasis [46], rheumatoid arthritis [47], and basal cell carcinoma [48]. In an interesting study, Nguyen and Banga studied the transdermal electrotransport of MTX through human cadaver skin [49]. The authors used cathodal ITP to deliver negatively charged MTX into the skin and also assessed the influence of EO on the drug transport via anodal ITP [49]. Silver (Ag)/silver chloride (AgCl) electrodes were dipped in the drug solution but were not allowed to touch the skin to prevent burns [49]. Iontophoretic studies were conducted using 0.4 mA/sq · cm current density for 60 min and this eletrotransport led to a significant rise in transepidermal water loss and a remarkable decrease in skin electrical resistance [49]. The authors reported that MTX did not penetrate the intact skin barrier in the passive group (0.00 ± 0.00 μg/cm^2) due to ionization at physiological pH, relatively high molecular weight, and hydrophilicity ($\log P = -1.85$). In contrast, cathodal ITP increased the transdermal iontophoretic drug transport

(0.54 ± 0.07 μg/cm^2) [49]. This was attributed to the repulsion by the cathode (AgCl) in the donor chamber of the ITP system. The electroreplusion is in turn caused by the negative charge of MTX at physiological pH (pKa = 5.6, 4.8, and 3.8) [49]. The authors also observed that anodal ITP significantly increased the transcutaneous flux of MTX into the receiver compartment (4.74 ± 0.62 μg/cm^2) in comparison with cathodal ITP (0.54 ± 0.07 μg/cm^2) [49]. It was postulated that EO in anodal ITP had a more significant influence on MTX transport than electrorepulsion in cathodal ITP [49]. In a different research project, the iontophoretic permeation of MTX across pig skin was also investigated [46]. The authors used cathodal ITP to increase the MTX skin penetration and accumulation compared to the passive permeation [46] The influence of ionic strength on the percutaneous delivery of MTX was also studied by altering NaCl concentration in the donor solution (0, 50, or 100 mM). Iontophoretic transport decreased with increasing ionic strength: nevertheless, the differences were statistically significant only when current density was 0.5 mA/cm^2 and the drug concentration in the donor solution was 2.0 mg/mL [46].

Penbutolol sulfate

Penbutolol is a noncardioselective beta-adrenoceptor blocking agent [50]. We investigated the effect of ITP on the permeation of penbutolol sulfate across pig ear skin [51]. The rationale was that EM would be sufficient to increase the transdermal delivery of this therapeutic agent [51]. We used a constant current power source together with Ag and Ag/AgCl electrodes to deliver current (0.1, 0.2, or 0.3 mA) [51]. The passive percutaneous flux of penbutolol (PBL) was 7.65 μg/cm^2/h, while the amounts of the drug delivered following ITP (0.11, 0.17, and 0.22 mA/cm^2) for 6 h were 87.36, 137.51, and 201.12 μg/cm^2, respectively [51]. Penbutolol sulfate has a pKa of 9.26 [52] and a positive charge at physiological pH. EM was postulated to be the main contributor to the iontophoretic delivery of PBL and there was a direct relationship between applied current density and percutaneous iontophoretic flux enhancement [51].

Almotriptan malate

Almotriptan malate is a second-generation triptan medication that is highly selective to the 5-HT1B/1D receptor and utilized for the management of acute migraine attacks [53]. Recently, the effect of ITP on the transdermal delivery of almotriptan malate was studied [54]. The investigators studied the influence of the following current densities: 0.25 and 0.50 mA/cm^2 [54]. Following the application of a current density of 0.25 mA/cm^2, there was a statistically significant increase (180-fold) in percutaneous drug transport compared to passive diffusion. When the current density of 0.50 mA/cm^2

was employed, there was a significant enhancement in transdermal flux, not only in comparison with control (411-fold), but also when compared with the current density of 0.25 mA/cm^2 (2.28-fold) [54]. The authors postulated that the decrease in drug flux observed following the discontinuation of ITP confirmed that EO and electrorepulsion were the main mechanisms by which transdermal delivery of the drug was enhanced [54]. The proportionality of transdermal drug flux to current density was also documented [54]. In addition, transport number values were calculated for almotriptan, with a low increase from 0.0218 (0.25 mA/cm^2) to 0.0249 (0.50 mA/cm^2). According to the authors, the competition between ions was negligible and this was ascribed to the salt bridges used in the transdermal iontophoretic experiments [54]. Although the effect of pH was not specifically addressed in this study, the authors observed that ITP can increase the permeation of ionized/charged drugs across the skin.

3-Fluoroamphetamine

Psychostimulant abuse is a significant public health issue in the United States, with 1.6 million Americans reporting current nonmedical use of stimulants such as methamphetamine [55]. Substitute-agonist therapies mimic major properties of the abused drug and may help in reducing craving a well as withdrawal and facilitating abstinence [55]. 3-Fluoroamphetamine is basic drug with a pKa of 9.97 and at a pH of 4.0 (formulation pH), it is cationic and thus, anodal ITP was used for iontophoretic delivery [55]. It was reported that anodal ITP led to the highest drug transport in comparison with other enhancement techniques such as microneedles or chemical sorption promoters (Fig. 9.3) [55].

Acyclovir

Acyclovir (ACV) is a synthetic purine nucleoside analog, with two pKa values of 2.41 ± 0.27 (N-7) and 9.06 ± 0.88 [56]. The drug is used for the therapy of varicella zoster [56] and herpes simplex [48] infections. Chen and coworkers studied the effect of ITP on the transcutaneous penetration of ACV [57]. Following ITP-assisted local administration of amino acid ester prodrugs of ACV (ACV-X, where X = Val, Arg, or Ile), the authors quantified the drug content as a function of skin depth [57]. Assay of ACV and prodrugs as a function skin depth was carried out by cryotoming and snap-freezing skin samples to obtain fine or coarse lamellae with a thickness of either 20 or 100 μm [57]. Passive transport of ACV or penciclovir (PCV) from commercial ointment or cream following 60 min of administration led to moderate skin delivery ($Q_{DEP,ACV}$ and $Q_{DEP,PCV} < 2$ $nmol/cm^2$ [57]. In comparison, electrotransport of ACV-Ile or ACV-Arg for only 10 min at 0.25 mA/cm^2 led to a significantly greater deposition of ACV species at the

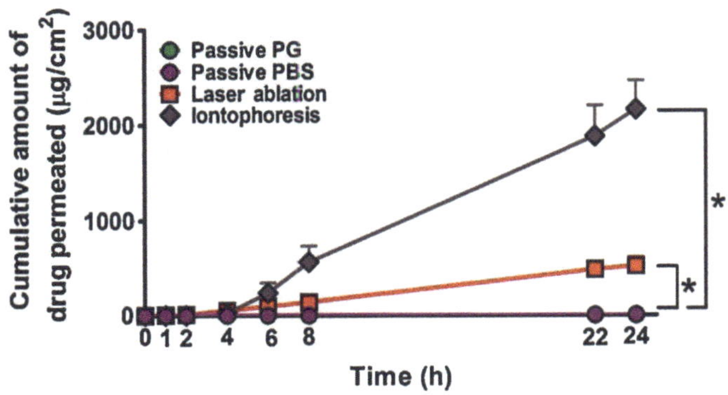

* signifies statistical difference ($P < .05$) between the groups, unpaired Student's *t*-test

FIGURE 9.3 Effect of ITP and ablative laser treatment on transdermal permeation of 3-fluoroamphetamine (PAL-353) across dermatomed human skin. *Reproduced with permission from Puri A, et al., Effects of chemical and physical enhancement techniques on transdermal delivery of 3-fluoroamphetamine hydrochloride. Int J Pharm 2017;528(1–2):452–62.*

same skin depths (100–200 μm): for ACV-Ile, $-Q_{DEP,ACV}$ and $Q_{DEP,ACV\text{-}Ile}$ were 17.2 ± 6.9 and 8.2 ± 1.3 nmol/cm^2, respectively [57]. Interestingly, higher-resolution biodistribution studies, with 20 μm lamellae, showed that electrotransport at 0.25 mA/cm^2 for only 5 min of ACV-Arg or ACV-Ile led to the transport of significant quantities of ACV species to the basal epidermis and adjacent layers ($Q_{DEP,ACV}$ was 4.0 ± 1.6 and 6.1 ± 1.7 nmol/cm^2, respectively) [57].

Hydrogels are semisolid preparations frequently used for the formulation of iontophoretic systems, serving as a base or reservoir of active pharmaceutical ingredients [57]. In the same study [57], hydrogels were used for the iontophoretic transport of these aminoacid prodrugs. A transparent and viscous carbopol hydrogel was utilized for the formulation of ACV-Ile (0.22% w/w) and the application of short-duration ITP for 5 min at 0.25 mA/cm^2 on the ACV-Ile hydrogel led to a statistically similar deposition of ACV species in full-thickness pig and human skin (13.3 ± 1.5 and 12.4 ± 1.4 nmol/cm^2, respectively) [57]. But hydrogels also have limitations as the presence of water in this drug delivery system might reduce ester prodrug stability making storage challenging. To deal with this issue, the authors also investigated fast dissolving films prepared from carbopol and loaded the films with ACV prodrugs [57]. When mild electric current used in conjunction with a fast dissolving film loaded with ACV-Ile, the $Q_{DEP,ACV}$ was 29.1 ± 1.0 nmol/cm^2 while the quantity of the drug in the basal epidermis was 2.7 ± 0.1 nmol/cm^2 [56]. ITP of ACV-Ile from hydrogel, fast dissolving film or aqueous solution, for a short period of 5 minutes led to ACV blood levels in the basal epidermis and neighboring areas that exceeded therapeutic concentration range [57].

Another approach for the iontophoretic delivery of ACV was adopted by Xu et al. [58]. The authors combined ITP with an ion-exchange membrane (Ionac) with the aim of limiting the transdermal diffusion of counterions and enhancing the iontophoretic delivery of ACV [58]. The rationale of this approach is that endogenous competing counterions can lower the efficiency of transdermal ITP [58]. For ACV, a twofold increase in transcutaneous flux across human epidermal membrane was documented following the combination of ITP with the ion-exchange membrane in comparison with ITP alone [58]. In this study, the contribution of EO to drug transport was less than 10% [58]. In another research project, Volpato and colleagues investigated the influence of electrotransport on ACV distribution in different layers of the skin [59]. The principal goal of the study was to achieve higher ACV concentrations in the basal epidermis—the site for herpes simplex lesions [59]. The investigations were carried out at the pH of 7.4 (the drug was not ionized) and 3.0 (20% of the drug was cationic) [59]. From the transdermal transport profiles of ACV, it was shown that ITP enhanced the transcutaneous delivery of the drug at both pH 7.4 and pH 3.0, while the passive permeation rates of the drug at pH 7.4 and 3.0 were low [59]. The ITP-driven ACV transcutaneous flux value normalized by donor concentration was 5.42×10^{-3} cm/h at pH 3; passive delivery at pH 3.0 was 0.06×10^{-3} cm^{-h}, while ITP-enhanced transport at pH 7.4 was 2.70×10^{-3} cm^{-h}. The passive transport of the drug at pH 7.4 was 0.3×10^{-3} cm/h [59].

Granisetron

Granisetron (GST) is a highly selective 5-HT3 receptor blocker, which is utilized for the management of vomiting and nausea induced by chemotherapy and radiotherapy [60]. GST has a molecular weight of 348.9 and a dissociation constant (pKa) of 9.4 [61]. Cázares-Delgadillo et al. studied the influence of current density (0.1, 0.2, and 0.3 mA/cm^2) and drug concentration (5, 10, 20, and 40 mM) on the iontophoretic permeation of GST across porcine ear skin [61]. The cumulative amount of the drug delivered in vitro from the 20 mM (1.41 ± 0.62 $\mu g/cm^2/min$) and 40 mM (2.50 ± 0.79 $\mu g/cm^2/min$) solution was significantly higher than that at 5 mM (0.39 ± 0.13 $\mu g/cm^2/min$) and 10 mM (0.57 ± 0.06 $\mu g/cm^2/min$) [61]. Raising the current density from 0.1 to 0.3 mA/cm^2 led to about 4.2-fold transcutaneous permeation enhancement [61]. The most optimal GST permeation rate was achieved at 0.3 mA/cm^2 without sodium ions, and the transcutaneous drug delivery rate was 2.93 ± 0.62 $\mu g/cm^2/min$ [61]. By simultaneously carrying out ITP of acetaminophen and GST, the authors were able to calculate the contributions of EM (EM) and EO (EO) to overall iontophoretic flux [61]. The authors reported that EM was the major mechanism of ITP and it contributed to

71%–86% of the overall granisetron transport [61]. The total iontophoretic flux (J_{tot}) of GST was determined by using the following equation [61]:

$$J_{tot} = J_{EM} + J_{EO} = \left(\frac{I_d}{F} x \frac{u_{\mathrm{GST}}}{\sum_1^i z_i u_i c_i} + v_w \right) c_{\mathrm{GST}} \tag{9.7}$$

where J_{EM} and J_{EO} are the contributions of EM and electrosmosis to the total permeation rate. J_{EM} is related to the current density (I_d), by Faraday's constant (F), and it is proportional to the concentration (c_{GST}) and mobility (u_{GST}) of the molecule. $z_i u_i$, andc_i are the corresponding values for the other electric charge carriers. J_{EO} is obtained by multiplying the drug concentration, c_{GST} and the solvent flow linear velocity v_w [61].

Memantine

Memantine (MMT) is an adamantine derivative and a *N*-methyl-D-aspartate (NMDA) receptor antagonist used for the pharmacotherapy of Alzheimer's disease (AD) [62–64]. The drug is a small lipophilic molecule (MW = 215.76 g/mol, log P_{oct} = 3.28) and also a weak base (pKa = 10.42) [65]. These properties in combination with the high ratio of the ions (99.95% at pH 7.4 and 100% at pH 5.4) provide the leverage to drive MMT across the skin with mild electric current [65]. A transdermal drug delivery system loaded with MMT may be useful for AD patients. Since the SC hinders the transport of medications, several scientists have investigated different approaches toward enhancing the delivery of MMT. One of the investigated techniques is ITP. Recently, Rio-Sancho and coworkers evaluated the effect of ITP on the transcutaneous permeation of memantine hydrochloride [65]. A current density of 0.5 mA/cm^2 and Ag/AgCl electrodes were used to deliver the drug through dermatomed pig ear skin for 8 h [65]. Saline bridges were employed to prevent competition between memantine hydrochloride and sodium ions in the donor solution. The passive transdermal flux of memantine hydrochloride was 7.10 ± 1.50 μg/cm^2/h, while ITP with a current density of 0.5 mA/cm^2 led to a marked enhancement of the transdermal flux of MMT (55.9 ± 5.8 μg/cm^2/h) [65]. The researchers also reported facilitated permeation rate of MMT (158 ± 6 μg/cm^2/h) following decreased ionic strength of the donor solution (HEPES, 20 mM, pH 5.4] [65].

Ketoprofen

It has been documented that, for certain Nonsteroidal anti-inflammatory drugs (NSAIDs) such as flurbiprofen and piroxicam, more than 99% of the drug transported into the skin is eliminated through the circulatory system [66]. Most NSAIDs are anionic at the pH of 7.4 and cathodal iontophoretic delivery of NSAIDs is the obvious choice [66]. However, the physicochemical properties of some of these drugs such as ketoprofen are so low that therapeutically relevant concentrations especially in deep tissues are not always achieved. As an illustration, ketorolac delivery was not optimal probably because of prompt skin clearance as well as high plasma protein binding [66]. But most NSAIDs possess a carboxyl functional group, capable of forming an ester prodrug and thus imparting more optimal physicochemical properties in comparison with the parent drug [66]. Ketoprofen (MW = 254.3) is a propionic acid-based prodrug with a pKa of 5.9 in a 3:1 solution of methanol and water [67]. Lobo and Yan recently synthesized a ketoprofen (KT) cationic ester prodrug and delivered it via ITP across human epidermal membrane and full-thickness rat skin [66]. Cathodal ITP at 0.2 mA setting was deployed for KT penetration, while anodal ITP was utilized for the percutaneous transport of ketoprofen choline chloride (KCC) [66].

The transdermal penetration of KT was superior to that of KCC [66]. Significantly, no KCC was detected in the receptor compartment in 6 h, and only a small quantity of the parent drug was found in the receptor compartment at the 6th hour [66]. The absence of compounds in the receiver chamber was attributed to the cationic and hydrophilic quaternary ammonium species of the prodrug, which does not easily cross the SC [66]. The transdermal flux obtained following anodal ITP of KCC was higher compared to that obtained via cathodal ITP [66]. When 0.2 mA electric current was used, anodal ITP transported a larger amount of the prodrug KCC through the human epidermal membrane (HEM) compared to the quantity of KT transported via cathodal ITP [66]. The prodrugs possessed low plasma protein binding and significantly, it was shown that a vasoconstrictor can be coiontophoretically transported across the HEM with the ketoprofen cationic prodrug [66]. Furthermore, cathodal ITP enhanced the transport of KT by more than 60-fold compared to KT flux across HEM delivered under passive conditions [66]. Also noteworthy was the fact that KT flux from the cathodal ITP was five times less than the KCC flux from the anodal ITP. The authors noted that the skin is negatively charged at the pH of 7.4, and that following anodal ITP, EO can also serve as an additional percutaneous transport enhancer for the positively charged KCC molecules [66].

Panus and colleagues also investigated the percutaneous delivery of KT across human cadaver skin [67]. The in vitro intracutaneous permeation of KT following anodal and cathodal ITP (0.5 mA/cm^2, 3 h) was 232.1 ± 27.1 μg/cm^2 and 275.0 ± 141.0 μg/cm^2 respectively [67]. In comparison, passive intracutaneous permeation of KT was 40.7 ± 42.1 μg/cm^2 [67]. The authors observed that only cathodic ITP led to the transdermal iontophoretic penetration of KT across cadaver skin [67]. Interestingly, the authors investigated the cathodal iontophoretic transport under clinically relevant conditions (0.28 mA/cm, 40 min) and increased KT concentration to 300 mg/mL [67]. The studies were carried out in humans and KT was detected (0.88 ± 0.42 μg/mL) in the forearm veins of the ipsilateral arm [67].

The cumulative urinary excretion of conjugated and unconjugated KT was 790 μg at the 16 h time point following ketoprofen ITP (0.28 mA/cm, 40 min) [67]. In another research project, Tashiro et al. used cathodal ITP to deliver KT in rats [68]. The applied electrical current values were 0.14 and 0.70 mA/cm^2 and the application times were 5, 15, 30, 60, and 90 min [68]. The drug content in the systemic vein, skin, and cutaneous vein was then quantified. The authors used a modified physiological pharmacokinetic model to calculate the transfer rate of ketoprofen from the skin to cutaneous blood (R_{SC}) [68]. The modified mathematical equations used were [68]:

$$R_{sc} = Q_b(C_{b\ \mathrm{systemic}} - C_{p\ \mathrm{systemic}}) \tag{9.8}$$

$$R_{sc} = Q_b \frac{C_b}{C_p}\left(C_{p\ \mathrm{cutaneous}} - C_{p\ \mathrm{systemic}}\right) \tag{9.9}$$

where Q_b is the flow rate of cutaneous blood and Q_bC_b/C_p refers to the effective plasma flow rate [68]. $C_{b\ \mathrm{systemic}}$ and $C_{p\ \mathrm{systemic}}$ were used by the authors to describe blood and plasma concentration in the cutaneous vein, respectively [68]. Electrical current effect on drug transfer to cutaneous blood was calculated by comparing R_{SC} during passive diffusion and that achieved following iontophoretic transport. The absorption of the medication into the skin, the transport of the drug from the skin into cutaneous blood, and the movement of the drug into systemic circulation were determined in a stepwise fashion by assaying drug concentration in the skin, cutaneous vein, and systemic vein, respectively [68]. The authors reported that the amount of KT absorbed into the skin increased after ITP and a steady-state concentration was achieved at 30 min regardless of the applied current [68]. The authors also observed that cutaneous plasma concentration reached a steady state in 15 min in contrast to systemic plasma concentration, which did not reach steady state in 90 min [68]. Another important observation was that R_{sc} was approximately proportional to electrical current. The enhancement ratio values for 0.14 and 0.70 mA/cm^2 current densities (vs passive diffusion) were 17 and 73, respectively [68].

Peptide dendrimers are made up of amino acids connected by peptide/amide bonds and they are widely used in biology and nanotechnology [69,70]. Peptide dendrimers can self-assemble due to the presence of several peptide bonds in their structure [69]. The advantages of this group of carriers include lower toxicity, cost-effective production, and biodegradability [69]. An interesting research involving the utilization of ITP for the delivery of ketoprofen conjugated to peptide dendrimers was reported by Hegde et al. [69]. The authors used Fmoc solid-phase peptide synthesis to prepare peptide dendrimers conjugated to ketoprofen with either 2+ or 4+ charge [69]. The authors synthesized conjugates from either arginine (D1 and D3) or lysine (D2 and D4) and their diffusion through the male Swiss Albino mouse skin was investigated [69]. Horizontal diffusion cells were utilized in vitro electrotransport experiments while Ag and AgCl rods were employed as anode and cathode, respectively. The authors used a constant current of 0.38 mA/cm^2 in the studies and dispersions of ketoprofen or D1, D2, D3, and D4 conjugates in 4-(2-hydroxyethyl)piperazine-1-ethanesulfonic acid (HEPES) solution of pH 7.4 were placed in the donor chamber [69].

For in vivo studies, the mice were classified into two groups—one group was given ketoprofen, while the second group underwent ITP) [69]. The authors reported that $68.06 \pm 3.62\ \mu g/cm^2$ of ketoprofen was transported across the skin passively at the end of 24 h ($Q_{24\ h}$), while among the conjugates, the following quantities of ketoprofen were transported at the end of 6 h [$Q_{24\ h}$ ($\mu g/cm^2$): D2 (49.62 ± 2.92) >D4 (19.20 ± 0.89) N>D1 (6.45 ± 0.40) N>D3 (2.21 ± 0.19) [69]. The authors postulated that lipophilicity of the penetrant determined the extent of skin permeation [69]. It was reported higher skin transcutaneous penetration was induced by higher lipophilicity of the molecules. The significance of molecular weight (MW) and charge of the conjugates was also highlighted. A higher penetration rate was documented with D2 conjugate (low MW and higher charge of 4 +) [69]. In contrast, less transport was observed with the D3 conjugate (higher MW and lower charge of 2 +) while the permeation of D1 (arginine 4 + ; MW = 878.52) and D4 (lysine 2 + ; MW = 930.50) did not reflect the proportional dependency on charge and MW [69]. When cathodic ITP was used, ($Q_{6\ h}$) was found to be $96.60 \pm 5.12\ \mu g/cm^2$. However, the $Q_{6\ h}$ ($\mu g/cm^2$) values following anodic ITP with different conjugates were: D2 (711.49 ± 39.14) > D4 (341.23 ± 16.43) >D3 (89.50 ± 4.99) > D1 (50.91 ± 2.98) [69]. The authors observed that D2 conjugate (with high positive charge and low MW) displayed the most superior iontophoretic percutaneous penetration rate but the trend was not observed with the other conjugates [69]. In a study of the relationship between lipophilicity and permeation rate, it was documented that D2 and D4 conjugates with relatively more superior partition coefficient values (higher lipophilicity) displayed higher iontophoretic delivery rates but again, the trend was not observed for D1 and D4 [69]. Intriguingly, there was a good correlation between the zeta potential values of the dendrimeric conjugates and the $Q_{6\ h}$ values obtained following ITP. The dendrimeric conjugates had the following zeta potential: D2 >D4 > D3 >D1 and this was in tandem with $Q_{6\ h}$ values observed following ITP [69]. Overall, the transdermal delivery of peptide dendrimers is a complex process and lipophilicity, molecular weight, and charge alone cannot adequately explain the permeation rate mechanism.

Dexamethasone

Dexamethasone is a corticosteroid medication utilized in clinical practice for the management of rheumatoid arthritis, immune thrombocytopenia, Crohn's disease, asthma, and ulcerative colitis [71]. The ester prodrug dexamethasone sodium phosphate (DSP) was synthesized from dexamethasone (DXM) with the aim of modifying DXM lipophilicity. Dexamethasone (log P = 1.83) has a higher log P value compared to the water-soluble DSP (log P = 1.64) [72]. In addition, the drug has two pKa values (1.89 and 6.18) and recently, Filipovic et al. used cathodal ITP to facilitate the transcutaneous flux of this molecule across porcine skin [13]. The authors studied the influence of different drug concentrations, current densities, and delivery time on the transcutaneous flux of DSP [13]. The following variables were studied by the investigators: initial drug loading (2, 4, and 8 mg), duration (1, 2, and 4 h), and current density (0.3, 0.4, and 0.5 mA/cm^2) [13]. The authors reported that higher drug loadings led to the skin delivery of more DSP [13]. In addition, the authors also carried out numerical simulations to examine the relationship between the experimental and theoretical methods of studying transcutaneous ITP of DSP in a pig skin model [13]. The investigators used the Nernst–Planck equation to calculate the transdermal flux of the drug and reported that numerical computations correlated well with experimentally determined values [13].

In another study, Joshi et al. used cutaneous microdialysis to measure interstitial fluid concentrations of DSP following ITP in humans [72]. It was reported that drug samples obtained from microdialysis sites following ITP in seven out of eight subjects had levels of DSP and DXM above 50 ng/mL, while no sample obtained at the passive site contained a detectable quantity of either DSP or DXM [72]. It was shown that cathodal ITP delivered remarkably more detectable quantities of DSP solution across human skin compared to passive permeation [72]. In another study, Cázares-Delgadillo and coworkers evaluated the iontophoretic transport of dexamethasone sodium phosphate (DSP) and examined the potential of using the cathodal iontophoretic technique for the transport of therapeutic quantities of the medication for the therapy of vomiting induced by cancer treatment [73]. The authors investigated the electrotransport of DSP across 750 μm pig skin in vitro in relation to current density (0.1, 0.3, and 0.5 mA/cm^2) and concentration (10, 20, and 40 mM) [73]. Raising the concentration of DSP from 10 to 40 mM led to about fourfold enhancement in cumulative transport (35.65 ± 23.20 and 137.90 ± 53.90 $\mu g/cm^2$, respectively) [73]. A good proportionality was also documented between the cumulative quantity of DSP transported and the administered current density. In particular, a rise in current density from 0.1 to 0.5 mA cm^2 led to a 12-fold enhancement in DSP transport following 7 h of mild current application. Intriguingly, there was no remarkable difference between the quantities of transcutaneously extracted DSP at 0.1, 0.3, and 0.5 mA/cm^2 [73]. The authors postulated that the lack of any influence of current density on the quantity of DSP retained in the skin may be attributed to the negative charge of the skin and that the deposition of cationic and anionic medications may take place by a different mechanism [73].

Donepezil

AD is a debilitating neurodegenerative disorder usually accompanied by oxidative stress, protein aggregation and misfolding, neuro-inflammatory processes, and mitochondrial abnormalities [74]. This pathological condition is characterized by the presence of neurofibrillary tangles and amyloid plaques which accumulate in the brain, leading to cognitive decline that deteriorates with time [75]. Donepezil is a centrally acting, reversible acetylcholinesterase blocker that is used for therapy of AD [76,77]. The base form of donepezil (DP has a log P of 3.08–4.11 and cannot cross the skin passively at therapeutically effective levels [77]. Recently, Saluja and coworkers investigated the transport of donepezil hydrochloride (DP HCl) (MW = 415.96, log P = 4.27) across hairless rat skin following the use of WEDD, which is a proprietary system for ITP [78]. DP was not detected following passive transdermal delivery but blood levels of 0.086 ± 0.02, 0.202 ± 0.046, and 0.304 ± 0.137 μg/mL were quantified at 24 h with current levels of 0.13 mA (0.026 mA/cm^2), 0.26 mA (0.052 mA/cm^2), and 0.39 mA (0.078 mA/cm^2), respectively [78]. Transdermal flux was proportional to current density. The authors explained that this was due to elevated current densities, providing a higher electromotive force for the percutaneous transport of ions [78].

ITP was also used to deliver donepezil hydrochloride from poly(D,L-lactide-co-glycolide) (PLGA) nanoparticles [1]. The authors used chitosan hydroxypropyltrimonium chloride (CS) to coat the drug-loaded PLGA nanoparticles, thus imparting a positive surface charge [1]. Uncoated and CS-coated nanoparticles with average volume diameters of 80.2 ± 30.1 and 117.7 ± 60.6 nm were used in the experiments [1]. Ex vivo skin deposition research was conducted with abdominal rat skin with or without ITP [1]. Ag/AgCl electrodes were utilized for ITP with constant current set at 0.25 mA/cm^2 for 2 h. The authors reported that when ITP was not used, the amount of DP that was deposited in the skin following the use of CS-coated nanoparticles was 5.3 times more than that of DP solution. It was also documented that DP concentration in the rat skin following ITP and the administration of CS-coated nanoparticles was 1.9 times more than that of CS-coated nanoparticles with no accompanying ITP [1]. Furthermore, the amount of DP deposited in the skin following ITP increased by 2.2 times when CS-coated nanoparticles were used [1]. The authors postulated that CS-coated nanoparticles with ITP were beneficial for the percutaneous transport of cationic drugs [1]. In a different research project, Lee et al. also examined the effect of propylene glycol (PG) on the ITP-mediated transcutaneous penetration of DP [79]. The project was carried out to study how PG influences transdermal EM and electroosmotic volume flow of drugs following ITP [79]. The influence of PG on the permeation of a cationic drug, donepezil hydrochloride (DH) across hairless mouse skin was studied [79].

The authors reported that anodal delivery resulted in a higher permeation rate compared to cathodal ITP and passive DH administration, showing the critical role played by EM in the transdermal iontophoretic permeation of DH [79]. With increase in the concentration of PG, there was a decline in the anodal permeation rate of DH decreased and this was ascribed to medium viscosity increase [79].

3-Fluoroamphetamine

In 2006, 2.1 million Americans reportedly used cocaine and 1.9 million used methamphetamine showing the severity and public health challenge of psychostimulant abuse [80]. Currently, there are no FDA-approved pharmacotherapies for the treatment of stimulant dependence [80]. It is known that psychoactive compounds such as cocaine block dopamine (DA), norepinephrine (NE), and serotonin (SER) transporters [81]. It has been suggested that substrate-based DA/NE releasers such as 3-fluoroamphetamine may be useful for the management of cocaine dependency or cocaine-use disorder [55]. 3-Fluoroamphetamine (PAL-353) possesses a molecular weight of 189.66 g/mol, a distribution coefficient (log D) from -1.086 to -0.498, and a dissociation constant (pKa) of 9.97 [55]. Recently, Puri et al. investigated the influence of anodal ITP on the percutaneous permeation of 3-fluoroamphetamine hydrochloride across dermatomed human skin [55]. Ag and AgCl electrodes were positioned in the donor and receiver chambers, respectively. PAL-353 is cationic and basic in nature with a pKa of 9.97 at a pH of 4.0 (formulation pH), and thus, anodal ITP was used by the researchers [55]. Anodal ITP (0.5 mA/cm^2 for 4 h) dramatically enhanced the transport of PAL-353 (2159.43 ± 301.14 mg/cm^2) compared to its passive penetration from phosphate-buffered saline (PBS) solution (3.94 ± 0.53 mg/cm^2) [55]. There was a 548-fold increase in the cumulative transport of PAL-353 following ITP in comparison with passive transport [55]. It was suggested that increased hydration, the concentration and type of ions, direct electric field effects, and dissipation of heat during ITP lead to SC disorganization and enhanced drug permeation [55]. ITP had the highest permeation rate compared to other drug enhancement approaches such as microneedles and laser ablation [55].

From the foregoing, it is obvious that ITP has considerable advantages. However, there are also limitations as the relationship between iontophoretic flux and current density is proportional up till a certain threshold. Flux enhancement has to be carried out while maintaining safety. Several parameters are known to impact iontophoretic drug transport, including electrode size, as well as the amount and time of current application [37]. Others are the drug solution pH, the type of ITP, charge, and drug ionization [37]. These variables have to be chosen rationally to obtain the desired results.

Magnetophoresis

Magnetophoresis refers to the utilization of a magnetic field (5–300 mT) for enhanced drug penetration across the skin. In this scenario, diamagnetic medications such as lidocaine are repelled from the magnetic field into the skin [82]. The main mechanisms driving magnetophoresis are magnetokinesis and magnetohydrokinesis. Diamagnetic compounds are typically repelled from an external magnetic field across a biological membrane such as the human skin [83]. Magnetokinesis refers to forced movement of drug molecules under an applied magnetic field. Magnetorepulsion and magnetohydrokinesis contribute to magnetokinesis in most cases. Magnetorepulsion is the forced movement of drug molecules induced by the repulsive force experienced by a diamagnet in the presence of an external magnetic field [83].

It has been hypothesized that magnetohydrokinesis-assisted drug permeation is caused by water flux across a membrane due to an external magnetic field [83]. Murthy et al. investigated the magnetophoretic transcutaneous transport of lidocaine [83]. Skin penetration experiments were conducted in vitro across pig epidermis using different magnetic field strengths. Magnetophoretic transport depended on the applied magnetic field strength [83]. An equation showing the link between lidocaine hydrochloride (LH) transport increase and magnetic field strength was given: $EF = 0.027S + 1$, ($R2 = 0.92$) where EF is the flux enhancement factor and S is the magnetic field strength [83]. Terbutaline sulfate is another diamagnetic compound that has been investigated as a potential candidate for magnetophoretic delivery across the skin [84]. Transdermal formulations loaded with terbutaline and different concentrations of isopropyl myristate (IPM) were investigated in vitro and the researchers reported that the solution with 4% IPM led to a transcutaneous flux of 5.10 ± 0.21 μg/cm^2/h [84]. When magnetophoresis was carried out with a magnet possessing the strength of 1×10^{-4} T, a permeation flux value of 5.26 ± 0.31 μg/h/cm^2 was achieved. The study showed that magnetophoresis had a comparable impact on transdermal drug flux similar to what was obtained with IPM [84].

ETP

Transdermal ETP entails applying HV electric pulses to the skin to facilitate drug delivery [85]. Some authors have reported flux increases that are up to four orders of magnitude for three polar molecules—erythrosine derivative (1025 Da, −1 charge), calcein (623 Da, −4 charge), and Lucifer yellow (457 Da, −2 charge) with molecular weights up to 1025 and electric charge between −4 and −1 [86]. ETP can (1) reduce skin resistance, (2) disorganize SC lipid bilayers, and (3) enhance skin hydration [87] but these changes are partially reversible. A correlation has been established between domains of high current density and the presence of skin appendages [88]. Two parallel current routes through the skin are thought to exist: one pathway goes through appendages and the second permeates the SC lipid-corneocyte matrix [88]. At a voltage value close to 1 V, the electric potential reduction across each epithelial cell membrane lining the appendageal ducts is about 250 mV and this is adequate for ETP [88]. Significant effects have been observed at applied potentials of approximately several hundred volts with the skin resistance reducing by 1000-fold during a brief ($<10\ \mu s$) time interval [88]. The main reduction in resistance took place at voltages that were lower than 70 V [88].

ETP facilitates drug transport by perturbing the SC layer of the skin in contrast to ITP [89]. ITP directly transports drug molecules into the skin through electrorepulsion [89]. Several categories of electrodes are used for ETP. The orientation, shape, size, and spacing of electrodes can be modulated. When utilized for transdermal drug delivery, electrodes can be placed on the skin surface or it can be used to pierce the skin before voltage application [8]. ETP of intact skin involves transmitting electrical pulses that are 10–1000 V in magnitude and can last for about 10^{-6}–10^{-3} s [90]. A pulse with those characteristics should not induce muscle contraction, pain, burn, external injury, or electric shock but should be capable of forming temporary pores in the SC lipid bilayers [90] ETP entails the administration of an HV electric pulse (50 V) with a short time frame (typically 1–100 ms) on the surface of the skin [89]. The technique is based on an electrical field of a short pulse duration (micro- to milliseconds) and a relatively high intensity, usually over 100 V/cm [91]. The resistance of a heat-stripped skin sample with an area of 0.69 cm^2 is between 50 and 250 kΩ [92]. Skin resistance depends on appendage density. If most of the resistance is in the SC and its thickness (h_{SC}) is about 15 μm, the resistivity of the SC is between 0.23 and 1.15 M$\Omega \cdot$m [92]. To put it into perspective, a 150 mM saline solution possesses a resistivity of approximately 0.72 $\Omega \cdot$m and that of the viable dermis is approximately 150 $\Omega \cdot$m [92]. When the voltage across the SC reaches about 60 V, an electric disruption connected to ETP is likely to occur [92]. There is usually a dramatic reduction in SC resistance within less than 1 μs upon the administration of an HV pulse [87].

By subjecting the skin to ETP pulses, the SC undergoes a structural change that leads to a significant surge in electrical conductivity, electrophoretic mobility, and molecular diffusivity [93]. pH values for the upper side of the SC, SC ceramides, and fatty acids are 5, 5.8, and 6.2, respectively [94]. Moreover, the SC constitutes the principal barrier and contributes significantly to the skin's electrical resistance (5–25 kΩ/cm^2) [95]. The SC is made up of about 100 bilayer membranes in series, and the electric disruption linked to significant permeation enhancement has been documented for high transdermal voltages (30–100 V) [96]. In ETP-mediated transdermal experiments, exponential decay electric field pulses (30–100 V transdermal voltages, 100 V–1500 V applied voltage, and 1 ms to hundreds of ms pulse duration) are typically used [97].

About 100 multilamellar bilayers of the SC require approximately 100 V pulses for ETP, or approximately 1 V per bilayer [17]. When the SC is subjected to a certain voltage (60 V $< R_{skin} <$ 120 V, all areas with decreased ETP threshold voltage will undergo ETP [98]. The primary pores through the multilamellae are minute ($r_{pore} \approx$ 1 nm) [98]. The critical pore radius at which the electric field decrease is equivalent to 1/e of the difference between the field within an electrically created pore and the undisturbed field is approximately 3 nm [98]. Transient skin ETP takes place when the applied external electric field is more than the critical transmembrane potential (TMP) [99,100]. At the cellular level, ETP leads to imperfections in cell membrane when the TMP is greater than the membrane breakdown voltage [101]. These flaws in the membrane lead to increased permeability and conductivity. ETP enhances transdermal drug delivery primarily due to two mechanisms: (1) creation of electropores and (2) rapid transport of molecules through the pores by electrophoresis and EO [102].

Even though the observed alterations in membrane characteristics linked to ETP have been elucidated with models involving temporary water pathways, the microscopic observation of these pores is challenging because electropores are thought to be sparse (<0.1% of surface area), small (<10 nm), and typically short-lived (microseconds to seconds), making their microscopic characterization very difficult [103]. As soon as a membrane is charged to ETP levels, water is squeezed into the lipid region due to the substantial difference in dielectric constant ($\varepsilon_{lipid} \approx 2$, $\varepsilon_{water} \approx 87$) [98]. Once a water channel (electropore) is formed, intra-pore water becomes polarized, leading to pore stabilization. Since it is energetically disadvantageous to have water and lipid chains inside the pores, the lipids creating the pore edge are aligned in such a manner that their head groups face the pore, leading to the creation of a hydrophilic surface [98]. A pore typically expands in the presence of an electric field. The pore is stable when a critical radius is achieved, even when the electric field is no longer present [98].

There were recent research reports in which computational studies based on molecular dynamics were used as potent tools to study pore formation through the simulation of lipid bilayers subjected to an external electrical field [91]. Even though numerous models have been developed to predict the spatial distribution and size of pores, the molecular basis of pore formation remains is not completely elucidated [91]. ETP pulse times are normally tens to hundreds of ms long such that the effect of EO is marginal in comparison to electrophoresis [93]. When an electric pulse is applied, the contribution of diffusion to transdermal transport is less than that of electrophoresis and this has been theoretically demonstrated to be negligible in the permeation of a high molecular–weight and charged solute at small time scales [93]. Nevertheless, after the administration of a series of pulses or at time intervals between pulses, diffusion becomes the only mechanism of transport [93].

During ETP, pulses with voltage values that are higher than the SC breakdown potential (75−100 V) are administered, leading to the formation of transient pores in the skin's lipid bilayers [95]. Enhanced skin permeability can be obtained by utilizing electric pulses of either long duration at low intensity (i.e., hundreds-of-ms-long pulses with up to 100 V pulse voltage) or short duration at high intensity (i.e., hundreds-of-μs-long pulses with hundreds-of-volts pulse voltage) or [104]. The use of the first category of pulses leads to the formation of areas with increased permeability within the SC that are relatively large (up to hundreds of μm) and long-lasting (induced by thermal effects of the electric pulses), while the use of the second type of pulses results in the formation of cell-sized routes through the SC [104]. During ETP, local transport regions (LTRs) are created in the "defective" SC areas [105]. These regions of "defects" are subsequently enlarged by resistive (Joule) heating [105]. Phase transition and lipid fluidization occur because of the ETP of lipid bilayers [82]. New pores or water pathways are thus formed within the SC [82].

ETP of the skin requires HV (typically higher than 50 V) [106]. It has been shown that when the voltage drop across the SC exceeds a critical value (above 30 V), the skin undergoes a sudden rise in penetrability by up to four orders of magnitude within a short period of time (less than 10 μs) [93]. Ionic and molecular penetration across the skin that is subjected to several HV pulses is mostly restricted to LTRs [105]. LTR size is a function of the cumulative pulse duration, while LTR density is controlled by pulse amplitude [105]. The anatomical changes associated with the use of short pulses are probably linked to nanoscale aqueous defects in the SC's lipid structure [105]. These alterations are followed by enhanced SC conductivity, which takes place within less than ~10 s, when the voltage drop across the SC exceeds 50 V [105]. Electric pulse also creates an electrophoretic driving force, such that there is an increased transport of highly charged molecules such as heparin [107]. In particular, the DC portion of an administered electric field gives rise to an electrophoretic force that drives molecular transport [100]. ETP-assisted transdermal delivery is a function of the distance between electrodes, number of electric pulses, duration, amplitude, and shape [85].

Skin properties can sometimes be altered at HV, which may result in nonlinear dependence of transdermal flux on voltage [106]. In most cases, these changes are reversible but the time taken to recover may vary significantly [106]. Traditionally, iterative experiments that study the influence of number of applied pulses, pulse duration, and electric field strength on the transport of extrinsic molecules are used to optimize ETP parameters [108]. Pulse duration, voltage, and number of electric impulses have to be properly chosen to achieve optimal transdermal transport [109]. Increase in the skin's penetrability to molecules correlates well with the number of pulses applied regardless of the pulse type [93]. Electric pulses can be either low voltage (LV) or HV. Numerous studies have focused on ETP-assisted transport of different molecules to skin, using multielectrode arrays, needle-free microelectrodes, noninvasive needle-free electrodes, invasive needle electrodes, or plate electrodes [110]. Electrode design (tips in the case of needle electrodes) can differ considerably, and this affects the delivery efficiency as well as the extent of the skin injury [110].

There are two forms of voltage output from ETP equipment—square-wave or exponential decay pulses [17]. Exponential decaying pulses decline at a rate proportional to its current value. These pulses have a short but higher voltage initially, followed by a long LV tail [82]. On the other hand, a square-wave is a periodic waveform in which the amplitude fluctuates at a constant periodicity between fixed maximum and minimum values, with equivalent duration at minimum and maximum [111]. The square-wave pulse may have HV or LV. It has been known to cause a moderate, temporary, and reversible damage to the skin barrier [82]. The exponential decay waveform entails full discharge of the capacitor into a resistor, whereas square-wave pulse is frequently generated by a partial discharge of a large capacitor [17]. In the case of an exponential waveform generator, the voltage of a capacitor C discharging into a resistor R is subject to an exponential decay law [17]:

$$V = V_0 \cdot \exp\left(\frac{-t}{RC}\right) \tag{9.10}$$

Electric pulse length is characterized by the 1/e time constant, which is the time required for the initial voltage to decay to 1/e:one-third of the initial value [17]. This time constant is usually calculated as a product of R and C, where R is the total resistance into which the capacitor discharges and C is the capacitance of the storage capacitor in the generator [17]. The optimization of parameters is a crucial challenge when converting ETP into practical applications [91]. When extended electric pulses and high electrical voltages are administered, tissue impairment may take place via cell overheating or irreversible dielectric breakdown, which is usually linked to necrosis [91].

Research has shown that few long-duration, LV, ETP pulses (e.g., 200 ms, 50 V) can transport medications across the skin in a more efficient manner compared to many HV, short-duration pulses (e.g., 100 V, 1 ms) [112]. Nonetheless, long-duration pulses can also induce marked local heating of the skin and are linked to increased skin sensation and irritation [112]. The transport efficiency of ETP is a function of several parameters such as the frequency, amplitude, duration, and shape of electric pulses, as well as the orientation, spacing, shape, and size of electrodes [8]. For optimal efficacy while at the same time preventing adverse events, researchers have to carefully fine-tune ETP parameters (pulse duration, field strength, and electrode dimensions) based on target tissue peculiarities [91]. For the most part, the aim of ETP is to increase drug transport using a procedure that is satisfactory for in vivo human studies; the protocol should neither injure the skin nor cause pain [112]. Usually, the administered voltage is 50–150 V, even though researchers have used higher voltages for transcutaneous experiments in vitro [112]. The voltage across the electrodes divided by the electrode spacing is called the field strength, and a correction for the voltage reduction at the electrode interface may sometimes be required [113]. An average of 6–10 pulses having a field strength of approximately 100–200 V/cm and lasting from 20 to 40 ms is postulated to be optimal for in vivo tissue ETP [91]. During ETP, the total charge transported is [113]:

$$Q = I_p \times \tau \times n \tag{9.11}$$

Where Q is the total charge, I_p is the current permeating the skin during pulse application as determined by oscilloscope, τ is the pulse length, and n is the number of applied pulses [113].

To create aqueous pathways measurements in the order of micrometers, a large pulse amplitude is required and this is usually obtained via square-wave, HV, and short-duration pulses or with the first portion of exponentially decaying HV pulses [105]. Conversely, LV, long-duration, and square-wave pulses or the long LV tail of exponentially decaying pulses lead to larger cumulative pulse energy and can result in the formation of SC domains with increased permeability that are comparatively long-lasting and large (up to hundreds of mm) [105]. Square-wave pulses are beneficial because they can be used to independently control the pulse length and pulse amplitude; optimized pulse parameters for ETP comprise eight square waves at a frequency of 1 Hz with a duration of 100 μs [114]. Previously, experiments were carried out with repetitive exponentially decaying pulses with varying durations, amplitudes, and numbers because (1) capacitor technology that generates exponentially decaying pulses is less complicated compared to the technology used for the delivery of square-wave pulses, and (2) the long LV tail of exponentially decaying pulses induces the electrophoretic portion of the pulse and is linked to Joule heating, further facilitating percutaneous drug transport [105]. Nonetheless, researchers are more predisposed to the use of square-wave pulses because with this mode of ETP, it is easier to control pulse parameters [105].

Although ETP has been extensively studied, certain aspects of the technique have not been elucidated. Despite the progress made in the experimental as well as the theoretical domains, there are still no techniques to measure certain ETP parameters [115]. The disappearance and contraction of pores as well as the kinetics of pore expansion are not well explained. Nonetheless, substantial advances in understanding ETP mechanisms have been made [115]. The following phenomena are typically observed following skin ETP: (1) modulation of the magnitude of skin transport and this is usually achieved by regulating the parameters of HV pulses as well as the physicochemical properties of the drug, (2) large flux enhancement for many different compounds, and (3) fast and responsive transport of drug molecules [97]. Skin permeation of molecules induced by HV ETP is very responsive, with lag times to reach steady-state fluxes and onset times for molecular transport measured in minutes [97]. Several research groups have assessed skin ETP safety in humans and animal models [116]. Moderate and reversible skin reactions were documented after the administration of 15 pulses of 200 ms and 250 V pulses in hairless rats [117]. In another study, ETP with 60 pulses (150 V, 1 ms) in human subjects did not result in pain [118]. A drawback of ETP is that advanced electronic instrumentation is required and this adds more complexity and cost. On the other hand, advances in electrode design that can result in nerve stimulation reduction, patch-based microelectronic systems, and low-cost batteries will engender progress in transdermal ETP [107]. Skin ETP has witnessed numerous technological advances, especially in the area of electrode design [119]: the utilization of needle-based electrodes rather than plate electrodes to circumvent HV; using closely spaced microelectrodes to restrict the electric field to the SC, thus decreasing muscle stimulation and potential pain; the use of elastic microneedles as electrodes, leading to a good coverage of the surface of the tissue as well as LV ETP [119].

Transdermal EP is an important physical enhancer for the transport of hydrophilic, lipophilic, neutral, or charged compounds across the skin [109]. Over the past few decades, there has been a marked increase in the number of transdermal ETP studies. Scientists have used this mode of drug delivery enhancement to increase the transcutaneous flux values of low and high molecular–weight medications. Even though regulatory authorities have not approved a transdermal drug delivery system based on ETP, numerous laboratories are active in this area of research. In the next section, specific examples of the application of transdermal ETP will be discussed.

ETP-mediated transdermal delivery of doxepin

Doxepin, a tricyclic antidepressant, is widely used for the management of depression and has also shown antianxiety and antihistamine properties [120]. The drug can also be used for the topical management of postherpetic neuralgia [116]. An ETP technique using 30 pulses (120 V, 10 ms) for doxepin and doxepin-hydroxypropyl-β-cyclodextrin (HPCD) complex delivery across pig epidermis was recently documented [116]. Experiments with vertical Franz-type diffusion cells were conducted to measure permeation and resistance across pig epidermis [116]. The authors placed concentric ring-shaped Ag/AgCl electrodes 2 mm away from pig epidermis in the receiver and donor chambers [116]. ETP-assisted transport of doxepin across pig epidermis was investigated using a solution of doxepin-HPCD complex in PBS (CDS) and the pure drug solution (PDS) [116]. The total quantity of the medication that penetrated the skin from PDS (passive penetration across pig epidermis in 20 min) was 0.16 ± 0.03 μg/cm^2 [116]. In comparison with the control formulation, the quantity of drug delivered by ETP using PDS was approximately 100-fold higher (16.77 ± 2.52 μg/cm^2). Conversely, the quantity of doxepin delivered via penetration within 20 min from the doxepin-hydroxy-propyl-β-cyclodextrin complex solution (CDS) control could not be detected, and it was 4.82 ± 1.08 μg/cm^2 from CDS following the use of ETP [116].

Using ETP to transport calcein

Zorec and coworkers investigated the effect of ETP on the percutaneous transport of a hydrophilic model molecule (calcein) [104]. ETP was carried out with square-wave pulses. The comparison of different pulse protocols and their effect on skin and subsequent passive calcein delivery through pig skin is shown in Fig. 9.4. Porcine skin was subjected to continuous pulses (spacing between pulses: 100 μs; pulse duration: 100 μs; amplitude: 200 V) for either 15 or 5 s. The pulses were administered pairwise between six surrounding electrodes (cathodes) and a middle electrode (anode), pairwise. ETP for either 15 or 5 s was a potent technique for enhancing drug transport. This technique markedly increased the transport of calcein from ethosomes, liposomes, and solution, in comparison to passive permeation. Moreover, there was a synergistic calcein flux enhancement from ethosomes combined with ETP in comparison with other combinations [104].

Delivering fentanyl across the human skin with ETP

Conjeevaram et al. investigated the influence of ETP on the percutaneous transport of fentanyl [113]. The ETP technique entailed the application of 15

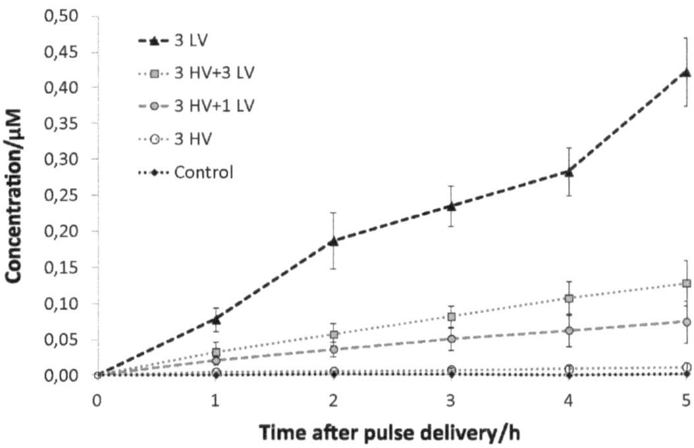

FIGURE 9.4 Comparison of different pulse protocols and their effect on skin and subsequent passive calcein delivery through pig skin. *Reproduced with permission from Zorec B, et al., Skin ETP for transdermal drug delivery: the influence of the order of different square wave electric pulses. Int J Pharm 2013;457(1):214–23.*

exponential pulses (at 1 pulse/min) of 500 V (applied voltage) for 200 ms at time zero and, in some cases, repeating at 1.5 and 2.5 h) [113]. The transport of fentanyl through human epidermis could not be detected following passive penetration. In the study, pulses (1 pulse/min) were administered [113]. ETP provided transdermal flux that was three times higher than that achieved by ITP and 270 times greater compared to passive delivery [113]. The lag time of delivery was also significantly less than that achieved by ITP. Thus ETP may allow for an even quicker onset of analgesia by rapid delivery of fentanyl within minutes compared to an hour to couple of hours with ITP and several hours to a day with passive delivery [113]. The authors also observed that using the high-intensity ETP protocol in an in vivo setting would require careful development of electrodes and pulsing protocols to avoid intolerable electrical sensations and develop a patient compliant, cost-effective delivery device [113]. The intensity required for in vivo delivery will, however, be less than the in vitro protocol since the electrodes do interface directly with the skin and an equivalent transdermal voltage can be reached at a lower setting [113].

Percutaneous transport of metoprolol with ETP

Metoprolol is a beta-receptor blocking agent that is utilized for the therapy of high blood pressure [121]. The drug slows down the heart rate and reduces stress on the arteries and the heart [121]. Metoprolol has a molecular weight of 267, a pKa of 9.7, and a partition coefficient of 0.6 [122]. Vanbever and coworkers studied the effect of ETP on the transcutaneous permeation of metoprolol [122]. The researchers investigated the effect of pulse time, number of pulses, pulse type, and pulse voltage on ETP-assisted transdermal delivery of metoprolol (MTP) across hairless rat skin in vitro using an exponentially decaying pulse [122]. ETP enhanced MTP transport in comparison to permeation across untreated skin. Increasing the number of twin pulses (300 V, 3 ms; followed after 1 s by 100 V, 620 ms) from 1 to 20 enhanced drug permeation [122]. Single pulse (100 V, 620 ms) was similar to twin pulses (2200, 1100, or 300 V, 3 ms; followed after 1 s by 100 V, 620 ms) in terms of effectiveness [122]. To evaluate the effect of pulse voltage on MTP transport, five single pulses (each 1 min apart) were administered to hairless rat skin using different voltages from 24 to 450 V (pulse time 620 ms) [122]. The authors observed that the voltage threshold required to enhance MTP transport was approximately 24 V under those ETP conditions [122].

When the voltage of five pulses (620 ms) was raised from 24 to 250 V, the amount of MTP that diffused through the skin went up roughly in proportion to the square of the voltage. From 74 to 250 V, MTP amount increased linearly with the voltage. There was a linear increase in the amount of the drug transported as the pulse duration of five 100 V single pulses was varied by the authors from 80 to 700 ms. The threshold of the pulse time was about 80 ms under those conditions [122]. It was inferred that voltage regulates the amount of drug transported because of the presence of a linear correlation between pulse voltage and cumulative amount of MTP that permeated the skin after 4 h [122]. The influence of pulse time on MTP delivery was evaluated by changing the pulse duration of five 100 V single pulses from 80 to 700 ms (each pulse 1 min apart) [122]. The cumulative amount of the medication that permeated the skin after 4 h was enhanced in proportion with pulse time [122].

ETP-mediated transdermal delivery of nalbuphine

Nalbuphine (NBN) is a κ-agonist and μ-antagonist used for the therapy of acute and chronic pain [123,124]. The drug is injected every 3–6 h because of its short elimination half-life and low oral bioavailability [124,125]. Fang et al. studied the effect of ETP on the percutaneous transport of NBN and its prodrugs (nalbuphine decanoate, nalbuphine enanthate, nalbuphine pivalate, and nalbuphine propionate) [125]. The permeation profiles of the compounds under the influence of assorted electrical factors were studied with the aim of unraveling the mechanisms of ETP-mediated percutaneous transport of NBN and its prodrugs [125]. The effect of pulse number, pulse voltage, and pulse duration as well as different skin barriers (furry Wistar rat skin, delipidized skin, SC-stripped skin, and intact hairless mouse skin) were investigated [125]. The prodrugs were fully transformed into the parent drug after penetrating the skin. ETP markedly increased the transcutaneous penetration of NBN and its prodrugs [125]. The enhancement ratios were largest for NBN, while the four prodrugs displayed comparable permeability values following ETP [125]. The use of higher pulse voltages led to higher total cumulative amount. For each penetrant, there was a linear correlation between the total quantity of drug that was transported and the applied voltage, with correlation coefficients of 0.981 for NBN, 0.990 for nalbuphine enanthate, and 0.985 for nalbuphine propionate [125]. It was noted that the different applied voltages may change skin pore dimensions that may influence drug transport rates [125]. The highest linear correlation was observed for NBN, indicating that the drug delivery process correlated well with molecular size or pulsing voltage. It has been suggested that longer pulse duration may lead to the formation of larger pores and as a result increase transdermal drug delivery rates [125].

The effect of ETP on the transdermal permeation of doxorubicin

Blagus studied the influence of two amplitude values (360 and 570 V) on the skin delivery of doxycycline [110]. ETP of mouse skin was carried out with multiarray electrodes capable of providing electric pulses with different amplitudes (from 70 to 570 V) [110]. The authors used transdermal patches, saturated with doxorubicin (DOX) for the ETP experiments. The administration of electric pulses led to increased percutaneous transport [110]. Transdermal delivery was enhanced up to the amplitude of 360 V and declined at higher amplitudes (460 and 570 V) [110]. Skin delivery was a function of electric pulse amplitude with the higher amplitude creating larger areas of enhanced permeability and also a higher amount of DOX in the skin [110]. Another proof of ETP-assisted skin transport of DOX delivery was seen in the treated portion of the skin, where DOX destroyed hair follicles resulting in transient alopecia (lasting ~4 days) [110]. Skin injury was more prominent when the tape stripping technique was used, since DOX was administered directly to the epidermis following the removal of the SC. When DOX was administered via ETP, a crust was observed within 48 h [110]. When DOX was injected subcutaneously, only a mild skin injury was recorded at the site of drug administration [110].

Delivery of iron with ETP

A reduction in the body iron concentration may sometimes lead to iron deficiency anemia (IDA) [126]. IDA occurs as a consequence of physiologic loss of iron from body, poor absorption, or insufficient dietary intake of iron. Transcutaneous transport of iron can be employed to tackle the adverse events linked to oral and parenteral iron delivery and can also be used to enhance patient compliance [127]. Ferric pyrophosphate (FPP) is a water-soluble and stable compound that is known to trigger the direct transformation of transferrin to ferritin, thus boosting iron exchange between transferrin molecules [126]. Vaka and colleagues investigated the influence of ETP on the transcutaneous absorption of FPP [126]. The authors applied electric pulses (120 V, 100 pulses) with varied frequencies (1 or 5 Hz) and pulse lengths (1, 10, or 100 ms) to pig epidermis [126]. In the study, pulse number (100 pulses) and pulse voltage (120 V) were fixed, while different frequency and pulse length values were used. Aliquots of the receptor chamber fluid were taken immediately after stopping the electric pulses to determine the amount of ETP-mediated FPP transport [126]. There was marked increase in the transport of FPP, when the frequency was increased at the pulse length of 1 and 10 ms [126]. At 100 ms, the transdermal delivery of FPP was not statistically different between 1 and 5 Hz. Furthermore, the delivery using a pulse duration of 100 ms was also not markedly different from that of 10 ms [126].

ETP-mediated transdermal delivery of Kb-binding ovalbumin-peptide SIINFEKL

Zhao and coworkers used the Kb-binding ovalbumin (OVA)-peptide SIINFEKL to generate cytotoxic T-lymphocytes response in mice [128].

The authors placed murine skin between the donor and receiver chambers of Franz diffusion cells and treated the skin with electric pulses (15 pulses, 1 m at 1 s interval, 100 V followed by a DC potential to provide electric current measuring 1 mA/cm^2 for 10 min) [128]. A higher proportion of rhodamine-labeled OVA peptide was found in the skin if the anionic lipid 1,2-dimyristoyl-3-phosphatidylserine (DMPS) was in the donor compartment during electric pulsing in comparison to the protocol that did not incorporate DMPS. Application of electric pulses without DMPS led to approximately an equivalent quantity of the compound in the skin (about 5%) compared to the protocol without pulsing (control) [128]. The quantities detected in the receptor compartment fluid were comparable with or with no electric pulsing. Ostensibly, more rhodamine-OVA diffused into, instead of permeating full-thickness, murine skin when pulsing was carried out with DMPS [128]. In the study, the Kb-binding OVA-peptide SIINFEKL transported by ETP remained largely in the skin rather than permeating the tissue [128]. This is beneficial for targeting antigen-presenting cells in the skin [128].

Transcutaneous transport of neostigmine via ETP

Neostigmine (NSN) is an anticholinesterase agent used for the management of neuromuscular blockade [129]. Even though newer compounds with anticholinesterase activity have been recently synthesized, NSN has certain benefits such as low cost, the availability of clinical reference data, and a far-ranging elimination of the effects of nondepolarizing neuromuscular blocking agents [129]. NSN induces gastrointestinal motility but possesses low bioavailability following oral ingestion [109]. NSN methylsulfate (log $P = -2.2$, $MW = 334.39$ g/mol) crosses the skin poorly principally due to its low transport across the SC. Recently, Berko et al. compared the effect of NSN methylsulfate on cecal contraction following percutaneous ETP and intravenous delivery in anesthetized rats [109]. The authors used implantable strain gauge sensors to determine cecal contractions. The Mezoforte Duo EP device -a polypropylene-covered treating headpiece equipped with a plate electrode indirectly connected with the treated skin surface- was used for ETP [109]. The device utilizes a pulsed electromagnetic field [109]. ETP protocol involved 1800 V_{pp} (peak-to-peak voltage) pulses (5 ms), followed by 20 ms break. Pulses were administered on the surface of the abdomen for 2 min (2200 periods/min), allowing the transdermal absorption of the applied neostigmine-containing hydrogel, with only a dry film layer left on the skin surface [109]. A waiting period of 10 min was observed before the next ETP-delivered drug dose. Both ETP-assisted and intravenous neostigmine (0.2–66.7 μg/kg) enhanced cecal contractions in a dose-dependent fashion [109]. For the highest dose and the low doses, NSN plasma concentrations were similar after the two methods of delivery, whereas an insignificantly higher concentration was detected at 20 μg/kg dose following intravenous administration in comparison with ETP [109]. The authors concluded that the action of NSN following intravenous and ETP-mediated administration was similar [109].

Skin delivery of sinomenine hydrochloride by ETP

Sinomenine, an alkaloid isolated from the medicinal plant *sinomenium acutum*, possesses immunosuppressive, antiangiogenic, antirheumatic, and anti-inflammatory activities [130]. It has been revealed that the side effects of sinomenine hydrochloride (SH) which manifested in certain animals after administration may be linked to fast SH distribution to internal organs [131]. It was reasoned that the local application to joints may be a useful drug delivery approach for the management of osteoarthritis and rheumatoid arthritis. Feng and coworkers used ETP for the skin delivery of SH [131]. Percutaneous penetration studies in vitro and in the clinic were used to optimize ETP parameters for SH. The authors investigated the influence of pulse intensity, pulse waveform and pulse frequency on the SH ETP [131]. Furthermore, fluorescence microscopy as well as hematoxylin and eosin staining were conducted to elucidate the mechanism by which ETP enhanced skin transport. Exponential waveform, a frequency of 3 KHz and an intensity of 10 were the optimal ETP parameters in vitro [131]. Utilizing these parameters, the authors enhanced the percutaneous penetration of SH by 1.9–10.1-fold in murine skin and by 1.6–47.1-fold in miniature porcine skin in comparison to passive transport [131]. In clinical studies, the synovial fluid concentration of SH was 20.84 ng/mL following ETP. It was postulated by the authors that ETP pulses loosened the SC and enhanced the skin's intercellular spaces [131]. ETP-mediated skin structure alterations decreased skin barrier properties and enhanced SH transport [131].

Skin delivery of methotrexate via ETP

Wong and coworkers used ETP to increase the transdermal permeation of MTX [132]. The aim was to increase the skin diffusion of the drug for the management of neoplastic diseases and psoriasis. The authors positioned electrodes either on a porcine skin sample placed between chambers of a vertical diffusion cell or on excised porcine skin in a side-by-side diffusion cell [132]. The authors administered 60 rectangular pulses at 1 Hz, 1 ms, and 120 V across the pig skin sample [132]. MTX remained on the surface of the skin for 10 min to facilitate permeation across the created pores. When the authors used the second electrode technique (side-by-side), application of pulses without chemical enhancers led to a 2.5-fold permeation enhancement, while the addition of anionic lipid enhancers led to a 4.4-fold increase in comparison with passive delivery [132]. The simultaneous use of ITP did not result in a dramatic increase in skin transport. The drug penetration profiles demonstrated that more than 50% of the drug was restricted to the epidermis and the papillary dermis [132]. To decrease tissue resistance, 40°C hyperthermia was used and skin permeation was boosted 11-fold to 53 μg/cm^2 (transdermal flux was 290 μg/cm^2/h) [132].

Percutaneous transport of tetracaine via ETP

Tetracaine (2-dimethylaminoethyl-4-butylaminobenzoate), which is marketed as a salt (hydrochloride), is an amino ester used clinically for the induction of local anesthesia [133]. Hu and colleagues studied the impact of ETP on the transdermal penetration of tetracaine (TCN) across rat skin [134]. The authors used the OX4-1 ETP device that is capable of generating square-wave pulses. The researchers varied the voltage between 70 and 130 V and the pulse frequency was set at 1, 2, 4, 8, 10, 20, or 40 pulses/min [134]. Different pulse times were also used in the study. The influence of ETP on the delivery of TCN through rat skin in vitro was investigated with side-by-side diffusion cells. The authors compared skin fluxes of the drug obtained following passive transport, ITP, and ETP [134]. ETP (pulse time 0.4 s, voltage 130 V, pulse frequency 40 pulses/min, square-wave pulse) enhanced the transdermal permeation of TCN. The transcutaneous flux of the drug at 0.25 h after ETP (pulse number 400) was 54.6 ± 6.0 μg/cm^2 in comparison with passive transport (8.2 ± 0.5 μg/cm^2/h). Furthermore, the transdermal fluxes of TCN were higher when pulse number was raised [134].

ETP-mediated transcutaneous permeation of alniditan

Alniditan (ADN) is a benzopyran derivative and a 5-HT receptor agonist used for the management of migraine [135]. The drug has a pK of 8.3 and 11.5, the molecular weight of 302.4, and a $P_{oct/water}$ (pH 8) of 1.59 [136]. It is a selective vasoconstrictor that acts mainly on the 5-HT1D serotoninergic receptor [136]. Due to low oral bioavailability, numerous research groups have investigated alternative modes of delivery. Jadoul et al. used factorial design to study the effect of ETP on the transcutaneous permeation of alniditan across full-thickness rat abdominal skin. To carry out ETP, the authors connected platinum electrodes to an exponential decay pulse generator (Easyject Plus). Applied voltage (V), the number of pulses (N), and time constant (τ) were investigated. The time interval between the maximum voltage and the time point at which the voltage reaches 37% of its highest value is called the time constant [136]. The quantity of transferred charges (Q) was determined using the sum of the integral of $I(t)dt$ of each pulse. The electrical energy administered to the electrodes can be estimated [136]:

$$E = N_{\tau}(V_i^2 - V_f^2)/2R_{cell} \tag{9.12}$$

where R_{cell} refers to the diffusion cell total resistance. The effect of time constant (approximately 100 and 500 ms), voltage (100 and 200 V), and the number of pulses (5 and 10, with an interpulse time of 1 min) was studied [136]. The permeation rate of alniditan was increased by two orders of magnitude through the use of HV electrical pulses. The number of pulses, pulse duration, and voltage allowed the investigators to control drug delivery [136]. Permeation during and after the administration of electrical pulses was shown to be important for ETP-mediated alniditan transport across the skin [136].

ETP-assisted skin permeation of heparin

Prausnitz and coworkers have provided evidence showing increased transdermal transport of heparin (HPN) following ETP [137]. The authors investigated the transdermal permeation of radiolabeled heparin across human skin SC following the use of HV pulses. The authors administered millisecond pulses (150–350 V) 12 times/min over 1 h and observed enhanced HPN flux rates of 100–500 μg/cm^2/h [137]. Following ETP, the human skin samples continued to display marked HPN transport over a one-day time frame even after ETP was discontinued, possibly due to the skin alteration by highly charged macromolecules [137]. Assay of the transported heparin showed that there was a propensity for the skin permeation of lower molecular–weight HPN, but overall, the drug still maintained biological effect [137]. The researchers showed that ETP delivered therapeutically relevant dose of HPN (200–1000 units/h over a 100 cm^2 area of human skin) [137].

Transdermal delivery of domperidone via ETP

Domperidone (DMP) is a peripheral dopamine D_2-receptor blocker used for the stimulation of breast milk production and management of GERD, nausea, gastric dysmotility, and vomiting [138]. Studies with hairless rat skin in vitro were conducted with a solution of DMP in 9.5% (v/v) ethyl alcohol [139]. Platinum electrodes (1 cm^2) were connected to device Easyject Plus with the cathode placed in the receptor compartment and the anode placed in the donor chamber. The use of five HV (250 V, 700 ms) pulses enhanced DMP transport across hairless rat abdominal skin by a factor of 70 [139]. DMP permeation rate by ETP (1.5 μg/cm^2/h) was comparable to that achieved with chemical penetration enhancer (CPEs) but the lag time was lower. Be that as it may, electrically facilitated flux was too low for therapeutic application due to the low aqueous solubility of DMP [139].

ETP-mediated transdermal penetration of diphtheria toxoid

Diphtheria toxoid (DT) is usually made from diphtheria toxin [140]. The toxin is transformed by formaldehyde into the immunogenic but nontoxic

DT [140]. Misra et al. compared the ETP-mediated immunogenic effect induced by the lipophilic and low molecular–weight myristylated peptide (MYR) and DT; a molecule with lower lipophilicity and higher molecular weight [90]. The authors employed 10 pulses (100 V, 1 ms, interpulse interval of 1 s) for this set of experiments [90]. MYR or DT given either intradermally (i.d.) or transdermally via ETP elicited significantly different responses. ETP route evoked higher responses to MYR compared to intradermal immunization, but less effect was elicited by DT [90]. Intraperitoneal (i.p.) immunization induced higher responses against MYR compared to those elicited by ETP. The authors suggested that ETP can be used as a method for skin vaccination (without adjuvants), particularly with weak, low molecular–weight antigens [90].

Percutaneous transport of insulin via ETP

Type 1 diabetes (T1DM) is characterized by the loss of pancreatic beta cells resulting in the lack of endogenic insulin production. In contrast, patients with type 2 diabetes (T2DM) do not have adequate compensation by pancreatic beta cells and do have peripheral insulin resistance [141]. Several transdermal formulations of insulin have been investigated. An interesting approach involves the use of ETP to increase insulin delivery. The impact of ETP on the transdermal delivery of insulin was studied [142]. The authors studied five insulin dosage forms and administered them to hyperglycemic rabbits. The influence of ETP parameters on blood glucose concentration of rabbits was compared with those of untreated rabbits [142]. When the field strength was reduced from 200 to 100 V/cm and the number of pulses increased from 15 to 60 pulses with the drug concentration of 50 IU/mL. Increased insulin concentration from 50 to 70 IU/mL led to a significant decrease in blood glucose concentration in comparison with the control samples [142]. Under practically all experimental scenarios, the authors observed optimal performance for insulin solution with ETP (without CPEs) [142].

ETP-mediated percutaneous delivery of andrographolide

Andrographolide (AGE) can be isolated from the medicinal plant *Andrographis paniculata* [143]. AGE possesses antiinflammatory, anticancer, antibacterial, and antiviral properties [143]. Several attempts are being made by investigators to find alternative routes for AGE delivery. Zhang and coworkers studied the influence of ETP on the transcutaneous permeation of AGE across rabbit skin [144]. The authors used a low-cost, fully programmable, and portable device for pulse generation. ETP-assisted transcutaneous targeted delivery (100 V, 60 pulses at 1 Hz interpulse period of 2 min, 10 ms) of AGE-loaded liposomes was administered to the rodents [144]. Following the use of different electric pulse parameters and input voltage, alterations in the skin, as well as other adverse events, were examined [144]. Skin ETP significantly enhanced the transcutaneous delivery of liposomes with entrapped AGE across rabbit skin. AGE was rapidly distributed into the lungs. By varying the magnitude of the electric pulse parameters and input voltage, the authors reported that ETP under 100 V (2 and 5 mA) was safe and well tolerated, and there was no skin erythema following the use of this form of enhancement [144].

The effect of ETP on the percutaneous absorption of genistein

Genistein is an isoflavone isolated from the dyer's broom, *Genista tinctorial* [145]. The compound is available soy products and has been shown to revamp pathophysiologic pathways that are usually impaired in metabolic syndrome, obesity, and cancer [145]. Genistein (GEN) is also referred to as a phytoestrogen due to its structural resemblance to 17β-oestradiol [146]. Lyotropic liquid crystals (LLCs) are nanosystems prepared from oil, water, surfactants, and cosurfactants [146]. The major benefits of LLCs are their thermodynamic stability, the possibility of storage for a protracted period of time with no phase separation, as well as resemblance to colloidal systems present in living organisms [146]. LLCs can also increase the transport of pharmacological agents into the skin or transdermally into the bloodstream [146].

ETP was used to deliver GEN and LLC-GEN across diverse membranes. Investigations were conducted with Franz diffusion cells across excised human epidermis ex vivo, chick chorioallantoic membrane ex ovo, and a synthetic membrane in vitro [146]. Ex vivo Raman spectroscopy and in vivo attenuated total reflection-Fourier transform infrared (ATR-FTIR) spectroscopy were also utilized to investigate the percutaneous transport of GEN-loaded LLCs across different membranes in the presence or absence of ETP [146]. An ETP device was used to generate HV pulses (5, 20 ms interpulse period) [146]. GEN delivery was carried out via EP with 700 or 900 V and different application times (1 or 2 min). Plots of the cumulative amount of GEN that permeated every square centimeter of the skin versus time (Q) were generated. The skin permeation flux (J) was determined from the slope of the concentration-time curves [146].

GEN diffusion across the synthetic membrane in vitro in 24 h was $713.26 \pm 90.73\ \mu g/cm^2$. A little quantity of the medication permeated the human epidermis ($8.93 \pm 1.81\ \mu g/cm^2$ after 24 h and $15.68 \pm 3.09\ \mu g/cm^2$ after 48 h). A combination of ATR-FTIR spectroscopy and tape stripping was used to investigate the transport of GEN within diverse layers of the SC. The most distinctive peaks in GEN ATR-FTIR were assigned to the ring A C–C stretch at 1518/cm, O7-H22 bend, the C = O stretch, and the C1 = C2 stretch at 1652/cm [146]. It was revealed that using ETP (700 V for 1 min) did not increase GEN transport across the skin compared to untreated skin.

This was attributed to the high viscosity of the drug carrier, which reduced the effectiveness of ETP on the skin [146]. Slightly deeper GEN permeation was obtained by using 900 V for 1 min, but the total quantity of GEN was not higher than was obtained following the use of the control LLC-GEN formulation [146]. Be that as it may, ETP at 700 V for 2 min led to a deeper permeation (twofold increase in flux). The most optimal GEN permeation profile was achieved with ETP (900 V for 2 min) which led to a threefold enhancement in the cumulative amount delivered in comparison with untreated skin [146]. Furthermore, GEN was not detected in the 5th and 6th tape strips, but the compound was seen in the 7th strip. The authors attributed this phenomenon to the electrical breakdown of the SC layers. In addition, the quantity of GEN that permeated went up when pulse voltage was elevated [146].

ETP-assisted skin transport of insulin

The concurrent influence of ETP and ITP on the transdermal penetration of insulin (ISN) was investigated in rats [147]. To examine the influence of ETP and/or IP on percutaneous penetration, ISN solutions (50 U/mL) with a pH 7 or 10 were studied. The investigators applied 10 ms, 300 V square-wave pulse (10 pulses) every second for 10 s. IP (0.4 mA/cm^2) and passive transport alone did not lead to the skin penetration of ISN at pH 7, while the use of ETP (10 ms, 150 or 300 V, 10 pulses) led to a high blood concentration of the drug. The concurrent utilization of EP and IP led to a further elevation of the plasma concentration of ISN in comparison with the use of only ETP [147]. Significantly, a further increase in the plasma concentration of ISN was recorded when the pH of the drug solution was raised to 10. This was ascribed to a higher nonassociation ratio of the monomers at pH 7. When ISN solution (pH 7) was administered on the skin, no transdermal delivery of the drug nor a marked alteration in blood glucose concentration was documented following the use of IP alone (0.4 mA/cm^2, 60 min) or ETP alone (300 V) [147]. On the other hand, when ISN solution (pH 10) was administered, the plasma drug concentration was enhanced by ETP alone and it reached about 50 μU/mL at 240 min from the beginning of the study. The investigators also assessed the combined effect of IP and ETP on the transcutaneous permeation of ISN. IP (0.4 mA/cm^2) was carried out for 1 h after EP (10 pulses, 10 ms, 150 or 300 V) at pH 7. The IP-assisted transdermal delivery of the drug was significantly higher following pretreatment with ETP, and its influence was a function of the applied voltage (10 pulses of 150 or 300 V). In addition, the concentration of glucose in the blood markedly decreased following the synergistic application of the two techniques (IP and ETP) to about 23% in the 150-V category and to about 53% in the 300-V category 120 min after delivery compared to the initial concentration indicating enhanced plasma insulin concentration [147].

The influence of ETP on the transcutaneous penetration of terazosin

Sharma and coworkers investigated the parameters that impact ETP-assisted percutaneous penetration of terazosin hydrochloride (TH) across hairless rat skin [148]. The researchers revealed that pulse length, voltage, and number of pulses were the three most relevant factors [148]. The authors reported that it was important to use five or more exponentially decaying pulses, with a decay time constant of 20 ms at 88 $\pm$ 2.5 V to cause a significant increase in drug delivery to the skin, with no alteration in the external appearance of the tissue [148]. It was also noted by the researchers that the use of electrodes with larger area resulted in the achievement of similar voltages across the skin with less applied voltage [148]. In another study, the ability to reverse ETP effect was examined in vitro by the same research group [149]. The skin's reversal from increased permeability to the base level following the cessation of ETP was utilized as a mechanistic index as well as an initial safety index [149]. The maximum transport of TH took place during electric pulsing [149]. ETP-assisted transport with a wire electrode (electrode area, 0.56 cm^2) using a pulse length of 20 ms and 20 pulses at U_{skin}, 0 88 V did not lead to any skin injury. Raising the pulse length to 60 ms, while maintaining the remaining parameters, induced a visible alteration in the outer appearance of the skin [149]. On the other hand, when a spiral electrode (large-area electrode, 2.74 cm^2) at 60-ms pulse length was used, injury to the skin was minimal. This can be ascribed to the more consistent current flow over the skin [149].

ETP-mediated delivery of vaccines against *Trypanosoma cruzi*

Trypanosoma cruzi causes Chagas disease, which is rampant in Latin America. This parasite is transmitted to human beings through triatomines [150]. It is well established that several years after infection, 20%–35% of those affected will experience permanent lesions of the colon, peripheral nervous system, autonomous nervous system of the esophagus and/or heart [150]. Hegazy-Hassan et al. investigated the prophylactic effectiveness of TcVac1 vaccine administered by means of an intradermal ETP (IDE) technique [150]. DNA-prime/DNA-boost vaccine (TcVac1) vaccine was given to mice through intramuscular (IM) or IDE means, and the rodents were then infected with *T. cruzi* [150]. The mice were randomly assigned to treatment groups: group I, empty pcDNA3.1 plasmid (25 mg/mouse) via IDE with or without infection; group II, TcVac1 DNA vaccine (25 mg each from the five DNA plasmids composing the vaccine) via IDE with or without infection; group III, pcDNA3.1 plasmid (25 mg/mouse) via IM with or without infection; and group IV, TcVac1 DNA vaccine (25 mg each from the four DNA plasmids composing the vaccine/mouse) via IM with or without infection [150].

The investigators administered placebo (pcDNA3) or a DNA vaccine (TcVac1) to the animals by means of IDE or IM injection. ETP was carried out (five pulses, 0.125-ms bandwidth, 450 V/cm^2, and 0.050-ms pulse interval) [150]. The humoral immune response was assessed by determining anti-TcG4 IgG and anti-TcG2 subtypes by means of enzyme-linked immunosorbent assay. The authors examined cellular immune response by using the lymphocyte proliferation method. The authors reported that when TcVac1 IDE transport was used, it led to a significantly higher degree of antigen-specific antibody response (IgG2a + IgG2b > IgG1) and lymphocyte proliferation compared to IM transport. The results of the study showed that IDE enhanced the prophylactic efficacy of TcVac1 vaccine directed against *T. cruzi* infection in mice in comparison with the IM mode of delivery [150].

ETP-mediated skin delivery of pDNA vaccine that codes for the influenza nucleoprotein (PR8)

Schultheis and coworkers recently delivered pDNA vaccine that codes for the influenza nucleoprotein (NP; PR8) using a skin surface ETP (SEP)-based platform [151]. The authors used a vaccine plasmid that encodes the full-length NP obtained from the A/Puerto Rico/8 (H1N1) strain of influenza [151]. The SEP utilized in this research project was an electrode array comprising gold-plated trocar needles measuring 0.43 mm in diameter with a 1.5 mm spacing [151]. The investigators reported that all the pNP-immunized guinea pigs generated IgG antibodies reactive to the NP antigen. The authors utilized interferon-gamma (IFN-γ) enzyme-linked immune absorbent spot (ELISpot) assay to monitor and quantify cellular immune responses in a Hartley guinea pig model [151]. Peripheral blood cells were used in the test so that the change in time of the host immune response induced in a single guinea pig can be determined via blood collection instead of sacrificing multiple animals to obtain responder cells [151]. To avoid sacrificing an animal to monitor cellular responses, the authors obtained whole blood from the jugular vein and retrieved peripheral blood mononuclear cells (PBMCs) via density gradient centrifugation. The authors reported that 3 mL of peripheral blood produced between 2 and 4 million PBMCs. Furthermore, antigen-specific IFN-γ ELISpot reactions between PBMCs collected from vaccinated guinea pigs and splenocytes were comparable. Following the transport of the DNA vaccine to the guinea pig skin, swift and potent T cell responses were recorded. The index of the T cell immune response to NP antigen was 4840 IFN-γ + SFU's/10^6 PBMCs following the second vaccination. In addition, 2 weeks after a dose of pNP, an average of 700 IFN-γ + SFU's/10^6 PBMCs were recorded[150]. The number of IFN- γ spot-forming units was about 5000 per million cells subsequent to two vaccinations. Numerous NP-immunodominant T-cell epitopes conserved across some outbred guinea pigs were also described by the authors [151].

References

[1] Takeuchi I, et al. Iontophoretic transdermal delivery using chitosan-coated PLGA nanoparticles for positively charged drugs. Colloids Surf B Biointerfaces 2017;160: 520–6.

[2] Ita K. Transdermal iontophoretic drug delivery: advances and challenges. J Drug Target 2015;1–6.

[3] Lemos CN, et al. Iontophoresis-stimulated silk fibroin films as a peptide delivery system for wound healing. Eur J Pharm Biopharm 2018;128:147–55.

[4] Kalia YN, et al. Iontophoretic drug delivery. Adv Drug Deliv Rev 2004;56(5):619–58.

[5] Bernardi DS, et al. Effective transcutaneous immunization using a combination of iontophoresis and nanoparticles. Nanomedicine 2016;12(8):2439–48.

[6] Davoodi P, et al. Drug delivery systems for programmed and on-demand release. Adv Drug Deliv Rev 2018;132:104–38.

[7] Sage BH, Riviere JE. Model systems in iontophoresis — Transport efficacy. Adv Drug Deliv Rev 1992;9(2):265–87.

[8] Chen X. Current and future technological advances in transdermal gene delivery. Adv Drug Deliv Rev 2018;127:85–105.

[9] Yoshida NH, Roberts MS. Structure-transport relationships in transdermal iontophoresis. Adv Drug Deliv Rev 1992;9(2):239–64.

[10] Gelker M, et al. Influence of pulse characteristics and power density on stratum corneum permeabilization by dielectric barrier discharge. Biochim Biophys Acta Gen Subj 2019;1863(10):1513–23.

[11] Tyagi V, et al. Topical iontophoresis of buflomedil hydrochloride increases drug bioavailability in the mucosa: a targeted approach to treat oral submucous fibrosis. Int J Pharm 2019;569:118610.

[12] Pikal MJ. The role of electroosmotic flow in transdermal iontophoresis. Adv Drug Deliv Rev 2001;46(1–3):281–305.

[13] Filipovic N, et al. Computational and experimental model of transdermal iontophorethic drug delivery system. Int J Pharm 2017;533(2):383–8.

[14] Osman-Ponchet H, et al. Pretreatment of skin using an abrasive skin preparation pad, a microneedling device or iontophoresis improves absorption of methyl aminolevulinate in ex vivo human skin. Photodiagnosis Photodyn Ther 2017;20:130–6.

[15] Malinovskaja K, Laaksonen T, Hirvonen J. Controlled transdermal delivery of leuprorelin by pulsed iontophoresis and ion-exchange fiber. Eur J Pharm Biopharm 2014;88(3): 594–601.

[16] Djabri A, Guy RH, Delgado-Charro MB. Potential of iontophoresis as a drug delivery method for midazolam in pediatrics. Eur J Pharm Sci 2019;128:137–43.

[17] Banga AK, Bose S, Ghosh TK. Iontophoresis and electroporation: comparisons and contrasts. Int J Pharm 1999;179(1):1–19.

[18] Banerjee A, et al. Intestinal iontophoresis from mucoadhesive patches: a strategy for oral delivery. J Control Release 2019;297:71–8.

[19] Simon L, Ospina J, Ita K. Prediction of in-vivo iontophoretic drug release data from in-vitro experiments – insights from modeling. Math Biosci 2015;270:106–14.

[20] Mitragotri S. Devices for overcoming biological barriers: the use of physical forces to disrupt the barriers. Adv Drug Deliv Rev 2013;65(1):100–3.

[21] Wiedersberg S, Guy RH. Transdermal drug delivery: 30 + years of war and still fighting! J Control Release 2014;190:150–6.

[22] Myles ME, Neumann DM, Hill JM. Recent progress in ocular drug delivery for posterior segment disease: emphasis on transscleral iontophoresis. Adv Drug Deliv Rev 2005;57 (14):2063–79.

[23] Hughes L, Maurice DM. A fresh look at iontophoresis. Arch Ophthalmol 1984;102 (12):1825–9.

[24] Gratieri T, Kalia YN. Mathematical models to describe iontophoretic transport in vitro and in vivo and the effect of current application on the skin barrier. Adv Drug Deliv Rev 2013;65(2):315–29.

[25] Harden JL, Viovy JL. Numerical studies of pulsed iontophoresis through model membranes. J Control Release 1996;38(2):129–39.

[26] Sylvestre JP, et al. Iontophoresis of dexamethasone phosphate: competition with chloride ions. J Control Release 2008;131(1):41–6.

[27] Sieg A, Guy RH, Delgado-Charro MB. Electroosmosis in transdermal iontophoresis: implications for noninvasive and calibration-free glucose monitoring. Biophys J 2004;87 (5):3344–50.

[28] Marro D, et al. Contributions of electromigration and electroosmosis to iontophoretic drug delivery. Pharm Res 2001;18(12):1701–8.

[29] Li LC, Scudds RA. Iontophoresis: an overview of the mechanisms and clinical application. Arthritis Care Res 1995;8(1):51–61.

[30] Singh P, Maibach HI. Iontophoresis: an alternative to the use of carriers in cutaneous drug delivery. Adv Drug Deliv Rev 1996;18(3):379–94.

[31] Mudry B, Guy RH, Delgado-Charro MB. Transport numbers in transdermal iontophoresis. Biophys J 2006;90(8):2822–30.

[32] Marro D, et al. Optimizing iontophoretic drug delivery: identification and distribution of the charge-carrying species. Pharm Res 2001;18(12):1709–13.

[33] Dubey S, Kalia YN. Electrically-assisted delivery of an anionic protein across intact skin: cathodal iontophoresis of biologically active ribonuclease T1. J Control Release 2011;152 (3):356–62.

[34] Prakash J, et al. Numerical simulation of heat transfer in blood flow altered by electroosmosis through tapered micro-vessels. Microvasc Res 2018;118:162–72.

[35] Guy RH, et al. Iontophoresis: electrorepulsion and electroosmosis. J Control Release 2000;64(1–3):129–32.

[36] Roustit M, Blaise S, Cracowski JL. Trials and tribulations of skin iontophoresis in therapeutics. Br J Clin Pharmacol 2014;77(1):63–71.

[37] Byrne JD, Yeh JJ, DeSimone JM. Use of iontophoresis for the treatment of cancer. J Control Release 2018;284:144–51.

[38] Kotzki S, et al. Effect of continuous vs pulsed iontophoresis of treprostinil on skin blood flow. Eur J Pharm Sci 2015;72:21–6.

[39] Hayashi S, et al. Lidocaine transport through a cellophane membrane by alternating current iontophoresis with a duty cycle. Bioelectrochemistry 2009;74(2):315–22.

[40] Pikal MJ, Shah S. Study of the mechanisms of flux enhancement through hairless mouse skin by pulsed DC iontophoresis. Pharm Res 1991;8(3):365–9.

[41] Yan G, Li SK, Higuchi WI. Evaluation of constant current alternating current iontophoresis for transdermal drug delivery. J Control Release 2005;110(1):141–50.

[42] Vadlapatla R, Wong EY, Gayakwad SG. Electronic drug delivery systems: an overview. J Drug Deliv Sci Technol 2017;41:359–66.

[43] Nguyen J, et al. Pharmacokinetics and skin tolerability of intracutaneous zolmitriptan delivery in swine using adhesive dermally applied microarray. J Pharm Sci 2018;107(8):2192–7.

[44] Matuszewska A, et al. Effect of long-term administration of ranitidine, a histamine H2 receptor antagonist, on bone metabolism in young growing rats. Pharmacol Rep 2018;70 (5):951–4.

[45] Djabri A, Guy RH, Delgado-Charro MB. Transdermal iontophoresis of ranitidine: an opportunity in paediatric drug therapy. Int J Pharm 2012;435(1):27–32.

[46] Alvarez-Figueroa MJ, Delgado-Charro MB, Blanco-Mendez J. Passive and iontophoretic transdermal penetration of methotrexate. Int J Pharm 2001;212(1):101–7.

[47] Pincus T, Gibson KA, Castrejon I. Update on methotrexate as the anchor drug for rheumatoid arthritis. Bull Hosp Jt Dis 2013;71(Suppl. 1):S9–19 2013.

[48] Ita KB, et al. Dermal delivery of selected hydrophilic drugs from elastic liposomes: effect of phospholipid formulation and surfactants. J Pharm Pharmacol 2007;59(9):1215–22.

[49] Nguyen HX, Banga AK. Electrically and ultrasonically enhanced transdermal delivery of methotrexate. Pharmaceutics 2018;10(3).

[50] Bernard N, Cuisinaud G, Sassard J. Determination of penbutolol and its hydroxylated metabolite in biological fluids by reversed-phase high-performance liquid chromatography. J Chromatogr 1982;228:355–61.

[51] Ita KB, Banga AK. In vitro transdermal iontophoretic delivery of penbutolol sulfate. Drug Deliv 2009;16(1):11–14.

[52] <https://books.google.com/books?isbn = 1483290697>.

[53] Youssef N, et al. A novel nasal almotriptan loaded solid lipid nanoparticles in mucoadhesive in situ gel formulation for brain targeting: preparation, characterization and in vivo evaluation. Int J Pharm 2018;548(1):609–24.

[54] Calatayud-Pascual MA, et al. Effect of iontophoresis on in vitro transdermal absorption of almotriptan. Int J Pharm 2011;416(1):189–94.

[55] Puri A, et al. Effects of chemical and physical enhancement techniques on transdermal delivery of 3-fluoroamphetamine hydrochloride. Int J Pharm 2017;528(1–2):452–62.

[56] Bejgum BC, Johnson PR, Stagner WC. Acyclovir chemical kinetics with the discovery and identification of newly reported degradants and degradation pathways involving formaldehyde as a degradant and reactant intermediate. Int J Pharm 2018;535(1–2):172–9.

[57] Chen Y, et al. Cutaneous biodistribution of ionizable, biolabile aciclovir prodrugs after short duration topical iontophoresis: targeted intraepidermal drug delivery. Eur J Pharm Biopharm 2016;99:94–102.

[58] Xu Q, et al. Ion-exchange membrane assisted transdermal iontophoretic delivery of salicylate and acyclovir. Int J Pharm 2009;369(1–2):105–13.

[59] Volpato NM, et al. In vitro acyclovir distribution in human skin layers after transdermal iontophoresis. J Control Release 1998;50(1–3):291–6.

[60] Wang J, et al. Granisetron protects polymicrobial sepsis-induced acute lung injury in mice. Biochem Biophys Res Commun 2019;508(4):1004–10.

[61] Cazares-Delgadillo J, et al. Using transdermal iontophoresis to increase granisetron delivery across skin in vitro and in vivo: effect of experimental conditions and a comparison with other enhancement strategies. Eur J Pharm Sci 2010;39(5):387–93.

[62] Lemire P, et al. Cognitive changes under memantine according to vitamin D status in Alzheimer patients: an exposed/unexposed cohort pilot study. J Steroid Biochem Mol Biol 2018;175:151–6.

[63] Stojiljković MP, et al. Prophylactic potential of memantine against soman poisoning in rats. Toxicology 2019;416:62–74.

[64] Kanasty R, et al. A pharmaceutical answer to nonadherence: once weekly oral memantine for Alzheimer's disease. J Control Release 2019;303:34–41.

[65] del Rio-Sancho S, et al. Transdermal absorption of memantin – effect of chemical enhancers, iontophoresis, and role of enhancer lipophilicity. Eur J Pharm Biopharm 2012;82(1):164–70.

[66] Lobo S, Yan G. Improving the direct penetration into tissues underneath the skin with iontophoresis delivery of a ketoprofen cationic prodrug. Int J Pharm 2018;535(1–2):228–36.

[67] Panus PC, et al. Transdermal iontophoretic delivery of ketoprofen through human cadaver skin and in humans. J Control Release 1997;44(2):113–21.

[68] Tashiro Y, et al. Iontophoretic transdermal delivery of ketoprofen: effect of iontophoresis on drug transfer from skin to cutaneous blood. Biol Pharm Bull 2000;23(12):1486–90.

[69] Hegde AR, et al. Peptide dendrimer-conjugates of ketoprofen: synthesis and ex vivo and in vivo evaluations of passive diffusion, sonophoresis and iontophoresis for skin delivery. Eur J Pharm Sci 2017;102:237–49.

[70] Verma RP, Shandilya A, Haridas V. Peptide dendrimers with designer core for directed self-assembly. Tetrahedron 2015;71(46):8758–65.

[71] Chen S, et al. Dexamethasone prodrugs as potent suppressors of the immunostimulatory effects of lipid nanoparticle formulations of nucleic acids. J Control Release 2018;286:46–54.

[72] Joshi A, et al. Iontophoresis successfully delivers dexamethasone sodium phosphate to dermis as measured by microdialysis. J Pharm Sci 2014;103(1):191–6.

[73] Cazares-Delgadillo J, et al. Transdermal iontophoresis of dexamethasone sodium phosphate in vitro and in vivo: effect of experimental parameters and skin type on drug stability and transport kinetics. Eur J Pharm Biopharm 2010;75(2):173–8.

[74] van Greunen DG, et al. Targeting Alzheimer's disease by investigating previously unexplored chemical space surrounding the cholinesterase inhibitor donepezil. Eur J Med Chem 2017;127:671–90.

[75] Robinson N, Grabowski P, Rehman I. Alzheimer's disease pathogenesis: is there a role for folate? Mech Ageing Dev 2018;174:86–94.

[76] Gawel K, et al. Influence of cholinesterase inhibitors, donepezil and rivastigmine on the acquisition, expression, and reinstatement of morphine-induced conditioned place preference in rats. Behav Brain Res 2014;268:169–76.

[77] Kearney M-C, et al. Microneedle-mediated delivery of donepezil: potential for improved treatment options in Alzheimer's disease. Eur J Pharm Biopharm 2016;103:43–50.

[78] Saluja S, et al. A novel electronic skin patch for delivery and pharmacokinetic evaluation of donepezil following transdermal iontophoresis. Int J Pharm 2013;453(2):395–9.

[79] Lee SY, Jeong NY, Oh SY. Modulation of electroosmosis and flux through skin: effect of propylene glycol. Arch Pharm Res 2014;37(4):484–93.

[80] Kimmel HL, et al. Behavioral and neurochemical effects of amphetamine analogs that release monoamines in the squirrel monkey. Pharmacol Biochem Behav 2009;94(2):278–84.

[81] Clifford PS, et al. Perinatal lead exposure alters locomotion induced by amphetamine analogs in rats. Life Sci 2011;88(13–14):586–9.

[82] Wong TW. Electrical, magnetic, photomechanical and cavitational waves to overcome skin barrier for transdermal drug delivery. J Control Release 2014;193:257–69.

[83] Murthy SN, Sammeta SM, Bowers C. Magnetophoresis for enhancing transdermal drug delivery: mechanistic studies and patch design. J Control Release 2010;148(2):197–203.

[84] Murthy SN, Hiremath SR. Physical and chemical permeation enhancers in transdermal delivery of terbutaline sulphate. AAPS PharmSciTech 2001;2(1) E-TN1.

[85] Ita K. Perspectives on transdermal electroporation. Pharmaceutics 2016;8(1).

[86] Prausnitz MR, et al. Electroporation of mammalian skin: a mechanism to enhance transdermal drug delivery. Proc Natl Acad Sci U S A 1993;90(22):10504–8.
[87] Dujardin N, et al. In vivo assessment of skin electroporation using square wave pulses. J Control Release 2002;79(1–3):219–27.
[88] Chizmadzhev YA, et al. Electrical properties of skin at moderate voltages: contribution of appendageal macropores. Biophys J 1998;74(2 Pt 1):843–56.
[89] Zhao Z, et al. Transdermal immunomodulation: principles, advances and perspectives. Adv Drug Deliv Rev 2018;127:3–19.
[90] Misra A, Ganga S, Upadhyay P. Needle-free, non-adjuvanted skin immunization by electroporation-enhanced transdermal delivery of diphtheria toxoid and a candidate peptide vaccine against hepatitis B virus. Vaccine 1999;18(5–6):517–23.
[91] Huang D, Chen YS, Rupenthal ID. Overcoming ocular drug delivery barriers through the use of physical forces. Adv Drug Deliv Rev 2018;126:96–112.
[92] Pliquett UF, Martin GT, Weaver JC. Kinetics of the temperature rise within human stratum corneum during electroporation and pulsed high-voltage iontophoresis. Bioelectrochemistry 2002;57(1):65–72.
[93] Becker S, et al. Transdermal transport pathway creation: electroporation pulse order. Math Biosci 2014;257:60–8.
[94] Pliquett U. Mechanistic studies of molecular transdermal transport due to skin electroporation. Adv Drug Deliv Rev 1999;35(1):41–60.
[95] Zhang Y, et al. Advances in transdermal insulin delivery. Adv Drug Deliv Rev 2019;139:51–70.
[96] Denet A-R, Vanbever R, Préat V. Skin electroporation for transdermal and topical delivery. Adv Drug Deliv Rev 2004;56(5):659–74.
[97] Vanbever R, Preat VV. In vivo efficacy and safety of skin electroporation. Adv Drug Deliv Rev 1999;35(1):77–88.
[98] Pliquett U, Gusbeth C, Nuccitelli R. A propagating heat wave model of skin electroporation. J Theor Biol 2008;251(2):195–201.
[99] Ita K. Transdermal delivery of heparin: physical enhancement techniques. Int J Pharm 2015;496:240–9.
[100] Demiryurek Y, et al. Transport, resealing, and re-poration dynamics of two-pulse electroporation-mediated molecular delivery. Biochim Biophys Acta 2015;1848(8):1706–14.
[101] Voyer D, et al. Dynamical modeling of tissue electroporation. Bioelectrochemistry 2018;119:98–110.
[102] Prausnitz MR, et al. Rapid temporal control of transdermal drug delivery by electroporation. Pharm Res 1994;11(12):1834–7.
[103] Prausnitz MR. A practical assessment of transdermal drug delivery by skin electroporation. Adv Drug Deliv Rev 1999;35(1):61–76.
[104] Zorec B, et al. Combinations of nanovesicles and physical methods for enhanced transdermal delivery of a model hydrophilic drug. Eur J Pharm Biopharm 2018;127:387–97.
[105] Zorec B, et al. Skin electroporation for transdermal drug delivery: the influence of the order of different square wave electric pulses. Int J Pharm 2013;457(1):214–23.
[106] Kalluri H, Banga AK. Transdermal delivery of proteins. AAPS PharmSciTech 2011;12(1):431–41.
[107] Morales JO, et al. Challenges and future prospects for the delivery of biologics: oral mucosal, pulmonary, and transdermal routes. AAPS J 2017;19(3):652–68.
[108] Brown DW, et al. Development of an adaptive electroporation system for intratumoral plasmid DNA delivery. Bioelectrochemistry 2018;122:191–8.

[109] Berko S, et al. Electroporation-delivered transdermal neostigmine in rats: equivalent action to intravenous administration. Drug Des Dev Ther 2016;10:1695–701.

[110] Blagus T, et al. In vivo real-time monitoring system of electroporation mediated control of transdermal and topical drug delivery. J Control Release 2013;172(3):862–71.

[111] Ramaley L, Krause MS. Theory of square wave voltammetry. Anal Chem 1969;41 (11):1362–5.

[112] Banga AK, Prausnitz MR. Assessing the potential of skin electroporation for the delivery of protein- and gene-based drugs. Trends Biotechnol 1998;16(10):408–12.

[113] Conjeevaram R, Banga AK, Zhang L. Electrically modulated transdermal delivery of fentanyl. Pharm Res 2002;19(4):440–4.

[114] Impellizeri J, et al. Electroporation in veterinary oncology. Vet J 2016;217:18–25.

[115] Weaver JC, Chizmadzhev YA. Theory of electroporation: a review. Bioelectrochemistry Bioenerg 1996;41(2):135–60.

[116] Sammeta SM, Vaka SRK, Murthy SN. Transcutaneous electroporation mediated delivery of doxepin-HPCD complex: a sustained release approach for treatment of postherpetic neuralgia. J Control Release 2010;142(3):361–7.

[117] Vanbever R, et al. In vivo noninvasive evaluation of hairless rat skin after high-voltage pulse exposure. Skin Pharmacol Appl Skin Physiol 1998;11(1):23–34.

[118] Wong TW, et al. Painless electroporation with a new needle-free microelectrode array to enhance transdermal drug delivery. J Control Release 2006;110(3):557–65.

[119] Yang G, Zhang Y, Gu Z. Punching and electroporation for enhanced transdermal drug delivery. Theranostics 2018;8:3688–90.

[120] Patel NP, et al. Highly sensitive LC–MS/MS method to estimate doxepin and its metabolite nordoxepin in human plasma for a bioequivalence study. J Pharm Anal 2018;8 (6):378–85.

[121] Nguyen KT, Ita KB, Parikh SJ, Popova IE, Bair DA. Transdermal delivery of captopril and metoprolol tartrate with microneedles. Drug Deliv Lett 2014;4:236–43.

[122] Vanbever R, Lecouturier N, Preat V. Transdermal delivery of metoprolol by electroporation. Pharm Res 1994;11(11):1657–62.

[123] Omar Mostafa M, Makram Botros J, Khaleel AM Sayed. Effect of dexmedetomidine versus nalbuphine as an adjuvant on paravertebral block to manage postoperative pain after mastectomies. Anesth Pain Med 2018;8(2):e13308.

[124] Liu FI, et al. Biodegradable polymeric microspheres for nalbuphine prodrug controlled delivery: in vitro characterization and in vivo pharmacokinetic studies. Int J Pharm 2003;257(1–2):23–31.

[125] Sung KC, et al. Transdermal delivery of nalbuphine and its prodrugs by electroporation. Eur J Pharm Sci 2003;18(1):63–70.

[126] Vaka SR, Shivakumar HN, Murthy SN. Constant voltage 'Iron'tophoresis. Pharm Dev Technol 2011;16(5):483–8.

[127] Modepalli N, et al. Transdermal iron replenishment therapy. Ther Deliv 2015;6(6): 661–8.

[128] Zhao YL, et al. Induction of cytotoxic T-lymphocytes by electroporation-enhanced needle-free skin immunization. Vaccine 2006;24(9):1282–90.

[129] Luo J, et al. Reevaluation and update on efficacy and safety of neostigmine for reversal of neuromuscular blockade. Ther Clin Risk Manag 2018;14:2397–406.

[130] Zhao B, et al. Sinomenine hydrochloride attenuates the proliferation, migration, invasiveness, angiogenesis and epithelial-mesenchymal transition of clear-cell renal cell carcinoma cells via targeting Smad in vitro. Biomed Pharmacother 2017;96:1036–44.

[131] Feng S, et al. Controlled release of optimized electroporation enhances the transdermal efficiency of sinomenine hydrochloride for treating arthritis in vitro and in clinic. Drug Des Devel Ther 2017;11:1737–52.

[132] Wong TW, et al. Pilot study of topical delivery of methotrexate by electroporation. Br J Dermatol 2005;152(3):524–30.

[133] Ridruejo C, et al. Electrochemical oxidation of anesthetic tetracaine in aqueous medium. Influence of the anode and matrix composition. Chem Eng J 2017;326:811–19.

[134] Hu Q, et al. Enhanced transdermal delivery of tetracaine by electroporation. Int J Pharm 2000;202(1–2):121–4.

[135] De Vries P, et al. The antimigraine agent alniditan selectively constricts porcine carotid arteriovenous anastomoses via 5-HT1B/1D receptors. Eur J Pharmacol 1998;351(2):193–201.

[136] Jadoul A, et al. Transdermal alniditan delivery by skin electroporation. J Control Release 1998;54(3):265–72.

[137] Prausnitz MR, et al. Transdermal delivery of heparin by skin electroporation. Biotechnology (N Y) 1995;13(11):1205–9.

[138] Bor S, et al. A meta-analysis on the cardiac safety profile of domperidone compared to metoclopramide. United Eur Gastroenterol J 2018;6(9):1331–46.

[139] Jadoul A, Préat V. Electrically enhanced transdermal delivery of domperidone. Int J Pharm 1997;154(2):229–34.

[140] Schipper P, et al. Diphtheria toxoid and N-trimethyl chitosan layer-by-layer coated pH-sensitive microneedles induce potent immune responses upon dermal vaccination in mice. J Control Release 2017;262:28–36.

[141] Ita K. Insights into the percutaneous penetration of antidiabetic agents. J Drug Target 2017;25(2):102–11.

[142] Mohammad EA, et al. Electroporation parameters for successful transdermal delivery of insulin. Am J Ther 2015;23(6):e1560–7.

[143] Kim AY, et al. Andrographolide suppresses TRIF-dependent signaling of toll-like receptors by targeting TBK1. Int Immunopharmacol 2018;57:172–80.

[144] Wu M, et al. Low-voltage electroporation mediated transcutaneous targeted delivery of liposomes with entrapped andrographolide. J Control Release 2013;172(1):e16.

[145] Mukund V, et al. Genistein: its role in metabolic diseases and cancer. Crit Rev Oncol Hematol 2017;119:13–22.

[146] Balazs B, et al. ATR-FTIR and Raman spectroscopic investigation of the electroporation-mediated transdermal delivery of a nanocarrier system containing an antitumour drug. Biomed Opt Express 2016;7(1):67–78.

[147] Tokumoto S, Higo N, Sugibayashi K. Effect of electroporation and pH on the iontophoretic transdermal delivery of human insulin. Int J Pharm 2006;326(1–2):13–19.

[148] Sharma A, et al. Transdermal drug delivery using electroporation. I. Factors influencing in vitro delivery of terazosin hydrochloride in hairless rats. J Pharm Sci 2000;89(4):528–35.

[149] Sharma A, et al. Transdermal drug delivery using electroporation. II. Factors influencing skin reversibility in electroporative delivery of terazosin hydrochloride in hairless rats. J Pharm Sci 2000;89(4):536–44.

[150] Hegazy-Hassan W, et al. TcVac1 vaccine delivery by intradermal electroporation enhances vaccine induced immune protection against Trypanosoma cruzi infection in mice. Vaccine 2019;37(2):248–57.

[151] Schultheis K, et al. Characterization of guinea pig T cell responses elicited after EP-assisted delivery of DNA vaccines to the skin. Vaccine 2017;35(1):61–70.

Chapter 10

Sonophoresis

Transdermal sonophoresis refers to the utilization of ultrasound (US) for enhanced percutaneous flux of medications [1–5]. The typical experimental setup for sonophoresis is shown in Fig. 10.1 while a commercially available sonophoretic device (Sonoprep) is shown in Fig. 10.2.

A longitudinal compression wave with a frequency greater than 20 kHz is called an US wave [6] and this can be regarded as a pressure wave with frequencies higher than human hearing. In audio sound, a pressure wave is propagated through a medium such as water or air [7]. Normal human hearing is in the range of 60–20,000 Hz [8]. US is not electromagnetic in nature and requires a medium for transmission, whereas electromagnetic waveforms can be transmitted across a vacuum [8]. Ultrasonic waves can be absorbed, refracted (bent), reflected, and focused [7]. US causes vibrations within the epidermal layers, thereby increasing the kinetic energy of drug molecules [9]. Because its wavelength is in the order of few millimeters, US can be focused on very restricted areas [10]. In particular, low-frequency sonophoresis (LFS) (under 100 kHz for skin permeation) can lead to the creation of the so-called cavitational bubbles in the skin [1]. Consequently, there is transdermal drug delivery enhancement via the generation of small pores, the disorganization of lipid bilayers in the skin [1], and by causing convection across the skin [11]. Alvarez-Román and coworkers used infrared spectroscopy to investigate the horny layer of the skin following the application of US and showed that a good proportion (about 30%) of stratum corneum (SC) intercellular lipids, linked to the barrier function of the skin, were expunged following the use of low-frequency US [12]. High-frequency (1–20 MHz), intermediate-frequency (200–700 kHz), and low-frequency US have found broad human applications [13].

Sonophoresis using an amplitude between 1 and 5 bar and a frequency range between 20 kHz and 16 MHz has been utilized for drug delivery enhancement [14]. Indeed, it has been documented that as the US frequency rises from 19.6 to 58.9 kHz, the breaching of the SC moves from a single position to multiple spots, thus presenting a more homogeneous area for drug transport [14]. The US generated may be either continuous or pulsed. To create a continuous US, an alternating voltage of the right frequency is administered to a transducer leading to the continuous production of an US

Transdermal Drug Delivery. DOI: https://doi.org/10.1016/B978-0-12-822550-9.00010-7

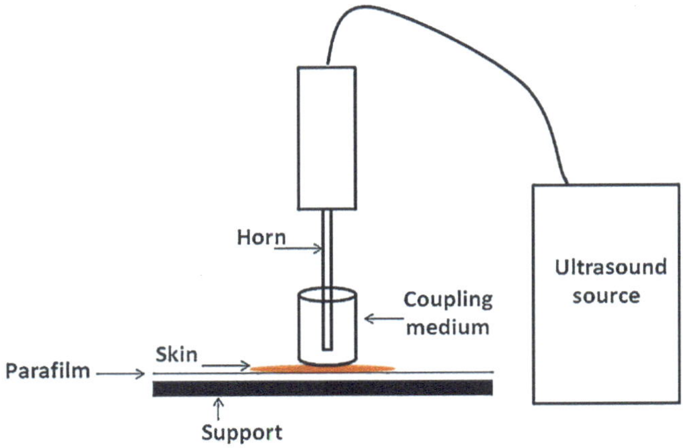

FIGURE 10.1 The experimental setup for sonophoresis. *Reproduced with permission from Herwadkar A, et al. Low frequency sonophoresis mediated transdermal and intradermal delivery of ketoprofen. Int J Pharm 2012;423(2):289–96.*

FIGURE 10.2 A commercially available sonophoretic device (Sonoprep). *Reproduced with permission from Azagury A, et al. Ultrasound mediated transdermal drug delivery. Adv Drug Deliv Rev (2014)72;127–43.*

with an equal frequency [15]. When short spurts of alternating voltage are repeatedly administered to an ultrasonic transducer, pulsed sonophoresis is propagated [15]. Increase in transcutaneous flux by sonophoresis depends on different parameters including duty cycle (the ON time for US), application time, frequency, radiating diameter of the transducer, and intensity [16,17]. Terahara and coworkers investigated the influence of horn distance and US intensity on LFS [18]. The authors carried out research with full-thickness porcine skin to assess skin conductivity and drug permeability increase following the application of US with different parameters [18]. Pig skin was pretreated with a US (20 or 40 kHz) using a sonicator and the authors found out that increase in skin conductivity was conversely proportional to the distance of the horn from the skin [18]. It was also revealed that with the increase in US intensity, skin conductivity also rose up to a certain threshold [18]. Furthermore, the intensities at which the highest enhancement took place were approximately 17 W/cm^2 for 40 kHz and 14 W/cm^2 for 20 kHz [18]. Sonophoresis is typically carried out via a sonicator in a duty cycle with pulsing or continuous mode. Pulsing is used to reduce heat accumulation induced by sonophoresis [14].

Percutaneous drug transport facilitated by low-frequency US ($f < 100$ kHz) is more efficient in comparison with high-frequency sonophoresis [19]. It has been observed that the weakening of an ultrasonic wave is inversely proportional to its frequency, and it can be inferred that with a rise in frequency, there is less US penetration into the skin [8]. Furthermore, there is an inverse relationship between US frequency and cavitational effects [6,20]. The spatial and temporal power densities during the utilization of low-frequency US are between 0.125 and 3 W/cm^2 [13]. Schoellhammer observed that when US in combination with chemical penetration enhancers are applied to the skin, localized transport regions (LTRs) are formed [21]. These regions are characterized by a high rate of the SC disruption [21]. The authors postulated that an alternative approach for reducing US application times and increasing LTR formation involves using a second US horn to create additional bubbles in the acoustic field adjoining the skin [21]. When the researchers simultaneously used two US horns with frequencies between 20 kHz and 3 MHz, there was increased cavitation activity in comparison with the use of a single ultrasonic horn [21]. The authors demonstrated that porcine skin samples subjected to dual-frequency US for 4 min possessed an LTR that was similar to single-frequency samples treated for 6 min. It was inferred that utilizing low- and high-frequency US at the same time reduces the application time needed to achieve an LTR of equivalent magnitude [21]. Furthermore, when the authors used high-frequency US, contiguous LTRs were formed while the use of low-frequency US alone led to the creation of noncontiguous LTRs [21].

Transdermal sonophoretic experiments are often conducted with Franz diffusion cells. A coupling medium is normally used to apply US to the skin [6,22]. Ultrasonic waves are generated by a transducer equipped with a piezoelectric crystal that changes electric energy into mechanical energy in the form of sound wave-generating oscillations [8]. LFS depends on the mode of

US application [23]. The two most commonly used protocols are: (1) the simultaneous mode, with the medication dissolved in the US coupling medium, and (2) the pretreatment mode, which entails the administration of US followed by the passive transport of the medication to the skin via a transdermal patch [23]. Simultaneous application of US increases percutaneous permeation in two ways: (1) facilitated diffusion through altered anatomic structures in the skin and (2) US-mediated convection [16]. Different parameters can be evaluated when these sonophoretic experiments are carried out: total solutes transported, alterations in the mass transport properties of the skin as well as the skin electrical resistivity changes [24]. In laboratory experiments, pig skin is usually positioned under the sonicator horn with the epidermis facing the horn [2]. The horn is then positioned in the coupling medium. Following sonophoretic pretreatment, diffusion studies with the skin sample are then carried out [2]. During US experiments, researchers often change receptor fluids due to US-induced heating [24]. Recently, Robertson and Becker suggested several changes aimed at optimizing transdermal sonophoretic experiments [24] including the use of uniform US field as well as the control of temperature [24].

Input parameters often influence sonophoretic transport: US frequency, US pressure amplitude (intensity), distance from the transducer to the skin, application time, and temperature [24]. With LFS, the degree of skin disruption, and the facilitated transdermal, can be regulated by altering US parameters [23]. Although LFS has several advantages, there are also limitations. The two main challenges hindering the broad clinical use of this enhancement technique are the nonportability of current sonophoretic equipment as well as the US application time [25]. The utilization of low-profile cymbal transducers that can be integrated into patches can help in resolving portability issues while the simultaneous application of high- and low-frequency US can reduce the treatment time [25]. SonoPrep received approval from the Food and Drug Administration (FDA) in 2004 for the topical delivery of lidocaine (a drug used for local anesthesia induction) [26].

Mechanism of transdermal sonophoresis

It is worth mentioning that the specific mechanisms through which US enhances transcutaneous drug penetration are still poorly understood even though the following phenomena are known to take place: cellular-level effect, acoustic streaming (AS), cavitation, and rectified diffusion (RD) [2].

Acoustic streaming

AS refers to a steady fluid flow caused by the dissipation of high amplitude acoustic waves [27]. It has been suggested that part of the energy lost through acoustic attenuation is imparted to the fluid as a steady momentum [27].

AS can take place in the form of boundary layer scale Schlichting, wavelength scale Rayleigh, or container scale Eckart streaming [28]. Boundary layer–driven streaming is thought to be induced by effects between solid boundaries and an acoustically excited fluid [29]. In Eckart streaming, a steady-state velocity is generated by the absorption of an ultrasonic wave in a viscous liquid [30]. Schlichting streaming refers to a vortex flow inside a viscous boundary [28]. It has been established that a sound wave in a fluid can cause vibrations close to its equilibrium position back and forth and with time, a time-independent flow will be created in the acoustic field, which is called AS [31]. Rayleigh streaming occurs because of energy dissipation in the viscous boundary layer of the waveguide and other solid surfaces present [28]. The velocity of AS is proportional to the surface area and intensity of the US source as well as the medium attenuation coefficient but inversely proportional to medium bulk viscosity and sound velocity in the medium [32]. It is also known that AS can reduce the effect of ultrasonic heating because it facilitates thermal convection [32]. AS is more prominent at higher sound intensities and it is also nonlinear in nature. Streaming can occur as a result of dissipation in the bulk medium or dissipation near boundaries.

Cavitation

When US is applied to a fluid, sinusoidal sound waves are generated and minuscule gas bubbles grow within the fluid once the local pressure falls below the liquid vapor pressure [33]. Once the bubble attains a critical size, there is implosion that results in cavitation [33]. It has been asserted that this violent inertial cavitation activity near the skin surface leads to microscopic defects in the lamellar lipid structure of the SC [34]. Essentially, cavitation refers to the propagation of gas bubbles, which vibrate and may collapse at the skin surface, thus disorganizing and/or producing an aqueous route through the horny layer of the skin [35]. Typically, low-pressure cavities are created in the liquid medium and these vacuum bubbles briefly vibrate, and then asymmetrically collapse with great ferocity [10]. Cavitating microbubbles form the route through which pressure wave energy pressure is concentrated to create forces that breach cell membranes [7]. The formed microjets and/or shock waves can breach the skin barrier by forming and expanding defects in the SC [16]. Cavitation may be stable (steady expansion and oscillation of bubbles) or inertial (fast growth and implosion of cavitation bubbles) [36]. The repeated oscillation of gas globules over a handful of acoustic cycles occurs during stable cavitation while inertial cavitation entails significant bubble growth during the rarefactional ultrasonic half-cycle, with an ensuing ferocious implosion during the compressional half-cycle under the impact of the surrounding medium inertia [2]. Stable cavitation bubbles remain for a comparatively huge number of acoustic cycles, where the bubble radius fluctuates around a certain equilibrium value, defined by the frequency used for US generation [37]. Such stable oscillation (repeatable over many cycles) forms a circulating fluid flow (called microstreaming) around the bubble with shear rates and velocities proportional to the oscillation amplitude [7]. Transient cavitation gas globules grow more rapidly, enlarging twice to thrice their resonant size, where they vibrate unstably, and finally implode in one compression half-cycle [37].

Sonophoresis-mediated increase in skin permeability is caused by cavitation, which is inversely proportional to ultrasonic frequency [21]. When a US is applied to an elastic medium, the solvent molecules move longitudinally, resulting in a sequence of rarefaction and compression phases [38]. During the compression step, the solvent molecules collide with each other [38]. During the rarefaction step, the solvent molecules are pulled apart by negative pressure leading to the creation of cavitation bubbles [38]. During cavitation there are shock waves, liquid jets, and high-pressure differentials that combine to rupture materials present in the liquid medium [33]. Under these conditions, the created pressures can be as high as 10^9 Pa while jet velocities can be larger than 100 m s^{-1} [38]. Indeed, high-pressure cores that emit shock waves with amplitudes exceeding 10 kbar are known to be created during the bubble implosion [39]. Research has shown that microjets form when a flat solid surface induces bubble involution and these microjets can attain speeds of hundreds of meters per second [39]. Interestingly, microjet distortions of bubble implosion are impacted by the surface confronted by the gas globules [39]. If the resonant size of the bubble (diameter of approximately 150 μm at 20 kHz) is less than the surface, the ensuing implosion will be in the form of a microjet [39].

It has been demonstrated that cavitation bubbles can form liquid microjets oriented toward the surface of the skin [14]. There is usually pressure build-up as well as asymmetry in the surrounding bubbles resulting in the creation of microjets [14]. Shock waves formed by inertial cavitation can induce structural changes in the skin keratinocyte–lipid interface leading to the formation of diffusion pathways through which medications can be transported [40]. In addition, the vibrations of cavitation bubbles can lead to dramatic water transport into disordered lipid parts of the skin and this can result in the creation of water pathways in the intercellular lipids of the skin's horny layer [14]. The following phenomena are usually observed during cavitation [6]: (1) tiny gas globules already present in a liquid grow or pulsate; (2) due to sound pressure variations, gas bubbles are created on nuclei or in the bulk; (3) other categories of growth occur due to splitting, or interaction of gas bubbles due to sound pressure waves in the liquid medium [6]. High-frequency US tends to create bubbles with less radii than that formed by LFS [6]. As an illustration, when US at 20 kHz is applied, the linear resonant bubble radius of air bubbles in water is 150 μm, whereas at

3 MHz, the radius is 1 μm [6]. Resonance frequency determines the cavitation bubble size that is adequate [41,42]:

$$R_r = \frac{1}{2\pi f_r}\left(\frac{3kp}{\rho}\right)^{\frac{1}{2}} \tag{10.1}$$

where R_r is the bubble resonant radius, f_r is the resonant frequency inversely proportional to R_r, k is the polytropic coefficient, p is the liquid static pressure(undisturbed), and ρ is the density of the fluid [41]. Furthermore, bubble size determines the acoustic energy released during cavitation [41,43]:

$$\frac{E_{ac}}{\left(\frac{4}{3}\right)\pi P_{ha^3_{\max}}} = \frac{1}{27}\left(\frac{2P_h}{\rho c^2}\right)^{\frac{1}{2}}\left(\frac{P_h}{Q}\right)^{\beta} \tag{10.2}$$

where E_{ac} is the acoustic energy, P_h is the flow field local pressure, a is the radius of the bubble, c is the velocity of the sound, Q is the gas partial pressure in the bubble for radius $a_{\max}$, and β is an empirical index, $0<\beta<3/2$ [41,43]. It has been inferred from this equation that violent bubble collapses are usually induced by low-frequency waves [41].

Rectified diffusion

RD is another contributory factor to US-induced transdermal drug delivery flux enhancement. RD is a bubble expansion occurrence in US fields [44]. When subjected to an oscillating pressure wave, a gas globule of the appropriate size goes through compression and expansion [44]. During the contraction phase, bubble gas concentration rises leading to gas diffusion from the bubble [45]. The scenario during the expansion stage is different: with a reduction in concentration, gas is transported into the bubble. Because there is more gas ingress during expansion than egress during contraction, there will be a net rise in gas quantity in the bubble over an entire cycle [45]. In RD, the net quantity of gas diffusing into a bubble during its growth is larger than the outward diffusion of gas during contraction phase [37]. During RD, the gas bubble facing a negative-pressure half-cycle of an US field typically expands due to gas expansion inside the bubble [6]. Furthermore, a proportion of the liquid enclosing the bubble is transported through the boundary layer and vaporizes, inducing a rise in the amount of gas in the bubble [6]. Vapor and/or gas is also transported in and out of the bubble due to pressure gradient between the exterior and the interior portions of the bubble [44]. With time, the gas globule will implode to a size less than what it was in its previous state [6]. Numerous effects contribute to the disparate transport in and out of the bubble [44]. The "area effect" is the result of the impact of surface area on the mass diffusion while the "shell effect" derives from the liquid–air mass transfer boundary thickness [44].

Cellular-level effect

Spatial peak temporal average, noncavitational low-intensity sonophoretic exposures of less than 100 mW/cm^2 can alter cell and tissue biology with no contributions from stable or inertial cavitation [46]. It is increasingly being recognized that biological membranes can absorb mechanical energy in acoustic field and transform it into contractions and expansions of the intramembrane area [2,46]. During intramembrane cavitation, there is a direct proportional relationship between the maximum area strain and acoustic pressure amplitude as well as an inverse proportionality between the maximum area strain and the square root of the frequency [2,46]. It has been hypothesized in the literature that intramembrane hydrophobic space between two lipid monolayer leaflets deflates and inflates repeatedly under the influence of sonophoresis [46]. Consequently, the two leaflets rupture when the acoustic negative pressure is greater than the molecular attractive forces between the two leaflets [46]. Krasovitski et al. hypothesized that in a biomembrane, intracellular defects (nanometric and micrometric) can occur (under suitable conditions) as a result of an oscillating acoustic pressure wave (millimeter wavelength) [46].

Thermal effect

Sonophoresis generates heat and promotes drug delivery into the skin [47]. Temperature-mediated impact of US on the skin occurs as a result of the conversion and transfer of mechanical energy created by a piezoelectric crystal vibration [48]. When ultrasonic energy is absorbed by the human body, there is a local rise in temperature that is determined by rate of heat removal by blood flow, duration of exposure, intensity, US frequency, conduction, and the area of the US beam [40]. Attenuation of an ultrasonic wave leads to the heating of the medium that is crossed by the wave [49]. Significantly, the increase in temperature can enhance transdermal drug delivery by: (1) increasing drug absorption; (2) widening points of entry of the skin (e.g., hair follicles and sweat glands); (3) elevating the kinetic energy and diffusivity of active pharmaceutical ingredients; and (4) improving blood circulation of blood in the affected portion of the skin [49]. However, the forecasting of the actual temperature increase following sonophoresis is challenging without the specific knowledge of the convection and conduction properties of the biological tissue as well as clear-cut acoustic absorption coefficient data [48].

It was recently reported in the literature that US administration at three different intensity levels (10%, 25%, and 70% corresponding to 4.5, 8.1, and 15 W cm) for 2 h at 20 kHz (at a duty cycle of 0.1 on, 0.9 off) raised donor solution temperature [48]. When superior intensities (8.1 and 15 W cm) were used, there were temperature increases of approximately 10°C and 20°C, at the end of a 2-h experimental period [48]. In terms of frequency, when

10 MHz US was deployed in another set of experiments, there were no measurable temperature changes (<2°C) over 2 h [50]. Furthermore, the heating profile of the sonicator was simulated 2 h without activating the probe with the objective of delineating the effect of temperature to US-mediated permeation rate increase [48]. They manually controlled diffusion cell temperature so as to simulate the temperature effect of US [48]. It was reported that 20 kHz US at an intensity of 15 W cm significantly increased skin permeability. The amount of mannitol transported in 2 h across the full-thickness porcine ear skin increased 35-fold from 6.2 ± 4.3 to 211 ± 105 nmol [48]. Significantly, the temperature "control" experiment showed that approximately 25% of this transdermal flux enhancement was attributable to thermal heating [48].

Transdermal sonophoretic delivery of therapeutic agents

Several researchers have studied the impact of US on the percutaneous transport of drugs and vaccines [9,51,52]. In this section, specific therapeutic agents will be discussed. The list is by no means exhaustive but illustrates the importance of this mode of transdermal drug delivery enhancement. Table 10.1 shows the effect of US on transdermal drug delivery.

TABLE 10.1 Effect of ultrasound on transcutaneous drug transport.

Therapeutic agent(s) or model compound(s)	Skin model(s)	Method	References
Methotrexate	Human skin	Sonophoresis	[51]
Gemcitabine	Mouse skin	Sonophoresis	[9]
Sinomenine hydrochloride	Pig skin	Sonophoresis	[41]
Penbutolol sulfate	Pig skin	Sonophoresis	[57]
Propranolol	Human skin	Sonophoresis	[60]
Ketoprofen	Mouse skin	Sonophoresis	[61]
Diclofenac	Rat skin	Sonophoresis	[65]
Galantamine	Mouse skin	Sonophoresis	[71]
Rivastigmine	Pig skin	Sonophoresis	[76]
Lercanidipine hydrochloride	Mouse skin	Sonophoresis	[79]
Insulin	Pig skin	Sonophoresis	[81]
Heparin	Pig skin	Sonophoresis	[88]
Caffeine	Pig skin	Sonophoresis	[93]

Methotrexate

Recently, Nguyen and Banga studied the impact of US on the transdermal permeation of methotrexate across dermatomed human skin [51]. The authors conducted sonophoresis using a low-frequency sonicator with a US intensity of 6.9 W/cm^2, an amplitude of 30%, a duty cycle of 100%, and a frequency of 20 kHz for 2 min [51]. A broader donor top—cylindrically shaped compartment, fabricated from glass (17.87 mm diameter), open from both sides to enclose the sonicator probe—was then positioned over the skin [51]. The authors reported that low-frequency US administration resulted in facilitated cumulative amount, percutaneous flux, and the permeability coefficient of MTX [51]. The cumulative amount transported in 24 h, transdermal flux, and permeability coefficient values were 161.92 ± 30.06 μg/cm^2, 6.81 ± 1.31 μg/cm^2/h, and $34.04 \pm 6.55 \times 10^{-4}$ (cm/h), respectively [51]. The formation of LTRs was suggested as a possible enhancement mechanism [51]. The authors also attributed the increased transdermal permeation parameters to acoustic microstreaming, cavitation, and radiation pressure force [51]. Any material positioned in the ultrasonic pathway and absorbs any or all of the beam energy undergoes radiation pressure force [15]. This steady force pushes the material in the direction in which the wave is generated [15]. It has been estimated that when a material fully absorbs ultrasonic waves, the radiation pressure force that this material is exposed to relates to intensity according to equation [15]:

$$F = \frac{P}{v} \tag{10.3}$$

where F is the radiation pressure force (in N), P is the intensity (in W), and v denotes ultrasonic speed in that medium (in m/s) [15]. Radiation pressure is usually measured by determining the force expended by an US beam on a perfect sound absorbing target [15].

Gemcitabine

Gemcitabine (GEM), a deoxycytidine antimetabolite, is used for the management of a broad class of solid tumors such as those that affect the breast, lung (nonsmall cell), pancreas, ovary, and bladder [53]. In the blood, gemcitabine is quickly deaminated into the inactive metabolite of 2′,2′-difluorodeoxyuridine, which is then rapidly eliminated from the body [54]. The result is a very short plasma half-life of gemcitabine at 8–17 min in humans following intravenous administration [53]. Recently, Baji et al. studied the transdermal sonophoretic transport of GEM across mouse skin [9]. The authors generated low-frequency US via a probe sonicator with the transducer positioned in the donor compartment [9]. The tip of the ultrasonic probe was kept at a distance of 3–5 mm from the skin and an On/Off cycle of 1 s was used [9]. A GEM concentration of 5 mg/mL was used for experiments and the investigators tested different amplitudes of 20, 30, or 40 W with the aim of assessing the influence of various factors on the transcutaneous flux of GEM [9]. The effect of different US amplitudes on the skin permeation of gemcitabine hydrochloride is shown in Fig. 10.3. The authors documented a linear relationship between US amplitude and the transdermal permeation of GEM. The highest cumulative amount of GEM that was transported at the end of 30 min (Q_{30min}) was achieved following the use of the US amplitude of 40 W [9] and the value was 108.22 ± 5.34 [9]. When the amplitude of 30 and 20 W were used, the Q_{30min} values were 98.96 ± 3.39 and 14.41 ± 2.26, respectively [9]. Keeping a constant amplitude of 40 W, the authors also examined the effect of concentration (5, 10, 15, 25, or 50 mg/mL in 4-(2-hydroxyethyl)-1-piperazineethanesulfonic acid (HEPES) buffer pH 7.4) on the transdermal sonophoretic transport of GEM [9]. The transdermal sonophoretic penetration of GEM depended on the concentration. The authors reported that the highest amount of GEM transported was observed at a concentration of 50 mg/mL (Q_{30min} of 950.24 ± 38.61 μg/cm^2) and the least amount transported was detected at a concentration of 5 mg/mL (108.22 ± 18.34 μg/cm^2) [9].

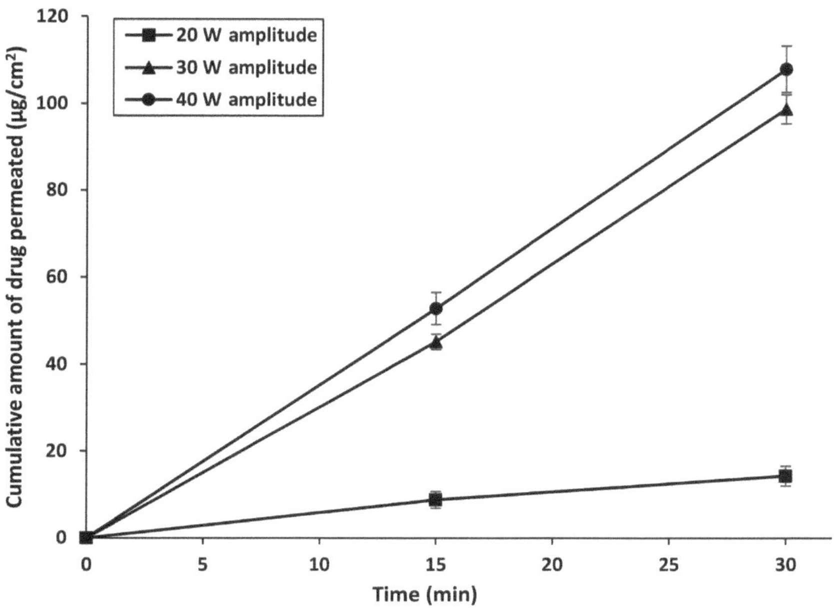

FIGURE 10.3 Effect of different ultrasound amplitude on the skin permeation of gemcitabine hydrochloride. *Reproduced with permission from Baji S, et al. Skin permeation of gemcitabine hydrochloride by passive diffusion, iontophoresis and sonophoresis: in vitro and in vivo evaluations. J Drug Deliv Sci Technol 2018;47:49–54.*

Sinomenine

Sinomenine (SIN) is derived from the Chinese medicinal herb *Sinomenium acutum* and it is widely utilized for the management of rheumatoid arthritis (RA) [55]. Sinomenine hydrochloride (SIN-HCL) is soluble in water (118 mg/mL) and has a molecular weight of 365.88, a log P of 1.34 and a pKa of 7.98 [41,56]. Yin and coworkers investigated the influence of single-frequency (20 or 800 kHz) and dual-frequency (20 + 800 kHz) US on the percutaneous transport of sinomenine hydrochloride across pig skin [41]. The authors designed a special Franz diffusion cell with two ultrasonic probes (with different frequencies) used at the same time for permeation experiments [41]. It was reported that the use of this experimental setup synergistically increased the permeability of sinomenine hydrochloride over 12 h [41]. In particular, both single-frequency (20 and 800 kHz used separately) and dual-frequency (20 and 800 kHz together) US pretreatment significantly increased the transdermal permeation of SIN-HCL compared to passive permeation [41]. When pig skin was subjected to dual-frequency US before permeation studies, the 12-h cumulative quantity of SIN transported was 4.3, 8.3, and 17.6 times higher than that achieved with 20, 800 kHz single-frequency US or passive samples, respectively [41]. The authors postulated that dual-frequency sonophoresis facilitated transient cavitation inside the skin and near the surface of the skin [41]. Cavitation bubbles near the skin surface can lead to the formation of microjets that can potentially broaden the skin pores [41]. Furthermore, cavitation inside the skin can increase the density of aqueous channels [41].

Penbutolol

Serum penbutolol concentration of 268 ng/mL at 0.9 h after dosing and a half-life of 4.5 h are documented in the literature [57]. The elimination half-life of approximately 1.6 h and a total clearance of 16.6 mL/min/kg body weight have also been highlighted [57]. We have studied the impact of US on percutaneous transport of penbutolol sulfate across split-thickness pig skin [57]. US-mediated transport at a frequency of 20 kHz enhanced the percutaneous permeation of the drug by 3.5-fold ($27.37 \pm 9.03\ \mu g/cm^2/h$) in comparison to passive transport ($7.82 \pm 1.72\ \mu g/cm^2/h$) [57]. The flux increase was not statistically significant [57].

Propranolol

β-adrenoceptor blockers decrease blood pressure by decreasing renin release, leading to a decreased plasma volume and vasodilatation [58]. Another important effect of this class of therapeutic agents is the reduction of cardiac output [58]. Propranolol (PRO) is a non-selective beta receptor blocker which is employed for the management of cardiac arrhythmias, hypertension and angina pectoris [59]. The half-life of the drug is approximately 4 h and that entails frequent dosing to maintain therapeutic drug concentration [59]. Furthermore, the oral bioavailability of PRO is less than 23% due to considerable first-pass effect [59]. PRO is a suitable candidate for the percutaneous route of administration and recently, Guo and coworkers studied the influence of sonophoresis on the transcutaneous permeation of the drug [60]. The authors used 2^4 statistical fractional factorial design to study the influence of probe to skin distance, US treatment time, and duty cycle on the delivery of the drug through isolated human abdominal cadaver skin [60]. PRO gel was prepared from oleic acid (chemical penetration promoter) and chitosan (polymer). Interestingly, a skin permeation rate of 245 μg/cm^2 and a deposition rate of 81.66 μg/cm^2 were achieved with a PRO gel in the absence of a permeation enhancer and without US (controlled condition) while the same formulation had permeation value of the 330 μg/cm^2 and deposition value of 152.90 μg/cm^2 following transdermal sonophoresis [60].

Ketoprofen

In an interesting set of experiments, Manikkath et al. studied the influence of US used alone and in combination with peptide dendrimers on the percutaneous transport of ketoprofen [61]. A distance of 3–5 mm was kept between the sonicator probe tip and freshly excised mouse skin [61]. The following sonophoretic parameters were used: time: 30 min, on/off cycle: 1 s "on," followed by 1 s "off," power: 7–8/cm^2 watts, amplitude: was set at 30. The authors combined transdermal sonophoresis with dendrimers [61] and reported that when US was used alone, the transported amount of the drug across mouse skin in 30 min ($Q_{0.5}$) was 118.67 ± 15.28 μg and this was more greater than the amount transported in 24 h following passive transport (51.88 ± 5.07 μg) [61]. Interestingly, when US and dendrimers were applied together, it was revealed that the quantity of the drug that was transported in 30 min using dendrimer and US was significantly greater than the amount transported in 24 h without US [61]. Furthermore, when US was combined with dendrimer pretreatment, significantly higher penetration rates of the drug were achieved. The authors ascribed the results to the creation of acoustic cavities that leads to the formation of aqueous conduits in the mouse skin lipid bilayers [61]. It is noteworthy that the authors also sought to link sonophoretic ketoprofen transport with partition coefficient by utilizing an equation previously developed by Mitragotri and colleagues [62]:

$$e \sim \frac{K_{o/w}^{0.75}}{\left(4X10^4\right)P_P} \tag{10.4}$$

where e is the sonophoretic permeation rate, $K_{o/w}$ is the octanol-water partition coefficient of the drug, and P_P is the drug's passive skin permeability (cm/h) [62].

Diclofenac

Diclofenac (DF) is a nonsteroidal antiinflammatory drug with a log P (octanol/water partition coefficient) value of 4.5, a melting point of 156°C–158°C, a molecular weight of 296.2, and a pKa value of 4.2 [63]. The water solubility of diclofenac sodium at 32°C is 37 mg/mL [63]. Aldwaikat and Alarjah investigated the effect of sonophoresis on the transcutaneous permeation of diclofenac sodium across EpiDerm [64]. Transcutaneous drug permeation experiments were conducted with this 3D skin equivalent in vitro [64]. The influence of US horn distance from the skin, amplitude, US frequency, mode of sonication, and application time on transdermal drug delivery rates was studied. The researchers reported a fivefold increase in the transcutaneous transport of diclofenac sodium across EpiDerm [64]. It was documented that the highest transdermal transport was obtained using power of 20 kHz US and 20% amplitude in a continuous mode for 5 min [64]. An alternative approach involving the combination of US with microbubbles (US-MB) has also been documented [65]. The authors examined the effect of diclofenac administered from different drug delivery systems on male Sprague-Dawley rats with adjuvant-induced RA [65]. Liao et al. randomly divided rats with RA into five groups: (1) diclofenac-carbopol gel, (2) US with microbubbles plus diclofenac-carbopol gel, (3) carbopol gel alone, (4) US plus diclofenac-carbopol gel, and (5) US plus carbopol gel [65]. A significantly higher rate of recovery on day 10 was achieved in the US-MB plus diclofenac-carbopol gel group compared to other treatment groups [65]. It was concluded that by combining US and MB, there was increased delivery of diclofenac sodium gel that led to the inhibition of an arthritic ankle [65].

Recently, Huang et al. used the statistical Plackett–Burman design (PBD) to study the influence of probe distance from the skin, US application time, coupling media concentration, and duty cycle on the skin delivery of diclofenac (DF) from a dendrimer formulation [66]. PBD assumes that each factor is independent and can be described by the first-order model [67]:

$$Y = \beta_0 + \sum \beta_1 + X_1 \tag{10.5}$$

where Y is the predicted target response, β_0 is the model intercept, β_1 is the regression coefficient, and X_1 is an independent parameter [67]. The authors found out that the cumulative amount of the drug that crossed the rat abdominal skin following the application of DF gel without dendrimer and US (passive delivery) was 56.69 μg/cm^2 [66]. It was also reported that the cumulative amount of the drug that penetrated rat skin after 24 h following the administration of DF-loaded dendrimer gel in the absence of US was 257.3 μg/cm^2 [66]. Strikingly, the cumulative amount of diclofenac that was transported across rat abdominal skin was 935.21 μg/cm^2 when US and dendrimer gel were used concurrently [66].

Galantamine

Galantamine is a slightly lipophilic tertiary amine with a pKa of 8 [68]. The drug is an acetylcholinesterase blocker used for the management of Alzheimer's disease (AD) [69]. Galantamine (GLT) modulates nicotinic acetylcholine receptors allosterically [70]. Recently, Rangsimawong and coworkers investigated the effect of sonophoresis on the delivery of galantamine across hairless mouse skin [71]. The skin was continuously sonicated for 2 min (100% duty cycle, 25% amplitude) and the applied acoustic intensity was 1.90 W/cm^2 [71]. Noteworthy is the fact that after the application of GLT solution, the drug was not detected in the receiver compartment at 8 h, while the simultaneous use of US led to a significant rise in the concentration of the drug in the receiver chamber [71].

Rivastigmine

The symptoms of dementia include cognitive disfunction, severe memory disorder, and impaired processing of emotions [72,73]. Rivastigmine (RVS) is an acetyl and butyrlcholinesterase inhibitor with a phenylcarbamate structure and it is utilized for the management of AD [74]. RVS is a good candidate for transdermal delivery because of the following properties: low molecular weight (400.43), short half-life (1.5 h), and a low dose(1.5–6 mg twice daily) [75]. Exelon has received regulatory approval by the FDA as a transdermal therapeutic system with rivastigmine as the active pharmaceutical ingredient [76]. Recently, Yu and coworkers studied the impact of US on the percutaneous penetration of rivastigmine across pig skin [76]. In vitro permeation studies were conducted with vertical diffusion cells and a US probe generating 20-kHz US at an acoustic intensity of 4 W was used to treat the pig skin for 2.5 min [76]. The coupling medium contained 2.5% of sodium carboxymethyl cellulose and 30% of glycerol. It was reported that sonophoresis significantly facilitated rivastigmine delivery through the back skin of suckling pigs [76]. The steady-state transdermal flux and magnitude of RVS transport through excised skin 24 h after sonophoresis was 3.10 and 2.99 times greater than passive control [76]. Specifically, the in vitro transdermal sonophoretic steady-state flux was 0.31 ± 0.03 μg/cm^2/h in comparison with the control (0.10 ± 0.02 μg/cm^2/h) while the extent of rivastigmine delivery across pig skin was 6.00 ± 0.56 μg/cm^2/h in comparison to passive control (2.01 ± 0.35 μg/cm^2/h) [76]. The authors also evaluated the pharmacokinetic profile of the drug in male Sprague-Dawley rats following transdermal sonophoretic administration [76]. For the sonophoresis group, the US probe was used to treat the skin for 10 min. The C_{max} was 0.83 ± 0.16 μg/mL and the $AUC_{0 \rightarrow 24\ h}$ was 12.35 ± 1.99 μg · h/mL following the application of US and these pharmacokinetic values were considerably greater than that of the control group (0.28 ± 0.07 μg/mL and 4.14 ± 1.12 μg/mL, respectively) [76].

Lercanidipine hydrochloride

Hypertension, which is the most common chronic disorder seen in primary care, is a risk factor for cardiovascular (CV) mortality and morbidity [77]. It has been suggested that reducing systolic pressure by 10 mm of mercury (mmHg) or diastolic pressure by 5 mmHg can significantly decrease the risk of adverse CV events [77]. Lercanidipine (LRDP) is a dihydropyridine calcium channel antagonist utilized for the pharmacotherapy of high blood pressure [78]. The drug induces peripheral vasodilatation by blocking calcium transport through L-type calcium channels in CV smooth muscle cells [78]. Recently, it was reported that US substantially raised the cumulative amount of LRDP transported across murine skin compared to passive diffusion [79]. Synergistic transport was documented by the authors when sonophoresis was used in combination with penetration enhancers [79].

Insulin

Human insulin has a molecular weight of 5808 and is made up of A chain with 21 amino acid residues, B chain with 30 amino acid residues connected by one intra-A-chain disulfide bond and two interchain disulfide bonds [80]. This protein is used for the pharmacotherapy of diabetes mellitus. Patients who suffer from diabetes typically use insulin injections, and it would be advantageous to have a transdermal formulation of this therapeutic agent. The use of sonophoresis for transdermal flux improvement was reported for insulin [81,82]. The rationale is that US-assisted percutaneous transport of insulin is a less invasive and less painful option compared to subcutaneous insulin injections [81].

Recently, Feiszthuber and colleagues assessed the influence of cavitation on the transcutaneous permeation of insulin [81]. The authors placed soluble Actrapid insulin that was fluorescently labeled on the surface of skin mimetics and 10% duty cycle, 265 kHz focused US was applied to these mimetics [81]. Actrapid, which is a neutral, fast-acting crystalline insulin, was chosen because it is commercially available as a clear solution and it is easier to label it with fluorophores [81]. Two types of skin models were utilized—pig skin subjected to 1.00 and 1.40 MPa peak rarefactional focal pressure (PRFP) US and 3% agar hydrogel, exposed to a range of US pressures (0.25–1.40 MPa PRFP) in the presence and absence of cavitation nuclei that was inserted within the agar hydrogel at a concentration of 0.05% w/v [81].

The authors found out that in agar gel, both insulin concentration and permeation depth only increased substantially when there was inertial cavitation, with a reported facilitated flux of 40% [81]. When pig skin was investigated, the quantity of fluorescent insulin was more in US-treated epidermis in comparison to the controls, but no dramatic increase in the penetration distance was observed [81].

Boucaud et al. also studied the impact of sonophoresis on the delivery of insulin across hairless rat skin [82]. The authors studied the effect of 20 kHz US deployed with different pulse length, US intensity, and application time values on the delivery of insulin in vivo across hairless rat skin [82]. It was postulated that US-mediated flux increase depended on US pulse length and energy dose [82]. It was suggested that the driving force for US-induced flux enhancement was cavitation. A significant reduction in blood glucose level was obtained with the application of less than 15 min of transdermal sonophoresis and was comparable to the effect obtained following the subcutaneous administration of 0.5 U insulin. When hairless rat skin was exposed to sonophoresis prior to insulin administration, there was no significant reduction in blood glucose level, implying that enhanced transcutaneous permeation of insulin took place principally during sonophoresis [82].

In another interesting set of experiments, cymbal arrays were used by Smith and Shung to provide sonophoresis-assisted percutaneous delivery of insulin in rats [83]. The cymbal-shaped ultrasonic transducer ($f = 20$ kHz) weighed less than 22 g and was $37 \times 37 \times 7$ mm in size. There were four groups of the rodents for the experiments: in the first control group, insulin was placed in the reservoir in the absence of sonophoresis while saline in combination with sonophoresis [spatial peak, temporal-peak intensity (I_{SPTP}) = 100 mW/cm^2 for 60 min] was in the reservoir of the second control group [83]. Rats in the third group were given insulin combined with 60 min of sonophoresis ($I_{SPTP} = 100$ mW/cm^2), while rodents in the fourth group were given insulin with 20-min US ($I_{SPTP} = 100$ mW/cm^2) [83]. The authors documented a decrease in the glucose level in 1 h from the baseline to -267.5 ± 61.9 mg/dL for the 60-min US group [83]. Intriguingly, rats in the group exposed to US for 20 min had relatively similar result when compared with the 60-min US group. The US intensity was the same with the added possibility of using a shorter US exposure time for transdermal transport [83]. Tachibana and Tachibana investigated the effect of sonophoresis on the transcutaneous transport of insulin [84]. The concentration of glucose in the blood was quantified before and after application of US and insulin [84]. The skin surface of hairless mice was subjected to 48 kHz sonophoresis between 3000–5000 and 5000–8000 Pa for 5 min [84]. When lower energy oscillations were generated, the concentration of glucose in the blood quickly declined to 34% $\pm$ 11.9% of the control values in 2 h, while exposure of the rats to higher energy vibrations led to a blood glucose level that was 22.4% $\pm$ 3.9% of control values at 2 h [84].

Heparin

Heparin is an anticoagulant administered as an injection for the pharmacotherapy of thrombosis [85]. Some investigators have used sonophoresis to enhance the transdermal delivery of heparin [86]. In one study, 55 kHz US for a short period of not more than 60 s was utilized to increase the transcutaneous flux of heparin having an average molecular weight of 3000 Da [87]. The researchers showed that the transdermal flux following sonophoresis was 0.058 U cm^2/h [87] compared to passive flux that was essentially zero [87]. Mitragotri and Kost studied the effect of US on the transcutaneous permeation of heparin across pig skin [88]. The authors applied 20 kHz US pulses (5 s on, 5 s off) possessing an intensity of 7 W/cm^2 [88]. This intensity is obtained during the "on" period of US (that is the spatially averaged pulse average values or I_{SAPA}) [88]. There was a 50-fold rise in the porcine skin electrical conductivity following the application of US and the percutaneous permeation of heparin was approximately 21-fold higher through US-treated skin in comparison with that through nonsonicated skin [88]. The authors observed that following the application of US, approximately 24 mg of heparin was delivered across the skin in 24 h, and that is equivalent to a bioavailability of approximately 16% [88]. Using the sonophoretic mode of delivery, approximately 72 mg of heparin can permeate the skin in 24 h from a patch with heparin solution at a concentration of 150 mg/mL and an area of 10 cm^2 [88]. In another set of experiments, Le et al. applied 20 kHz US at an intensity of 7.4 W/cm^2 to porcine skin using two different surfactants: dodecyl pyridinium chloride (DPC) and sodium lauryl sulfate (SLS) at a single US frequency [86]. To study the effect of surface charge, the authors chose the two surfactants, DPC and SLS because they possess the same tail group but the electric charge is not the same: DPC is positively charged while SLS is negatively charged [86]. The authors reported that US increased the long-term permeation rate of heparin by a factor of 13 although sonophoresis had little influence on transcutaneous permeation of heparin during the first hour [86]. It was also reported that when DPC was combined with US, there was an increase in the steady-state permeation rate of heparin by about 10-fold, while the flux increase quantified after 1 h was approximately threefold [86].

Histamine

Histamine (HIS) is a bioactive amine that is usually prepared via the decarboxylation of histidine and it regulates gastric juice secretion, circadian rhythm, neurotransmission, and immunomodulation as well as cell growth and differentiation [89]. HIS has also been utilized for drug hypersensitivity investigation in allergy testing [35]. Maruani et al. studied the transdermal delivery of histamine following the application of US [35]. The ultrasonic probe was used in the pulsed mode at a frequency of 36 kHz for 5 min to reduce heating [35]. Ten participants took part in the study. Three zones, corresponding to no US, US_1 ($I1 = 2.72\ W/cm^2$), and US_2 ($I2 = 3.50\ W/cm^2$), were delineated in the right forearms of the subjects [35]. Induced papule area, which correlated with histamine penetration, served as the primary endpoint in the study, while the secondary endpoints were pruritus and papule measurement as determined by echography [35]. The secondary endpoints showed skin edema that resulted from histamine absorption. Arm zones with no US had no histamine-generated papules in 9 of 10 patients, whereas papules were present in arm zones with US (US_1 or US_2) [35]. After 30 min, papule area was considerably bigger compared with the controls (no US). Papules with larger mean sizes were formed when higher US intensities ($US_2 > US_1$) were used but the authors observed that the differences were not statistically significant [35]. There were more cases of skin edema when US was used, and no edema was detected after histamine application in the absence of US. The median values of edema were higher when higher doses of US (US_2) were used in comparison with US_1 [35]. Significantly, no pruritus was detected following histamine administration (without US). In contrast, after the application of US_1, pruritus was observed in 7 out of 10 cases [35]. In the case of US_2, the researchers detected pruritus in seven cases but there the condition did not last longer than 2 or 24 h [35].

Caffeine

It has been suggested that caffeine (1,3,7-trimethylxanthine) can reduce the motor and nonmotor signs of Parkinson's disease and also prevent the onset and progression of the disease [90]. Other pharmacological effects of caffeine include enhancement of mood and alertness, improvement of performance during exercise, and improvement of cognitive functions such as awareness, reaction time, problem-solving, and decision-making [90]. The potential anticancer effects of caffeine are also well-documented [91]. Caffeine does not possess the properties of an ideal skin penetrant because it is hydrophilic with a log P of -0.07 [92].

Recently, Sarheed and Rasool studied the influence of various sonication parameters on the penetration of caffeine across full-thickness pig skin [93]. The authors used 20 kHz with three different duty cycles (10%, 33%, and 100%), varying application time (from 5 s to 10 min), and two distinct US application modes (either pretreatment or simultaneously with drug administration) [93]. In one instance, the skin was subjected to contrasting US application modalities with the spatial-average temporal-peak intensity set at $3.7\ W/cm^2$ while sonophoresis in the continuous wave mode was conducted for either 0 (control), 5, 30, 120, or 600 s [93]. In the second set of experiments, pulsed sonophoresis in 1 s on: 2 s off mode (33% duty cycle) was carried out for 30 or 120 s. The third set of experiments entailed the use of sonophoresis with a 10% duty cycle (1 s on: 9 s off mode) over 300 or 1200 s [93].

When using the simultaneous US application mode, sonophoresis was carried out immediately after topical administration of caffeine solution. The experiments revealed a mean Kp of 11.7×10^{-4} cm/h when no US was used. In contrast, when simultaneous use of sonophoresis was carried out for 5, 30, 120, or 600 s, caffeine transdermal delivery rate was almost doubled, although the influence was only statistically significant for the two longest US administration modes [93]. When pretreatment sonophoresis was carried out for 5, 30, 120, and 600 s, there was increased steady-state penetration of caffeine by 1.9-, 3.4-, 3.1-, and 1.5-fold, respectively, in comparison to passive transport [93]. It was also reported by the authors that concurrent sonication with pulsed US (33% duty cycle for 90 and 360 s) increased the average permeability coefficient by 1.3 times and 2.09 times, respectively [93]. When the pretreatment regime was used (33% duty cycle), 90 and 360 s of sonophoresis increased caffeine transport by 1.4- and 1.78-fold, respectively. It is important to reiterate that statistically significant permeability coefficient increase was associated with a longer duration of US application. Pulsed US form (10% duty cycle) applied concurrently with drug administration for 300 s resulted in a significant 3.88-fold enhancement in the average caffeine Kp, compared to passive penetration [93].

In another interesting set of experiments, Boucaud and colleagues investigated the influence of LFS on caffeine delivery across human and hairless rat skin in vitro [94]. The authors used 20 kHz sonophoresis with a mean intensity of 2.5 W/cm^2 in either a continuous or pulsed mode [94]. It was established that low-frequency US enhanced the transdermal delivery of the drug across hairless rat and human skin. The transdermal delivery of caffeine increased when continuous and pulsed modes of US administration were used [94].

Scientists have not always agreed on the use of the terms "sonophoresis" and "sonoporation." In an interesting publication, Robertson et al. have stated that US-enhanced percutaneous drug transport can be divided into two groups: sonophoresis and sonoporation [95]. According to the authors, the US field and the penetrant are administered to the skin at the same time in a sonophoresis experiment [95]. In sonoporation (also called pretreatment sonophoresis), US is administered by researchers to the skin for a definite period of time to enhance its permeability. The US transducer is subsequently removed, and a solution of the penetrant is administered to the transiently permeabilized skin [95].

References

[1] Guignot F, et al. Early steps of cryopreservation of day one honeybee (Apis mellifera) embryos treated with low-frequency sonophoresis. Cryobiology 2018;83:27–33.

[2] Ita K. Recent progress in transdermal sonophoresis. Pharm Dev Technol 2015;22(4):458–66.

[3] Azagury A, et al. Ultrasound mediated transdermal drug delivery. Adv Drug Deliv Rev 2014;72:127–43.

[4] Snook KA, et al. Transdermal delivery of enfuvirtide in a porcine model using a low-frequency, low-power ultrasound transducer patch. Ultra Med Biol 2019;45 (2):513–25.

[5] Herwadkar A, et al. Low frequency sonophoresis mediated transdermal and intradermal delivery of ketoprofen. Int J Pharm 2012;423(2):289–96.

[6] Polat BE, et al. Ultrasound-mediated transdermal drug delivery: mechanisms, scope, and emerging trends. J Control Rel 2011;152(3):330–48.

[7] Pitt WG, Husseini GA, Staples BJ. Ultrasonic drug delivery—a general review. Expert Opin Drug Deliv 2004;1(1):37–56.

[8] Vranic E. Sonophoresis-mechanisms and application. Bosn J Basic Med Sci 2004;4 (2):25–32.

[9] Baji S, et al. Skin permeation of gemcitabine hydrochloride by passive diffusion, iontophoresis and sonophoresis: in vitro and in vivo evaluations. J Drug Deliv Sci Technol 2018;47:49–54.

[10] Srivastava SK, et al. Micromotors for drug delivery in vivo: the road ahead. Adv Drug Deliv Rev 2018;138:41–55.

[11] Banga AK. New technologies to allow transdermal delivery of therapeutic proteins and small water-soluble drugs. Am J Drug Deliv 2006;4(4):221–30.

[12] Alvarez-Román R, et al. Skin permeability enhancement by low frequency sonophoresis: lipid extraction and transport pathways. J Pharm Sci 2003;92(6):1138–46.

[13] Ahmadi F, et al. Bio-effects and safety of low-intensity, low-frequency ultrasonic exposure. Prog Biophys Mol Biol 2012;108(3):119–38.

[14] Wong, T.W., Electrical, magnetic, photomechanical and cavitational waves to overcome skin barrier for transdermal drug delivery. J Control Rel 2014;193:257–69.

[15] Meidan VM, Walmsley AD, Irwin WJ. Phonophoresisis it a reality? Int J Pharmaceutics 1995;118(2):129–49.

[16] Ogura M, Paliwal S, Mitragotri S. Low-frequency sonophoresis: current status and future prospects. Adv Drug Deliv Rev 2008;60(10):1218–23.

[17] Pamornpathomkul B, et al. Transdermal delivery of fluorescein isothiocyanate-dextrans using the combination of microneedles and low-frequency sonophoresis. Asian J Pharm Sci 2015;10(5):415–24.

[18] Terahara T, et al. Dependence of low-frequency sonophoresis on ultrasound parameters; distance of the horn and intensity. Int J Pharm 2002;235(1–2):35–42.

[19] Dragicevic N, Maibach H. Combined use of nanocarriers and physical methods for percutaneous penetration enhancement. Adv Drug Deliv Rev 2018;127:58–84.

[20] Mitragotri S, Blankschtein D, Langer R. Transdermal drug delivery using low-frequency sonophoresis. Pharm Res 1996;13(3):411–20.

[21] Schoellhammer CM, et al. Rapid skin permeabilization by the simultaneous application of dual-frequency, high-intensity ultrasound. J Control Rel 2012;163(2):154–60.

[22] Huang D, Chen YS, Rupenthal ID. Overcoming ocular drug delivery barriers through the use of physical forces. Adv Drug Deliv Rev 2018;126:96–112.

[23] Polat BE, Blankschtein D, Langer R. Low-frequency sonophoresis: application to the transdermal delivery of macromolecules and hydrophilic drugs. Expert Opin Drug Deliv 2010;7(12):1415–32.

[24] Robertson J, Becker S. Motivations for a custom apparatus for sonophoresis experimentation. IFAC-PapersOnLine 2015;48(20):100–5.

[25] Schoellhammer CM, et al. Applicability and safety of dual-frequency ultrasonic treatment for the transdermal delivery of drugs. J Control Rel 2015;202:93–100.
[26] Vadlapatla R, Wong EY, Gayakwad SG. Electronic drug delivery systems: an overview. J Drug Deliv Sci Technol 2017;41:359–66.
[27] Castro A, Hoyos M. Study of the onset of the acoustic streaming in parallel plate resonators with pulse ultrasound. Ultrasonics 2016;66:166–71.
[28] Kuznetsova LA, Coakley WT. Applications of ultrasound streaming and radiation force in biosensors. Biosens Bioelectron 2007;22(8):1567–77.
[29] Doinikov AA, Thibault P, Marmottant P. Acoustic streaming induced by two orthogonal ultrasound standing waves in a microfluidic channel. Ultrasonics 2018;87:7–19.
[30] Cosgrove JA, et al. PIV applied to eckart streaming produced by a medical ultrasound transducer. Ultrasonics 2001;39(6):461–4.
[31] Tang Q, Hu J. Diversity of acoustic streaming in a rectangular acoustofluidic field. Ultrasonics 2015;58(0):27–34.
[32] Frenkel V, et al. Preliminary investigations of ultrasound induced acoustic streaming using particle image velocimetry. Ultrasonics 2001;39(3):153–6.
[33] Amirante R, et al. Acoustic cavitation by means ultrasounds in the extra virgin olive oil extraction process. Energy Procedia 2017;126:82–90.
[34] Robertson J, Squire M, Becker S. Circulation cooling in continuous skin sonoporation at constant coupling fluid temperatures. Ultra Med & Biol 2020;46(1):137–48.
[35] Maruani A, et al. Efficiency of low-frequency ultrasound sonophoresis in skin penetration of histamine: a randomized study in humans. Int J Pharm 2010;385(1–2):37–41.
[36] Zhao Z, et al. Transdermal immunomodulation: principles, advances and perspectives. Adv Drug Deliv Rev 2018;127:3–19.
[37] Frenkel V. Ultrasound mediated delivery of drugs and genes to solid tumors. Adv Drug Deliv Rev 2008;60(10):1193–208.
[38] Wang T, et al. Ultrasound-negative pressure cavitation extraction of phenolic compounds from blueberry leaves and evaluation of its DPPH radical scavenging activity. Food Bioprod Process 2018;108:69–80.
[39] Wolloch L, Kost J. The importance of microjet vs shock wave formation in sonophoresis. J Control Rel 2010;148(2):204–11.
[40] Park D, et al. Sonophoresis in transdermal drug deliverys. Ultrasonics 2014;54(1):56–65.
[41] Yin L, et al. Enhancing percutaneous permeability of sinomenine hydrochloride using dual-frequency sonophoresis. J Drug Deliv Sci Technol 2016;36:62–7.
[42] Monnier H, Wilhelm AM, Delmas H. Influence of ultrasound on mixing on the molecular scale for water and viscous liquids. Ultrason Sonochem 1999;6(1–2):67–74.
[43] Rahimi M, et al. Experimental investigation on proper use of dual high-low frequency ultrasound waves—advantage and disadvantage. Chem Eng Process: Process Intensif 2014;78:17–26.
[44] Leong T, Ashokkumar M, Kentish S. The growth of bubbles in an acoustic field by rectified diffusion. Handbook of Ultrasonics and Sonochemistry. Singapore: Springer Singapore; 2016. p. 69–98.
[45] Lavon I, et al. Bubble growth within the skin by rectified diffusion might play a significant role in sonophoresis. J Control Rel 2007;117(2):246–55.
[46] Krasovitski B, et al. Intramembrane cavitation as a unifying mechanism for ultrasound-induced bioeffects. Proc Natl Acad Sci U S A 2011;108(8):3258–63.
[47] Lee H, et al. Device-assisted transdermal drug delivery. Adv Drug Deliv Rev 2017;.
[48] Merino G, et al. Frequency and thermal effects on the enhancement of transdermal transport by sonophoresis. J Control Rel 2003;88(1):85–94.

[49] Polat BE, et al. A physical mechanism to explain the delivery of chemical penetration enhancers into skin during transdermal sonophoresis — insight into the observed synergism. J Control Rel 2012;158(2):250–60.
[50] Merino G, Kalia YN, Delgado-Charro MB, Guy RH. Mechanism of enhanced transdermal transport by low-frequency sonophoresis. The role of local heating. In: Proceedings of the 27th international symposium on controlled release of bioactive material; 2000. p. 942–43.
[51] Nguyen HX, Banga AK. Electrically and ultrasonically enhanced transdermal delivery of methotrexate. Pharmaceutics 2018;10(3):E117.
[52] Tezel A, et al. Low-frequency ultrasound as a transcutaneous immunization adjuvant. Vaccine 2005;23(29):3800–7.
[53] Yang C, et al. Poly (l-glutamic acid)-g-methoxy poly (ethylene glycol)-gemcitabine conjugate improves the anticancer efficacy of gemcitabine. Int J Pharm 2018;550 (1–2):79–88.
[54] Zhang P, et al. A carbon nanotube-gemcitabine-lentinan three-component composite for chemo-photothermal synergistic therapy of cancer. Int J Nanomed 2018;13:3069–80.
[55] Yuan Y, et al. Protective effects of sinomenine on CFA-induced inflammatory pain in rats. Med Sci Monit 2018;24:2018–24.
[56] Wang J, et al. Preparation of mixed monoterpenes edge activated PEGylated transfersomes to improve the in vivo transdermal delivery efficiency of sinomenine hydrochloride. Int J Pharm 2017;533(1):266–74.
[57] Ita KB, Popova IE. Influence of sonophoresis and chemical penetration enhancers on percutaneous transport of penbutolol sulfate. Pharm Dev Technol 2015;1–6.
[58] Waller JR, Waller DG. Drugs for systemic hypertension and angina. Medicine 2018;46 (9):566–72.
[59] Al-Kassas R, et al. Transdermal delivery of propranolol hydrochloride through chitosan nanoparticles dispersed in mucoadhesive gel. Carbohydr Polym 2016;153:176–86.
[60] Guo L, Wang PP, Li QQ. Development of sonophoresis mediated transdermal drug delivery system for propranolol. Lat Am J Pharm 2016;35(9):2041–9.
[61] Manikkath J, et al. Influence of peptide dendrimers and sonophoresis on the transdermal delivery of ketoprofen. Int J Pharm 2017;521:110–19.
[62] Mitragotri S, Blankschtein D, Langer R. An explanation for the variation of the sonophoretic transdermal transport enhancement from drug to drug. J Pharm Sci 1997;86 (10):1190–2.
[63] Goh CF, Lane ME. Formulation of diclofenac for dermal delivery. Int J Pharmaceutics 2014;473(1):607–16.
[64] Aldwaikat M, Alarjah M. Investigating the sonophoresis effect on the permeation of diclofenac sodium using 3D skin equivalent. Ultrason Sonochem 2015;22:580–7.
[65] Liao A-H, et al. Efficacy of combined ultrasound-and-microbubbles-mediated diclofenac gel delivery to enhance transdermal permeation in adjuvant-induced rheumatoid arthritis in the rat. Ultrasound Med Biol 2016;42(8):1976–85.
[66] Huang B, et al. Dendrimer-coupled sonophoresis-mediated transdermal drug-delivery system for diclofenac. Drug Des Devel Ther 2015;9:3867–76.
[67] Li X, et al. An efficient homogenate-microwave-assisted extraction of flavonols and anthocyanins from blackcurrant marc: optimization using combination of Plackett-Burman design and Box-Behnken design. Ind Crop Prod 2016;94:834–47.
[68] Park CW, et al. Investigation of formulation factors affecting in vitro and in vivo characteristics of a galantamine transdermal system. Int J Pharm 2012;436(1–2):32–40.

[69] Peters O, et al. Combined treatment with memantine and galantamine-CR compared with galantamine-CR only in antidementia drug naive patients with mild-to-moderate Alzheimer's disease. Alzheimers Dement 2015;1(3):198–204.
[70] Coyle J, Kershaw P. Galantamine, a cholinesterase inhibitor that allosterically modulates nicotinic receptors: effects on the course of Alzheimer's disease. Biol Psychiatry 2001;49 (3):289–99.
[71] Rangsimawong W, et al. Enhancement of galantamine HBr skin permeation using sonophoresis and limonene-containing PEGylated liposomes. AAPS PharmSciTech 2018;19 (3):1093–104.
[72] Penhasi A, Gomberg M. A specific two-pulse release of rivastigmine using a modified time-controlled delivery system: a proof of concept case study. J Drug Deliv Sci Technol 2018;47:404–10.
[73] Guzman-Velez E, Feinstein JS, Tranel D. Feelings without memory in Alzheimer disease. Cogn Behav Neurol 2014;27(3):117–29.
[74] Değirmenci Y, Keçeci H. Visual hallucinations due to rivastigmine transdermal patch application in Alzheimer's disease; The First Case Report. Int J Gerontol 2016;10 (4):240–1.
[75] Malaiya MK, et al. Controlled delivery of rivastigmine using transdermal patch for effective management of Alzheimer's disease. J Drug Deliv Sci Technol 2018;45: 408–14.
[76] Yu ZW, Liang Y, Liang WQ. Low-frequency sonophoresis enhances rivastigmine permeation in vitro and in vivo. Pharmazie 2015;70(6):379–80.
[77] Grassi G, et al. Lercanidipine in the management of hypertension: an update. J Pharmacol Pharmacother 2017;8(4):155–65.
[78] Antza C, Stabouli S, Kotsis V. Combination therapy with lercanidipine and enalapril in the management of the hypertensive patient: an update of the evidence. Vasc Health Risk Manag 2016;12:443–51.
[79] Shetty PK, et al. Transdermal delivery of lercanidipine hydrochloride: effect of chemical enhancers and ultrasound. Curr Drug Deliv 2013;10(4):427–34.
[80] Hossain MA, Bathgate RAD. Challenges in the design of insulin and relaxin/insulin-like peptide mimetics. Bioorg Med Chem 2018;26(10):2827–41.
[81] Feiszthuber H, et al. Cavitation-enhanced delivery of insulin in agar and porcine models of human skin. Phys Med Biol 2015;60(6):2421–34.
[82] Boucaud A, et al. Effect of sonication parameters on transdermal delivery of insulin to hairless rats. J Control Rel 2002;81(1–2):113–19.
[83] Smith NB, Lee S, Shung KK. Ultrasound-mediated transdermal in vivo transport of insulin with low-profile cymbal arrays. Ultrasound Med Biol 2003;29(8):1205–10.
[84] Tachibana K, Tachibana S. Transdermal delivery of insulin by ultrasonic vibration. J Pharm Pharmacol 1991;43(4):270–1.
[85] Motlekar NA, Youan BB. The quest for non-invasive delivery of bioactive macromolecules: a focus on heparins. J Control Rel 2006;113(2):91–101.
[86] Le L, Kost J, Mitragotri S. Combined effect of low-frequency ultrasound and iontophoresis: applications for transdermal heparin delivery. Pharm Res 2000;17(9):1151–4.
[87] Lanke SS, Strom JG, Banga AK. Enhancement of transdermal delivery of heparin by various physical and chemical enhancement techniques. Crit Rev Ther Drug Carr Syst 2009;26(6):581–606.
[88] Mitragotri S, Kost J. Transdermal delivery of heparin and low-molecular weight heparin using low-frequency ultrasound. Pharm Res 2001;18(8):1151–6.

[89] Comas-Baste O, et al. New approach for the diagnosis of histamine intolerance based on the determination of histamine and methylhistamine in urine. J Pharm Biomed Anal 2017;145:379–85.
[90] Tej G, Nayak PK. Mechanistic considerations in chemotherapeutic activity of caffeine. Biomed Pharmacother 2018;105:312–19.
[91] Shakeel F, Ramadan W. Transdermal delivery of anticancer drug caffeine from water-in-oil nanoemulsions. Colloids Surf B Biointerfaces 2010;75(1):356–62.
[92] Luo L, Lane ME. Topical and transdermal delivery of caffeine. Int J Pharm 2015;490(1–2):155–64.
[93] Sarheed O, Rasool BK. Development of an optimised application protocol for sonophoretic transdermal delivery of a model hydrophilic drug. Open Biomed Eng J 2011;5:14–24.
[94] Boucaud A, et al. In vitro study of low-frequency ultrasound-enhanced transdermal transport of fentanyl and caffeine across human and hairless rat skin. Int J Pharm 2001;228(1–2):69–77.
[95] Robertson J, Squire M, Becker S. A thermoelectric device for coupling fluid temperature regulation during continuous skin sonoporation or sonophoresis. AAPS PharmSciTech 2019;20(4):147.

Chapter 11

Laser and other ablation technologies

Skin laser ablation is a thermal technique that entails eliminating the SC layer through the transient administration of laser beam to the skin [1]. The enhancement of percutaneous flux with fully ablative lasers was first reported in 1987 [2]. Manstein and coworkers subsequently introduced fractional photothermolysis that entailed the use of focused laser beams to form microscopic conduits, while sparing the tissue surrounding each conduit [3]. Laser poration involves the utilization of high-energy light source to form well-defined ablated regions in a tissue. Pulsed lasers are normally used since their duration and power can be adjusted to control tissue removal [2]. It is relevant to know individual drug biodistribution in skin structures and distinct skin layers with the aim of achieving targeted laser-mediated drug transport. Presently, most clinical trials involving lasers examine the total drug accumulation in the skin [2].

In recent times, laser-mediated microporation of the stratum corneum (SC) has been used to enhance (trans)dermal drug transport [4]. When a fractional laser is employed, several microscopic channels are formed in the skin. These zones of treatment are surrounded by normal tissue. Because the laser beam resurfaces 5% to 20% of the skin surface, the tissue heals faster. In addition, full epidermal wounds are not induced [4]. Recently, several areas of medicine, such as oncology, dentistry, surgery, dermatology, and ophthalmology, have witnessed increased use of laser for either diagnosis or treatment [5]. Lasers discharge monochromatic, high-intensity, and narrow radiation that interacts with particular chromophores in the skin such as water, hemoglobin, or melanin to cause precise and clinically useful tissue destruction measuring a few micrometers in depth with decreased adverse effects [6]. Pigments and water in the skin usually convert laser energy to heat [1]. Based on laser time and intensity, it is possible to heat the skin to hundreds of degrees in a short time (micro to milliseconds) and thus breach the SC [1]. When utilizing laser energy, there is no need to use additional mechanical devices on the skin [7]. One of the advantages of lasers is that it can be used for precise tissue removal like a sharp-edged chisel, thus reducing collateral damage to the neighboring tissues [7]. The aim is usually to

Transdermal Drug Delivery. DOI: https://doi.org/10.1016/B978-0-12-822550-9.00011-9

take away the upper skin layers and form conduits that facilitate the delivery of topically administered medications. Lasers have been found to be safe for the topical management of certain dermatological disorders such as warts or keloids as well as aesthetic effects like the removal of age spots or the reduction of wrinkles [7]. The formation of photomechanical waves and direct ablation are laser-skin interactions that facilitate the percutaneous transport of medications [8]. Photomechanical waves refer to unipolar compressional waves that are generated as a result of intense laser application [8]. These are waves that measure hundreds of atmospheres in magnitude and can last from nano to microseconds. They may deform and permeabilize cells and tissues but the exact nature of the interactions is poorly understood [8]. Direct ablation disintegrates the SC because of the effect of high energy [8]. Furthermore, the application of laser energy to the skin can lead to their excitation and explosive evaporation from the epidermis, which subsequently results in the creation of microconduits (MCs) [9]. Since the duration of the energy pulse is usually less than the thermal relaxation time of water, there is insignificant heat transfer and hence thermal injury—to the adjacent tissues [9]. In an interesting study, Bachhav et al. investigated the transport of four proteins (equine heart cytochrome c, recombinant human growth hormone expressed in *Escherichia coli*, urinary follicle-stimulating hormone, and fluorescein isothiocyanate (FITC)-labeled bovine serum albumin) by using a scanning Er:YAG diode−pumped laser (P.L.E.A.S.E., Precise Laser Epidermal System) [9]. The authors found out that no protein transport (deposition or permeation) occurred across intact skin but the use of P.L.E.A.S.E. led to total delivery after 24 h of 48.2 ± 8.9, 8.1 ± 4.2, 0.2 ± 0.1, and $273.3 \pm 30.6\ \mu g/cm^2$ for Cyt c, hGH, FSH, and FITC-BSA, respectively, using 900 pores/135.9 cm^2 [9].

Lasers have been investigated for the percutaneous transport of medications due to its good acceptability, avoidance of first pass effect as well as noninvasiveness [5]. Laser-mediated drug delivery can be classified into four groups [10]: (1) Nonablative dermal remodeling lasers (NDRLs) have nonaqueous chromophores and have been utilized to enhance drug delivery. Lasers such as the neodymium-doped YAG laser (1064 nm) or the 585/595-nm pulsed dye laser used for the management of vascular disorders are also regarded as NDRLs [10]; (2) nonablative fractional lasers (NAFLs) such as erbium fiber laser (1550 nm) [10]; (3) ablative fractional lasers (AFLs) are lasers that, when used fractionally, can form regions of thermal damage, which are called microscopic treatment zones; (4) fully ablative lasers, such as the erbium-doped yttrium aluminum garnet (Er:YAG) laser ($\lambda = 2940$ nm) or the carbon dioxide (CO_2) laser ($\lambda = 10{,}600$ nm), whose principal chromophore is water and have been used for the heating as well as complete vaporization of the skin. Erbium:yttrium-aluminum-garnet (Er:YAG) laser is utilized for percutaneous drug transport enhancement because it has a wavelength that is comparable to the main absorption wavelength of water thus resulting in heat radiation [1]. Er:YAG laser emits light in the near-infrared spectral region ($\lambda = 2940$ nm) and this radiation is highly absorbed by water present in the skin [11]. Another advantage of this technique is that Er:YAG laser can ablate the SC with the least possible lingering thermal injury [12,13].

Light from CO_2 and Er:YAG lasers can be absorbed by water molecules leading to the formation of MCs in the SC due to water vaporization. Be that as it may, thermal injury and/or irritation at the site of administration as well as neighboring tissues may result from photothermal effects [8]. Er:YAG and CO_2 are infrared lasers that can heat the skin to temperatures above 100°C and expel vapor [14]. The Er:YAG laser has an absorption coefficient of 2×10^7/cm and due to water absorption, it takes less energy to cause tissue ablation [14]. Not much energy is required to create conduits with the Er:YAG systems and there is usually minimal thermal damage around the conduits. In contrast, the CO_2 laser has an absorption coefficient of 2×10^6/cm and requires higher energies for tissue ablation, leading to more thermal injury (coagulation zone) around the ablated conduits in comparison with Er:YAG [14]. Table 11.1 shows the effect of laser irradiation on transdermal drug delivery.

Ganti and Banga investigated the effect of NAFL on the in vitro percutaneous permeation of diclofenac sodium and sumatriptan succinate across dermatomed human skin [6]. Transdermal delivery of the drug across untreated skin led to the percutaneous transport of 22.80 ± 0.64 and 72.61 ± 50.35 mg/cm^2 of sumatriptan succinate and diclofenac sodium, respectively [6]. NAFL significantly enhanced the transport of diclofenac sodium and sumatriptan succinate to 575.66 ± 207.18 and 498.32 ± 97.54 mg/cm^2, respectively [6]. Lee et al. investigated the effect of Er:YAG laser on the transdermal permeation of nalbuphine and indomethacin [15]. These therapeutic agents possess identical molecular weights but were chosen as model hydrophilic (nalbuphine) and lipophilic (indomethacin) compounds. The authors irradiated nude mouse skin with a laser possessing an energy of 0.35–0.60 J. This was done to evaluate the influence of Er:YAG laser on the integrity of the skin [15]. The fluences utilized for experiments ranged from 0.91 to 1.56 J/cm [15]. SC thickness and epidermis following laser treatment were proportional to laser energy. The authors reported a marked enhancement in the transport of the investigated drugs across laser-pretreated skin [15]. The laser had more influence on the transdermal penetration of the hydrophilic nalbuphine that normally possesses low skin permeability. The laser spot size and intensity were relevant parameters for the modulation of transdermal delivery. Indomethacin flux across SC-stripped skin was 3.82-fold greater than drug flux across untreated skin [15]. Enhanced laser intensity (laser spot size of 7 mm) led to a higher increase in nalbuphine flux. In the skin samples irradiated with 0.35-J laser using different laser spot sizes, the transdermal delivery of nalbuphine was enhanced in the following order: $7 > 5 > 3.5 > 2$ mm [15].

TABLE 11.1 The influence of laser treatment on percutaneous drug delivery.

Therapeutic agent(s) or model compound(s)	Skin model(s)	Method	References
Diclofenac sodium and sumatriptan succinate	Human skin	Nonablative fractional laser	[6]
Tretinoin, imiquimod, 5-aminolevulinic acid, peptide, quantum dots (QD), dextran	Mouse and pig skin	Nonablative fractional erbium:glass (Er:glass) laser	[16]
Lysozyme	Mouse skin	Erbium:yttrium aluminum garnet (Er:YAG) laser	[12]
Diclofenac	Human skin, pig skin	Er:YAG laser	[17]
Tranexamic acid	Pig skin	CO2 laser, nonfractionated ablative Er:YAG laser	[18]
Basiliximab, antithymocyte globulin	Human skin, pig skin	Erbium:YAG fractional laser	[19]
Human growth hormone (hGH)	Pig skin	Er:YAG laser	[20]
Cisplatin(CIS) and 5-fluorouracil	Pig skin	Ablative fractional laser	[22]
Prednisone	Pig skin	Er:YAG laser	[23]
Ovalbumin	Mouse skin	Ablative fractional laser	[24]
Hepatitis B surface antigen	Mouse skin	Ablative fractional infrared laser	[27]
2-Phospho-L-ascorbic acid trisodium salt (SAP), magnesium L-ascorbic acid-2-phosphate (MAP-2) and L-ascorbic acid 2-phosphate sesquimagnesium salt (MAP-1)	Pig skin	CO_2 and Er:YAG laser irradiation	[29]

In another study, the efficacy and safety of the nonablative fractional erbium:glass (Er:glass) laser as a drug delivery enhancement technique were explored [16]. Nude mouse and pig skin samples were used for the experiments. The influence of Er:glass laser on the transcutaneous flux of quantum dots (QD), dextran, peptide, tretinoin, imiquimod, and 5-aminolevulinic acid (ALA) in vitro and in vivo was investigated [16]. The fractional laser selectively formed photothermal dots deep into the dermis while leaving the epidermis and the SC intact [16]. In comparison with untreated skin, ALA percutaneous flux increased 1200-fold following laser treatment [16]. Flux increase following laser treatment declined with increased penetrant lipophilicity. The skin deposition of the extremely lipophilic tretinoin increased only twofold following laser application [16]. Conversely, there was a 10-fold increase in peptide transport following laser treatment in comparison with flux across untreated skin. The skin transport of dextran (MW $\geq$ 40 kDa) was also facilitated with Er:glass laser. Furthermore, nonablative laser was used to transport QD with a diameter of 20 nm into skin samples. The authors reported that the barrier properties of the skin were restored 8–60 h after laser application and this was proportional to laser spot densities. Significantly, the laser treatment did not induce any *Staphylococcus aureus* or *Pseudomonas aeruginosa* infection [16].

Lee and coworkers investigated the transcutaneous penetration of vaccines and peptides following the use of a single pulse of an Er:YAG laser [12]. The percutaneous flux of peptides across laser-treated skin using different fluences was 3–140-fold greater than what was obtained across untreated skin [12]. The lipophilicity, peptide sequence, and molecular size influenced transdermal flux values. Confocal laser scanning microscopy was used by the authors to demonstrate a significant enhancement in the skin accumulation of peptides following exposure to laser radiation [12]. The authors applied laser to mouse skin and then carried out skin vaccination with a lysozyme antigen. Lysozyme (MW 14,307 Da) with 129 amino acids was utilized for in vivo skin immunization [12]. Initially, lysozymes linked to FITC were examined in an in vitro skin transport study. No lysozyme was transported across untreated skin during 12 h apparently due to large molecular weight [12]. The application of 1.4 and 1.7 J/cm^2 laser radiation resulted in a normalized flux of 0.081 ± 0.021 and 0.098 ± 0.039 nmol/cm^2/h, respectively [12]. The authors also determined serum antibody titers for different rodent groups. The control group (neither laser nor lysozyme) displayed no or insignificant titers on the plot profiles. Mice that were topically administered lysozyme exhibited a measurable Immunoglobulin G (IgG) response. Serum IgG is increased significantly by threefold following laser exposure. Serum IgG for 1.4 and 1.7 J/cm^2 were similar [12].

Bachhav and coworkers used laser treatment to form MCs in the skin thus enhancing the transdermal flux of diclofenac [17]. The laser system deployed in these experiments (P.L.E.A.S.E.) employs an Er:YAG laser that emits light at 2940 nm [17]. This is analogous to a principal water absorption peak; the excitation and ensuing water evaporation in the epidermis result in MC formation with no thermal injury to the neighboring tissues [17]. Transdermal permeation of diclofenac from propylene glycol, aqueous solution, and commercially available formulations across untreated and laser-treated pig and human skin samples was investigated [17]. After 24 h, the cumulative drug transport across skin samples with 150, 300, 450, and 900 shallow pores (50–80 μm) was 3.7-, 7.5-, 9.2-, and 13-fold higher compared to intact skin [17]. The authors revealed that cumulative permeation depended on laser fluence: permeation (g/cm^2) = 11.35 Fluence (J/cm^2) + 352.3. After 24 h, the application of laser measuring 22.65, 45.3, 90.6, and 135.9 J/cm^2 in fluence values led to diclofenac permeation of 539.6 ± 78.1, 934.5 ± 451.5, 1451.9 ± 151.3, and 1858.6 ± 308.5 $\mu g/cm^2$, respectively. Be that as it may, there was no statistically significant influence of laser fluence on skin accumulation. Drug transport from the commercially available gel dosage forms was significantly greater across laser-treated skin samples [e.g., for Solaraze, the cumulative transport after 24 h across treated (900 pores/135.9 J/cm^2) and intact skin was 974.9 ± 368.8 and 8.2 ± 3.8 $\mu g/cm^2$, respectively] [17].

In an interesting study, Hsiao et al. evaluated the delivery of tranexamic acid following laser treatment with either CO_2 laser pretreatment or conventional nonfractionated ablative Er:YAG laser [18]. Dorsal pig skin was pretreated with either CO_2 or Er:YAG laser. The authors used scanning electron microscopy to evaluate skin surface disruption [18]. The depth of penetration of fluorescein isothiocyanate (a reporter molecule) into the skin was determined by confocal laser scanning microscopy. Fluency-linked enhancement in the transcutaneous flux of the drug was conducted by the researchers using Franz diffusion cells. Percutaneous transport of tranexamic acid increased proportionally with Er:YAG laser fluency hike [18]. Transcutaneous permeation was greater when exposure to CO_2 laser was carried out compared to Er:YAG laser pretreatment, but a "ceiling effect" was documented and the use of increased wattage did not induce additional enhancement in transcutaneous drug transport [18]. Exposure to CO_2 laser resulted in a deeper and more pervasive skin rupture compared to Er:YAG laser pretreatment [18].

Yu et al. used fractional laser ablation to deliver therapeutic antibodies into the skin [19]. The authors investigated the laser-mediated transport of basiliximab and antithymocyte globulin (ATG)–therapeutic agents approved by regulatory authorities for immunosuppression. In vitro permeation experiments were carried out with dermatomed human abdominal and pig ear skin samples; the authors also performed animal experiments using C57 BL/10 SCSnJ mice and reported in vitro/in vivo correlation [19]. The transdermal delivery of antibodies was investigated using enzyme-linked immunosorbent assay. By raising the pore number from 300 to 450 and 900, the total antibody delivery was enhanced for ATG, from 1.18 ± 0.10 to 3.98 ± 0.64 and 4.97 ± 0.83 $\mu g/cm^2$, respectively—corresponding to 19.7-,

66.3-, and 82.8-fold increases in flux values compared to untreated skin [19]. Raising laser fluence from 22.65 to 45.3 and 135.9 J/cm^2 also increased total ATG transport from 1.70 ± 0.65 to 4.97 ± 0.83 and 8.70 ± 1.55 μg/cm^2, respectively [19].

The percutaneous permeation of human growth hormone (hGH) through laser-porated dermatomed pig ear skin was studied [20]. The transport of hGH was investigated using several micropore densities and laser fluences. Transdermal delivery was carried out in vitro using vertical Franz diffusion cells and dermatomed pig ear skin exposed to ablative laser (2940 nm; P.L. E.A.S.E) [21]. The influence of several fluences (34.1, 45.4, and 68.1 J/cm^2) at 10% pore density as well as several micropore densities (5%, 10%, and 15%) at a fluence of 34.1 J/cm^2 on the delivery of hGH were examined [20]. After 48 h, 77.12 ± 10.77 μg/cm^2 of hGH was transported into the receptor chamber following the administration of 45.4 J/cm^{2}laser, which was significantly greater than that documented with the 34.1 J/cm^2 group (53.13 ± 1.75 μg/cm^2) [20]. The use of fluence of 68.1 J/cm^2 led to a transport of 90.94 ± 3.93 μg/cm^2 that was significantly greater than that from the 34.1 J/cm^2 group ($P < .05$), but lower compared to the 45.4 J/cm^2 group [20]. When micropore density was raised from 5% to 15%, hGH transport went up significantly from 7.1 ± 2.63 to 95.89 ± 13.43 μg/cm^2 after 48 h [20]. The differences in laser micropore density and fluence impacted hGH transport through dermatomed laser-microporated pig skin [20].

In another study, Wenande and coworkers assessed the influence of AFL on the skin delivery and biodistribution of cisplatin (CIS) and 5-fluorouracil (5-FU) [22]. The authors evaluated the toxicity, biodistribution, and pharmacokinetics of the two drugs either alone or in combination following the application of AFL to pig skin in vivo. It was reported that fractional CO_2 laser application (852 μm ablation depth, 196 microchannels/cm^2) resulted in a fast drug uptake in 1500 μm deep skin layers, with a sixfold increase in peak CIS concentration versus intact skin [22]. In like manner, maximum 5-FU accumulation was recorded within an hour of AFL application, and this was superior to peak accumulation in nonlaser–treated skin sample that was subjected to topical drug administration for 5 days. On the whole, this deeper and faster skin drug uptake led to significantly enhanced inflammatory and histopathological effects [22]. Quantitative histopathologic analyses carried out by the authors showed markedly increased cellular apoptosis and decreased epidermal proliferation following AFL-mediated drug transport, especially after combined 5-FU + cisplatin treatment [22]. When administered alone or simultaneously, 5-FU and cisplatin uptake was accelerated and boosted by AFL in vivo, with the greatest effect in deep skin layers [22]. The authors showed that enhanced potency of 5-FU and cisplatin chemotherapy combined with increased skin permeation by AFL may lead to a beneficial topical treatment approach for nonmelanoma skin cancer [22].

Yu et al. studied the effect of laser irradiation on the transdermal permeation kinetics of prednisone [23]. The authors employed the Painless Laser Epidermal System (P.L.E.A.S.E.) that can create preprogrammed micropores with specific depths in a few seconds [23]. The researchers investigated the effect of pore depth and pore number on the transdermal delivery of prednisone across pig skin [23]. Transport studies were conducted utilizing full thickness pig ear skin samples at room temperature for 24 h. The quantity of the drug that was retained in the skin was also assayed. The overall quantity of the drug transported was computed from the sum of the quantities that penetrated the skin as well as what was obtained from the skin through extraction [23]. The researchers noted that fluence can be employed to modulate pore depth in the skin. At the lowest energy of 4.53 J/cm^2, the investigators eliminated only the SC; at 22.65 J/cm^2, a steady presence of pores in the viable epidermis was observed; and at 135.9 J/cm^2, the pores extended into the dermal–epidermal junction and often permeated the dermis [23]. Significantly, it was demonstrated that prednisone delivery across intact skin was poor and could not be quantified. Nonetheless, drug transport across and retention in porated skin characterized by the presence of 450, 900, and 1800 pores were 60.85 ± 14.05, 107.93 ± 14.41, and 197.18 ± 29.62 μg/cm^2, respectively [23]. Accordingly, a fourfold enhancement in the number of formed pores led to a corresponding increase in drug transport. It is important to note that for this particular set of experiments, the number of pores was fixed at 900. There was a marked increase in drug penetration following exposure to P.L.E.A.S.E. laser irradiation. Elevating fluence from 22.65 to 45.3 J/cm^2 resulted in an almost threefold enhancement in drug transport—47.54 ± 4.90 to 135.59 ± 6.85 μg/cm^2. But a further twofold increase in fluence to 90.6 J/cm^2 led to only about 20% enhancement in transdermal drug delivery (162.21 ± 7.14 μg/cm^2) [23].

Several researchers and regulatory authorities have expressed safety concerns regarding the use of full-surface laser ablation for transdermal drug delivery. To address this problem, Chen and coworkers studied the influence of AFL on the transport of a model vaccine ovalbumin (OVA) [24]. It was documented that exposure to AFL led to the formation of several self-renewable MCs in the skin as well as the creation of routes for vaccine and drug transport into the dermis. The use of AFL led to a higher transdermal drug and vaccine flux values compared to tape stripping. Furthermore, a higher amount of methylene blue, sulforhodamine B (SRB), or OVA was retrieved from AFL-exposed skin compared to tape-stripped skin or control skin. SRB, a hydrophilic model compound with a molecular mass of approximately 560 Da, was first used by the authors to examine transdermal permeation across AFL-treated or tape-stripped skin samples. SRB penetrated laser-treated skin 30 min following the skin application of a gauze patch coated with SRB, as shown by images of pink-colored SRB only in AFL-treated skin (none in control skin), with the greatest density found in MCs formed from laser application. Even in the proximity of individual MC, the concentration of the tested compound (SRB) was greater than what was observed in control skin, ostensibly due to drug diffusion from the MC. The research also revealed that the quantity of SRB in the skin after 0.5 h following patch administration to AFL-treated skin using fluence values of 2.5 mJ 5%, 2.5 mJ 15%, 5.0 mJ 5%, or 5.0 mJ 15% was 5.83 ± 0.44, 15.17 ± 1.73, 10.36 ± 0.72, or 31.37 ± 4.72 μg/cm^2, respectively. This corresponds to a 12-, 30-, 21-, or 63-fold enhancement in comparison to the control value (0.50 ± 0.17 μg/cm^2). The quantities of SRB in mildly tape-stripped or slightly invasive tape-stripped skin samples were 1.09 ± 0.24 or 3.09 ± 0.17 μg/cm^2, respectively. The maximum quantity of SRB in the skin was 9.62 ± 1.06 μg/cm^2 in 2.5 mJ 5% group and 15.91 ± 1.10 in 5.0 mJ 5% group following 6 h of patch administration whereas SRB quantity was at the greatest level at 25.18 ± 2.90 μg/cm^2 in 2.5 mJ 15% group and 31.37 ± 4.72 μg/cm^2 in the 5.0 mJ 15% group after 1 or 0.5 h of patch application. respectively [24]. When the researchers coated Texas Red−conjugated OVA (TR-OVA) onto a patch and administered same to laser-exposed skin for 0.5 or 3 h, TR-OVA was visible, after 0.5 h of patch administration, in both the epidermis and in the upper dermis encompassing the MCs. There was a continuous horizontal and vertical distribution into all dermal tissue in 3 h. The authors reported no dermal transport of TR-OVA in both tape-stripped and control groups in the first 30 min of patch administration, even though TR-OVA transport in the upper dermis was found in 3 h after patch application following more invasive tape stripping. The quantity of TR-OVA in the skin increased in laser-exposed skin following patch administration and achieved a maximum concentration in 3 h in all groups exposed to AFL, which was substantially greater than what was achieved with the tape-stripped or the nonlaser−exposed control groups [24]. Laser exposure enhanced the transdermal transport of TR-OVA by about $8 \sim 15$ times within 3 h in comparison to the control group, while slightly invasive tape stripping, but not mild tape stripping, enhanced TR-OVA permeation only by less than four times during equivalent time frame. Significantly, the authors did not find substantial difference between each tape-stripping group and the control groups. Furthermore, there was no statistically significant difference between the two tape-stripping groups. Clearly, AFL enhanced the percutaneous penetration of OVA compared to tape stripping [24].

In another report, Engelke and colleagues employed the P.L.E.A.S.E. apparatus to ablate pig skin ($\lambda = 2940$ nm) and gain access to the viable skin layers [25]. The investigators achieved a four to fivefold enhancement in water permeation (TEWL) across excised porcine skin compared to nonlaser−treated skin. Measured TEWL values were similar to those obtained with human skin in vivo. Significantly, enhanced water diffusion increased the dissolution of all topically administered Polyvinyl alcohol (PVA)-based film dosage forms within 6 h. In experiments using untreated pig skin samples, the authors did not observe film dissolution [25]. PVA blends with crosslinked carbomer, carboxymethyl cellulose as well as PVA films were used for the permeation studies. Rhodamine B-labeled dextran 70 kDa or fluorescein isothiocyanate were utilized by the investigators as macromolecular and low molecular weight model compounds, respectively. A patch was formed from the polymer films that subsequently induced fast drug release upon dissolution. Enhanced transdermal delivery of the loaded compounds through laser-treated pig skin was thus achieved [25].

Two major limitations of conventional allergen-specific immunotherapy are poor patient compliance and a protracted treatment schedule [25]. In an effort to address this challenge, an infrared laser equipment was used to form several micropores on dorsal mouse skin. These pores possessed specific depth, density, and number [25]. The authors then administered grass pollen allergen Phl p 5 using a patch with or without the T helper 1-promoting CpG oligodeoxynucleotide 1826 as an adjuvant or by subcutaneous injection [25]. Sensitization experiments that entailed parenteral administration of allergen (with alum as an adjuvant), followed by intranasal delivery, were studied as a potential bulwark against allergic immune responses. Presensitized mice underwent treatment either through the classic technique that utilizes subcutaneous injection or through micropores formed by a laser source [25]. The authors used enzyme-linked immunosorbent assay (ELISA) to evaluate sera for IgG and a basophil mediator release method to quantify Immunoglobulin E (IgE). Cytokine levels from supernatants of bronchoalveolar lavage fluids and re-stimulated lymphocytes were determined with flow cytometry. The cellular constitution of lavage fluids was also examined via flow cytometry. Administration of antigen through micropores led to T helper 2-biased immune responses [25].

The incorporation of CpG (short synthetic single-stranded DNA molecules containing CpG motifs) provided a balanced response thus circumventing allergic sensitization, that is expression of T helper 2 cytokines, airway inflammation, and IgE induction [25]. The effectiveness of immunotherapy via the transdermal route was similar to subcutaneous injection, but was superior in terms of the repression of preexisting IgE responses. The same research group had previously shown that transdermal vaccination through laser-formed MCs can induce a T helper 2-biased serological configuration including the generation of IL-4 secreting TH2 cells and the secretion of IgE, both of which can be stifled by adding toll-like receptor (TLR) agonists such as CpG ODN [26]. CpG is a DNA molecule a portion of which has cytosine triphosphate deoxynucleotide ("C") followed by guanine triphosphate deoxynucleotide ("G"). The authors utilized the P.L.E.A.S.E. system for the creation of aqueous micropores in the skin. The device combines the capability to alter the depth, density, and number of MCs with precise laser scanning features [26]. The feasibility of transdermal immunization using laser-generated micropores for specific immune responses was studied and the results were compared to classic subcutaneous injection. By directing the vaccine to different layers of the skin, the researchers were able to induce T cell polarization bias, which can be modified by the incorporation of adjuvants [26].

Scheiblhofer et al. used an ablative fractional infrared laser to introduce Hepatitis B surface antigen (HBsAg) into BALB/c mice [27]. CRM197, CpG ODN1826, enterotoxin subunit B of *E. coli* (LT-B), monophosphoryl lipid A, and alum were employed as adjuvants. The effect of various pore densities (5%–15%) and fluences (2.1 to 16.8 J/cm^2) was studied [27]. The immunogenicity of HBsAg and the marketed conjugate vaccines Menveo as well as ActHIB administered via the transdermal route were compared to the classic intramuscular injection [27]. Antigen-specific antibody titers were measured with luminometric ELISA. Antibody titers against HBsAg depended upon pore depth and reached a maximum value when the authors employed a fluence of 8.4 J/cm^2. There was no correlation between pore density and immunogenicity. The use of alum as an adjuvant significantly decreased antibody titers following transcutaneous immunization (TCI), while adjuvantation with other ingredients only caused insignificant alterations in overall IgG titers [27]. CpG and LT-B shifted the immune response polarization as shown by the reduced IgG1/IgG2a ratios. HBsAg/LT-B administered through TCI engendered antibody titers comparable to the intramuscular injection of HBsAg/alum. It was shown by the authors that TCI with optimal laser features (fluency, exposure time, etc.) induced high antibody titers. The addition of adjuvants did not lead to any significant boost in titers. It was inferred from the data that marketed vaccines without alum can be used for an efficacious TCI via laser-generated MCs, without the need to reformulate them [27].

The efficacy of epicutaneous allergen-specific immunotherapy (EPIT) is compromised by significant skin reactions. Recently, Kumar and coworkers prepared a patch partially coated with a powder mixture of 1,25-dihydroxyvitamin D3, CpG, and OVA model allergen (VD3). The authors named this EPIT technique as μEPIT [28]. The skin delivery of the patch onto laser-treated skin led to enhanced transport while reducing allergen leakage into the blood similar to the currently used subcutaneous immunotherapy (SCIT) [28]. Furthermore, only three doses of μEPIT over 14 days could adequately block allergen-specific IgE responses in mice with OVA-induced airway hyperresponsiveness. This response was could not be achieved by eight doses of SCIT over 21 days [28]. The authors noted that μEPIT most likely increased IgG2a production indicating TH1-biased immune responses and caused the production of a high concentration of T-regulatory (T_{reg}) cells. Immune tolerance was proven by a significant decrease in airway wall thickness as well as neutrophil and eosinophil infiltration into the respiratory airway. The μEPIT constitutes a painless and novel technology for the management of IgE-mediated allergic disorders with less local skin reaction and a reduced risk of anaphylaxis [28].

In another interesting study, Huang et al. studied the effect of two lasers (CO_2 and Er:YAG) on the percutaneous delivery of three vitamin C derivatives, 2-phospho-L-ascorbic acid trisodium salt (SAP), magnesium L-ascorbic acid-2-phosphate (MAP-2), and L-ascorbic acid 2-phosphate sesquimagnesium salt (MAP-1) across porcine dorsal skin [29]. Alterations in transport across laser-exposed skin were studied with confocal scanning electron microscopy. The percutaneous permeation of vitamin C derivatives was investigated. Fluxes of MAP-1, MAP-2, and SAP across Er:YAG laser-treated skin were 15–27-fold, 48–123-fold, and 22–56-fold higher, respectively, than their fluxes across untreated skin [29]. The permeation rates of MAP-1, MAP-2, and SAP across CO_2 laser-treated skin were 28–36-fold, 116–156-fold, and 79–102-fold higher, respectively, than their fluxes across untreated skin. For the Er:YAG laser, the optimal fluency was 3.8 J/cm^2 for MAP-1 and 5 J/cm^2 for MAP-2 and SAP, respectively [29]. Conversely, the optimal fluency for the CO_2 laser was 5 W for all the three derivatives [29].

Heat

An interesting method of increasing skin permeability involves heating the skin [30,31]. It has been asserted that either very short exposures at high temperatures or long exposures at moderate temperatures can increase percutaneous transport [30]. Thermal ablation entails the noninvasive removal of small sections of the SC leading to enhanced skin permeability [32]. This increase in transdermal flux is ascribed to the formation of micrometer-scale conduits in the skin [32]. Usually, investigators heat the skin surface and as a result the tissue is vaporized leading to the removal of the SC. Because the thermal exposure of the skin is short, SC temperature gradient is so steep that while the surface of the skin is very hot, the viable epidermis, the dermis, and the subcutaneous layer are not subjected to a substantial increase in temperature [32].

Skin ablation is interesting because of the simple concept of removing the SC layers for enhanced drug permeation [33]. Because a significantly high level of energy is needed to damage the outer layers of skin, it is important to cautiously regulate the amplitude and exposure time of the applied energy to prevent undesirable injury to the inner skin layers [34]. Thermal ablation can be accomplished by using different technologies including lasers as well as microfabricated resistive and radiofrequency (RF) electrical heating elements [32]. Lasers can heat the skin at a timescale of microseconds, but bulky and costly devices are usually employed for this purpose. The laser directs high-level energy at a designated location to penetrate the skin. Gold nanorods absorb near-infrared light and generate an intense heat, which can damage the outer layer of the skin [34]. Compared to a continuous-wave laser, the pulsed laser only increases the temperature of the skin surface and causes less damage to the inner skin. It is important to emphasize that microfabricated resistive and RF approaches require heating elements that are in contact with the skin and heat application is accomplished at a timescale of milliseconds [32].

Molecular transport across a membrane usually increases with a rise in temperature [35]. Heat can potentially facilitate follicular drug transport by rendering the sebum more permeable to drug permeation [36]. Furthermore, there may be a positive relationship between skin temperature and the penetration of topically applied therapeutic agents [35]. As an illustration, subjecting the skin to 40°C for 4 h has been shown to enhance human skin permeability to a hydrophobic drug (fentanyl) by fourfold through a mechanism that is hypothesized to involve lipid fluidization of the SC [30,37]. In that study by Shomaker and coworkers, six healthy adult volunteers received a fentanyl 25-μg/h transdermal patch with and without local heat for 240 min followed by patch application without heat for an additional 20 h [37]. Blood was drawn at baseline and every hour for 24 h. Peak plasma concentration (C_{max}) of the drug was assayed and the area under the curve of the plasma drug concentration versus time curve was measured [37]. In another research work, exposing pig skin to 80°C for 15 s resulted in a 12-fold increase in permeability of a hydrophobic model compound (butanol) across porcine skin [30,38]. In the study, hairless mice were burned dorsally for 15 s on a metal surface kept at 80°C. The temperature and time conditions were selected to induce a deep partial-thickness to full thickness damage on the animal. Mice were sacrificed daily after burn over a 14-day period and the skin transport of 3H-methanol and 14C-butanol through the excised eschar was determined [38].

In another interesting work, Lee et al. developed a novel microfabricated device that can quickly convert electrical energy into mechanical and thermal energy via the ejection of a jet of superheated steam at the skin on a timescale of the order of 100 μs [32]. The authors showed that by capacitively discharging electric current directly via a few microliters of water in a microchamber allows very rapid and efficient heating of the water, which results in extremely rapid and efficient heat transfer to the skin upon ejection from the device [32]. Significantly, steam temperature was utilized to regulate the depth of tissue removal and the windows mask localized tissue removal to micrometer-scale conduits on the skin surface (lateral control) [32]. The use of a conductive mask hindered physical contact between the skin surface and the ejectate, which ultimately did not allow black particles entrained in the steam jet to contact and discolor the skin [32]. Interestingly, while skin ablation of spots measuring approximately 100 μm in diameter were obtained through the thickness of the SC, the utilization of diverse ablation operating parameters and different mask sizes can result in different degrees of tissue removal [32]. Park and colleagues also analyzed the effects of temperature and duration of heating on skin permeability [30]. A very strong dependence of skin transport on temperature was demonstrated, such that a twofold increase in absolute temperature (i.e., 25°C = 298K; 315°C = 588K; 588K/298K = 1.97) corresponded to a 760-fold increase in skin permeability. There was a weaker dependence on the duration of heating over the range examined. On the other hand, a 50-fold variation in heating time (i.e., 100 ms to 5 s) had no influence at some temperatures and resulted in up to a sixfold enhancement at other temperatures [30]. Haine et al. adopted a unique thermal ablation approach in their study [39]. The photothermal effect of the gold nanorods by near-infrared radiation irradiation enhanced the skin temperature and increased the transport of a model protein through the SC into the skin. Specifically, the research project showed the capability a hydrogel system combined with a photothermal effect of gold nanorods to successfully increase the transdermal delivery of a model protein.

One of the thermal ablation techniques involves the use of RF. RF heating occurs in materials via energy transferred from the electric field to the charges in the material [33]. RF can be categorized as high frequency (> 500 kHz), medium frequency (25 ~ 500 kHz), and low frequency (1 ~ 25,000 Hz) [33]. RF ablation uses a high-frequency electrical current (100–500 kHz) for localized heating of the outer skin layer [34]. The method involves placing of a thin, needle-like electrode directly into a tissue [40]. During the application of RF energy, a frequency alternating current moves from the tip of the electrode into the tissue surrounding that electrode [40]. As the ions within the tissue attempt to follow the change in the direction of the alternating current, their movements result in frictional heating of the tissue, producing coagulative necrosis and tissue ablation [40]. Sintov et al. used RF high-voltage currents to ablate the outer layers of skin with the aim of enhancing the transdermal delivery of two drugs, granisetron hydrochloride and diclofenac sodium [40]. The RF currents formed MCs across the SC deep into the epidermis. The transdermal drug delivery experiments were first conducted in vitro using excised full thickness pig ear skin. An array of 100 microelectrodes/cm^2 was utilized in these experiments [40]. The percutaneous transport of both molecules significantly increased following pretreatment with the RF microelectrodes, in comparison with the permeation across the untreated control skin. The transdermal steady-state fluxes of 41.6 and 23.0 μg/cm^2/h were achieved for granisetron and diclofenac, respectively [40]. Similar experiments were carried out by the investigators in vivo. The administration of granisetron patches (3% in crosslinked hydrogel) onto rats' abdominal skin pretreated with RF electrodes led to a mean peak plasma level of 239.3 ± 43.7 ng/mL after 12 h, which was about 30 times higher than the plasma levels obtained by 24-h passive diffusion of the applied drug [40]. It was demonstrated that diclofenac plasma levels in pretreated rats were 1.22 ± 032 μg/mL after 3 h and this went up to 1.47 ± 0.33 μg/mL after 6 h in comparison to 0.16 ± 0.04 μg/mL levels measured after 6 h in untreated rats [40].

Abrasion utilizes sandpaper or pressurized particles to remove the SC [41]. Microdermabrasion (MDA) uses negative pressure and Al_2O_3 crystals to superficially peel off the outer surface of the skin [42]. MDA is an FDA-approved cosmetic procedure that was developed in the 1980s to decrease the appearance of superficial scars, tattoos, wrinkles, fine lines, and large pores [41]. The procedure is beneficial because it is quick and painless, and it is already approved by the FDA for other applications [41]. Another advantage is that usually there are fewer complications, less bleeding and there is no requirement for local anesthesia compared to other superficial peeling technologies [42]. Although various researchers have provided evidence showing that microdermabrasion increases transdermal drug delivery rate, a substantial limitation in the development of microdermabrasion for clinical use is the poor understanding of the influence of microdermabrasion on the skin [43].

In addition, current microdermabrasion equipment needs meticulous characterization to choose conditions that can selectively peel the SC for transdermal drug delivery applications [41]. From a mechanistic standpoint, microdermabrasion entails impinging sharp microparticles on the surface of the skin [43]. The particles are subsequently pulled out via vacuum into a waste vessel together with the abraded skin sample [43]. Specifically, MDA injures the SC by bombarding it with abrasive particles, such as sodium chloride or alumina under vacuum [41]. Microdermabrasion gently pulls the skin into a hand-piece by mild suction that induces the regulated movement of the crystals. Because it is a closed-loop procedure, particles as well as debris are collected in a container [33]. The impact of the particles on the skin is a function of the vacuum pressure and the flow rate [33]. From the standpoint of transdermal drug delivery, it is essential to fathom the influence of microdermabrasion on the skin layers in a way that facilitates the removal of the SC in a controlled manner with less collateral damage to the underlying layers of the viable epidermis [43].

Gill et al. histologically characterized the skin of human volunteers and rhesus macaques following microdermabrasion at different conditions. A rise in the number of treatment passes resulted in a greater tissue removal ranging from minimal effects to extensive damage to deeper layers of the skin. It is noteworthy that at moderate microdermabrasion conditions, selective yet full thickness removal of SC was accomplished with minimal damage to deeper skin layers [43]. The authors delivered a fluorescent compound (fluorescein) via microdermabraded skin and subsequently the authors reported that antibodies were generated against vaccinia virus after administration in monkeys [43]. In another interesting study, Andrews and coworkers evaluated the influence of time, microdermabrasion crystal flow rate, and applied suction pressure (dynamic and static modes) on the magnitude of SC removal from excised pig skin [41]. The authors did not only control the depth of tissue removal by utilizing different microdermabrasion parameters but also regulated the area of tissue removal by positioning a metal mask patterned with 125- or 250-μm pores to selectively expose small portions of the tissue to microdermabrasion [41]. Using microdermabrasion, various scientists have demonstrated enhanced permeation of freshly excised animal skin to low molecular weight compounds (<300 Da) reporting a 10–20-fold permeation rate increase [43].

Lee and coworkers studied the effect of microdermabrasion on the in vitro skin transport and deposition of ascorbic acid and magnesium ascorbyl phosphate, a prodrug of ascorbic acid [42]. The system used for microdermabrasion was equipped with aspiration-compression within a flexible tube, which was then linked to a machine and a hand-piece [42]. Al_2O_3 crystals were fired from the compression system through a nozzle at a vacuum pressure of 3 bar with the hand-piece in contact with nude mouse skin for 2, 3, or 4 s. The microcrystals were reabsorbed through an aspiration system and shunted to a waste storage [42]. The authors reported that microdermabrasion ablated the SC layers with minimal disruption of the skin barrier properties. Significantly, the flux and skin deposition of vitamin C across microdermabrasion-treated nude mouse skin were about 20-fold greater compared to that obtained across untreated skin [42].

5-aminolaevulinic acid (ALA) is utilized as a protoporphyrin IX-precursor for the photodynamic treatment of superficial skin cancer and cutaneous metastases of internal malignancies [44]. Fang et al. recently evaluated the influence of microdermabrasion on the transdermal delivery of ALA [44]. The transcutaneous penetration of ALA across microdermabrasion-treated skin was about 5–15-fold greater than that across untreated skin. Both the influence of ablation on the SC and ALA flux were proportional to the treatment duration of microdermabrasion [44].

References

[1] Zhao Z, et al. Transdermal immunomodulation: principles, advances and perspectives. Adv Drug Deliv Rev 2018;127:3–19.

[2] Haedersdal M, et al. Translational medicine in the field of ablative fractional laser (AFXL)-assisted drug delivery: a critical review from basics to current clinical status. J Am Acad Dermatol 2016;74(5):981–1004.

[3] Manstein D, et al. Fractional photothermolysis: a new concept for cutaneous remodeling using microscopic patterns of thermal injury. Lasers Surg Med 2004;34(5):426–38.

[4] Lee W-R, et al. Laser-assisted topical drug delivery by using a low-fluence fractional laser: imiquimod and macromolecules. J Control Rel 2011;153(3):240–8.

[5] Zorec B, et al. The effect of pulse duration, power and energy of fractional Er:YAG laser for transdermal delivery of differently sized FITC dextrans. Int J Pharmaceutics 2017;516(1):204–13.

[6] Ganti SS, Banga AK. Non-ablative fractional laser to facilitate transdermal delivery. J Pharm Sci 2016;105(11):3324–32.

[7] Gratieri T, et al. Next generation intra- and transdermal therapeutic systems: using non- and minimally-invasive technologies to increase drug delivery into and across the skin. Eur J Pharm Sci 2013;50(5):609–22.

[8] Yang R, et al. Getting drugs across biological barriers. Adv Mater 2017;29(37):1606596.
[9] Bachhav YG, Heinrich A, Kalia YN. Controlled intra- and transdermal protein delivery using a minimally invasive Erbium:YAG fractional laser ablation technology. Eur J Pharm Biopharm 2013;84(2):355–64.
[10] Alegre-Sanchez A, Jimenez-Gomez N, Boixeda P. Laser-assisted drug delivery. Actas Dermosifiliogr 2018;109(10):858–67.
[11] Shen J, et al. Combination of a 2940 nm Er:YAG laser with recombinant bovine basic fibroblast growth factor (rb-bFGF) and light-emitting diode-red light (LED-RL) for the treatment of striae alba: a pilot study. J Cosmet Dermatol 2018;17(2):176–83.
[12] Lee W-R, et al. Erbium:YAG laser enhances transdermal peptide delivery and skin vaccination. J Control Rel 2008;128(3):200–8.
[13] Gómez C, et al. Skin laser treatments enhancing transdermal delivery of ALA. J Pharm Sci 2011;100(1):223–31.
[14] Waibel JS, et al. Update of ablative fractionated lasers to enhance cutaneous topical drug delivery. Adv Ther 2017;34(8):1840–9.
[15] Lee WR, et al. Transdermal drug delivery enhanced and controlled by erbium:YAG laser: a comparative study of lipophilic and hydrophilic drugs. J Control Rel 2001;75(1–2):155–66.
[16] Lee W-R, et al. Non-ablative fractional laser assists cutaneous delivery of small- and macro-molecules with minimal bacterial infection risk. Eur J Pharm Sci 2016;92:1–10.
[17] Bachhav YG, Heinrich A, Kalia YN. Using laser microporation to improve transdermal delivery of diclofenac: increasing bioavailability and the range of therapeutic applications. Eur J Pharm Biopharm 2011;78(3):408–14.
[18] Hsiao CY, et al. Skin pretreatment with conventional non-fractional ablative lasers promote the transdermal delivery of tranexamic acid. Dermatol Surg 2016;42(7):867–74.
[19] Yu J, Kalaria DR, Kalia YN. Erbium:YAG fractional laser ablation for the percutaneous delivery of intact functional therapeutic antibodies. J Control Rel 2011;156(1):53–9.
[20] Song Y, et al. Transdermal delivery of human growth hormone via laser-generated micropores. Drug Deliv Transl Res 2018;8(2):450–60.
[21] Song Y, et al. Transdermal delivery of cimetidine across microneedle-treated skin: effect of extent of drug ionization on the permeation. J Pharm Sci 2017;106(5):1285–92.
[22] Wenande E, et al. Laser-assisted delivery enhances topical uptake of the anticancer agent cisplatin. Drug Deliv 2018;25(1):1877–85.
[23] Yu J, et al. Using controlled laser-microporation to increase transdermal delivery of prednisone. J Control Rel 2010;148(1):e71–3.
[24] Chen X, et al. Facilitation of transcutaneous drug delivery and vaccine immunization by a safe laser technology. J Control Rel 2012;159(1):43–51.
[25] Engelke L, Winter G, Engert J. Application of water-soluble polyvinyl alcohol-based film patches on laser microporated skin facilitates intradermal macromolecule and nanoparticle delivery. Eur J Pharm Biopharm 2018;128:119–30.
[26] Weiss R, et al. Transcutaneous vaccination via laser microporation. J Control Rel 2012;162(2):391–9.
[27] Scheiblhofer S, et al. Skin vaccination via fractional infrared laser ablation—optimization of laser-parameters and adjuvantation. Vaccine 2017;35(14):1802–9.
[28] Kumar MNK, Zhou C, Wu MX. Laser-facilitated epicutaneous immunotherapy to IgE-mediated allergy. J Control Rel 2016;235:82–90.
[29] Huang CH, et al. Transdermal delivery of three vitamin C derivatives by Er:YAG and carbon dioxide laser pretreatment. Lasers Med Sci 2013;28(3):807–14.

[30] Park JH, et al. The effect of heat on skin permeability. Int J Pharm 2008;359(1–2):94–103.

[31] Mitragotri S. Temperature dependence of skin permeability to hydrophilic and hydrophobic solutes. J Pharm Sci 2007;96(7):1832–9.

[32] Lee JW, et al. Microsecond thermal ablation of skin for transdermal drug delivery. J Control Rel 2011;154(1):58–68.

[33] Aljuffali IA, Lin CF, Fang JY. Skin ablation by physical techniques for enhancing dermal/transdermal drug delivery. J Drug Deliv Sci Technol 2014;24(3):277–87.

[34] Lee H, et al. Device-assisted transdermal drug delivery. Adv Drug Deliv Rev 2017;127:35–45.

[35] Shahzad Y, et al. Breaching the skin barrier through temperature modulations. J Control Rel 2015;202:1–13.

[36] Caserta F, Brown MB, McAuley WJ. The use of heat and chemical penetration enhancers to increase the follicular delivery of erythromycin to the skin. Eur J Pharm Sci 2019;132:55–62.

[37] Shomaker TS, Zhang J, Ashburn MA. Assessing the impact of heat on the systemic delivery of fentanyl through the transdermal fentanyl delivery system. Pain Med 2000;1(3):225–30.

[38] Flynn GL, et al. Permeability of thermally damaged skin v- permeability over the course of maturation of a deep partial-thickness wound. Burn Incl Therm Inj 1982;8(3):196–202.

[39] Haine AT, et al. Enhancement of transdermal protein delivery by photothermal effect of gold nanorods coated on polysaccharide-based hydrogel. Eur J Pharm Biopharm 2017;119:91–5.

[40] Sintov AC, et al. Radiofrequency-driven skin microchanneling as a new way for electrically assisted transdermal delivery of hydrophilic drugs. J Control Rel 2003;89(2):311–20.

[41] Andrews SN, et al. Optimization of microdermabrasion for controlled removal of stratum corneum. Int J Pharm 2011;407(1):95–104.

[42] Lee W-R, et al. Lasers and microdermabrasion enhance and control topical delivery of Vitamin C. J Investig Dermatol 2003;121(5):1118–25.

[43] Gill HS, et al. Selective removal of stratum corneum by microdermabrasion to increase skin permeability. Eur J Pharm Sci 2009;38(2):95–103.

[44] Fang JY, et al. Enhancement of topical 5-aminolevulinic acid delivery by erbium:YAG laser and microdermabrasion: a comparison with iontophoresis and electroporation. Br J Dermatol 2004;151(1):132–40.

Chapter 12

Mathematical modeling of transdermal drug delivery

Several researchers have developed robust mathematical models for describing and predicting transdermal drug delivery with the aim of reducing animal experiments [1]. It is critical to understand transdermal drug delivery mechanisms from both experimental and theoretical standpoints [2]. In silico modeling of percutaneous permeation has been used by several researchers to reduce and refine transdermal experiments. This can accelerate product design and provide more reliable safety assessment. In addition, mathematical equations can assist researchers in elucidating transdermal transport mechanisms [1]. Several methods, including analytical and numerical statistical techniques such as finite element modeling, finite difference modeling, finite volume modeling as well as quantitative structure–permeation relationship (QSPR) modeling, are routinely used to characterize transdermal permeation [3]. Typically, research scientists use easily accessible physical constants such as solvation parameters, lipophilicity, and molecular weight (MW) as well as mathematical models to predict the apparent permeability coefficient of various compounds [4]. Specifically, multiple linear regression models are used to establish a relationship between a dependent variable and two or more independent variables by fitting a linear equation to experimental data [5]. The dependent variable y has been calculated by using a multiple regression equation and the following independent variables $x_1, x_2, x_3 \ldots x_p$ with the following parameters $\alpha_0, \alpha_1, \alpha_2 \ldots \alpha_p$ [5]:

$$y = \alpha_0 + \alpha_1 x_1 + \alpha_2 x_2 \tag{12.1}$$

Potts and Guy used a multiple regression method that uses permeant octanol/water partition coefficient (log P) as well as molecular volume (MV) or MW to compute permeability coefficient ($\log K_p$) data for a group of compounds [6]. The researchers derived the following equation:

$$\log K_p = (0.71 \times \log P) - (0.0061 \times \text{MW}) - 2.7 \tag{12.2}$$

where log Kp is the logarithm of the permeability coefficient, log P is the logarithm of the octanol–water coefficient, and MW is the molecular weight [6]. One shortcoming of the Potts and Guy equation is that K_p is sometimes

Transdermal Drug Delivery. DOI: https://doi.org/10.1016/B978-0-12-822550-9.00012-0

overpredicted for highly lipophilic molecules and the permeability coefficient of these compounds can, at least partially, be subjected to change by the viable skin layers beneath the stratum corneum (SC). A modified equation was derived by Cleek and Bunge to account for permeability coefficient (K_p, mod) of highly lipophilic compounds [7]:

$$K_p\text{mod}(\text{cm/hr}) = \frac{K_p}{\left\{\dfrac{1 + \left(K_p \times \sqrt{\text{MW}}\right)}{2.6}\right\}} \tag{12.3}$$

Diffusion models typically use Fick's second law of diffusion to predict drug concentrations locally and temporally [4]. Drug diffusion through a transdermal device and the skin can be regarded as Fickian transport through a simple homogeneous membrane [2] or a heterogeneous multilayer membrane [8]. Transdermal drug delivery is a complex process and tremendous effort has been devoted toward the development of mathematical models capable of describing and more importantly predicting the process. Most transdermal drug delivery models are referred to as physiologic because they use the concept of compartments [9]. A principal category is composed of pharmacokinetic models, which employ ordinary differential equations to characterize permeation without a spatial resolution of the compartments [9]. In diffusion models, partial differential equations (PDE) [9] are employed to resolve spatial variations of solute concentrations and also to describe time evolution of the concentration profile. These models are derived from first principles such as mass balance and Fick's laws of diffusion [9]. Fick's first law describes steady-state diffusion phenomena and can predict transdermal drug delivery, especially when there is no significant depletion in the system [10]:

$$Q = \frac{DAT\Delta C_s}{h} \tag{12.4}$$

Eq. (12.3) links the quantity of solute, Q, crossing the skin membrane of area, A, over a time period, T, with a constant concentration gradient across the skin, C_s. Other terms in the equation are the diffusion coefficient in the skin membrane, D, and the path length, h [11]. Eq. (12.3) is often depicted by researchers using steady-state skin flux, J_{ss}, defined as [11]:

$$J_{ss} = \frac{Q}{AT} = \frac{D\Delta C_s}{h} \tag{12.5}$$

In QSPR studies, most authors usually calculate the permeability coefficient (K_p) that is the steady-state flux of a drug across the skin (J_{ss}) normalized by the concentration gradient, C_v [11]:

$$K_p = \frac{J_{ss}}{C_v} \tag{12.6}$$

Nonsteady-nstate diffusion can be described with Fick's second law that uses a time-dependent method [10]:

$$Q(t) = AKhC\left[D\frac{t}{h^2} - \frac{1}{6} - \frac{2}{\pi^2}\sum_{n=1}^{\infty}\frac{(-1)^n}{n^2}\exp\left(\frac{-Dn^2\pi^2t}{h^2}\right)\right] \quad (12.7)$$

where $Q(t)$ is the amount that enters the receiver compartment from the donor compartment across a membrane at a given time (t), A is the surface diffusion area, K is the partition coefficient of the penetrant between the donor vehicle and the membrane, h is the membrane thickness, D is the diffusion coefficient of the penetrant across the membrane, and C is the penetrant concentration in the donor solution [12]. One- or two-compartmental pharmacokinetic models can be employed to calculate rate constants from physiological and physicochemical parameters such as skin thickness, blood flow, diffusion, and partition coefficients [4]. Mathematical models are used to characterize diffusion in the SC either as a series of discrete compartments or a continuum [10]. Consequently, the physiological complexities of the SC can be substantially decreased by using the compartmental technique. With this approach, the skin is regarded as well-stirred compartments, each of which has uniformly distributed solute concentration [10].

Compounds with a balanced partition coefficient (that is with a log P between 1 and 3) are associated with optimal transdermal penetration rates [11]. Knowing that skin transport processes can be mathematically modeled with Fick's first law, Higuchi derived mathematical equations that are used to characterize transdermal delivery as a passive transport process through vehicle and membrane layers in series [11,13]. Using fundamental physicochemical principles, the author emphasized the relevance of the thermodynamic activity of the permeating compound [11,13]. Mathematical modeling of skin permeability can assist in elucidating skin transport mechanisms [10].

Mathematical modeling also enables researchers to design optimal experiments, study the variables that impact skin permeation, predict permeability of given compounds, and understand the physical/chemical processes that control transdermal penetration [14]. Modeling can help in designing appropriate doses, exposure times, or sampling intervals [10]. But the validity of a mathematical model depends on the ability to predict experimental observations [10]. It has been recognized that there are often differences between in vivo (where the SC regulates intercellular passive diffusion rate) and in vitro data [15]. Furthermore, even mathematical models based on human in vivo data can significantly differ from experimental data underlining the complicated nature of the transdermal drug delivery process [15]. Modeling of transdermal delivery is an ethical and viable option to laboratory experiments [5]. In vivo skin transport experiments are viewed as gold standard, but are challenging to conduct and assess because of ethical issues and the complicatedness of the process [5]. Moreover, transdermal drug delivery across human skin is significantly impacted by the type and magnitude of electric charge of the drug molecule that is difficult to consider using most of the proposed mathematical models. Most transdermal mathematical modeling investigations only examine a single series of molecules. This often hinders the broad application of the proposed models as they are only valid for a specific group of medications, rather than all medications. Transdermal drug delivery models differ substantially in scope, ranging from simple models that regard the SC (or sometimes the entire skin) as one compartment to those that take into consideration the anatomical complicatedness of the skin (e.g., the presence of corneocytes, the existence of keratin within the corneocytes, or the availability of lipids) [11].

Mathematical operations, quantities, and relations feature in mathematical models [5]. Mathematical terms are used to depict the quantitative relationships between the different processes that constitute percutaneous drug transport [5]. Tsakovska et al. discussed two major classes of predictive models for transdermal drug delivery: (1) mechanistic models that take into consideration the heterogeneous structure of the skin when developing mathematical equations to describe solute permeation. These equations are derived from first principles such as mass balance and depend on additional assumptions such as Fick's laws of diffusion (2) QSPR models that link a compound's permeability coefficient to chemical structure (physicochemical properties and other structural descriptors). With this class of mathematical models, statistical techniques are used to build quantitative correlations and experimental data are utilized or the development of skin permeability equations [16].

Goyal and colleagues categorized transdermal mathematical models into mechanistic and empirical [5]. The following equation is used to link steady-state flux (J_{ss}) of a solute (from the donor solution to the receiver solution across a skin model) to the concentration gradient between the donor and receiver solutions [17]:

$$J_{ss} = K_p(C_d - C_r) \tag{12.8}$$

where C_d and C_r are concentrations of the solute in the donor and receiver solutions, respectively [17]. Assuming that the SC is a homogenous thin membrane, experimentally determined skin permeability of a compound can be linked to the effective diffusivity D_{sc} and the SC—water partition parameter $K_{sc/w}$ of the compound as follows [17]:

$$K_p = \frac{K_{sc/w} D_{sc}}{h_{sc}} \tag{12.9}$$

where h_{sc} is pseudo-homogenous SC membrane thickness.

QSPR models are typically used to correlate the physicochemical and/or structural properties of a series of chemicals to statistically determined skin permeability data [17]. A QSPR model that can be used to predict skin permeability was suggested by Kasting and coworkers who assumed that solute partition property in the SC conforms with the linear free energy theory and can be expressed via the power law relationship [18]:

$$K_{sc/w} = K_{ow}^{\psi} \tag{12.10}$$

where K_{ow} is the octanol–water partition coefficient of chemical and ψ is constant. The second assumption is that the effective diffusion coefficient in the pseudo-homogenous membrane SC obeys the free volume theory and can be expressed via an exponential function [18]:

$$D = D_o \exp(-\zeta.V) \tag{12.11}$$

where V is the MV, whereas D_o and ζ are constant. By combining Eqs. (12.8–12.10), a general QSPR model of skin permeability can be written as follows [17]:

$$\log K_p(\mathrm{cm/s}) = a + b.\log K_{ow} + c.V \tag{12.12}$$

Artificial neural network

Artificial neural network (ANN) can be used to deal with certain mathematical modeling challenges especially those that cannot be solved with analytical methods [19]. ANN is made up of artificial neurons or nodes with a parallel structure. For each independent variable, the ANN has one input layer containing one node, one or more hidden layers, where the data are processed, and one output layer, including one node for each dependent variable [19]. ANN can be used for the nonlinear mapping of dependent and independent variables without knowing the correlation between targeted responses a priori. The use of ANN is an easier computational and mathematical model motivated by anatomic and physiologic features of the biological neural network. There is usually an input layer (independent variables), several hidden layers, and an output layer (response variables) [20]. Each layer is made up of several intertwined processing units known as neurons and signals are relayed as a result of neuronal interactions [20]. Outside sources relay information to the input layer, these input data weighted singly will then be processed in the hidden layer and subsequently, the output data will be generated based on the total of weighted data from input layer adjusted by a sigmoid transfer function [20]. Prediction of the skin permeability of selected xenobiotics with ANN was carried out with Değim and coworkers [21]. The authors used an equation based on computed octanol–water partition coefficient (log K_{oct}) of permeants, their partial charges, and MW as well as permeability coefficients (log K_p) derived from different literature sources. The equation was used to predict the skin permeability for

40 compounds ($r^2 = 0.672$) [21]. An efficient ANN was created and it generated log K_p values that exhibited good correlation with experimentally determined values ($r^2 = 0.997$). Human skin was used to study the permeation profiles of selected compounds that have not been previously investigated (etodolac, famotidine, nimesulide, nizatidine, ranitidine). Their permeability coefficients were experimentally determined and compared with values predicted with a partial charge equation and a trained ANN [21]. ANN modeling was relevant for the prediction of log K_p of these compounds [21].

Transdermal drug delivery takes place on a spectrum of scale or pecking order [5]. Distinct phases of solute transport have different length scales. Four distinct length scales have been identified in the skin [9]: (1) processes at the (macro-)molecular level (1–10 nm); (2) subcellular level (0.1 μm) or cellular level (1–10 μm); (3) processes on the membrane level (0.1–1 mm), as well as the (4) compartmental/environmental level (1 cm) or in the body (1 m) [9]. Even though certain mathematical models can, in principle, be used to describe drug permeation across the skin with sufficient accuracy, they cannot be used for quick computation practically because they are complicated [22]. Some mathematical models are derived by fitting experimentally determined permeabilities with optimally selected parameters. These models are used for the prediction of drug permeabilities, but they do not possess a physical meaning and thus the models can be viewed as being only relevant from a statistical calculus standpoint [22]. Some researchers have used mathematical modeling to study transport processes and theoretically elucidate percutaneous transport [23]. When this approach is used, diffusion equations are derived from Fick's first and second laws of diffusion [23]. Recently, some authors have used multidimensional diffusion models to describe the more complex aspects of transdermal delivery, such as infinite and finite dosing as well as multilayer barrier systems [23].

Macroscopic models

Macroscopic models view the skin as a homogeneous region while more complicated microscopic models focus on the SC and regard it as corneocytes embedded in anisotropic lipid bilayers or a brick-and-mortar structure with impermeable or permeable corneocyte "bricks" immersed in an isotropic, homogeneous lipid phase "mortar" [3]. Macroscopic models usually assume that the vehicle and the skin are homogeneous membrane layers positioned sequentially through which diffusional processes take place through a single route or a mixture of independent routes [9]. These models consider the skin as a multilamellar structure in which each skin layer is assumed to possess effective properties K_{eff} and D_{eff} for a given penetrant [14]. Penetrant concentration changes with one spatial coordinate (depth x), and transient skin absorption is usually described using those models [14]. Penetrant concentration changes with one spatial coordinate (depth x), and transient skin absorption is usually described using those models [9]. Hence, transient one-dimensional diffusion problems can be formulated, and at times a second spatial dimension is incorporated to model a donor source or finite patch administered to the skin surface. These equations can be solved via the method of lines or the finite difference method [9]. The most fundamental category of macroscopic models can be viewed as one-dimensional diffusion equations that can be solved with a closed form of the analytical method. However, in certain instances, for example, when lateral diffusion is accounted for, the macroscopic model may be modified to incorporate two spatial dimensions [9]. Using the diffusion equation (Eq. 12.11) as the initial point for mathematical analysis, Frasch and Barbero highlighted a macroscopic problem where concentration (C) changes in only one direction, taken to be the x direction perpendicular to the surface of the skin whereas diffusivity (D) is constant:

$$\frac{\partial C}{\partial t} = D\frac{\partial^2 C}{\partial x^2} \tag{12.13}$$

If C is initially 0 everywhere (the skin starts out free of penetrant) and an instantaneous partitioning of the chemical between vehicle and membrane (quantified by membrane-vehicle partition coefficient, K_{mv}) gives rise to a constant membrane concentration of penetrant positioned close to the donor solution at $K_{mv}C_0$; and C at the receiver surface ($x = h$) is 0 for all time (sink condition in the receiver chamber), then either a method of lines or a finite difference method can be used to solve Eq. (12.11). If both the region of interest and the time are divided into equally spaced points along both t- and x-axes satisfying the condition:

$$t_n = t_0 + n\Delta tn = 0, 1 \ldots N$$

$$x_j = x_0 + j\Delta tj = 0, 1 \ldots N$$

Then an approximation Eq. (12.11) will be:

$$\frac{C\left(x_j, t_{n+1}\right) - C(x_j, t_n\big)}{\Delta t} = D\left[\frac{C\left(x_{j+1}, t_n\right) - 2C\left(x_j, t_n\right) + C\left(x_{j-1}, t_n\right)}{(\Delta x)^2}\right] \tag{12.14}$$

When a combination of the forward Euler and the backward Euler method (also called the Crank–Nicholson method) is employed, the solution becomes [14]:

$$\frac{C\left(x_j, t_{n+1}\right) - C(x_j, t_n\big)}{\Delta t} = \frac{D}{2}\left[\frac{\left[C\left(x_{j+1}, t_n\right) - 2C\left(x_j, t_n\right) + C\left(x_{j-1}, t_n\right)\right] + \left[C\left(x_{j+1}, t_{n+1}\right) - 2C\left(x_j, t_{n+1}\right) + C\left(x_{j-1}, t_{n+1}\right)\right]}{(\Delta x)^2}\right] \tag{12.15}$$

Although transdermal mathematical modeling equations are complex, computer software can be utilized to solve them. Ultimately, the utility of these equations lies in the ability to predict transdermal flux values and reduce the number of experiments.

References

[1] Kattou P, et al. Development of a two-dimensional model for predicting transdermal permeation with the follicular pathway: demonstration with a caffeine study. Pharm Res 2017;34(10):2036–48.

[2] Rim JE, Pinsky PM, van Osdol WW. Multiscale modeling framework of transdermal drug delivery. Ann Biomed Eng 2009;37(6):1217–29.

[3] Wen J, Koo SM, Lape N. How sensitive are transdermal transport predictions by microscopic stratum corneum models to geometric and transport parameter input? J Pharm Sci 2018;107(2):612–23.

[4] Hansen S, et al. In-silico model of skin penetration based on experimentally determined input parameters. Part I: experimental determination of partition and diffusion coefficients. Eur J Pharm Biopharm 2008;68(2):352–67.

[5] Goyal N, Thatai P, Sapra B. Surging footprints of mathematical modeling for prediction of transdermal permeability. Asian J Pharm Sci 2017;12(4):299–325.

[6] Potts RO, Guy RH. Predicting skin permeability. Pharm Res 1992;9(5):663–9.

[7] Cleek RL, Bunge AL. A new method for estimating dermal absorption from chemical exposure. 1. General Approach. Pharm Res 1993;10(4):497–506.

[8] Barbero AM, Frasch HF. Effect of stratum corneum heterogeneity, anisotropy, asymmetry and follicular pathway on transdermal penetration. J Control Rel 2017;260:234–46.

[9] Naegel A, Heisig M, Wittum G. Detailed modeling of skin penetration—an overview. Adv Drug Deliv Rev 2013;65(2):191–207.

[10] Amarah AA, et al. Compartmental modeling of skin transport. Eur J Pharm Biopharm 2018;130:336–44.

[11] Mitragotri S, et al. Mathematical models of skin permeability: an overview. Int J Pharm 2011;418(1):115–29.

[12] Luu E, et al. The influence of microneedles on the percutaneous penetration of selected antihypertensive agents: diltiazem hydrochloride and perindopril erbumine. Curr Drug Deliv 2018;15(10):1449–58.

[13] Higuchi T. Physical chemical analysis of percutaneous absorption process from creams and ointments. J Soc Cosmet Chem 1960;11:85–97.

[14] Frasch HF, Barbero AM. Application of numerical methods for diffusion-based modeling of skin permeation. Adv Drug Deliv Rev 2013;65(2):208–20.

[15] Waters LJ, Shahzad Y, Stephenson J. Modelling skin permeability with micellar liquid chromatography. Eur J Pharm Sci 2013;50(3–4):335–40.

[16] Tsakovska I, et al. Quantitative structure-skin permeability relationships. Toxicology 2017;387:27–42.

[17] Chen L, Han L, Lian G. Recent advances in predicting skin permeability of hydrophilic solutes. Adv Drug Deliv Rev 2013;65(2):295–305.

[18] Kasting GB, Smith RL, Cooper EB. Effect of lipid solubility and molecular size on percutaneous absorption. In: Shroot B, Schaefer H, editors. Skin Pharmacokinetics. Basel: Karger; 1987. p. 138–53.

[19] Kavuncuoglu H, et al. Prediction of the antimicrobial activity of walnut (Juglans regia L.) kernel aqueous extracts using artificial neural network and multiple linear regression. J Microbiol Methods 2018;148:78–86.
[20] Alara OR, et al. Efficient extraction of antioxidants from Vernonia cinerea leaves: Comparing response surface methodology and artificial neural network. Beni-Suef Univ J Basic Appl Sci 2018;7(3):276–85.
[21] Değim T, et al. Prediction of skin penetration using artificial neural network (ANN) modeling. J Pharm Sci 2003;92(3):656–64.
[22] Kontturi K, Murtomäki L. Mechanistic model for transdermal transport including iontophoresis. J Control Rel 1996;41(3):177–85.
[23] Bezrouk A, et al. SAMPA: a free software tool for skin and membrane permeation data analysis. Toxicol In Vitro 2017.

Index

Note: Page numbers followed by "*f*" and "*t*" refer to figures and tables, respectively.

D

E

H

I

N

U

V

W

FSC
www.fsc.org
MIX
Papier | Fördert gute Waldnutzung
FSC® C083411

Kolibri 360 GmbH
Ferdinand-Jühlke-Straße 7
99095 Erfurt, Deutschland
produktsicherheit@kolibri360.de